SIR GAWAIN A
GREEN KNI

O.

Special attention Bks. I. IV

I 342-865

The Lady of the Castle visits Sir Gawain

(See p. xiii)

Sir Gawain and the Green Knight

EDITED BY

J. R. R. TOLKIEN AND E. V. GORDON

SECOND EDITION

REVISED BY

NORMAN DAVIS

OXFORD

AT THE CLARENDON PRESS

Oxford University Press, Ely House, London W.1

GLASGOW NEW YORK TORONTO MELBOURNE WELLINGTON
CAPE TOWN SALISBURY IBADAN NAIROBI LUSAKA ADDIS ABABA
BOMBAY CALCUTTA MADRAS KARACHI LAHORE DACCA
KUALA LUMPUR HONG KONG TOKYO

FIRST EDITION 1925
REPRINTED 1930 (with CORRECTIONS)
1936, 1946, 1949, 1952, 1955, 1960, 1963, 1966
SECOND EDITION 1967

FIRST ISSUED AS A PAPERBACK 1968
REPRINTED 1968

PRINTED LITHOGRAPHICALLY IN GREAT BRITAIN
AT THE UNIVERSITY PRESS, OXFORD
BY VIVIAN RIDLER
PRINTER TO THE UNIVERSITY

PREFACE TO THE SECOND EDITION

THE first edition of this book was published in 1925, and last substantially corrected in 1936. A number of things in it had naturally come to need revision. E. V. Gordon died in 1938; Mrs. Gordon has consented to my attempting the task. J. R. R. Tolkien, long ago my teacher and now my much honoured friend, has allowed me a free hand in revising his work and has generously given me the use of his later notes. Many of these I have incorporated, but other changes are my own and for the final blend I am alone responsible. I have tried above all to maintain the central concern of the first edition with the author's words. Fashions in the 'interpretation' of *Gawain* have changed often and violently in the past twenty years or so, and an edition is not the place to attempt another opinion. But I have expanded the introductory account of the known analogues, for these too are matters of fact.

The willingness of the Clarendon Press to reset the book has made possible some changes of policy in text and footnotes. The most important is the replacement of ʒ by ẓ where that is the letter intended. In other features of spelling the practice of the first edition is unchanged. Though there is much to be said for normalizing spelling, in the way to which everyone is accustomed in editions of Chaucer, there is also a place for a text that will show something of the appearance of the unique manuscript and enable readers who are interested to judge the problems that its forms may present. The other most noticeable change is the distinction of type marking the lesser coloured initial capitals— though Madden's division into four main parts is retained.

The major event in *Gawain* scholarship since this book was first published has been the appearance of Sir Israel Gollancz's edition of the poem for the Early English Text Society in 1940. I have naturally made full use of it, and have acknowledged what I have adopted from it. In addition to more recent discussions of particulars of the text, I have taken the opportunity to look again at earlier work, notably (though not only) by C. Brett, O. F. Emerson, J. R. Hulbert, T. A. Knott, F. P. Magoun, H. L. Savage, and Mrs. E. M. Wright; and I have collated the text with the manuscript again. The outcome of all this is that in comparison with the first edition there are a few different readings, some new emendations, and a rather larger number of different interpretations of particular words and passages.[1]

The bibliography has been altered, but remains highly selective. It is designed to guide the reader to reference books that will help him to understand the poem in its setting, and to editions of texts referred to more than once in the notes. In recent years the flow of articles on the poem has grown to a flood, and any bibliography of them would be out of date before it was printed. Only books are therefore given, and the numerous current bibliographies must be consulted for the rest. For work up to 1940 Gollancz's bibliography is excellent.

My thanks are due to many colleagues for suggesting revisions, and especially to Mr. C. A. Robson for invaluable help with the Old French forms in appendix and glossary. I salute, *forbe al þyng*, Professor Tolkien's *fraunchyse and felaȝschyp* in letting this be done to his book.

N. D.

Oxford, August 1966

---

[1] The principal textual changes are as follows. New readings are offered in 611 *peruyng*, 624 *in tent*, 649 *inore*. Gollancz's readings in 960 *treleted*, 984 *wayned*, 2171 *saue*, 2198 *roffe*, 2290 *rynez*, 2440 *ȝonder*, 2445 *Bertilak*, Brett's in 1493 *deuayed*, and Emerson's in 2173 *forȝ* are accepted. New emendations are made in 157, 210, 660, 726, 785, 815, 960, 1183, 1265–6, 1396, 1440, 1623; and emendations proposed by others are newly adopted in 11, 100, 171, 440, 946, 971, 1334, 1719, 1878, 2511. Forms previously emended are restored in 646, 734, 881, 1595. Punctuation is significantly altered in 452, 896, 1296, 1395, 1457, 1861.

PREFACE TO THE FIRST EDITION

THE first endeavour of this edition has been to provide the student with a text which, treating the unique manuscript with all due respect, is yet pleasant for the modern reader to look at, and is free (as are few Middle English texts) from a litter of italics, asterisks, and brackets, the trail of the passing editor. The second has been to provide a sufficient apparatus for reading this remarkable poem with an appreciation as far as possible of the sort which its author may be supposed to have desired. Much of the literature that begins to gather about *Sir Gawain and the Green Knight*, though not without interest, has little bearing on this object, and many of the theories held, or questions asked, about the poem have here been passed over or lightly handled—the nature and significance of the 'test'; the sources, near and remote, of the story's elements and details; the identity, character, life, and other writings of the author (who remains unknown); his immediate motive in writing this romance; and so on.

On the other hand, the more linguistic part of the apparatus, which is principally directed towards determining, as precisely as possible, the meaning of the author's actual words (in so far as the manuscript is fair to him), is in proportion more extensive. The glossary, for instance, bulks unusually large. But to a certain extent the author has made this inevitable. While a full glossary is still essential for students of any Middle English text that merits a close and scholarly attention, the vocabulary and idiom of *Sir Gawain* deserve as much as even Chaucer's best work (which has not received it) a full and careful analysis—one even fuller and more careful than has here been possible. The language is idiomatic, and the vocabulary rich. There are approximately[1] as many distinct individual words as there are lines in the poem: a new word for every line.

Our thanks are due to Mr. J. F. Sharpe for his kindness in answering questions concerning the geography of lines 696–700; to Mr. C. T. Onions for his help on several points, and for his constant interest; to Mr. K. Sisam for personal advice and help;

[1] Words about 2690; lines 2530.

to Sir Walter Napier for the loan of the late Professor Napier's notes. The general debt of a pupil, still freshly remembering Napier's skill in the elucidation of the difficult language of the poems of this manuscript, is thus greatly increased. Though not much of the present edition is derived directly from this source, it is noteworthy that many of the suggestions made independently by others are there found anticipated but unpublished.

J. R. R. T.
E. V. G.

CONTENTS

INTRODUCTION

Sir Gawain and the Green Knight (abbreviated below to *Gawain*) is the last of four poems in MS. Cotton Nero A. x, Art. 3, in the British Museum, a vellum manuscript measuring about $6\frac{3}{4} \times 4\frac{7}{8}$ in. (*c*. 170 × 125 mm.). It was formerly bound together with two unrelated manuscripts, but was rebound separately in November 1964, and now bears the distinguishing mark *Art. 3* on spine and fly-leaf. In the rebinding the gatherings have been separately stitched to stiff guards, so that the collation can be clearly seen. It begins with a bifolium, continues with seven gatherings of twelve leaves, each with a catchword at the end, and ends with a gathering of four leaves. The foliation was made, and also revised, while the book was part of the composite volume; so that the first leaf now bears the old number 37 in ink, which is struck out and replaced by 41 in pencil. The old foliation, which was used by Madden and Morris in the first editions of the poems, is still generally used in referring to them (as, for example, in Gollancz's facsimile and editions, and in Gordon's *Pearl*) and it has therefore been retained in this edition. *Gawain*, excluding the illustrations, is on ff. 91ᵃ to 124ᵇ, following *Pearl*, *Purity* (or *Cleanness*), and *Patience*. The poems are all written in the same small sharp hand, which is dated by general consent about 1400. The size and spacing of the writing varies a good deal in the course of the manuscript, but there are always 36 lines to each full page, on ruled lines between bounding lines. (*Gawain* begins low on the page with only 25.) In *Gawain* the short 'bob' lines, which metrically follow each group of long lines, are written to the right of the long lines, sometimes opposite the last of these but often two or three lines up. In a few places another hand has retraced some letters. The ink has faded considerably and some lines were blotted against the opposite page when the text was written, so that reading is often difficult. The first transcribers, Madden and Morris, deserve great credit for their care and accuracy. The manuscript has been reproduced in facsimile by the Early English Text Society, with an introduction by Sir Israel Gollancz (1922).

In a few places the manuscript has deteriorated since the facsimile was made; in particular, at the top of f. 92ᵇ the ink has been lost from several words which are complete in the facsimile.

The history of the manuscript is obscure. The earliest record of it is in the catalogue of the library of Henry Savile of Bank in Yorkshire (1568–1617); but how it came to be there, and how Sir Robert Cotton acquired it, are alike unknown. On f. 91ᵃ, above the beginning of *Gawain*, the words *Hugo de* are written in a fifteenth-century hand, but we do not know what they mean.

The poems bear no titles in the manuscript, and those by which they are known were given by modern editors. They are clearly separated by large capital letters, coloured blue and red, at the beginning of each—that of *Pearl*, beginning the written part of the manuscript, extends over 14 lines, the others over 8, and flourishes on each run to the foot of the page; and they are further separated by illustrations. Each poem is divided internally by smaller coloured capitals, which in *Gawain* vary in size and elaboration. The initial letters of lines 491, 1126, and 1998, though not all of the same size (the first is of 4 lines, the others 6), are given approximately equal prominence by long horizontal flourishes which extend right across the page, taking up the space ruled for a line of writing and so making a clear break in the sequence of the lines. These breaks come at points in the text at which the sense calls for a substantial pause. Madden was clearly right in accepting them as structural divisions of the poem having the authority of the author, and later editors have followed him in numbering them as separate parts. (There are no numbers in the manuscript.) But there are also five smaller coloured initials, extending over three lines, with simpler ornament and without the flourishes across the page or the accompanying space. These are at lines 619 (the description of Gawain's shield), 763 (Gawain's approach to Bertilak's castle), 1421 (the boar-hunt), 1893 (the last part of the fox-hunt), and 2259 (the return blow at the Green Chapel). Though each of these may be held to mark a distinct stage in the story, or an important transition, there are equally important stages which are not so marked; and these lesser capitals can hardly have been so systematically planned by the scribe as the major ones were.[1]

[1] L. L. Hill, 'Madden's Divisions of *Sir Gawain* and the "large initial capitals" of *Cotton Nero A. X*', *Speculum* xxi (1946), 67–71, argues from the occurrence

The four poems are accompanied by crude illustrations, which are now somewhat rubbed and indistinct. All precede the poems they illustrate except for three relating to *Gawain*, and all occupy a full page except one half-page picture concerning *Patience*. There are four illustrations to *Pearl*, two to *Purity*, two to *Patience*, and four to *Gawain*. The first of the *Gawain* pictures, preceding the text, shows Gawain taking the axe from King Arthur, who is standing at the high table with the Queen on his left; and also the beheading scene in front of the dais with the Green Knight on horseback holding up his severed head—all this is combined in one picture. The other three illustrations are at the end of the poem. The first of these (which is the clearest of all, and is re-produced here as the frontispiece) shows one of the lady's stealthy visits to Gawain. Above the picture is written, in a hand different from that of the scribe of the poems but contemporary with it:

Mi minde is mukul on on þat wil me noȝt amende
Sum time was trewe as ston and fro schame couþe hir defende.

These lines have no relevance to the situation in the poem. The next illustration shows Gawain on horseback at the Green Chapel, with the Green Knight, holding his axe, above; it is very in-distinct. The last depicts Gawain on his return to Camelot, in the act of kneeling before Arthur, Guenever, and a courtier. A curious feature of the illustrations is that they fail to illustrate some of the most significant features of the text—in particular, the Green Knight's face and hair are not green, and his hair and beard are no longer than Arthur's.

There is no external evidence of the place where the manuscript was written. From its linguistic forms (using the word in its widest sense) scholars have mostly agreed that it must have come from the north-west midlands, with a leaning towards Lancashire; and that there was probably no important difference between the language of the scribe and that of the poet. Professor Angus McIn-tosh, on the evidence of localized documents from the north-west midland area, concluded that '*Gawain and the Green Knight*, as it stands in MS Cotton Nero A x, can only *fit* with reasonable pro-priety in a very small area either in SE Cheshire or just over the

---

of the smaller coloured capitals that 'there is no absolute four-fold division of *Gawain*'. But this gives too little weight to the distinctive forms of the large capitals and the words of the text where they appear.

border in NE Staffordshire'.[1] Acceptance of so precise a location must await publication of the supporting documents, but it would be widely admitted to be in the right general area.

THE STORY

Gawain stands first among medieval English romances, and high among romances at large, in the strength of its plot. Even the greatest Arthurian stories, French no less than English—such as Chrétien's *Yvain* or the prose *Perlesvaus*—present strings of adventures which, though sometimes systematically 'interlaced', are often only loosely connected with each other or with the main theme. This discursive incoherence is apparently inherited from the older Celtic narratives from which so much of the Arthurian legend derives.[2] It is conspicuous in the stories of the Welsh *Mabinogion*, which though told with great subtlety and power are even less unified in structure than French or English romances. But in *Gawain* there are no adventures brought in simply for their own sake. Though the hero's two long journeys gave obvious openings for many, the author resisted the temptation:

> And mony aventure in vale, and venquyst ofte,
> þat I ne tyȝt at þis tyme in tale to remene.
>
> (2482–3)

There are two 'adventures', the first (occupying the first and fourth divisions of the poem) of the Green Knight's challenge and the ensuing beheading match, the second (in the second and third divisions) of the temptation of Gawain by the lady at the castle of Bertilak de Hautdesert. The outcome of the beheading match, and so the life of Gawain, is made to depend—though Gawain does not know it—on his conduct at the castle; and the temptation, primarily a test of chastity and of honourable behaviour towards a host, becomes through the additional device of the 'exchange of winnings' yet another trial both of courage and of truth to the pledged word. The intricacy with which each element is linked to the other—the three blows of the return match to the three mornings of the temptation, the 'nirt in þe nek' to the failure to fulfil the contract of exchange, even the green and gold of the

---

[1] 'A New Approach to Middle English Dialectology', *English Studies* xliv (1963), 1–11, esp. p. 5.

[2] See especially R. S. Loomis in the books noted in the Bibliography.

girdle gleaming in the castle bedroom, where Gawain had no cause to associate it with his mysterious adversary at Camelot (and where only an unusually alert reader is likely at once to recall where he last met those colours)—is almost equal to the interlocking of the pentangle itself, 'vchone halched in oþer, þat non ende hade' (657). Many readers have been disappointed that this admirable unity should in the end be ascribed simply to the malignity of Morgan le Fay; but it is no less sufficient a motive than that of many another Arthurian adventure, except the great ones of the Grail and the *Morte* itself.

Incidents resembling both the adventures are found separately in other romances earlier than *Gawain*, and in three English poems which are later. Elements of both of them even occur together in one or two of the earlier texts. But no other story yet discovered embodies the distinguishing master-stroke of *Gawain* by which the outcome of the temptation determines the conclusion of the beheading match, and there is no close analogue at all to the exchange of winnings.

The 'sources and analogues' have been summarized and discussed very fully (though highly speculatively) by G. L. Kittredge in *A Study of Gawain and the Green Knight*, more briefly by Mabel Day in the introduction to Gollancz's edition, and by Laura Hibbard Loomis in chapter 39 of *Arthurian Literature in the Middle Ages*. (For particulars of these books, and others mentioned below, see the Bibliography.) The following outline points out only the most notable features.

The theme of the beheading match occurs first in a Middle Irish prose narrative called *Fled Bricrend*, 'Bricriu's Feast'; the earliest manuscript dates from about 1100, but the story is evidently much older. The heroes of Ulster compete for 'the champion's portion', and among their contests are two distinct episodes in which each of them faces a challenge to behead a superhumanly strong opponent on condition that he shall submit to a return blow the next day. In the first account the incident occurs away from the king's court. Only Cuchulainn takes up the challenge. He keeps his word to come back and receive the blow, and his opponent, after three strokes of the axe which do not harm him, declares him champion. In the second account (separately headed 'The Champion's Bargain') the scene is the royal court. Three of the heroes in turn behead the challenger, but fail to appear for the return blow. Then Cuchulainn accepts the challenge, and keeps his word. This time he receives one stroke with the back of the axe, and again is judged to be champion. In both versions the challenger can change his shape, and when his head is cut off he picks it up and goes away without replacing it on his shoulders. Besides these two features the points of special resemblance to *Gawain* are the fierceness of the challenger, his declared wish to test the courage of the heroes of whom he has heard so much, and his use of an axe.

All the other stories in which this extraordinary challenge appears are romances associated with Arthur, most of them in French and of the thirteenth century:

1. *Le Livre de Caradoc*, part of the anonymous first continuation of the *Perceval* which Chrétien de Troyes left unfinished. The 'long' version of this text is closest to *Gawain* of all the analogues. (It has been claimed to be the direct source of the beheading incident;[1] but the differences between the two narratives appear too great for this to be accepted.) The main points of agreement are these: Arthur and Guenever are at table ready for a feast, but Arthur, according to his custom, waits for a marvel before beginning it. The challenger rides into the hall on horseback and first addresses Arthur, but Caradoc undertakes the adventure. The period between the blows is a year, and when the challenger delays his return blow Caradoc accuses him of cowardice. In the prose version of this story, known first from the text printed in Paris in 1530 as *Perceual le galloys*, the challenger is dressed in green satin. Differences from *Gawain*, in addition to the identity of the hero, are these: The feast is at Pentecost, not Christmas, and at 'Cardoil', not Camelot. The challenger is an urbane knight, who enters singing and greets Arthur courteously, and his weapon is a sword. He replaces his head on his shoulders. The hero makes no journey, for the return blow takes place at Arthur's court; and, though there are interruptions, there are no feints. The challenger turns out to be Caradoc's father, who declares that he spares him on this account.

2. The French prose *Perlesvaus* includes an episode about

---

[1] See esp. L. D. Benson, 'The source of the Beheading Episode in *Sir Gawain and the Green Knight*', *M.P.* lix (1961), 1–12, and further in *Art and Tradition in Sir Gawain and the Green Knight*, pp. 16–37.

Lancelot (ed. Nitze and Jenkins, pp. 136–8, 283–6). In a waste city a young knight with an axe proposes an exchange of blows, and Lancelot duly beheads him. The body disappears, but a year later Lancelot keeps his promise to return and is met by the knight's brother, who appears sharpening his axe. Lancelot shrinks from the first blow, and is reproached; while he prepares for another a lady appeals for his life, and the knight drops the axe and praises his fidelity. In addition to the difference of setting, and the introduction of the knight's brother, there is the important development that the incident leads to the disenchantment of the waste city.

3. *La Mule sans Frein*, or *La Damoisele à la Mule*, by Paien de Maisières, embodies an episode (ll. 496–1035) in which Gauvain— his first appearance in this role—is challenged in a strange castle to a beheading match by a *vilain* armed with a *jusarme*. When Gauvain keeps his promise to meet the return blow the next day the challenger lifts his axe but does not strike him.

4. *Diu Crône*, a High German poem by Heinrich von dem Türlin, contains another version, fuller than Paien's, of the same story (ll. 13004–185). Instead of the boor it is an enchanter named Gansguoter who challenges Gawain to a beheading match. He replaces his head, and at the return meeting the next day he aims two blows at Gawain without striking him.

5. *Hunbaut*, another French romance, again has Gawain as its hero, and a *vilain* who challenges him to a beheading match (ll. 1462–1539). It differs from other versions in that the return blow never takes place. Gawain holds his opponent back from his severed head so that he cannot pick it up, and he dies.

All these variants of the beheading theme clearly derive ulti-mately from an Irish story like that found in *Fled Bricrend*,[1] in which it was a test of courage and honour. No such clear descent can be found for the theme of the temptation of a knight by a lady. R. S. Loomis has observed[2] that something like an analogue appears, together with other features resembling aspects of *Gawain*, in the story of Pwyll and Arawn in the *Mabinogion*, so that this

---

[1] See further Alice Buchanan, 'The Irish Framework of *Gawain and the Green Knight*', *P.M.L.A.* xlvii (1932), 315–38.

[2] *Wales and the Arthurian Legend*, ch. vi, and *Development of Arthurian Romance*, p. 157.

theme also would seem to be Celtic in origin. Yet the resemblance is distant—the lady makes no approach, and nothing is said of a test—and the *Gawain* episode could not have been derived from this story as it stands. Incidents a good deal closer to *Gawain* are contained in many Arthurian stories, of which the most significant are these:

1. *Lanzelet*, a verse translation from Anglo-Norman by the Swiss Ulrich von Zatzikhoven in the late twelfth century, contains an episode in which three knights in bed are tempted by their host's daughter (tr. Webster, pp. 34–43). Two of them reject her, but Lancelot willingly yields. The essential difference from the situation in *Gawain*—apart from the conduct of the hero—is that the girl behaves not as the agent of the host but against his wishes. In the morning he angrily challenges Lancelot to a singular duel in which they are to throw knives at each other in turn (somewhat in the manner of the beheading match), and he is himself killed.

2. In *Yder*, another French romance, a queen on her husband's instructions tests Yder's virtue by making outspoken advances to him in the hall where he has fallen asleep (ll. 185–510). He emphasizes his rejection of her by knocking her down with a kick in the stomach, to the amusement and satisfaction of the courtiers who are present. Apart from its remarkable crudity this tale differs essentially from *Gawain* in that Yder has been warned by the king that he is to be tested in this way; and the incident takes place in public. ·

3. In the prose romance of *Lancelot del Lac* the hero meets various sexual temptations. The closest to *Gawain* is an episode in which Morgain la Fée, having attempted without success to win Lancelot from his devotion to Guenever, sends her maid to try to seduce him while he is in bed. Despite repeated passionate appeals, she fails. Lancelot does not behave with Gawain's *cortaysye* —when she finally kisses him, 'il saut sus si angoisseus que por vn poi qu'il nissi du sens et corut a s'espee, et li dist que se elle ne fust femme il li copast la teste' (*Vulgate Version*, iv, p. 127).

Temptations in some ways similar appear in *Hunbaut* (ll. 490–846) and in *Le Chevalier à l'Épée* (ll. 1–848), in both of which Gawain is concerned. In both tales the host is the instigator, but openly—in *Hunbaut* he makes Gawain kiss his daughter, in *Le Chevalier* go to bed with her. In *Hunbaut* he is angry when Gawain kisses her four times; in *Le Chevalier* Gawain is restrained by the girl's warning that a magic sword above the bed will kill him if he comes too close, but he does go far enough to be wounded by it twice. In these stories the sense of the incident is quite different from that of the temptation scenes in *Gawain*, and they are to be classed rather with the 'imperious host' theme. The same is true of *Sir Gawain and the Carl of Carlisle*, an English romance, in two versions, of a date later than our poem.[1] Here the hero is ordered to bed with his host's wife, but prevented by him from intercourse with her; the host's daughter is sent to him instead.

This last poem has been held to embody an association of the two themes in *Sir Gawain and the Green Knight*, for in the version of it in the Percy Folio manuscript (written about 1650) it concludes with a beheading. The Carl, a hideous giant, tells Gawain to cut off his head, and when he does so the Carl is freed from a spell and restored to the form of a man. Another late text, *The Turk and Gawain*, also in the Percy manuscript, tells how a dwarf comes to Arthur's court with a challenge to anyone who will 'give a buffet and take another'. The incident of the 'buffet' itself has been lost from the manuscript, so that its nature is unknown; but evidently Gawain gives it. He then goes away with the dwarf, who after various adventures asks him to cut off his head. Like the Carl, the dwarf is thereby restored to knightly shape. These versions evidently depend on a special development of the beheading theme, in which the notion of an apparently desperate return blow as a test of courage and honour has been replaced by that of a mere technique of disenchantment. The nearest to this in earlier texts is the disenchantment of the waste city in *Perlesvaus*, but that was attributable to Lancelot's fidelity to his promise, not to the blow itself. These two later poems, therefore, deviate considerably from the tradition seen in *Gawain*, and throw little light upon it. The other late English text is the ballad of *The Green Knight*, which is evidently a debased and contaminated version of *Gawain* itself.

It is apparent, then, that though elements of the two adventures, and others in some ways like them, are scattered fairly widely in Arthurian story—sometimes, as in *Lanzelet* and *Hunbaut*, both

---

[1] See A. Kurvinen's edition, esp. pp. 95–101.

adventures in the same romance—they are nowhere organically linked as in *Gawain*. Further, though the device of the exchange of winnings has been tentatively derived from the medieval Latin poem *Miles Gloriosus*, the agreement there is for sharing rather than exchange and it is not close enough to be a credible source. The components of the plot thus appear in so diverse and dispersed forms that it is fruitless to speculate about precisely how and when they came to be united.

We cannot know whether the English poet found the combined plot worked out in a French romance now lost, or whether he devised the combination himself. That he knew French romances intimately is beyond question, from his language as well as his story; but his use of French terms and even idioms (such as *cros Kryst* 762, *for alle lufez* 1786) does not mean that he took them from a particular model. Since it is the linking of the two main themes, by means of the exchange bargain, which expresses the moral of the poem, this feature of the story would surely appeal especially to a man who probably wrote also the moral poems *Purity* and *Patience*. It may well be to his own ingenuity that we owe the superbly successful interlocking.

There remain other striking features of *Gawain* which have no analogues in any of the romances that embody the leading adventures—notably the colour of the Green Knight and his horse, and the strange conception of the Green Chapel. The greenness of the Knight, and his holly 'bob', are no doubt ultimately drawn from popular belief in a 'green man'; but attempts to relate his role in the poem to ritual, or to myths of the dying year,[1] cannot be reconciled with the sources or with the story as it is told. The lonely 'chapel' may have been in part suggested by the hermitages and chapels which so often figure in French quest stories,[2] but it is nothing like a hermitage in the poem.

Whatever the form in which the poet found his plot, there is little doubt that he transformed the handling of it. It is characteristic of the French verse romancers to tell their stories, however rambling, in a comparatively plain, spare style, sometimes with perceptive use of brief description, often with subtly developed

---

[1] See especially J. Speirs, *Medieval English Poetry. The non-Chaucerian Tradition* (1957), p. 219.

[2] See G. V. Smithers, 'What *Sir Gawain and the Green Knight* is about', *M.Æ.* xxxii (1963), 171–89.

dialogue, but seldom enriching atmosphere with material expanded far beyond the demands of the tale, as the *Gawain* poet with such evident relish describes luxuries of dress and entertainment, the excitement and expertise of the hunts, the grim grandeur of winter landscape. In his eye for colour, light, and movement, his ear for the delicate nuances of cultivated talk, and above all his warm and quick appreciation of minds and motives, the poet utterly transcends anything we know that could have served him as a source. Though an ancient tale of magic is the mainspring of his plot, magic concerns him not as a theme but as a device. It is understanding of man, not the supernatural, that gives his poem its power.

For all the coherence of the plot in its main lines, some particulars must be admitted to raise questions that are never resolved. The author demonstratively delays his narrative while he explains the significance of the pentangle, which is thereby given great weight—'I am in tent yow to telle, þof tary hyt me schulde' (624). But he never returns to the subject, as he might have done, for example, to comment explicitly on the relation of the pentangle to the green belt that Gawain wore at the end 'in tokenyng he watz tane in tech of a faute'; the pentangle itself is not even mentioned by name after the elaborate account of it ending at 665. Again, though Gawain's prayer to the Virgin to guide him to shelter (737, 753–8) is fully in keeping with his devotion as expressed especially by her image on his shield (649), the poet does not dwell on the unexpected circumstance that his prayer is answered by the appearance of the very castle in which he is to undergo so severe a temptation that he would probably succumb to it without Mary's protection (1769);[1] and further, Mary is never mentioned again (except for the use of her name as an oath) in the rest of the poem—Gawain gives no thanks for her care for him, and we hear no more of his devotion. On the other hand the narrative is not without its superfluities, most conspicuous in the descriptions of the hunts and the breaking of the deer, which are extended, for enjoyment, rather beyond the bounds of reasonable elaboration. A perfectly completed structure the poem is not; but it approaches it more nearly than any other of its kind in Middle English.

---

[1] This interpretation, now generally accepted, has been challenged; see the note on this line.

RELATED POEMS

The identity of the author of *Gawain* remains wholly unknown. Speculation has not ended, but in the complete absence of evidence none of it persuades.

Gawain is closely related in most features of language and style to two of the other three poems in the manuscript, and in many qualities to the third as well. It is in detail nearest to *Purity*, which tells the stories of the Flood, the destruction of Sodom and Gomorrah, and the fall of Belshazzar to demonstrate God's hatred of 'uncleanness'—which embraces the sacrilege of Belshazzar as well as the 'filth of the flesh' punished in the other two events. The poem lacks the close-knit structure of *Gawain*, but the handling of diction and verse is very similar—most strikingly in the use of particular words and phrases in elaborate descriptions: the account of Arthur's New Year feast (*Gawain* 114 ff.) might almost be an alternative draft for Belshazzar's feast (*Purity* 1401 ff.), and some characteristic architectural details of Bertilak's castle (*Gawain* 787 ff.) reappear on the 'couered cowpes as casteles arayed' brought into Belshazzar's hall (*Purity* 1458 ff.).

Both *Purity* and *Patience* are written in alliterative lines of the same structure as the long lines in *Gawain*. They are not divided into stanzas as *Gawain* is, though they tend to fall into groups of four. Some critics, especially Gollancz, have concluded that the poet intended to write these two poems in quatrains; but the pattern is not regularly observed throughout either.

Patience is shorter, better organized, and more personal than *Purity*. It is a free and lively paraphrase of the story of Jonah, as an illustration, by its contrary, of the value of patience. But it is less directly didactic than *Purity*, which addresses the reader almost as a preacher might:

> þus vpon þrynne wyses I haf yow þro schewed
> þat vnclannes tocleues in corage dere
> Of þat wynnelych Lorde þat wonyes in heuen.

In *Patience* the poet takes the lesson to himself:

> For þy when pouerte me enprecez and paynez innoȝe
> Ful softly with suffraunce saȝttel me bihouez.

Again his descriptive gifts are notably displayed in depicting the storm at sea, and still more imaginatively in following Jonah's itinerary inside the whale. In this poem, too, there is more than a technical and linguistic resemblance to *Gawain*. The poet sometimes lightens the gravity of the scene with a humorous comment, much in the manner of such passages as the opening exchanges at the Green Chapel.

The first poem in the manuscript, *Pearl*, differs considerably from these, and indeed from any other medieval English poem. It is in the first place an elegy, in the form of a dream allegory, on the poet's little daughter who had died in her second year; but it embodies a passionately felt debate upon the right of the innocent to salvation by the grace of God, which leads to a vision of the heavenly Jerusalem. The poet is brought to reconciliation with his loss and submission to God's will. The form of the poem is almost uniquely intricate. Instead of the unrhymed alliterative line the poet here uses four-stress rhyming lines in twelve-line stanzas, embellished by alliteration and with a complex system of stanza linking. Despite these technical restrictions the movement of the poem is swifter and more lyrical than that of the others; and the poet's anguish, in his grief and his religious doubts, is most movingly conveyed. Though *Pearl* thus stands apart in both theme and technique from its companion poems, there is much in it, particularly in the richness of its diction and in its vivid scenes of light and colour, that is like them.

All four pieces are written in the same dialect and show many parallels of word and phrase. In alliterative poetry, and poetry strongly coloured by the alliterative tradition as *Pearl* is, the large common stock of material makes it especially hard to know whether 'parallel passages' imply common authorship, imitation, or simply the use of familiar conventions and set pieces. Examples of similar details in poems which otherwise differ markedly may be seen in Mabel Day's comparison of the poems in this manuscript with *The Wars of Alexander*,[1] or Morris's comparison of passages in *Purity* and *Patience* with *The Destruction of Troy*,[2] or the hunting scene at the beginning of *The Parlement of the Thre Ages* beside the end of the deer-hunt in *Gawain* (1319 ff.).[3] Among the poems of MS. Nero A. x the similarities are such that most readers find

---

[1] *Gawain*, ed. Gollancz, pp. xiii–xviii.

[2] *Early English Alliterative Poems*, pp. x–xi.

[3] See further Oakden, *Alliterative Poetry*, ii; R. A. Waldron, 'Oral Formulaic Technique and Middle English Alliterative Poetry', *Speculum* xxxii (1957), 792–804.

it simplest to assume common authorship. Apart from the details of language and metre, and shared excellences of style, some devices of form suggest it also—*Gawain*, *Patience*, and *Pearl* all conclude with lines almost identical with their opening lines, and *Gawain* and *Pearl* both contain 101 stanzas. More significantly, there is much common ground in themes and attitudes. The moral narratives *Purity* and *Patience*, composed essentially of biblical paraphrase, have obvious affinities with each other and it is easy to believe that the same man wrote both. The theological concern of *Pearl* associates it with them. The underlying moral seriousness of *Gawain*, for all its surface lightheartedness, is in keeping with them all. Dorothy Everett summed up admirably what is probably the prevailing view: 'It seems easier to assume a common author than to suppose that two or more men writing in the same locality and the same period, and certainly closely associated with one another, possessed this rare, and, one would think, inimitable quality.'[1]

The poem *St. Erkenwald*, which survives in a single paper manuscript (British Museum, Harley 2250) of perhaps the last quarter of the fifteenth century, shows a number of features of language and metre which resemble—remarkably, considering the interval between the manuscripts—the four poems of MS. Nero A. x. Its narrative of Erkenwald's intercession for a pre-Christian judge, written in alliterative lines arranged predominantly in quatrains, might be held to share the theological interests of *Pearl* and the external form of *Purity*. Many critics have in fact come to believe that it was written by the same poet. But the similarities are by no means so close as those among the four poems of the Nero manuscript, and the general tone and style of *St. Erkenwald* do not warrant this belief. Even the opening account of London, 'þe New Troie', seems unlikely to be from the same hand as the beginning of *Gawain*; and the whole poem is duller work altogether.[2]

From the four poems of the Nero manuscript a poet emerges who knew a great deal of the life and etiquette of noble households. In *Gawain* he shows a detailed, even technical, knowledge of hunting, of castle architecture, and of the armour and gear of a knight. In *Patience* he uses with an air of assurance the right

---

[1] *Essays on Middle English Literature* (Oxford, 1955), p. 68.
[2] See further L. D. Benson, 'The Authorship of *St. Erkenwald*', *J.E.G.P.* xiv (1965), 393–405.

terms for the parts of a ship. His reading was especially in the Vulgate Bible, from which comes much of the material of all the poems except *Gawain*; and the debate in *Pearl* implies an acquaintance with patristic theology as well. In *Purity* he cites 'Clopyngnel in þe compas of his clene Rose'—the *Roman de la Rose* by Jean de Meun or Clopinel—and the account of the Dead Sea in the same poem draws upon the French text of *Mandeville's Travels*. Whether or not he had any particular 'Brutus bokez' in mind as sources of *Gawain*, it is certain that he had read widely in French romance. His language, though strongly provincial in many of its words and forms, is yet highly sophisticated in its use of courtly terms and elegant modes of conversation. His mind was of a different cast from Chaucer's in obvious ways: he entirely lacked, for instance, Chaucer's deep interest in astrology and its associated sciences, and he had nothing to say about the great Boethian problems of foreknowledge and free will. But in learning, wit, and humanity he is a worthy companion.

DATE AND PLACE

Gawain cannot be dated precisely. The latest possible date is obviously that of the manuscript, which can hardly be later than 1400; but it is plainly not the author's original and there is no way of telling how often or at what interval it may have been copied. Internal evidence is vague. The elaboration of the castle architecture, especially the profusion of pinnacles, is typical of the late fourteenth century; the richness of costume and furnishings, and the style of armour, are appropriate to the same period though they would not in themselves exclude a rather earlier one—there is ample testimony to the cultivation of luxury in dress and household by the middle of the century. Even the lady's *tressour* (1739) is anticipated in one of the poems in MS. Harley 2253, which is now dated *c.* 1340 (Facsimile ed. N. R. Ker, E.E.T.S. 255 (1965), p. xxi and f. 106ᵛ; poem ed. F. J. Furnivall, E.E.T.S. 117 (1901), p. 511):

> Þe ryche ledies in huere bour
> Þat wereden gold on huere tressour.

Perhaps the repeated emphasis on complex design and lavish display is enough to imply a date towards the end of the century.

The state of the language, so far as that of the original can be detected from metre and rhyme, gives no more precise evidence than the content. It is clear that historical inflexional -e in disyllables had been largely dropped (see p. 133), so that in this particular the language is more advanced than that of London in the late fourteenth century. But though not much is known about the chronology of the loss of -e in different regions it certainly fell earlier in the north than in London, and its recessive condition in this text gives no firm indication of date. The general composition of the vocabulary, with its considerable proportion of French words current elsewhere in the second half of the fourteenth century, fits in well enough with the impression made by the descriptions. The most likely date, on these vague indications, is again in the latter part of the century.

The area of composition is a little less uncertain. The firmest evidence is the local knowledge shown by the author. In lines 691–702 he seems to know a good deal about the geography of North Wales and Wirral, and to expect that his audience will be interested in the district. Since some of the places he mentions cannot be identified, his complete accuracy is uncertain; but his selection of only this region to describe by name surely implies that he was writing not far from it.

The language contains many northerly features. There is an important group of words otherwise found mainly in northern and north-midland texts, and within this group a number which appear only in conspicuously northern and Scottish writers—such as *brent, farand, ron, snayp, snart, stang* (see p. 139). Some inflexions, confirmed by rhyme, are similarly northerly—the regular -*es*, -*ez* in 2 and 3 sg. of verbs (*cnokez* 414 : *strokes*), and occasionally in pl. (*hyƷes* 1351); the pron. *payres* 1019; the pres. part. ending -*ande* 1207, which is predominantly though not exclusively northerly; the shortened stem of 'take', *ta* 2357. The frequent preservation of unrounded *ā*, as *hame* 1534, *wape* 2355, shows familiarity with the northern tradition; the retention of *aw* from OE. *āw* (*knowe* 1645 : *lawe, drowe* with scribal *ow* for etymological *aw*) is characteristic of the north-west midlands[1] as well as the north more generally.

But other inflexions are as clearly midland, notably the pres.

[1] See A. H. Smith, *The Place-Names of the West Riding of Yorkshire,* vii (E.P.N.S. 36, 1962), p. 82.

pl. in -en of most verbs (though this does not appear in rhyme), and the pron. *ho* 'she', of which the initial is confirmed by alliteration in 948 and 2463, is typically north-west midland. Of sounds, the rounded vowel in *brode* 967 (:*Gode*) and the development of OE. *hw* to *w* shown by alliteration are again midland rather than northern. The distribution of some forms is uncertain. The past part. *tone* 2159 has its *o* unhistorically, and might be supposed to arise in a border area; but this very form and comparably anomalous ones are used even in some Scottish texts,[1] so that they must have been known and exploited as variants without necessary regional significance. OE. *a/o* followed by *ng* rhymes on /u/ in *stronge, longe* 34–36 : *tonge, fonge* 1315 : *ȝonge*. This is usually held to be typical of the west midlands,[2] but the evidence is slight and there are some cases in other areas.[3] Two words in the vocabulary are in modern times found in limited dialect areas: *kay* 422, recorded only in Lancashire and Cheshire, and *misy* 749, modern *mizzy*, only in south Lancashire: but survival in dialects is erratic and an unsafe guide to fourteenth-century conditions, so that these are less impressive than the larger number of words that can be seen to have been northern at the approximate date of the poem.

The language is not a simple and self-consistent local dialect. The author obviously used to some extent a traditional poetic vocabulary, and also combined with English and Scandinavian words of restricted currency many French words which cannot have been limited to a comparatively remote area. In somewhat the same way he took advantage of variants of form and pronunciation known extensively in the alliterative tradition. His language is to some extent eclectic; yet the basis of it is no doubt, as most scholars have long believed, a dialect of the north-west midlands.

---

[1] See J. Farish, *English Studies* xxxviii (1957), 1–6.
[2] As for example by A. H. Smith, *English Place-Name Elements*, I. xxxiv.
[3] See M. S. Serjeantson, *R.E.S.* vii (1931), 450–2.

THE TEXT

THE spelling of the manuscript is reproduced, except for correction of scribal errors. Emendations are indicated by footnotes, which give the forms in the manuscript and the names of those who proposed the principal emendations adopted. No emendations have been made on purely metrical grounds, for the details of the original metrical form are too uncertain; but a few have been made to restore alliteration. Corrections made by the original scribe are as a rule not recorded. Abbreviations have been expanded without notice. There is doubt about the meaning of only three of them: 1. The sign ꝫ, which normally means *-us*, occasionally serves as a mere equivalent of *-s*; see footnotes to 456, 2027. The pronoun 'us' is written *vꝫ* everywhere except 2246, where it is once *vs*. This may be a scribal eccentricity which should be printed *vs* throughout (so Magoun, *Anglia* lxi (1937), 129–30); yet since the abbreviation certainly stands for *-us* in many places some uncertainty remains, and the word is here shown as *vus* in the usual way. 2. The compendium *wᵗ* could stand for either *with* or *wyth*, both of which are used when the word is written out; *with* has been chosen as the simpler. 3. The crossed *q*, used in writing Latin for *quod*, is here expanded to *quoþ*. The word is nowhere so written in the manuscript, but cf. *cope* 776.

Word-division has been regularized without notice: words which stand divided in the manuscript, such as *in noȝe* 514, have been joined (one or two special collocations are hyphenated, as *as-tit* 31), and many which are written without space, such as *bisypeȝ* 17, have been separated. The long *i* is printed *j* except in *iwis* and the pronoun *I*. The manuscript does not distinguish in form between *ȝ* and *ȥ*, the form *ȝ* serving for both; but where the letter is *ȥ* it is so printed. Capital letters are used as in modern English, and punctuation—which does not exist in the manuscript—is supplied. The only diacritic introduced is an acute accent to mark an unaccented *e* when it stands for etymological *i* or OFr. *é*, as in *meré* 'merry', *bewté* 'beauty'.

The Beginning of the Text

MS. Cotton Nero A. x, Art. 3, folio 91 a

(*slightly reduced*)

SIR GAWAYN AND
ÞE GRENE KNYȜT

——◆◆◆◆◆——

I

SIÞEN þe sege and þe assaut watz sesed at Troye,
  þe borȝ brittened and brent to brondez and askez,
þe tulk þat þe trammes of tresoun þer wroȝt
Watz tried for his tricherie, þe trewest on erthe:
Hit watz Ennias þe athel, and his highe kynde,   5
þat siþen depreced prouinces, and patrounes bicome
Welneȝe of al þe wele in þe west iles.
Fro riche Romulus to Rome ricchis hym swyþe,
With gret bobbaunce þat burȝe he biges vpon fyrst,   *founds*
And neuenes hit his aune nome, as hit now hat;   10
Tirius to Tuskan and teldes bigynnes,
Langaberde in Lumbardie lyftes vp homes,
And fer ouer þe French flod Felix Brutus   *hill sides*
On mony bonkkes ful brode Bretayn he settez
      wyth wynne,   *bob*   15
   Where werre and wrake and wonder
   Bi syþez hatz wont þerinne,   *wheel*   *? sets tone for whole poem*
   And oft boþe blysse and blunder
   Ful skete hatz skyfted synne.

Ande quen þis Bretayn watz bigged bi þis burn rych,   20
Bolde bredden þerinne, baret þat lofden,
In mony turned tyme tene þat wroȝten.
Mo ferlyes on þis folde han fallen here oft
þen in any oþer þat I wot, syn þat ilk tyme.
Bot of alle þat here bult, of Bretaygne kynges,   25
Ay watz Arthur þe hendest, as I haf herde telle.

11 Tirius] *Silverstein*; *MS.* Ticius

B

Forþi an aunter in erde I attle to schawe,
þat a selly in siȝt summe men hit holden,
And an outtrage awenture of Arthurez wonderez.
If ȝe wyl lysten þis laye bot on littel quile,   30
I schal telle hit as-tit, as I in toun herde,
        with tonge,
    As hit is stad and stoken
    In stori stif and stronge,
    With lel letteres loken,   35
    In londe so hatz ben longe.

þis kyng lay at Camylot vpon Krystmasse
With mony luflych lorde, ledez of þe best,
Rekenly of þe Rounde Table alle þo rich breþer,
With rych reuel oryȝt and rechles merþes.   40
þer tournayed tulkes by tymez ful mony,
Justed ful jolilé þise gentyle kniȝtes,
Syþen kayred to þe court caroles to make.
For þer þe fest watz ilyche ful fiften dayes,
With alle þe mete and þe mirþe þat men couþe avyse;   45
Such glaum ande gle glorious to here,
Dere dyn vpon day, daunsyng on nyȝtes,
Al watz hap vpon heȝe in hallez and chambrez
With lordez and ladies, as leuest him þoȝt.
With all þe wele of þe worlde þay woned þer samen,   50
þe most kyd knyȝtez vnder Krystes seluen,
And þe louelokkest ladies þat euer lif haden,
And he þe comlokest kyng þat þe court haldes;
For al watz þis fayre folk in her first age,
        on sille,   55
    þe hapnest vnder heuen,
    Kyng hyȝest mon of wylle;
    Hit were now gret nye to neuen
    So hardy a here on hille.

Wyle Nw Ȝer watz so ȝep þat hit watz nwe cummen,   60
þat day doubble on þe dece watz þe douth serued.
Fro þe kyng watz cummen with knyȝtes into þe halle,

---

41 by] y *rubbed, former edd.* bi   43 make] ake *rewritten in another hand*
46 glaum ande] *Emerson; MS.* glaumande   58 were] werere

christian lay

þe chauntré of þe chapel cheued to an ende,
Loude crye watz þer kest of clerkez and oþer,
Nowel nayted onewe, neuened ful ofte;   f. 92ª
And syþen riche forth runnen to reche hondeselle,   *offer*   66
Ȝeȝed ȝeres-ȝiftes on hiȝ, ȝelde hem bi hond,
Debated busyly aboute þo giftes;   *lady, lady*
Ladies laȝed ful loude, þoȝ þay lost haden,
And he þat wan watz not wrothe, þat may ȝe wel trawe. *believe* 70
Alle þis mirþe þay maden to þe mete tyme;   *romantic ritual*
When þay had waschen worþyly þay wenten to sete,
þe best burne ay abof, as hit best semed,
Whene Guenore, ful gay, grayþed in þe myddes,   *seated*
Dressed on þe dere des, dubbed al aboute,   *decorated seat* 75
Smal sendal bisides, a selure hir ouer   *carpets rich silk, canopy*
Of tryed tolouse, of tars tapites innoghe,
þat were enbrawded and beten wyth þe best gemmes
þat myȝt be preued of prys wyth penyes to bye,
        in daye.   80
    þe comlokest to discrye
    þer glent with yȝen gray,   *glanced*
    A semloker þat euer he syȝe
truly Soth moȝt no mon say.

Bot Arthure wolde not ete til al were serued,   *courteous* 85
He watz so joly of his joyfnes, and sumquat childgered: *jovial high spirits*
His lif liked hym lyȝt, he louied þe lasse   *cheerful/busy*
Auþer to longe lye or to longe sitte,
So bisied him his ȝonge blod and his brayn wylde.
And also an oþer maner meued him eke   90
þat he þurȝ nobelay had nomen, he wolde neuer ete
Vpon such a dere day er hym deuised were
Of sum auenturus þyng an vncouþe tale,
Of sum mayn meruayle, þat he myȝt trawe,   *believe in*
Of alderes, of armes, of oþer auenturus,   95
Oþer sum segg hym bisoȝt of sum siker knyȝt   *knight*
To joyne wyth hym in iustyng, in jopardé to lay,
Lede, lif for lyf, leue vchon oþer,

81 discrye] discry *rewritten, over stain, in another hand, as in 43 opposite*
82 glent] e *in darker ink over another letter*   yȝen] n *rewritten*   88 longe
(*1st*)] lenge   95 Of (*1st*)] Of of

As fortune wolde fulsun hom, þe fayrer to haue.
þis watz þe kynges countenaunce where he in court were,   100
At vch farand fest among his fre meny
       in halle.   f. 92^b
     þerfore of face so fere
     He stiȝtlez stif in stalle,
     Ful ȝep in þat Nw ȝere   105
     Much mirthe he mas withalle.

Thus þer stondes in stale þe stif kyng hisseluen,
Talkkande bifore þe hyȝe table of trifles ful hende.
There gode Gawan watz grayþed Gwenore bisyde,
And Agrauayn a la dure mayn on þat oþer syde sittes,   110
Boþe þe kynges sistersunes and ful siker kniȝtes;
Bischop Bawdewyn abof biginez þe table,
And Ywan, Vryn son, ette with hymseluen.
þise were diȝt on þe des and derworþly serued,
And siþen mony siker segge at þe sidbordez.   115
þen þe first cors come with crakkyng of trumpes,
Wyth mony baner ful bryȝt þat þerbi henged;
Nwe nakryn noyse with þe noble pipes,
Wylde werbles and wyȝt wakned lote,
þat mony hert ful hiȝe hef at her towches.   120
Dayntés dryuen þerwyth of ful dere metes,
Foysoun of þe fresche, and on so fele disches
þat pine to fynde þe place þe peple biforne
For to sette þe sylueren þat sere sewes halden
       on clothe.   125
     Iche lede as he loued hymselue
     þer laght withouten loþe;
     Ay two had disches twelue,
     Good ber and bryȝt wyn boþe.

Now wyl I of hor seruise say yow no more,   130
For vch wyȝe may wel wit no wont þat þer were.
An oþer noyse ful newe neȝed biliue,
þat þe lude myȝt haf leue liflode to cach;

---

    100 þe *supplied* (Madden)   103–5 *Ink lost from many letters at the be-*
ginning of these lines, esp. stiȝtlez *no longer legible in MS. though clear in facsimile*
113 with] wit; *no space between* ette *and* wit, te *crowded in*   115 siker]
i *with accent, altered from* e   124 sylueren] syluener

For vneþe watz þe noyce not a whyle sesed,
And þe fyrst cource in þe court kyndely serued,   135
þer hales in at þe halle dor an aghlich mayster,
On þe most on þe molde on mesure hyghe;
Fro þe swyre to þe swange so sware and so þik,
And his lyndes and his lymes so longe and so grete,
Half etayn in erde I hope þat he were,   f. 93ª
Bot mon most I algate mynn hym to bene,   141
And þat þe myriest in his muckel þat myƷt ride;
For of bak and of brest al were his bodi sturne,
Both his wombe and his wast were worthily smale,
And alle his fetures folƷande, in forme þat he hade,   145
    ful clene;
    For wonder of his hwe men hade,
    Set in his semblaunt sene;
    He ferde as freke were fade,
    And oueral enker-grene.   150

Ande al grayþed in grene þis gome and his wedes:
A strayte cote ful streƷt, þat stek on his sides,
A meré mantile abof, mensked withinne
With pelure pured apert, þe pane ful clene
With blyþe blaunner ful bryƷt, and his hod boþe,   155
þat watz laƷt fro his lokkez and layde on his schulderes;
Heme wel-haled hose of þat same,
þat spenet on his sparlyr, and clene spures vnder
Of bryƷt golde, vpon silk bordes barred ful ryche,
And scholes vnder schankes þere þe schalk rides;   160
And alle his vesture uerayly watz clene verdure,
Boþe þe barres of his belt and oþer blyþe stones,
þat were richely rayled in his aray clene
Aboutte hymself and his sadel, vpon silk werkez.
þat were to tor for to telle of tryfles þe halue   165
þat were enbrauded abof, wyth bryddes and flyƷes,
With gay gaudi of grene, þe golde ay inmyddes.
þe pendauntes of his payttrure, þe proude cropure,
His molaynes, and alle þe metail anamayld was þenne,
þe steropes þat he stod on stayned of þe same,   170

137 on (2nd)] o uncertain   144 Both] Napier; MS. bot   157 same]
same grene   168 þe (2nd)] pe

And his arsounz al after and his aþel skyrtes,
þat euer glemered and glent al of grene stones;
þe fole þat he ferkkes on fyn of þat ilke,
  sertayn,
  A grene hors gret and þikke,   175
  A stede ful stif to strayne,
  In brawden brydel quik—
  To þe gome he watz ful gayn.   f. 93ᵇ

Wel gay watz þis gome gered in grene,
And þe here of his hed of his hors swete.   180
Fayre fannand fax vmbefoldes his schulderes;
A much berd as a busk ouer his brest henges,
þat wyth his hiȝlich here þat of his hed reches
Watz euesed al vmbetorne abof his elbowes,
þat half his armes þer-vnder were halched in þe wyse 185
Of a kyngez capados þat closes his swyre;
þe mane of þat mayn hors much to hit lyke,
Wel cresped and cemmed, wyth knottes ful mony
Folden in wyth fildore aboute þe fayre grene,
Ay a herle of þe here, an oþer of golde;   190
þe tayl and his toppyng twynnen of a sute,
And bounden boþe wyth a bande of a bryȝt grene,
Dubbed wyth ful dere stonez, as þe dok lasted,
Syþen þrawen wyth a þwong a þwarle knot alofte,
þer mony bellez ful bryȝt of brende golde rungen. 195
Such a fole vpon folde, ne freke þat hym rydes,
Watz neuer sene in þat sale wyth syȝt er þat tyme,
  with yȝe.
  He loked as layt so lyȝt,
  So sayd al þat hym syȝe;   200
  Hit semed as no mon myȝt
  Vnder his dynttez dryȝe.

Wheþer hade he no helme ne hawbergh nauþer,
Ne no pysan ne no plate þat pented to armes,
Ne no schafte ne no schelde to schwue ne to smyte, 205
Bot in his on honde he hade a holyn bobbe,

171 skyrtes] *Menner*; *MS.* sturtes 182 as] as as 203 hawbergh
hawbrgh

þat is grattest in grene when greuez ar bare,
And an ax in his oþer, a hoge and vnmete,
A spetos sparþe to expoun in spelle, quoso myȝt.
þe lenkþe of an elnȝerde þe large hede hade, 210
þe grayn al of grene stele and of golde hewen,
þe bit burnyst bryȝt, with a brod egge
As wel schapen to schere as scharp rasores,
þe stele of a stif staf þe sturne hit bi grypte,
þat watz wounden wyth yrn to þe wandez ende, f. 94ᵃ
And al bigrauen with grene in gracios werkes; 216
A lace lapped aboute, þat louked at þe hede,
And so after þe halme halched ful ofte,
Wyth tryed tasselez þerto tacched innoghe
On botounz of þe bryȝt grene brayden ful ryche. 220
þis haþel heldez hym in and þe halle entres,
Driuande to þe heȝe dece, dut he no woþe,
Haylsed he neuer one, bot heȝe he ouer loked.
þe fyrst word þat he warp, 'Wher is', he sayd,
'þe gouernour of þis gyng? Gladly I wolde 225
Se þat segg in syȝt, and with hymself speke
  raysoun.'
  To knyȝtez he kest his yȝe,
  And reled hym vp and doun;
  He stemmed, and con studie 230
  Quo walt þer most renoun.

Ther watz lokyng on lenþe þe lude to beholde,
For vch mon had meruayle quat hit mene myȝt
þat a haþel and a horse myȝt such a hwe lach,
As growe grene as þe gres and grener hit semed, 235
þen grene aumayl on golde glowande bryȝter.
Al studied þat þer stod, and stalked hym nerre
Wyth al þe wonder of þe worlde what he worch schulde.
For fele sellyez had þay sen, bot such neuer are;
Forþi for fantoum and fayryȝe þe folk þere hit demed. 240
þerfore to answare watz arȝe mony aþel freke,
And al stouned at his steuen and stonstil seten
In a swoghe sylence þurȝ þe sale riche;

210 lenkþe ... hede] hede ... lenkþe 236 glowande] lowande

As al were slypped vpon slepe so slaked hor lotez   245
   in hyȝe—
  I deme hit not al for doute,
  Bot sum for cortaysye—
  Bot let hym þat al schulde loute
  Cast vnto þat wyȝe.

þenn Arþour bifore þe hiȝ dece þat auenture byholdez,   250
And rekenly hym reuerenced, for rad was he neuer,
And sayde, 'Wyȝe, welcum iwys to þis place,
þe hede of þis ostel Arthour I hat;   f. 94ᵇ
Liȝt luflych adoun and lenge, I þe praye,
And quat-so þy wylle is we schal wyt after.'   255
'Nay, as help me,' quoþ þe haþel, 'he þat on hyȝe syttes,
To wone any quyle in þis won, hit watz not myn ernde;
Bot for þe los of þe, lede, is lyft vp so hyȝe,
And þy burȝ and þy burnes best ar holden,
Stifest vnder stel-gere on stedes to ryde,   260
þe wyȝtest and þe worþyest of þe worldes kynde,
Preue for to play wyth in oþer pure laykez,
And here is kydde cortaysye, as I haf herd carp,
And þat hatz wayned me hider, iwyis, at þis tyme.
ȝe may be seker bi þis braunch þat I bere here   265
þat I passe as in pes, and no plyȝt seche;
For had I founded in fere in feȝtyng wyse,
I haue a hauberghe at home and a helme boþe,
A schelde and a scharp spere, schinande bryȝt,
Ande oþer weppenes to welde, I wene wel, als;   270
Bot for I wolde no were, my wedez ar softer.
Bot if þou be so bold as alle burnez tellen,
þou wyl grant me godly þe gomen þat I ask
   bi ryȝt.'
  Arthour con onsware,   275
  And sayd, 'Sir cortays knyȝt,
  If þou craue batayl bare,
  Here faylez þou not to fyȝt.'

'Nay, frayst I no fyȝt, in fayth I þe telle,
Hit arn aboute on þis bench bot berdlez chylder.   280
If I were hasped in armes on a heȝe stede,

Here is no mon me to mach, for myȝtez so wayke.
Forþy I craue in þis court a Crystemas gomen,
For hit is ȝol and Nwe ȝer, and here ar ȝep mony:
If any so hardy in þis hous holdez hymseluen,   285
Be so bolde in his blod, brayn in hys hede,
þat dar stifly strike a strok for an oþer,
I schal gif hym of my gyft þys giserne ryche,
þis ax, þat is heué innogh, to hondele as hym lykes,
And I schal bide þe fyrst bur as bare as I sitte.   f. 95ª
If any freke be so felle to fonde þat I telle,   291
Lepe lyȝtly me to, and lach þis weppen,
I quit-clayme hit for euer, kepe hit as his auen,
And I schal stonde hym a strok, stif on þis flet,
Ellez þou wyl diȝt me þe dom to dele hym an oþer   295
        barlay,
    And ȝet gif hym respite,
    A twelmonyth and a day;
    Now hyȝe, and let se tite
    Dar any herinne oȝt say.'   300

If he hem stowned vpon fyrst, stiller were þanne
Alle þe heredmen in halle, þe hyȝ and þe loȝe.
þe renk on his rouncé hym ruched in his sadel,
And runischly his rede yȝen he reled aboute,
Bende his bresed broȝez, blycande grene,   305
Wayued his berde for to wayte quo-so wolde ryse.
When non wolde kepe hym with carp he coȝed ful hyȝe,
Ande rimed hym ful richely, and ryȝt hym to speke:
'What, is þis Arþures hous,' quoþ þe haþel þenne,
'þat al þe rous rennes of þurȝ ryalmes so mony?   310
Where is now your sourquydrye and your conquestes,
Your gryndellayk and your greme, and your grete wordes?
Now is þe reuel and þe renoun of þe Rounde Table
Ouerwalt wyth a worde of on wyȝes speche,
For al dares for drede withoute dynt schewed!'   315
Wyth þis he laȝes so loude þat þe lorde greued;
þe blod schot for scham into his schyre face
            and lere;

282 so] fo   283 gomen] gome *with stroke over third minim*   308 richely]
richley   312 gryndellayk] gry dellayk

He wex as wroth as wynde,
So did alle þat þer were.
Þe kyng as kene bi kynde
Þen stod þat stif mon nere,   320

Ande sayde, 'Haþel, by heuen, þyn askyng is nys,
And as þou foly hatz frayst, fynde þe behoues.
I know no gome þat is gast of þy grete wordes;   325
Gif me now þy geserne, vpon Godez halue,
And I schal bayþen þy bone þat þou boden habbes.'
Lyȝtly lepez he hym to, and laȝt at his honde.   f. 95^b
Þen feersly þat oþer freke vpon fote lyȝtis.
Now hatz Arthure his axe, and þe halme grypez,   330
And sturnely sturez hit aboute, þat stryke wyth hit þoȝt.
Þe stif mon hym bifore stod vpon hyȝt,
Herre þen ani in þe hous by þe hede and more.
Wyth sturne schere þer he stod he stroked his berde,
And wyth a countenaunce dryȝe he droȝ doun his cote,   335
No more mate ne dismayd for hys mayn dintez
Þen any burne vpon bench hade broȝt hym to drynk
       of wyne.
    Gawan, þat sate bi þe quene,
    To þe kyng he can enclyne: 340
    'I beseche now with saȝez sene
    Þis melly mot be myne.

'Wolde ȝe, worþilych lorde,' quoþ Wawan to þe kyng,
'Bid me boȝe fro þis benche, and stonde by yow þere,
Þat I wythoute vylanye myȝt voyde þis table,   345
And þat my legge lady lyked not ille,
I wolde com to your counseyl bifore your cort ryche.
For me þink hit not semly, as hit is soþ knawen,
Þer such an askyng is heuened so hyȝe in your sale,
Þaȝ ȝe ȝourself be talenttyf, to take hit to yourseluen,   350
Whil mony so bolde yow aboute vpon bench sytten,
Þat vnder heuen I hope non haȝerer of wylle,
Ne better bodyes on bent þer baret is rered.
I am þe wakkest, I wot, and of wyt feblest,
And lest lur of my lyf, quo laytes þe soþe—   355

336 hys] hẏs   343 Wawan] Gawan

Bot for as much as ȝe ar myn em I am only to prayse,
No bounté bot your blod I in my bodé knowe;
And syþen þis note is so nys þat noȝt hit yow falles,
And I haue frayned hit at yow fyrst, foldez hit to me;
And if I carp not comlyly, let alle þis cort rych
       bout blame.'   360
     Ryche togeder con roun,
     And syþen þay redden alle same
     To ryd þe kyng wyth croun,
     And gif Gawan þe game.   365

þen comaunded þe kyng þe knyȝt for to ryse;   f. 96ᵃ
And he ful radly vpros, and ruchched hym fayre,
Kneled doun bifore þe kyng, and cachez þat weppen;
And he luflyly hit hym laft, and lyfte vp his honde,
And gef hym Goddez blessyng, and gladly hym biddes   370
þat his hert and his honde schulde hardi be boþe.
'Kepe þe, cosyn,' quoþ þe kyng, 'þat þou on kyrf sette,
And if þou redez hym ryȝt, redly I trowe
þat þou schal byden þe bur þat he schal bede after.'
Gawan gotz to þe gome with giserne in honde,   375
And he baldly hym bydez, he bayst neuer þe helder.
þen carppez to Sir Gawan þe knyȝt in þe grene,
'Refourme we oure forwardes, er we fyrre passe.
Fyrst I eþe þe, haþel, how þat þou hattes
þat þou me telle truly, as I tryst may.'   380
'In god fayth,' quoþ þe goode knyȝt, 'Gawan I hatte,
þat bede þe þis buffet, quat-so bifallez after,
And at þis tyme twelmonyth take at þe an oþer
Wyth what weppen so þou wylt, and wyth no wyȝ ellez
       on lyue.'   385
     þat oþer onswarez agayn,
     'Sir Gawan, so mot I þryue
     As I am ferly fayn
     þis dint þat þou schal dryue.

'Bigog,' quoþ þe grene knyȝt, 'Sir Gawan, me lykes   390
þat I schal fange at þy fust þat I haf frayst here.
And þou hatz redily rehersed, bi resoun ful trwe,

365 Gawan] w *rewritten*   384 so] fo

Clanly al þe couenaunt þat I þe kynge asked,
Saf þat þou schal siker me, segge, bi þi trawþe,
þat þou schal seche me þiself, where-so þou hopes   395
I may be funde vpon folde, and foch þe such wages
As þou deles me to-day bifore þis douþe ryche.'
'Where schulde I wale þe,' quoþ Gauan, 'where is þy place?
I wot neuer where þou wonyes, bi hym þat me wroȝt,
Ne I know not þe, knyȝt, þy cort ne þi name.   400
Bot teche me truly þerto, and telle me how þou hattes,
And I schal ware alle my wyt to wynne me þeder,
And þat I swere þe for soþe, and by my seker traweþ.'   f. 96ᵇ
'þat is innogh in Nwe Ȝer, hit nedes no more',
Quoþ þe gome in þe grene to Gawan þe hende;   405
'Ȝif I þe telle trwly, quen I þe tape haue
And þou me smoþely hatz smyten, smartly I þe teche
Of my hous and my home and myn owen nome,
þen may þou frayst my fare and forwardez holde;
And if I spende no speche, þenne spedez þou þe better,   410
For þou may leng in þy londe and layt no fyrre—
       bot slokes!
    Ta now þy grymme tole to þe,
     And let se how þou cnokez.'
      'Gladly, sir, for soþe',
      Quoþ Gawan; his ax he strokes.   415

The grene knyȝt vpon grounde grayþely hym dresses,
A littel lut with þe hede, þe lere he discouerez,
His longe louelych lokkez he layd ouer his croun,
Let the naked nec to þe note schewe.   420
Gauan gripped to his ax, and gederes hit on hyȝt,
þe kay fot on þe folde he before sette,
Let hit doun lyȝtly lyȝt on þe naked,
þat þe scharp of þe schalk schyndered þe bones,
And schrank þurȝ þe schyire grece, and schade hit in twynne,   425
þat þe bit of þe broun stel bot on þe grounde.
þe fayre hede fro þe halce hit to þe erþe,
þat fele hit foyned wyth her fete, þere hit forth roled;
þe blod brayd fro þe body, þat blykked on þe grene;

425 schade] scade

And nawþer faltered ne fel þe freke neuer þe helder, 430
Bot styþly he start forth vpon styf schonkes, *undismayed*
And runyschly he raƷt out, þere as renkkez stoden,
LaƷt to his lufly hed, and lyft hit vp sone;
And syþen boƷez to his blonk, þe brydel he cachchez, *turns horse*
Steppez into stelbawe and strydez alofte, 435 *note*
And his hede by þe here in his honde haldez;
And as sadly þe segge hym in his sadel sette *steadily, leaning*
As non vnhap had hym ayled, þaƷ hedlez he were
      in stedde.
    He brayde his bulk aboute, 440
    þat vgly bodi þat bledde; f. 97ᵃ
    Moni on of hym had doute, *was afraid*
    Bi þat his resounz were redde. *by the time the words were uttered.* *note*

For þe hede in his honde he haldez vp euen,
Toward þe derrest on þe dece he dressez þe face, 445
And hit lyfte vp þe yƷe-lyddez and loked ful brode,
And meled þus much with his muthe, as Ʒe may now here: *'thou' form*
'Loke, Gawan, þou be grayþe to go as þou hettez, *ready*
And layte as lelly til þou me, lude, fynde, *to seek, faithful prince with honour*
As þou hatz hette in þis halle, herande þise knyƷtes; 450
To þe grene chapel þou chose, I charge þe, to fotte *make your way, to get* *note*
Such a dunt as þou hatz dalt—disserued þou habbez
To be Ʒederly Ʒolden on Nw Ʒeres morn. *promptly returned*
þe knyƷt of þe grene chapel men knowen me mony;
Forþi me for to fynde if þou fraystez, faylez þou neuer. *seeks* 455 *he seeks, cannot find*
þerfore com, oþer recreaunt be calde þe behoues.'
With a runisch rout þe raynez he tornez, *violent jerk*
Halled out at þe hal dor, his hed in his hande,
þat þe fyr of þe flynt flaƷe fro fole houes. *horse's (gen. s.)*
To quat kyth he becom knwe non þere, 460
Neuer more þen þay wyste from queþen he watz wonnen.
      What þenne?
    þe kyng and Gawen þare
    At þat grene þay laƷe and grenne,
    Ʒet breued watz hit ful bare *declared.* 465
    A meruayl among þo menne.

432 runyschly] ruyschly   438 he] ho   were] we   440 bulk]
Onions; MS. bluk   456 behoues] s *repr. by* -us *abbr.*

þaȝ Arþer þe hende kyng at hert hade wonder,
He let no semblaunt be sene, bot sayde ful hyȝe
To þe comlych quene wyth cortays speche,
'Dere dame, to-day demay yow neuer;   ~~dismay~~ dismay   470
Wel bycommes such craft vpon Cristmasse,
Laykyng of enterludez, to laȝe and to syng,
Among þise kynde caroles of knyȝtez and ladyez.
Neuer þe lece to my mete I may me wel dres,
For I haf sen a selly, I may not forsake.'   475
He glent vpon Sir Gawen, and gaynly he sayde,   *appropriately* *to the point* *note*
'Now sir, heng vp þyn ax, þat hatz innogh hewen';
And hit watz don abof þe dece on doser to henge,   *wall tapestry* f. 97ᵇ
þer alle men for meruayl myȝt on hit loke,
And bi trwe tytel þerof to telle þe wonder.   *note*   480
þenne þay boȝed to a borde þise burnes togeder,
þe kyng and þe gode knyȝt, and kene men hem serued
Of alle dayntyez double, as derrest myȝt falle;
Wyth alle maner of mete and mynstralcie boþe,   *note*
Wyth wele walt þay þat day, til worþed an ende   485
spent   in londe.   *came to pass*
          Now þenk wel, Sir Gawan,
danger   For woþe þat þou ne wonde   *neglect*
          þis auenture for to frayn
          þat þou hatz tan on honde.   490

II

gift   THIS hanselle hatz Arthur of auenturus on fyrst
          In ȝonge ȝer, for he ȝerned ȝelpyng to here. *challenge*
          Thaȝ hym wordez were wane when þay to sete wenten,
provide   Now ar þay stoken of sturne werk, stafful her hond. *cram-full*
          Gawan watz glad to begynne þose gomnez in halle,   495
          Bot þaȝ þe ende be heuy haf ȝe no wonder;
          For þaȝ men ben mery in mynde quen þay han mayn drynk,
swiftly, passes   A ȝere ȝernes ful ȝerne, and ȝeldez neuer lyke,
beginning   þe forme to þe fynisment foldez ful selden. *matches*
          Forþi þis ȝol ouerȝede, and þe ȝere after,   500
          And vche sesoun serlepes sued after oþer:
                    separated

After Crystenmasse com þe crabbed lentoun,
þat fraystez flesch wyth þe fysche and fode more symple;
Bot þenne þe weder of þe worlde wyth wynter hit þrepez,
Colde clengez adoun, cloudez vplyften,   505
Schyre schedez þe rayn in schowrez ful warme,
Fallez vpon fayre flat, flowrez þere schewen,
Boþe groundez and þe greuez grene ar her wedez,
Bryddez busken to bylde, and bremlych syngen
.For solace of þe softe somer þat sues þerafter   510
          bi bonk;
      And blossumez bolne to blowe
      Bi rawez rych and ronk,
      þen notez noble inno3e
      Ar herde in wod so wlonk.   f. 98ª

After þe sesoun of somer wyth þe soft wyndez   516
Quen Zeferus syflez hymself on sedez and erbez,
Wela wynne is þe wort þat waxes þeroute,
When þe donkande dewe dropez of þe leuez,
To bide a blysful blusch of þe bry3t sunne.   520
Bot þen hy3es heruest, and hardenes hym sone,
Warnez hym for þe wynter to wax ful rype;
He dryues wyth dro3t þe dust for to ryse,
Fro þe face of þe folde to fly3e ful hy3e;
Wroþe wynde of þe welkyn wrastelez with þe sunne,   525
þe leuez lancen fro þe lynde and ly3ten on þe grounde,
And al grayes þe gres þat grene watz ere;
þenne al rypez and rotez þat ros vpon fyrst,
And þus 3irnez þe 3ere in 3isterdayez mony,
And wynter wyndez a3ayn, as þe worlde askez,   530
          no fage,
      Til Me3elmas mone
      Watz cumen wyth wynter wage;
      þen þenkkez Gawan ful sone
      Of his anious uyage.   535

3et quyl Al-hal-day with Arþer he lenges;
And he made a fare on þat fest for þe frekez sake,
With much reuel and ryche of þe Rounde Table.

531 fage] *Onions; MS.* sage

Knyȝtez ful cortays and comlych ladies
Al for luf of þat lede in longynge þay were,   *knyȝt, prince*   540
Bot neuer þe lece ne þe later þay neuened bot merþe: *less readily*
Mony ioylez for þat ientyle iapez þer maden.   *noble*
For aftter mete with mournyng he melez to his eme,
And spekez of his passage, and pertly he sayde,   *openly*
'Now, lege lorde of my lyf, leue I yow ask;   *courtly respect*   545
ȝe knowe þe cost of þis cace, kepe I no more
trouble   To telle yow tenez þerof, neuer bot trifel;
Bot I am boun to þe bur barely to-morne
To sech þe gome of þe grene, as God wyl me wysse.'
þenne þe best of þe burȝ boȝed togeder,   550
Aywan, and Errik, and oþer ful mony,
Sir Doddinaual de Sauage, þe duk of Clarence,   f. 98ᵇ
Launcelot, and Lyonel, and Lucan þe gode,
Sir Boos, and Sir Byduer, big men boþe,
And mony oþer menskful, with Mador de la Port.   555
Alle þis compayny of court com þe kyng nerre
For to counseyl þe knyȝt, with care at her hert.
þere watz much derue doel driuen in þe sale   *severe, lament*
þat so worthé as Wawan schulde wende on þat ernde,
endure   To dryȝe a delful dynt, and dele no more   560
          wyth bronde.   *sword*
     þe knyȝt mad ay god chere,
     And sayde, 'Quat schuld I wonde?   *fear*
     Of destinés derf and dere   *grievous & pleasant*
     What may mon do bot fonde?'   *try*   565

He dowellez þer al þat day, and dressez on þe morn,
Askez erly hys armez, and alle were þay broȝt.
Fyrst a tulé tapit tyȝt ouer þe flet,
And miche watz þe gyld gere þat glent þeralofte;
þe stif mon steppez þeron, and þe stel hondelez,   570
Dubbed in a dublet of a dere tars,
And syþen a crafty capados, closed aloft,
þat wyth a bryȝt blaunner was bounden withinne.
þenne set þay þe sabatounz vpon þe segge fotez,
His legez lapped in stel with luflych greuez,   575
With polaynez piched þerto, policed ful clene,
Aboute his knez knaged wyth knotez of golde;

Queme quyssewes þen, þat coyntlych closed
His thik þrawen þyȝez, with þwonges to tachched;
And syþen þe brawden bryné of bryȝt stel ryngez   580
Vmbeweued þat wyȝ vpon wlonk stuffe,
And wel bornyst brace vpon his boþe armes,
With gode cowters and gay, and glouez of plate,
And alle þe godlych gere þat hym gayn schulde
   þat tyde;   585
  Wyth ryche cote-armure,
  His gold sporez spend with pryde,
  Gurde wyth a bront ful sure
  With silk sayn vmbe his syde.

When he watz hasped in armes, his harnays watz ryche: f. 99ª
þe lest lachet oþer loupe lemed of golde.   591
So harnayst as he watz he herknez his masse,
Offred and honoured at þe heȝe auter.
Syþen he comez to þe kyng and to his cort-ferez,
Lachez lufly his leue at lordez and ladyez;   595
And þay hym kyst and conueyed, bikende hym to Kryst.
Bi þat watz Gryngolet grayth, and gurde with a sadel
þat glemed ful gayly with mony golde frenges,
Ayquere naylet ful nwe, for þat note ryched;
þe brydel barred aboute, with bryȝt golde bounden;   600
þe apparayl of þe payttrure and of þe proude skyrtez,
þe cropore and þe couertor, acorded wyth þe arsounez;
And al watz rayled on red ryche golde naylez,
þat al glytered and glent as glem of þe sunne.
þenne hentes he þe helme, and hastily hit kysses,   605
þat watz stapled stifly, and stoffed wythinne.
Hit watz hyȝe on his hede, hasped bihynde,
Wyth a lyȝtly vrysoun ouer þe auentayle,
Enbrawden and bounden wyth þe best gemmez
On brode sylkyn borde, and bryddez on semez,   610
As papiayez paynted peruyng bitwene,
Tortors and trulofez entayled so þyk
As mony burde þeraboute had ben seuen wynter
   in toune.

590 *catchword* when he watz   591 oþer] ou*er*

þe cercle watz more o prys   615
þat vmbeclypped hys croun,
Of diamauntez a deuys
þat boþe were bry3t and broun.

THEN þay schewed hym þe schelde, þat was of schyr goulez
Wyth þe pentangel depaynt of pure golde hwez.   620
He braydez hit by þe bauderyk, aboute þe hals kestes,
þat bisemed þe segge semlyly fayre.
And quy þe pentangel apendez to þat prynce noble
I am in tent yow to telle, þof tary hyt me schulde:
Hit is a syngne þat Salamon set sumquyle   625
In bytoknyng of trawþe, bi tytle þat hit habbez,
For hit is a figure þat haldez fyue poyntez,   f. 99ᵇ
And vche lyne vmbelappez and loukez in oþer,
And ayquere hit is endelez; and Englych hit callen
Oueral, as I here, þe endeles knot.   630
Forþy hit acordez to þis kny3t and to his cler armez,
For ay faythful in fyue and sere fyue syþez
Gawan watz for gode knawen, and as golde pured,
Voyded of vche vylany, wyth vertuez ennourned
        in mote;   635
    Forþy þe pentangel nwe
    He ber in schelde and cote,
    As tulk of tale most trwe
    And gentylest kny3t of lote.

Fyrst he watz funden fautlez in his fyue wyttez,   640
And efte fayled neuer þe freke in his fyue fyngres,
And alle his afyaunce vpon folde watz in þe fyue woundez
þat Cryst ka3t on þe croys, as þe crede tellez;
And quere-so-euer þys mon in melly watz stad,
His þro þo3t watz in þat, þur3 alle oþer þyngez,   645
þat alle his forsnes he feng at þe fyue joyez
þat þe hende heuen-quene had of hir chylde;
At þis cause þe kny3t comlyche hade
In þe inore half of his schelde hir ymage depaynted,
þat quen he blusched þerto his belde neuer payred.   650

þe fyft fyue þat I finde þat þe frek vsed
Watz fraunchyse and fela3schyp forbe al þyng,
His clannes and his cortaysye croked were neuer,
And pité, þat passez alle poyntez, þyse pure fyue
Were harder happed on þat haþel þen on any oþer.   655
Now alle þese fyue syþez, for soþe, were fetled on þis kny3t,
And vchone halched in oþer, þat non ende hade,
And fyched vpon fyue poyntez, þat fayld neuer,
Ne samned neuer in no syde, ne sundred nouþer,
Withouten ende at any noke I oquere fynde,   660
Whereeuer þe gomen bygan, or glod to an ende.
þerfore on his schene schelde schapen watz þe knot
Ryally wyth red golde vpon rede gowlez,
þat is þe pure pentaungel wyth þe peple called   f. 100ᵃ
      with lore.   665
    Now grayþed is Gawan gay,
    And la3t his launce ry3t þore,
    And gef hem alle goud day,
    He wende for euermore.

He sperred þe sted with þe spurez and sprong on his way,   670
So stif þat þe ston-fyr stroke out þerafter.
Al þat se3 þat semly syked in hert,
And sayde soþly al same segges til oþer,
Carande for þat comly: 'Bi Kryst, hit is scaþe
þat þou, leude, schal be lost, þat art of lyf noble!   675
To fynde hys fere vpon folde, in fayth, is not eþe.
Warloker to haf wro3t had more wyt bene,
And haf dy3t 3onder dere a duk to haue worþed;
A lowande leder of ledez in londe hym wel semez,
And so had better haf ben þen britned to no3t,   680
Hadet wyth an aluisch mon, for angardez pryde.
Who knew euer any kyng such counsel to take
As kny3tez in cauelaciounz on Crystmasse gomnez!'
Wel much watz þe warme water þat waltered of y3en,
When þat semly syre so3t fro þo wonez   685
      þad daye.

658 fayld] f and d rewritten   659 nouþer] e lost   660 I oquere]
(?) jquere   683 cauelaciounz] cauelounz

He made non abode,
Bot wyȝtly went hys way;
Mony wylsum way he rode,
þe bok as I herde say.   690

Now ridez þis renk þurȝ þe ryalme of Logres,
Sir Gauan, on Godez halue, þaȝ hym no gomen þoȝt.
Oft leudlez alone he lengez on nyȝtez
þer he fonde noȝt hym byfore þe fare þat he lyked.
Hade he no fere bot his fole bi frythez and dounez,   695
Ne no gome bot God bi gate wyth to karp,
Til þat he neȝed ful neghe into þe Norþe Walez.
Alle þe iles of Anglesay on lyft half he haldez,
And farez ouer þe fordez by þe forlondez,
Ouer at þe Holy Hede, til he hade eft bonk   700
In þe wyldrenesse of Wyrale; wonde þer bot lyte
þat auþer God oþer gome wyth goud hert louied.   f. 100b
And ay he frayned, as he ferde, at frekez þat he met,
If þay hade herde any karp of a knyȝt grene,
In any grounde þeraboute, of þe grene chapel;   705
And al nykked hym wyth nay, þat neuer in her lyue
þay seȝe neuer no segge þat watz of suche hwez
            of grene.
      þe knyȝt tok gates straunge
      In mony a bonk vnbene,   710
      His cher ful oft con chaunge
      þat chapel er he myȝt sene.

Mony klyf he ouerclambe in contrayez straunge,
Fer floten fro his frendez fremedly he rydez.
At vche warþe oþer water þer þe wyȝe passed   715
He fonde a foo hym byfore, bot ferly hit were,
And þat so foule and so felle þat feȝt hym byhode.
So mony meruayl bi mount þer þe mon fyndez,
Hit were to tore for to telle of þe tenþe dole.
Sumwhyle wyth wormez he werrez, and with wolues als,   720
Sumwhyle wyth wodwos, þat woned in þe knarrez,
Boþe wyth bullez and berez, and borez oþerquyle,
And etaynez, þat hym anelede of þe heȝe felle;

697 neghe] noghe   705 chapel] clapel

? pathetic fallacy
winter / mood of G.

Nade he ben duȝty and dryȝe, and Dryȝtyn had serued,
Douteles he hade ben ded and dreped ful ofte.   725
For werre wrathed hym not so much þat wynter nas wors,
When þe colde cler water fro þe cloudez schadde,
And fres er hit falle myȝt to þe fale erþe;
Ner slayn wyth þe slete he sleped in his yrnes
Mo nyȝtez þen innoghe in naked rokkez,   730
þer as claterande fro þe crest þe colde borne rennez,
And henged heȝe ouer his hede in hard iisse-ikkles.
þus in peryl and payne and plytes ful harde
Bi contray caryez þis knyȝt, tyl Krystmasse euen,
            al one;   735
        þe knyȝt wel þat tyde
        To Mary made his mone,
        þat ho hym red to ryde
        And wysse hym to sum wone.   f. 101ᵃ

Bi a mounte on þe morne meryly he rydes   740
Into a forest ful dep, þat ferly watz wylde,
Hiȝe hillez on vche a halue, and holtwodez vnder
Of hore okez ful hoge a hundreth togeder;
þe hasel and þe haȝþorne were harled al samen,
With roȝe raged mosse rayled aywhere,   745
With mony bryddez vnblyþe vpon bare twyges,
þat pitosly þer piped for pyne of þe colde.
þe gome vpon Gryngolet glydez hem vnder,
þurȝ mony misy and myre, mon al hym one,
Carande for his costes, lest he ne keuer schulde   750
To se þe seruyse of þat syre, þat on þat self nyȝt
Of a burde watz borne oure baret to quelle;
And þerfore sykyng he sayde, 'I beseche þe, lorde,
And Mary, þat is myldest moder so dere,
Of sum herber þer heȝly I myȝt here masse,   755
Ande þy matynez to-morne, mekely I ask,
And þerto prestly I pray my pater and aue
            and crede.'
        He rode in his prayere,
        And cryed for his mysdede,   760

726 nas] was   727 schadde] schadden   732 iisse *altered from* ysse
751 seruyse] seruy

He sayned hym in syþes sere,
> And sayde 'Cros Kryst me spede!'

Nade he sayned hymself, segge, bot þrye,
Er he watz war in þe wod of a won in a mote,
Abof a launde, on a lawe, loken vnder bo3ez   765
Of mony borelych bole aboute bi þe diches:
A castel þe comlokest þat euer kny3t a3te,
Pyched on a prayere, a park al aboute,
With a pyked palays pyned ful þik,
þat vmbete3e mony tre mo þen two myle.   770
þat holde on þat on syde þe haþel auysed,
As hit schemered and schon þur3 þe schyre okez;
þenne hatz he hendly of his helme, and he3ly he þonkez
Jesus and sayn Gilyan, þat gentyle ar boþe,
þat cortaysly had hym kydde, and his cry herkened.   f. 101ᵇ
'Now bone hostel,' coþe þe burne, 'I beseche yow 3ette!'   776
þenne gerdez he to Gryngolet with þe gilt helez,
And he ful chauncely hatz chosen to þe chef gate,
þat bro3t bremly þe burne to þe bryge ende
      in haste.   780
   þe bryge watz breme vpbrayde,
   þe 3atez wer stoken faste,
   þe wallez were wel arayed,
   Hit dut no wyndez blaste.

þe burne bode on blonk, þat on bonk houed   785
Of þe depe double dich þat drof to þe place;
þe walle wod in þe water wonderly depe,
Ande eft a ful huge he3t hit haled vpon lofte
Of harde hewen ston vp to þe tablez,
Enbaned vnder þe abataylment in þe best lawe;   790
·And syþen garytez ful gaye gered bitwene,
Wyth mony luflych loupe þat louked ful clene:
A better barbican þat burne blusched vpon neuer.
And innermore he behelde þat halle ful hy3e,
Towres telded bytwene, trochet ful þik,   795
Fayre fylyolez þat fy3ed, and ferlyly long,

  774 sayn] say   777 gerdez] *Napier*; MS. gederez   785 blonk . . . bonk]
bonk . . . blonk   795 Towres] towre

With coruon coprounes craftyly sleȝe.
Chalkwhyt chymnees þer ches he innoȝe
Vpon bastel rouez, þat blenked ful quyte;
So mony pynakle payntet watz poudred ayquere,   800
Among þe castel carnelez clambred so þik,
þat pared out of papure purely hit semed.
þe fre freke on þe fole hit fayr innoghe þoȝt,
If he myȝt keuer to com þe cloyster wythinne,
To herber in þat hostel whyl halyday lested,   805
          auinant.
          He calde, and sone þer com
          A porter pure plesaunt,
          On þe wal his ernd he nome,
          And haylsed þe knyȝt erraunt.   810

'Gode sir,' quoþ Gawan, 'woldez þou go myn ernde
To þe heȝ lorde of þis hous, herber to craue?'
'ȝe, Peter,' quoþ þe porter, 'and purely I trowee   f. 102ᵃ
þat ȝe be, wyȝe, welcum to won quyle yow lykez.'
þen ȝede þe wyȝe ȝerne and com aȝayn swyþe,   815
And folke frely hym wyth, to fonge þe knyȝt.
þay let doun þe grete draȝt and derely out ȝeden,
And kneled doun on her knes vpon þe colde erþe
To welcum þis ilk wyȝ as worþy hom þoȝt;
þay ȝolden hym þe brode ȝate, ȝarked vp wyde,   820
And he hem raysed rekenly, and rod ouer þe brygge.
Sere seggez hym sesed by sadel, quel he lyȝt,
And syþen stabeled his stede stif men innoȝe.
Knyȝtez and swyerez comen doun þenne
For to bryng þis buurne wyth blys into halle;   825
Quen he hef vp his helme, þer hiȝed innoghe
For to hent hit at his honde, þe hende to seruen;
His bronde and his blasoun boþe þay token.
þen haylsed he ful hendly þo haþelez vchone,
And mony proud mon þer presed þat prynce to honour.   830
Alle hasped in his heȝ wede to halle þay hym wonnen,
þer fayre fyre vpon flet fersly brenned.
þenne þe lorde of þe lede loutez fro his chambre

803 innoghe] ĩnghe   813 trowee] trowoe   815 ȝerne and com *supplied*
832 fersly] ferfly, *apparently corrected*

For to mete wyth menske þe mon on þe flor;
Hé sayde, 'Ȝe ar welcum to welde as yow lykez   835
þat here is; al is yowre awen, to haue at yowre wylle
      and welde.'
   'Graunt mercy,' quoþ Gawayn,
   'þer Kryst hit yow forȝelde.'
   As frekez þat semed fayn   840
   Ayþer oþer in armez con felde.

Gawayn glyȝt on þe gome þat godly hym gret,
And þuȝt hit a bolde burne þat þe burȝ aȝte,
A hoge haþel for þe nonez, and of hyghe eldee;
Brode, bryȝt, watz his berde, and al beuer-hwed,   845
Sturne, stif on þe stryþþe on stalworth schonkez,
Felle face as þe fyre, and fre of hys speche;
And wel hym semed, for soþe, as þe segge þuȝt,
To lede a lortschyp in lee of leudez ful gode.
þe lorde hym charred to a chambre, and chefly cumaundez   f. 102ᵇ
To delyuer hym a leude, hym loȝly to serue;   851
And þere were boun at his bode burnez innoȝe,
þat broȝt hym to a bryȝt boure, þer beddyng watz noble,
Of cortynes of clene sylk wyth cler golde hemmez,
And couertorez ful curious with comlych panez   855
Of bryȝt blaunner aboue, enbrawded bisydez,
Rudelez rennande on ropez, red golde ryngez,
Tapitez tyȝt to þe woȝe of tuly and tars,
And vnder fete, on þe flet, of folȝande sute.
þer he watz dispoyled, wyth spechez of myerþe,   860
þe burn of his bruny and of his bryȝt wedez.
Ryche robes ful rad renkkez hym broȝten,
For to charge, and to chaunge, and chose of þe best.
Sone as he on hent, and happed þerinne,
þat sete on hym semly wyth saylande skyrtez,   865
þe ver by his uisage verayly hit semed
Welneȝ to vche haþel, alle on hwes
Lowande and lufly alle his lymmez vnder,
þat a comloker knyȝt neuer Kryst made
      hem þoȝt.   870

---

850 chefly] clesly   856 blaunner] *Gollancz*; *MS.* bla+7 *minims*+er *abbr.*
860 myerþe] er *abbr.*   862 hym] hem   865 hym] hyn

Wheþen in worlde he were,
Hit semed as he moȝt
Be prynce withouten pere
In felde þer felle men foȝt.

A cheyer byfore þe chemné, þer charcole brenned,   875
Watz grayþed for Sir Gawan grayþely with cloþez,
Whyssynes vpon queldepoyntes þat koynt wer boþe;
And þenne a meré mantyle watz on þat mon cast
Of a broun bleeaunt, enbrauded ful ryche
And fayre furred wythinne with fellez of þe best,   880
Alle of ermyn in erde, his hode of þe same;
And he sete in þat settel semlych ryche,
And achaufed hym chefly, and þenne his cher mended.
Sone watz telded vp a tabil on trestez ful fayre,
Clad wyth a clene cloþe þat cler quyt schewed,   885
Sanap, and salure, and syluerin sponez.
þe wyȝe wesche at his wylle, and went to his mete.   f. 103ᵃ
Seggez hym serued semly innoȝe
Wyth sere sewes and sete, sesounde of þe best,
Double-felde, as hit fallez, and fele kyn fischez,   890
Summe baken in bred, summe brad on þe gledez,
Summe soþen, summe in sewe sauered with spyces,
And ay sawes so sleȝe þat þe segge lyked.
þe freke calde hit a fest ful frely and ofte
Ful hendely, quen alle þe haþeles rehayted hym at onez,   895
      'As hende,
   þis penaunce now ȝe take,
   And eft hit schal amende.'
   þat mon much merþe con make,
   For wyn in his hed þat wende.   900

þenne watz spyed and spured vpon spare wyse
Bi preué poyntez of þat prynce, put to hymseluen,
þat he beknew cortaysly of þe court þat he were
þat aþel Arthure þe hende haldez hym one,
þat is þe ryche ryal kyng of þe Rounde Table,   905
And hit watz Wawen hymself þat in þat won syttez,

---

872 moȝt] myȝt   874 foȝt] fyȝt   877 þat] þa   883 chefly] cefly
884 tabil] tapit   893 sleȝe] sleȝez

Comen to þat Krystmasse, as case hym þen lymped.
When þe lorde hade lerned þat he þe leude hade,
Loude laȝed he þerat, so lef hit hym þoȝt,
And alle þe men in þat mote maden much joye   910
To apere in his presense prestly þat tyme,
þat alle prys and prowes and pured þewes
Apendes to hys persoun, and praysed is euer;
Byfore alle men vpon molde his mensk is þe most.
Vch segge ful softly sayde to his fere: 915
'Now schal we semlych se sleȝtez of þewez
And þe teccheles termes of talkyng noble,
Wich spede is in speche vnspurd may we lerne,
Syn we haf fonged þat fyne fader of nurture.
God hatz geuen vus his grace godly for soþe,   920
þat such a gest as Gawan grauntez vus to haue,
When burnez blyþe of his burþe schal sitte
              and synge.
        In menyng of manerez mere
        þis burne now schal vus bryng,   f. 103ᵇ
        I hope þat may hym here   926
        Schal lerne of luf-talkyng.'

Bi þat þe diner watz done and þe dere vp
Hit watz neȝ at þe niyȝt neȝed þe tyme.
Chaplaynez to þe chapeles chosen þe gate,   930
Rungen ful rychely, ryȝt as þay schulden,
To þe hersum euensong of þe hyȝe tyde.
þe lorde loutes þerto, and þe lady als,
Into a cumly closet coyntly ho entrez.
Gawan glydez ful gay and gos þeder sone;   935
þe lorde laches hym by þe lappe and ledez hym to sytte,
And couþly hym knowez and callez hym his nome,
And sayde he watz þe welcomest wyȝe of þe worlde;
And he hym þonkked þroly, and ayþer halched oþer,
And seten soberly samen þe seruise quyle.   940
þenne lyst þe lady to loke on þe knyȝt,
þenne com ho of hir closet with mony cler burdez.
Ho watz þe fayrest in felle, of flesche and of lyre,
And of compas and colour and costes, of alle oþer,

930 Chaplaynez] claplaynez

And wener þen Wenore, as þe wyȝe þoȝt.   945
Ho ches þurȝ þe chaunsel to cheryche þat hende.
An oþer lady hir lad bi þe lyft honde,
þat watz alder þen ho, an auncian hit semed,
And heȝly honowred with haþelez aboute.
Bot vnlyke on to loke þo ladyes were,   950
For if þe ȝonge watz ȝep, ȝolȝe watz þat oþer;
Riche red on þat on rayled ayquere,
Rugh ronkled chekez þat oþer on rolled;
Kerchofes of þat on, wyth mony cler perlez,
Hir brest and hir bryȝt þrote bare displayed,   955
Schon schyrer þen snawe þat schedez on hillez;
þat oþer wyth a gorger watz gered ouer þe swyre,
Chymbled ouer hir blake chyn with chalkquyte vayles,
Hir frount folden in sylk, enfoubled ayquere,
Toreted and treleted with tryflez aboute,   960
þat noȝt watz bare of þat burde bot þe blake broȝes,   f. 104ª
þe tweyne yȝen and þe nase, þe naked lyppez,
And þose were soure to se and sellyly blered;
A mensk lady on molde mon may hir calle,
           for Gode!   965
     Hir body watz schort and þik,
     Hir buttokez balȝ and brode,
     More lykkerwys on to lyk
     Watz þat scho hade on lode.

When Gawayn glyȝt on þat gay, þat graciously loked,   970
Wyth leue laȝt of þe lorde he lent hem aȝaynes;
þe alder he haylses, heldande ful lowe,
þe loueloker he lappez a lyttel in armez,
He kysses hir comlyly, and knyȝtly he melez.
þay kallen hym of aquoyntaunce, and he hit quyk askez 975
To be her seruaunt sothly, if hemself lyked.
þay tan hym bytwene hem, wyth talkyng hym leden
To chambre, to chemné, and chefly þay asken
Spycez, þat vnsparely men speded hom to bryng,
And þe wynnelych wyne þerwith vche tyme.   980
þe lorde luflych aloft lepez ful ofte,

946 Ho] *Wright*; *MS.* he   956 schedez] scheder   958 chalkquyte]
Onions; *MS.* mylkquyte   960 Toreted] toret   967 balȝ] bay   971 lent]
Andrew; *MS.* went

Mynned merthe to be made vpon mony syþez,
Hent heȝly of his hode, and on a spere henged,
And wayned hom to wynne þe worchip þerof,
þat most myrþe myȝt meue þat Crystenmas whyle—   985
'And I schal fonde, bi my fayth, to fylter wyth þe best
Er me wont þe wede, with help of my frendez.'
þus wyth laȝande lotez þe lorde hit tayt makez,
For to glade Sir Gawayn with gomnez in halle
      þat nyȝt,   990
    Til þat hit watz tyme
    þe lord comaundet lyȝt;
    Sir Gawen his leue con nyme
    And to his bed hym diȝt.

On þe morne, as vch mon mynez þat tyme   995
þat Dryȝtyn for oure destyné to deȝe watz borne,
Wele waxez in vche a won in worlde for his sake;
So did hit þere on þat day þurȝ dayntés mony:
Boþe at mes and at mele messes ful quaynt   f. 104^b
Derf men vpon dece drest of þe best.   1000
þe olde auncian wyf heȝest ho syttez,
þe lorde lufly her by lent, as I trowe;
Gawan and þe gay burde togeder þay seten,
Euen inmyddez, as þe messe metely come,
And syþen þurȝ al þe sale as hem best semed.   1005
Bi vche grome at his degré grayþely watz serued
þer watz mete, þer watz myrþe, þer watz much ioye,
þat for to telle þerof hit me tene were,
And to poynte hit ȝet I pyned me parauenture.
Bot ȝet I wot þat Wawen and þe wale burde   1010
Such comfort of her compaynye caȝten togeder
þurȝ her dere dalyaunce of her derne wordez,
Wyth clene cortays carp closed fro fylþe,
þat hor play watz passande vche prynce gomen,
      in vayres.   1015
    Trumpez and nakerys,
    Much pypyng þer repayres;
    Vche mon tented hys,
    And þay two tented þayres.

Much dut watz þer dryuen þat day and þat oþer,   1020
And þe þryd as þro þronge in þerafter;
þe ioye of sayn Jonez day watz gentyle to here,
And watz þe last of þe layk, leudez þer þoƷtén.
þer wer gestes to go vpon þe gray morne,
Forþy wonderly þay woke, and þe wyn dronken,   1025
Daunsed ful dreƷly wyth dere carolez.
At þe last, when hit watz late, þay lachen her leue,
Vchon to wende on his way þat watz wyƷe stronge.
Gawan gef hym god day, þe godmon hym lachchez,
Ledes hym to his awen chambre, þe chymné bysyde,   1030
And þere he draƷez hym on dryƷe, and derely hym þonkkez
Of þe wynne worschip þat he hym wayued hade,
As to honour his hous on þat hyƷe tyde,
And enbelyse his burƷ with his bele chere:
'Iwysse sir, quyl I leue, me worþez þe better   1035
þat Gawayn hatz ben my gest at Goddez awen fest.'   f. 105ᵃ
'Grant merci, sir,' quoþ Gawayn, 'in god fayth hit is yowrez,
Al þe honour is your awen—þe heƷe kyng yow Ʒelde!
And I am wyƷe at your wylle to worch youre hest,
As I am halden þerto, in hyƷe and in loƷe,   1040
          bi riƷt.'
          þe lorde fast can hym payne
          To holde lenger þe knyƷt;
          To hym answarez Gawayn
          Bi non way þat he myƷt.   1045

Then frayned þe freke ful fayre at himseluen
Quat derue dede had hym dryuen at þat dere tyme
So kenly fro þe kyngez kourt to kayre al his one,
Er þe halidayez holly were halet out of toun.
'For soþe, sir,' quoþ þe segge, 'Ʒe sayn bot þe trawþe,   1050
A heƷe ernde and a hasty me hade fro þo wonez,
For I am sumned myselfe to sech to a place,
I ne wot in worlde whederwarde to wende hit to fynde.
I nolde bot if I hit negh myƷt on Nw Ʒeres morne
For alle þe londe inwyth Logres, so me oure lorde help!   1055
Forþy, sir, þis enquest I require yow here,
þat Ʒe me telle with trawþe if euer Ʒe tale herde

1030 þe chymné] þehȳne   1032 þat] &   1037 merci] nerci
1044 answarez] answrez   1053 ne *supplied*

Of þe grene chapel, quere hit on grounde stondez,
And of þe knyƷt þat hit kepes, of colour of grene.
þer watz stabled bi statut a steuen vus bytwene   1060
To mete þat mon at þat mere, Ʒif I myƷt last;
And of þat ilk Nw Ʒere bot neked now wontez,
And I wolde loke on þat lede, if God me let wolde,
Gladloker, bi Goddez sun, þen any god welde!
ForÞi, iwysse, bi Ʒowre wylle, wende me bihoues,   1065
Naf I now to busy bot bare þre dayez,
And me als fayn to falle feye as fayly of myyn ernde.'
þenne laƷande quoþ þe lorde, 'Now leng þe byhoues,
For I schal teche yow to þat terme bi þe tymez ende,
þe grene chapayle vpon grounde greue yow no more;   1070
Bot Ʒe schal be in yowre bed, burne, at þyn ese,
Quyle forth dayez, and ferk on þe fyrst of þe Ʒere,
And cum to þat merk at mydmorn, to make quat yow likez   f. 105ᵇ
          in spenne.
     Dowellez whyle New Ʒeres daye,   1075
     And rys, and raykez þenne,
     Mon schal yow sette in waye,
     Hit is not two myle henne.'

þenne watz Gawan ful glad, and gomenly he laƷed:
'Now I þonk yow þryuandely þurƷ alle oþer þynge,   1080
Now acheued is my chaunce, I schal at your wylle
Dowelle, and ellez do quat Ʒe demen.'
þenne sesed hym þe syre and set hym bysyde,
Let þe ladiez be fette to lyke hem þe better.
þer watz seme solace by hemself stille;   1085
þe lorde let for luf lotez so myrry,
As wyƷ þat wolde of his wyte, ne wyst quat he myƷt.
þenne he carped to þe knyƷt, criande loude,
'Ʒe han demed to do þe dede þat I bidde;
Wyl Ʒe halde þis hes here at þys onez?'   1090
'Ʒe, sir, for soþe,' sayd þe segge trwe,
'Whyl I byde in yowre borƷe, be bayn to Ʒowre hest.'
'For Ʒe haf trauayled,' quoþ þe tulk, 'towen fro ferre,
And syþen waked me wyth, Ʒe arn not wel waryst
Nauþer of sostnaunce ne of slepe, soþly I knowe;   1095

1069 þat] þa   1092 Ʒowre] Ʒowe

Ȝe schal lenge in your lofte, and lyȝe in your ese
To-morn quyle þe messequyle, and to mete wende
When ȝe wyl, wyth my wyf, þat wyth yow schal sitte
And comfort yow with compayny, til I to cort torne;
      Ȝe lende,   1100
    And I schal erly ryse,
    On huntyng wyl I wende.'
    Gauayn grantez alle þyse,
    Hym heldande, as þe hende.

'Ȝet firre,' quoþ þe freke, 'a forwarde we make: 1105
Quat-so-euer I wynne in þe wod hit worþez to yourez,
And quat chek so ȝe acheue chaunge me þerforne.
Swete, swap we so, sware with trawþe,
Queþer, leude, so lymp, lere oþer better.'
'Bi God,' quoþ Gawayn þe gode, 'I grant þertylle,   1110
And þat yow lyst for to layke, lef hit me þynkes.'   f. 106ᵃ
'Who bryngez vus þis beuerage, þis bargayn is maked':
So sayde þe lorde of þat lede; þay laȝed vchone,
þay dronken and daylyeden and dalten vntyȝtel,
þise lordez and ladyez, quyle þat hem lyked;   1115
And syþen with Frenkysch fare and fele fayre lotez
þay stoden and stemed and stylly speken,
Kysten ful comlyly and kaȝten her leue.
With mony leude ful lyȝt and lemande torches
Vche burne to his bed watz broȝt at þe laste,   1125
     ful softe.
    To bed ȝet er þay ȝede,
    Recorded couenauntez ofte;
    þe olde lorde of þat leude
    Cowþe wel halde layk alofte.   1125

III

FUL erly bifore þe day þe folk vprysen,
  Gestes þat go wolde hor gromez þay calden,
And þay busken vp bilyue blonkkez to sadel,

Tyffen her takles, trussen her males,
Richen hem þe rychest, to ryde alle arayde,　　　　　1130
Lepen vp lyȝtly, lachen her brydeles,
Vche wyȝe on his way þer hym wel lyked.
þe leue lorde of þe londe watz not þe last
Arayed for þe rydyng, with renkkez ful mony;
Ete a sop hastyly, when he hade herde masse,　　　　1135
With bugle to bent-felde he buskez bylyue.
By þat any daylyȝt lemed vpon erþe
He with his haþeles on hyȝe horsses weren.
þenne þise cacheres þat couþe cowpled hor houndez,
Vnclosed þe kenel dore and calde hem þeroute,　　　1140
Blwe bygly in buglez þre bare mote;
Braches bayed þerfore and breme noyse maked;
And þay chastysed and charred on chasyng þat went,
A hundreth of hunteres, as I haf herde telle,
　　　　of þe best.　　　　　　　　　　　　　　　1145
　　　To trystors vewters ȝod,
　　　Couples huntes of kest;
　　　þer ros for blastez gode　　　　　　　f. 106ᵇ
　　　Gret rurd in þat forest.

At þe fyrst quethe of þe quest quaked þe wylde;　　1150
Der drof in þe dale, doted for drede,
Hiȝed to þe hyȝe, bot heterly þay were
Restayed with þe stablye, þat stoutly ascryed.
þay let þe herttez haf þe gate, with þe hyȝe hedes,
þe breme bukkez also with hor brode paumez;　　　1155
For þe fre lorde hade defende in fermysoun tyme
þat þer schulde no mon meue to þe male dere.
þe hindez were halden in with hay! and war!
þe does dryuen with gret dyn to þe depe sladez;
þer myȝt mon se, as þay slypte, slentyng of arwes—　1160
At vche wende vnder wande wapped a flone—
þat bigly bote on þe broun with ful brode hedez.
What! þay brayen, and bleden, bi bonkkez þay deȝen,
And ay rachches in a res radly hem folȝes,
Hunterez wyth hyȝe horne hasted hem after　　　　1165
Wyth such a crakkande kry as klyffes haden brusten.

1129 her (1st)] he　　　1137 þat] þat þat

What wylde so atwaped wyȝes þat schotten
Watz al toraced and rent at þe resayt,
Bi þay were tened at þe hyȝe and taysed to þe wattrez;
þe ledez were so lerned at þe loȝe trysteres,   1170
And þe grehoundez so grete, þat geten hem bylyue
And hem tofylched, as fast as frekez myȝt loke,
        þer-ryȝt.
      þe lorde for blys abloy
      Ful oft con launce and lyȝt,   1175
      And drof þat day wyth joy
      Thus to þe derk nyȝt.

þus laykez þis lorde by lynde-wodez euez,
And Gawayn þe god mon in gay bed lygez,
Lurkkez quyl þe daylyȝt lemed on þe wowes,   1180
Vnder couertour ful clere, cortyned aboute;
And as in slomeryng he slode, sleȝly he herde
A littel dyn at his dor, and dernly vpon;
And he heuez vp his hed out of þe cloþes,
A corner of þe cortyn he caȝt vp a lyttel,   f. 107ᵃ
And waytez warly þiderwarde quat hit be myȝt.   1186
Hit watz þe ladi, loflyest to beholde,
þat droȝ þe dor after hir ful dernly and stylle,
And boȝed towarde þe bed; and þe burne schamed,
And layde hym doun lystyly, and let as he slepte;   1190
And ho stepped stilly and stel to his bedde,
Kest vp þe cortyn and creped withinne,
And set hir ful softly on þe bed-syde,
And lenged þere selly longe to loke quen he wakened.
þe lede lay lurked a ful longe quyle,   1195
Compast in his concience to quat þat cace myȝt
Meue oþer amount—to meruayle hym þoȝt,
Bot ȝet he sayde in hymself, 'More semly hit were
To aspye wyth my spelle in space quat ho wolde.'
þen he wakenede, and wroth, and to hir warde torned,   1200
And vnlouked his yȝe-lyddez, and let as hym wondered,
And sayned hym, as bi his saȝe þe sauer to worthe,
       with hande.

1179 Gawayn] G: 1183 dernly] derfly   1199 in *illegible*

Wyth chynne and cheke ful swete,
Boþe quit and red in blande,   1205
Ful lufly con ho lete
Wyth lyppez smal laȝande.

'God moroun, Sir Gawayn,' sayde þat gay lady,
'Ȝe ar a sleper vnslyȝe, þat mon may slyde hider;
Now ar ȝe tan as-tyt! Bot true vus may schape,   1210
I schal bynde yow in your bedde, þat be ȝe trayst':
Al laȝande þe lady lanced þo bourdez.
'Goud moroun, gay,' quoþ Gawayn þe blyþe,
'Me schal worþe at your wille, and þat me wel lykez,
For I ȝelde me ȝederly, and ȝeȝe after grace,   1215
And þat is þe best, be my dome, for me byhouez nede':
And þus he bourded aȝayn with mony a blyþe laȝter.
'Bot wolde ȝe, lady louely, þen leue me grante,
And deprece your prysoun, and pray hym to ryse,
I wolde boȝe of þis bed, and busk me better;   1220
I schulde keuer þe more comfort to karp yow wyth.'
'Nay for soþe, beau sir,' sayd þat swete,   f. 107b
'Ȝe schal not rise of your bedde, I rych yow better,
I schal happe yow here þat oþer half als,
And syþen karp wyth my knyȝt þat I kaȝt haue;   1225
For I wene wel, iwysse, Sir Wowen ȝe are,
þat alle þe worlde worchipez quere-so ȝe ride;
Your honour, your hendelayk is hendely praysed
With lordez, wyth ladyes, with alle þat lyf bere.
And now ȝe ar here, iwysse, and we bot oure one;   1230
My lorde and his ledez ar on lenþe faren,
Oþer burnez in her bedde, and my burdez als,
þe dor drawen and dit with a derf haspe;
And syþen I haue in þis hous hym þat al lykez,
I schal ware my whyle wel, quyl hit lastez,   1235
        with tale.
    Ȝe ar welcum to my cors,
    Yowre awen won to wale,
    Me behouez of fyne force
    Your seruaunt be, and schale.'   1240

1208 gay] fayr   1213 gay] ay *damaged; only room for two letters*
1214 your] yourr, y *formed like* þ   wel *interlined in another hand*   1216 be]
he

'In god fayth,' quoþ Gawayn, 'gayn hit me þynkkez,
þaȝ I be not now he þat ȝe of speken;
To reche to such reuerence as ȝe reherce here
I am wyȝe vnworþy, I wot wel myseluen.
Bi God, I were glad, and yow god þoȝt,   1245
At saȝe oþer at seruyce þat I sette myȝt
To þe plesaunce of your prys—hit were a pure ioye.'
'In god fayth, Sir Gawayn,' quoþ þe gay lady,
'þe prys and þe prowes þat plesez al oþer,
If I hit lakked oþer set at lyȝt, hit were littel daynté;   1250
Bot hit ar ladyes innoȝe þat leuer wer nowþe
Haf þe, hende, in hor holde, as I þe habbe here,
To daly with derely your daynté wordez,
Keuer hem comfort and colen her carez,
þen much of þe garysoun oþer golde þat þay hauen.   1255
Bot I louue þat ilk lorde þat þe lyfte haldez,
I haf hit holly in my honde þat al desyres,
          þurȝe grace.'
      Scho made hym so gret chere,
      þat watz so fayr of face,   f. 108ᵃ
      þe knyȝt with speches skere   1261
      Answered to vche a cace.

'Madame,' quoþ þe myry mon, 'Mary yow ȝelde,
For I haf founden, in god fayth, yowre fraunchis nobele,
And oþer ful much of oþer folk fongen bi hor dedez,   1265
Bot þe daynté þat þay delen, for my disert nys euen,
Hit is þe worchyp of yourself, þat noȝt bot wel connez.'
'Bi Mary,' quoþ þe menskful, 'me þynk hit an oþer;
For were I worth al þe wone of wymmen alyue,
And al þe wele of þe worlde were in my honde,   1270
And I schulde chepen and chose to cheue me a lorde,
For þe costes þat I haf knowen vpon þe, knyȝt, here,
Of bewté and debonerté and blyþe semblaunt,
And þat I haf er herkkened and halde hit here trwee,
þer schulde no freke vpon folde bifore yow be chosen.'   1275
'Iwysse, worþy,' quoþ þe wyȝe, 'ȝe haf waled wel better,
Bot I am proude of þe prys þat ȝe put on me,
And, soberly your seruaunt, my souerayn I holde yow,

1255 þat] þat þᵗ   1262 An-] a-   1265 bi supplied   1266 nys euen] nysen

And yowre knyЗt I becom, and Kryst yow forЗelde.'
þus þay meled of muchquat til mydmorn paste,   1280
And ay þe lady let lyk as hym loued mych;
þe freke ferde with defence, and feted ful fayre—
'þaЗ I were burde bryЗtest', þe burde in mynde hade.
þe lasse luf in his lode for lur þat he soЗt
   boute hone,   1285
  þe dunte þat schulde hym deue,
  And nedez hit most be done.
  þe lady þenn spek of leue,
  He granted hir ful sone.

þenne ho gef hym god day, and wyth a glent laЗed,   1290
And as ho stod, ho stonyed hym wyth ful stor wordez:
'Now he þat spedez vche spech þis disport Зelde yow!
Bot þat Зe be Gawan, hit gotz in mynde.'
'Querfore?' quoþ þe freke, and freschly he askez,
Ferde lest he hade fayled in fourme of his castes;   1295
Bot þe burde hym blessed, and 'Bi þis skyl' sayde:
'So god as Gawayn gaynly is halden,   f. 108ᵇ
And cortaysye is closed so clene in hymseluen,
Couth not lyЗtly haf lenged so long wyth a lady,
Bot he had craued a cosse, bi his courtaysye,   1300
Bi sum towch of summe tryfle at sum talez ende.'
þen quoþ Wowen: "Iwysse, worþe as yow lykez;
I schal kysse at your comaundement, as a knyЗt fallez,
And fire, lest he displese yow, so plede hit no more.'
Ho comes nerre with þat, and cachez hym in armez,   1305
Loutez luflych adoun and þe leude kyssez.
þay comly bykennen to Kryst ayþer oþer;
Ho dos hir forth at þe dore withouten dyn more;
And he ryches hym to ryse and rapes hym sone,
Clepes to his chamberlayn, choses his wede,   1310
BoЗez forth, quen he watz boun, blyþely to masse;
And þenne he meued to his mete þat menskly hym keped,
And made myrry al day, til þe mone rysed,
  with game.
  Watz neuer freke fayrer fonge   1315
  Bitwene two so dyngne dame,

1281 as hym] ahў   1286 schulde] sculde   1304 so] fo   1315 Watz] wᵗ

þe alder and þe ȝonge;
Much solace set þay same.

And ay þe lorde of þe londe is lent on his gamnez,
To hunt in holtez and heþe at hyndez barayne;   1320
Such a sowme he þer slowe bi þat þe sunne heldet,
Of dos and of oþer dere, to deme were wonder.
þenne fersly þay flokked in folk at þe laste,
And quykly of þe quelled dere a querré þay maked.
þe best boȝed þerto with burnez innoghe,   1325
Gedered þe grattest of gres þat þer were,
And didden hem derely vndo as þe dede askez;
Serched hem at þe asay summe þat þer were,
Two fyngeres þay fonde of þe fowlest of alle.
Syþen þay slyt þe slot, sesed þe erber,   1330
Schaued wyth a scharp knyf, and þe schyre knitten;
Syþen rytte þay þe foure lymmes, and rent of þe hyde,
þen brek þay þe balé, þe bowelez out token
Lystily for laucyng þe lere of þe knot;   f. 109ᵃ
þay gryped to þe gargulun, and grayþely departed   1335
þe wesaunt fro þe wynt-hole, and walt out þe guttez;
þen scher þay out þe schulderez with her scharp knyuez,
Haled hem by a lyttel hole to haue hole sydes.
Siþen britned þay þe brest and brayden hit in twynne,
And eft at þe gargulun bigynez on þenne,   1340
Ryuez hit vp radly ryȝt to þe byȝt,
Voydez out þe avanters, and verayly þerafter
Alle þe rymez by þe rybbez radly þay lance;
So ryde þay of by resoun bi þe rygge bonez,
Euenden to þe haunche, þat henged alle samen,   1345
And heuen hit vp al hole, and hwen hit of þere,
And þat þay neme for þe noumbles bi nome, as I trowe,
        bi kynde;
    Bi þe byȝt al of þe þyȝes
    þe lappez þay lance bihynde;   1350
    To hewe hit in two þay hyȝes,
    Bi þe bakbon to vnbynde.

Boþe þe hede and þe hals þay hwen of þenne,
And syþen sunder þay þe sydez swyft fro þe chyne,

1333 bowelez] balez   1334 þe (1st)] Gollancz; MS. &   1344 So] fo

And þe corbeles fee þay kest in a greue;   1355
þenn þurled þay ayþer þik side þurȝ bi þe rybbe,
And henged þenne ayþer bi hoȝez of þe fourchez,
Vche freke for his fee, as fallez for to haue.
Vpon a felle of þe fayre best fede þay þayr houndes
Wyth þe lyuer and þe lyȝtez, þe leþer of þe paunchez,   1360
And bred baþed in blod blende þeramongez.
Baldely þay blw prys, bayed þayr rachchez,
Syþen fonge þay her flesche, folden to home,
Strakande ful stoutly mony stif motez.
Bi þat þe daylyȝt watz done þe douthe watz al wonen   1365
Into þe comly castel, þer þe knyȝt bidez
        ful stille,
    Wyth blys and bryȝt fyr bette.
    þe lorde is comen þertylle;
    When Gawayn wyth hym mette   1370
    þer watz bot wele at wylle.

Thenne comaunded þe lorde in þat sale to samen alle þe
        meny,   f. 109ᵇ
Boþe þe ladyes on loghe to lyȝt with her burdes
Bifore alle þe folk on þe flette, frekez he beddez
Verayly his venysoun to fech hym byforne,   1375
And al godly in gomen Gawayn he called,
Techez hym to þe tayles of ful tayt bestes,
Schewez hym þe schyree grece schorne vpon rybbes.
'How payez yow þis play? Haf I prys wonnen?
Haue I þryuandely þonk þurȝ my craft serued?'   1380
'Ȝe iwysse,' quoþ þat oþer wyȝe, 'here is wayth fayrest
þat I seȝ þis seuen ȝere in sesoun of wynter.'
'And al I gif yow, Gawayn,' quoþ þe gome þenne,
'For by acorde of couenaunt ȝe craue hit as your awen.'
'þis is soth,' quoþ þe segge, 'I say yow þat ilke: 1385
þat I haf worthyly wonnen þis wonez wythinne,
Iwysse with as god wylle hit worþez to ȝourez.'
He hasppez his fayre hals his armez wythinne,
And kysses hym as comlyly as he couþe awyse:

    1357 ayþer] aþer   1369 lorde] e *partly erased*   1376 Gawayn] Gaway
1386 þat] *Gollancz; MS.* &   wonnen *supplied*   1389 he] *Madden;*
MS. ho

'Tas yow þere my cheuicaunce, I cheued no more;   1390
I wowche hit saf fynly, þaȝ feler hit were.'
'Hit is god,' quoþ þe godmon, 'grant mercy þerfore.
Hit may be such hit is þe better, and ȝe me breue wolde
Where ȝe wan þis ilk wele bi wytte of yorseluen.'
'þat watz not forward,' quoþ he, 'frayst me no more.   1395
For ȝe haf tan þat yow tydez, trawe non oþer
      ȝe mowe.'
    þay laȝed, and made hem blyþe
    Wyth lotez þat were to lowe;
    To soper þay ȝede as-swyþe,   1400
    Wyth dayntés nwe innowe.

And syþen by þe chymné in chamber þay seten,
Wyȝez þe walle wyn weȝed to hem oft,
And efte in her bourdyng þay bayþen in þe morn
To fylle þe same forwardez þat þay byfore maden: 1405
Wat chaunce so bytydez hor cheuysaunce to chaunge,
What nwez so þay nome, at naȝt quen þay metten.
þay acorded of þe couenauntez byfore þe court alle;
þe beuerage watz broȝt forth in bourde at þat tyme,   f. 110ª
þenne þay louelych leȝten leue at þe last,   1410
Vche burne to his bedde busked bylyue.
Bi þat þe coke hade crowen and cakled bot þryse,
þe lorde watz lopen of his bedde, þe leudez vchone;
So þat þe mete and þe masse watz metely delyuered,
þe douthe dressed to þe wod, er any day sprenged,   1415
      to chace;
    Heȝ with hunte and hornez
    þurȝ playnez þay passe in space,
    Vncoupled among þo þornez
    Rachez þat ran on race.   1420

Sone þay calle of a quest in a ker syde,
þe hunt rehayted þe houndez þat hit fyrst mynged,
Wylde wordez hym warp wyth a wrast noyce;
þe howndez þat hit herde hastid þider swyþe,
And fellen as fast to þe fuyt, fourty at ones;   1425

1394 yor-] hor   1396 trawe] trawe ȝe   1406 Wat] þat   1412 crowen]
crowez

þenne such a glauer ande glam of gedered rachchez
Ros, þat þe rocherez rungen aboute;
Hunterez hem hardened with horne and wyth muthe.
þen al in a semblé sweyed togeder,
Bitwene a flosche in þat fryth and a foo cragge;   1430
In a knot bi a clyffe, at þe kerre syde,
þer as þe rogh rocher vnrydely watz fallen,
þay ferden to þe fyndyng, and frekez hem after;
þay vmbekesten þe knarre and þe knot boþe,
WyЗez, whyl þay wysten wel wythinne hem hit were,   1435
þe best þat þer breued watz wyth þe blodhoundez.
þenne þay beten on þe buskez, and bede hym vpryse,
And he vnsoundyly out soЗt seggez ouerþwert;
On þe sellokest swyn swenged out þere,
Long sythen fro þe sounder þat siЗed for olde,   1440
For he watz breme, bor alþer-grattest,
Ful grymme quen he gronyed; þenne greued mony,
For þre at þe fyrst þrast he þryЗt to þe erþe,
And sparred forth good sped boute spyt more.
þise oþer halowed hyghe! ful hyЗe, and hay! hay! cryed,   1445
Haden hornez to mouþe, heterly rechated;   f. 110ᵇ
Mony watz þe myry mouthe of men and of houndez
þat buskkez after þis bor with bost and wyth noyse
        to quelle.
    Ful oft he bydez þe baye,   1450
    And maymez þe mute inn melle;
    He hurtez of þe houndez, and þay
    Ful Зomerly Зaule and Зelle.

Schalkez to schote at hym schowen to þenne,
Haled to hym of her arewez, hitten hym oft;   1455
Bot þe poyntez payred at þe pyth þat pyЗt in his scheldez,
And þe barbez of his browe bite non wolde—
þaЗ þe schauen schaft schyndered in pecez,
þe hede hypped aЗayn were-so-euer hit hitte.

1426 glauer ande] glauerande   1433 þay *from offset*   1435 wythinne]
wytinne   1440 fro] for   siЗed] wiЗt   1441 breme *blotted and illegible*
bor *MS. now* hor, *but* h *prob. damaged* b   1442 ful grymme *prob. reading of*
offset   1443 þre at *from offset*   1444 sparred] *Menner, probable reading*
aided by offset (*previously read* sped him)   1445 þise oþer *from offset*
1447 myry] *four minims at beginning*

Bot quen þe dyntez hym dered of her dryȝe strokez,   1460
þen, braynwod for bate, on burnez he rasez,
Hurtez hem ful heterly þer he forth hyȝez,
And mony arȝed þerat, and on lyte droȝen.
Bot þe lorde on a lyȝt horce launces hym after,
As burne bolde vpon bent his bugle he blowez,   1465
He rechated, and rode þurȝ ronez ful þyk,
Suande þis wylde swyn til þe sunne schafted.
þis day wyth þis ilk dede þay dryuen on þis wyse,
Whyle oure luflych lede lys in his bedde,
Gawayn grayþely at home, in gerez ful ryche   1470
          of hewe.
     þe lady noȝt forȝate,
     Com to hym to salue;
     Ful erly ho watz hym ate
     His mode for to remwe.   1475

Ho commes to þe cortyn, and at þe knyȝt totes.
Sir Wawen her welcumed worþy on fyrst,
And ho hym ȝeldez aȝayn ful ȝerne of hir wordez,
Settez hir softly by his syde, and swyþely ho laȝez,
And wyth a luflych loke ho layde hym þyse wordez: 1480
'Sir, ȝif ȝe be Wawen, wonder me þynkkez,
Wyȝe þat is so wel wrast alway to god,
And connez not of compaynye þe costez vndertake,
And if mon kennes yow hom þe to knowe, ȝe kest hom of your
          mynde;   f. 111ᵃ
þou hatz forȝeten ȝederly þat ȝisterday I taȝtte   1485
Bi alder-truest token of talk þat I cowþe.'
'What is þat?' quoþ þe wyghe, 'Iwysse I wot neuer;
If hit be sothe þat ȝe breue, þe blame is myn awen.'
'Ȝet I kende yow of kyssyng,' quoþ þe clere þenne,
'Quere-so countenaunce is couþe quikly to clayme;   1490
þat bicumes vche a knyȝt þat cortaysy vses.'
'Do way,' quoþ þat derf mon, 'my dere, þat speche,
For þat durst I not do, lest I deuayed were;
If I were werned, I were wrang, iwysse, ȝif I profered.'
'Ma fay,' quoþ þe meré wyf, 'ȝe may not be werned,   1495

Ȝe ar stif innoghe to constrayne wyth strenkþe, ȝif yow lykez,
Ȝif any were so vilanous þat yow devaye wolde.'
'Ȝe, be God,' quoþ Gawayn, 'good is your speche,
Bot þrete is vnþryuande in þede þer I lende,
And vche gift þat is geuen not with goud wylle.   1500
I am at your comaundement, to kysse quen yow lykez,
Ȝe may lach quen yow lyst, and leue quen yow þynkkez,
          in space.'
          þe lady loutez adoun,
          And comlyly kysses his face,   1505
          Much speche þay þer expoun
          Of druryes greme and grace.

'I woled wyt at yow, wyȝe,' þat worþy þer sayde,
'And yow wrathed not þerwyth, what were þe skylle
þat so ȝong and so ȝepe as ȝe at þis tyme,   1510
So cortayse, so knyȝtyly, as ȝe ar knowen oute—
And of alle cheualry to chose, þe chef þyng alosed
Is þe lel layk of luf, þe lettrure of armes;
For to telle of þis teuelyng of þis trwe knyȝtez,
Hit is þe tytelet token and tyxt of her werkkez,   1515
How ledes for her lele luf hor lyuez han auntered,
Endured for her drury dulful stoundez,
And after wenged with her walour and voyded her care,
And broȝt blysse into boure with bountees hor awen—
And ȝe ar knyȝt comlokest kyd of your elde,   1520
Your worde and your worchip walkez ayquere,   f. 111b
And I haf seten by yourself here sere twyes,
Ȝet herde I neuer of your hed helde no wordez
þat euer longed to luf, lasse ne more;
And ȝe, þat ar so cortays and coynt of your hetes,   1525
Oghe to a ȝonke þynk ȝern to schewe
And teche sum tokenez of trweluf craftes.
Why! ar ȝe lewed, þat alle þe los weldez?
Oþer elles ȝe demen me to dille your dalyaunce to herken?
          For schame!   1530
          I com hider sengel, and sitte
          To lerne at yow sum game;

1508 woled] d *probably rewritten*   1513 lel layk] lellayk   1514 For]
r *illegible*   1516 ledes] des *illegible*   for] r *illegible*

Dos, techez me of your wytte,
Whil my lorde is fro hame.'

'In goud fayþe,' quoþ Gawayn, 'God yow forȝelde!   1535
Gret is þe gode gle, and gomen to me huge,
þat so worþy as ȝe wolde wynne hidere,
And pyne yow with so pouer a mon, as play wyth your knyȝt
With anyskynnez countenaunce, hit keuerez me ese;
Bot to take þe toruayle to myself to trwluf expoun,   1540
And towche þe temez of tyxt and talez of armez
To yow þat, I wot wel, weldez more slyȝt
Of þat art, bi þe half, or a hundreth of seche
As I am, oþer euer schal, in erde þer I leue,
Hit were a folé felefolde, my fre, by my trawþe.   1545
I wolde yowre wylnyng worche at my myȝt,
As I am hyȝly bihalden, and euermore wylle
Be seruaunt to yourseluen, so saue me Dryȝtyn!'
þus hym frayned þat fre, and fondet hym ofte,
For to haf wonnen hym to woȝe, what-so scho þoȝt ellez;   1550
Bot he defended hym so fayr þat no faut semed,
Ne non euel on nawþer halue, nawþer þay wysten
          bot blysse.
     þay laȝed and layked longe;
     At þe last scho con hym kysse,   1555
     Hir leue fayre con scho fonge
     And went hir waye, iwysse.

Then ruþes hym þe renk and ryses to þe masse,
And siþen hor diner watz dyȝt and derely serued.   f. 112ᵃ
þe lede with þe ladyez layked alle day,   1560
Bot þe lorde ouer þe londez launced ful ofte,
Swez his vncely swyn, þat swyngez bi þe bonkkez
And bote þe best of his brachez þe bakkez in sunder
þer he bode in his bay, tel bawemen hit breken,
And madee hym mawgref his hed for to mwe vtter,   1565
So felle flonez þer flete when þe folk gedered.
Bot ȝet þe styffest to start bi stoundez he made,
Til at þe last he watz so mat he myȝt no more renne,
Bot in þe hast þat he myȝt he to a hole wynnez
Of a rasse bi a rokk þer rennez þe boerne.   1570

He gete þe bonk at his bak, bigynez to scrape,
þe froþe femed at his mouth vnfayre bi þe wykez,
Whettez his whyte tuschez; with hym þen irked
Alle þe burnez so bolde þat hym by stoden
To nye hym on-ferum, bot ne3e hym non durst   1575
      for woþe;
    He hade hurt so mony byforne
    þat al þu3t þenne ful loþe
    Be more wyth his tusches torne,
    þat breme watz and braynwod bothe,   1580

Til þe kny3t com hymself, kachande his blonk,
Sy3 hym byde at þe bay, his burnez bysyde;
He ly3tes luflych adoun, leuez his corsour,
Braydez out a bry3t bront and bigly forth strydez,
Foundez fast þur3 þe forth þer þe felle bydez.   1585
þe wylde watz war of þe wy3e with weppen in honde,
Hef hy3ly þe here, so hetterly he fnast
þat fele ferde for þe freke, lest felle hym þe worre.
þe swyn settez hym out on þe segge euen,
þat þe burne and þe bor were boþe vpon hepez   1590
In þe wy3test of þe water; þe worre hade þat oþer,
For þe mon merkkez hym wel, as þay mette fyrst,
Set sadly þe scharp in þe slot euen,
Hit hym vp to þe hult, þat þe hert schyndered,
And he 3arrande hym 3elde, and 3edoun þe water   1595
    ful tyt.   f. 112ᵇ
    A hundreth houndez hym hent,
    þat bremely con hym bite,
    Burnez him bro3t to bent,
    And doggez to dethe endite.   1600

There watz blawyng of prys in mony breme horne,
He3e halowing on hi3e with haþelez þat my3t;
Brachetes bayed þat best, as bidden þe maysterez
Of þat chargeaunt chace þat were chef huntes.
þenne a wy3e þat watz wys vpon wodcraftez   1605
To vnlace þis bor lufly bigynnez.
Fyrst he hewes of his hed and on hi3e settez,

And syþen rendez him al roghe bi þe rygge after,
Braydez out þe boweles, brennez hom on glede,
With bred blent þerwith his braches rewardez.   1610
Syþen he britnez out þe brawen in bryȝt brode cheldez,
And hatz out þe hastlettez, as hiȝtly bisemez;
And ȝet hem halchez al hole þe haluez togeder,
And syþen on a stif stange stoutly hem henges.
Now with þis ilk swyn þay swengen to home;   1615
þe bores hed watz borne bifore þe burnes seluen
þat him forferde in þe forþe þurȝ forse of his honde
          so stronge.
       Til he seȝ Sir Gawayne
       In halle hym þoȝt ful longe;   1620
       He calde, and he com gayn
       His feez þer for to fonge.

þe lorde ful lowde with lote and laȝter myry,
When he seȝe Sir Gawayn, with solace he spekez;
þe goude ladyez were geten, and gedered þe meyny,   1625
He schewez hem þe scheldez, and schapes hem þe tale
Of þe largesse and þe lenþe, þe liþernez alse
Of þe were of þe wylde swyn in wod þer he fled.
þat oþer knyȝt ful comly comended his dedez,
And praysed hit as gret prys þat he proued hade,   1630
For suche a brawne of a best, þe bolde burne sayde,
Ne such sydes of a swyn segh he neuer are.
þenne hondeled þay þe hoge hed, þe hende mon hit praysed,
And let lodly þerat þe lorde for to here.   f. 113ª
'Now, Gawayn,' quoþ þe godmon, 'þis gomen is your awen   1635
Bi fyn forwarde and faste, faythely ȝe knowe.'
'Hit is sothe,' quoþ þe segge, 'and as siker trwe
Alle my get I schal yow gif agayn, bi my trawþe.'
He hent þe haþel aboute þe halse, and hendely hym kysses,
And eftersones of þe same he serued hym þere.   1640
'Now ar we euen,' quoþ þe haþel, 'in þis euentide
Of alle þe couenauntes þat we knyt, syþen I com hider,
          bi lawe.'
       þe lorde sayde, 'Bi saynt Gile,
       Ȝe ar þe best þat I knowe!   1645

1623 laȝter] laȝed   1624 Gawayn] G: 1639 hent *supplied*

3e ben ryche in a whyle,
Such chaffer and 3e drowe.'

þenne þay teldet tablez trestes alofte,
Kesten cloþez vpon; clere ly3t þenne
Wakned bi wo3ez, waxen torches;   1650
Seggez sette and serued in sale al aboute;
Much glam and gle glent vp þerinne
Aboute þe fyre vpon flet, and on fele wyse
At þe soper and after, mony aþel songez,
As coundutes of Krystmasse and carolez newe   1655
With al þe manerly merþe þat mon may of telle,
And euer oure luflych kny3t þe lady bisyde.
Such semblaunt to þat segge semly ho made
Wyth stille stollen countenaunce, þat stalworth to plese,
þat al forwondered watz þe wy3e, and wroth with hymseluen, 1660
Bot he nolde not for his nurture nurne hir a3aynez,
Bot dalt with hir al in daynté, how-se-euer þe dede turned
        towrast.
    Quen þay hade played in halle
    As longe as hor wylle hom last,   1665
    To chambre he con hym calle,
    And to þe chemné þay past.

Ande þer þay dronken, and dalten, and demed eft nwe
To norne on þe same note on Nwe 3erez euen;
Bot þe kny3t craued leue to kayre on þe morn,   1670
For hit watz ne3 at þe terme þat he to schulde.
þe lorde hym letted of þat, to lenge hym resteyed,   f. 113^b
And sayde, 'As I am trwe segge, I siker my trawþe
þou schal cheue to þe grene chapel þy charres to make,
Leude, on Nw 3erez ly3t, longe bifore pryme.   1675
Forþy þow lye in þy loft and lach þyn ese,
And I schal hunt in þis holt, and halde þe towchez,
Chaunge wyth þe cheuisaunce, bi þat I charre hider;
For I haf fraysted þe twys, and faythful I fynde þe.
Now "þrid tyme þrowe best" þenk on þe morne,   1680
Make we mery quyl we may and mynne vpon joye,
For þe lur may mon lach when-so mon lykez.'
þis watz grayþely graunted, and Gawayn is lenged,

Bliþe broȝt watz hym drynk, and þay to bedde ȝeden
        with liȝt.   1685
    Sir Gawayn lis and slepes
    Ful stille and softe al niȝt;
    þe lorde þat his craftez kepes,
    Ful erly he watz diȝt.

After messe a morsel he and his men token;   1690
Miry watz þe mornyng, his mounture he askes.
Alle þe haþeles þat on horse schulde helden hym after
Were boun busked on hor blonkkez bifore þe halle ȝatez.
Ferly fayre watz þe folde, for þe forst clenged;
In rede rudede vpon rak rises þe sunne,   1695
And ful clere costez þe clowdes of þe welkyn.
Hunteres vnhardeled bi a holt syde,
Rocheres roungen bi rys for rurde of her hornes;
Summe fel in þe fute þer þe fox bade,
Traylez ofte a traueres bi traunt of her wyles;   1700
A kenet kryes þerof, þe hunt on hym calles;
His felaȝes fallen hym to, þat fnasted ful þike,
Runnen forth in a rabel in his ryȝt fare,
And he fyskez hem byfore; þay founden hym sone,
And quen þay seghe hym with syȝt þay sued hym fast,   1705
Wreȝande hym ful weterly with a wroth noyse;
And he trantes and tornayeez þurȝ mony tene greue,
Hauilounez, and herkenez bi heggez ful ofte.
At þe last bi a littel dich he lepez ouer a spenne,   f. 114ᵃ
Stelez out ful stilly bi a strothe rande,   1710
Went haf wylt of þe wode with wylez fro þe houndes;
þenne watz he went, er he wyst, to a wale tryster,
þer þre þro at a þrich þrat hym at ones,
      al graye.
    He blenched aȝayn bilyue   1715
    And stifly start on-stray,
    With alle þe wo on lyue
    To þe wod he went away.

  1686 Gawayn] G: 1690 morsel] *four minims at beginning*   1693 bifore]
biforere   1700 traueres] trayteres   1706 hym] ym *illegible*
weterly] w *from offset, first* e *illegible*   1710 strothe] ro *rewritten*
1712 to] to to

Thenne watz hit list vpon lif to lyþen þe houndez,
When alle þe mute hade hym met, menged togeder: 1720
Suche a sorȝe at þat syȝt þay sette on his hede
As alle þe clamberande clyffes hade clatered on hepes;
Here he watz halawed, when haþelez hym metten,
Loude he watz ȝayned with ȝarande speche;
þer he watz þreted and ofte þef called,   1725
And ay þe titleres at his tayl, þat tary he ne myȝt;
Ofte he watz runnen at, when he out rayked,
And ofte reled in aȝayn, so Reniarde watz wylé.

And ȝe he lad hem bi lagmon, þe lorde and his meyny,
On þis maner bi þe mountes quyle myd-ouer-vnder,   1730
Whyle þe hende knyȝt at home holsumly slepes
Withinne þe comly cortynes, on þe colde morne.
Bot þe lady for luf let not to slepe,
Ne þe purpose to payre þat pyȝt in hir hert,
Bot ros hir vp radly, rayked hir þeder   1735
In a mery mantyle, mete to þe erþe,
þat watz furred ful fyne with fellez wel pured,
No hwez goud on hir hede bot þe haȝer stones
Trased aboute hir tressour be twenty in clusteres;
Hir þryuen face and hir þrote þrowen al naked,   1740
Hir brest bare bifore, and bihinde eke.
Ho comez withinne þe chambre dore, and closes hit hir after,
Wayuez vp a wyndow, and on þe wyȝe callez,
And radly þus rehayted hym with hir riche wordes,
          with chere: 1745
     'A! mon, how may þou slepe,
     þis morning is so clere?'   f. 114[b]
     He watz in drowping depe,
     Bot þenne he con hir here.

In dreȝ droupyng of dreme draueled þat noble,   1750
As mon þat watz in mornyng of mony þro þoȝtes,
How þat destiné schulde þat day dele hym his wyrde
At þe grene chapel, when he þe gome metes,
And bihoues his buffet abide withoute debate more;
Bot quen þat comly com he keuered his wyttes,   1755

1719 list vpon lif] *Morris*; *MS.* lif vpon list   1752 dele hym *supplied*
1755 com *supplied*

Swenges out of þe sweuenes, and swarez with hast.
þe lady luflych com laȝande swete,
Felle ouer his fayre face, and fetly hym kyssed;
He welcumez hir worþily with a wale chere.
He seȝ hir so glorious and gayly atyred,   1760
So fautles of hir fetures and of so fyne hewes,
Wiȝt wallande joye warmed his hert.
With smoþe smylyng and smolt þay smeten into merþe,
þat al watz blis and bonchef þat breke hem bitwene,
        and wynne.   1765
    þay lanced wordes gode,
    Much wele þen watz þerinne;
    Gret perile bitwene hem stod,
    Nif Maré of hir knyȝt mynne.   _NB._

For þat prynces of pris depresed hym so þikke,   1770
Nurned hym so neȝe þe þred, þat nede hym bihoued
Oþer lach þer hir luf, oþer lodly refuse.
He cared for his cortaysye, lest craþayn he were,
And more for his meschef ȝif he schulde make synne,
And be traytor to þat tolke þat þat telde aȝt.   1775
'God schylde,' quoþ þe schalk, 'þat schal not befalle!'
With luf-laȝyng a lyt he layd hym bysyde
Alle þe spechez of specialté þat sprange of her mouthe.
Quoþ þat burde to þe burne, 'Blame ȝe disserue,
Ȝif ȝe luf not þat lyf þat ȝe lye nexte,   1780
Bifore alle þe wyȝez in þe worlde wounded in hert,
Bot if ȝe haf a lemman, a leuer, þat yow lykez better,
And folden fayth to þat fre, festned so harde
þat yow lausen ne lyst—and þat I leue nouþe;   f. 115ᵃ
And þat ȝe telle me þat now trwly I pray yow,   1785
For alle þe lufez vpon lyue layne not þe soþe
        for gile.'
    þe knyȝt sayde, 'Be sayn Jon,'
    And smeþely con he smyle,
    'In fayth I welde riȝt non,   1790
    Ne non wil welde þe quile.'

'þat is a worde,' quoþ þat wyȝt, 'þat worst is of alle,

1770 prynces] prynce

Bot I am swared for soþe, þat sore me þinkkez.
Kysse me now comly, and I schal cach heþen,
I may bot mourne vpon molde, as may þat much louyes.'   1795
Sykande ho sweȝe doun and semly hym kyssed,
And siþen ho seueres hym fro, and says as ho stondes,
'Now, dere, at þis departyng do me þis ese,
Gif me sumquat of þy gifte, þi gloue if hit were,
þat I may mynne on þe, mon, my mournyng to lassen.'   1800
'Now iwysse,' quoþ þat wyȝe, 'I wolde I hade here
þe leuest þing for þy luf þat I in londe welde,
For ȝe haf deserued, for soþe, sellyly ofte
More rewarde bi resoun þen I reche myȝt;
Bot to dele yow for drurye þat dawed bot neked,   1805
Hit is not your honour to haf at þis tyme
A gloue for a garysoun of Gawaynez giftez,
And I am here an erande in erdez vncouþe,
And haue no men wyth no malez with menskful þingez;
þat mislykez me, ladé, for luf at þis tyme,   1810
Iche tolke mon do as he is tan, tas to non ille
      ne pine.'
        'Nay, hende of hyȝe honours,'
        Quoþ þat lufsum vnder lyne,
        'þaȝ I hade noȝt of yourez,   1815
        Ȝet schulde ȝe haue of myne.'

Ho raȝt hym a riche rynk of red golde werkez,
Wyth a starande ston stondande alofte
þat bere blusschande bemez as þe bryȝt sunne;
Wyt ȝe wel, hit watz worth wele ful hoge.   1820
Bot þe renk hit renayed, and redyly he sayde,
'I wil no giftez, for Gode, my gay, at þis tyme;   f. 115^b
I haf none yow to norne, ne noȝt wyl I take.'
Ho bede hit hym ful bysily, and he hir bode wernes,
And swere swyfte by his sothe þat he hit sese nolde,   1825
And ho soré þat he forsoke, and sayde þerafter,
'If ȝe renay my rynk, to ryche for hit semez,
Ȝe wolde not so hyȝly halden be to me,
I schal gif yow my girdel, þat gaynes yow lasse.'

1799 if] of   1810 tyme] tyne   1815 noȝt] oȝt   1825 swyfte by]
swyftel

Ho laȝt a lace lyȝtly þat leke vmbe hir sydez, 1830
Knit vpon hir kyrtel vnder þe clere mantyle,
Gered hit watz with grene sylke and with golde schaped,
Noȝt bot arounde brayden, beten with fyngrez;
And þat ho bede to þe burne, and blyþely bisoȝt,
þaȝ hit vnworþi were, þat he hit take wolde. 1835
And he nay þat he nolde neghe in no wyse
Nauþer golde ne garysoun, er God hym grace sende
To acheue to þe chaunce þat he hade chosen þere.
'And þerfore, I pray yow, displese yow noȝt,
And lettez be your bisinesse, for I bayþe hit yow neuer 1840
      to graunte;
      I am derely to yow biholde
      Bicause of your sembelaunt,
      And euer in hot and colde
      To be your trwe seruaunt.' 1845

'Now forsake ȝe þis silke,' sayde þe burde þenne,
'For hit is symple in hitself? And so hit wel semez.
Lo! so hit is littel, and lasse hit is worþy;
Bot who-so knew þe costes þat knit ar þerinne,
He wolde hit prayse at more prys, parauenture; 1850
For quat gome so is gorde with þis grene lace,
While he hit hade hemely halched aboute,
þer is no haþel vnder heuen tohewe hym þat myȝt,
For he myȝt not be slayn for slyȝt vpon erþe.'
þen kest þe knyȝt, and hit come to his hert 1855
Hit were a juel for þe jopardé þat hym iugged were:
When he acheued to þe chapel his chek for to fech,
Myȝt he haf slypped to be vnslayn, þe sleȝt were noble.
þenne he þulged with hir þrepe and þoled hir to speke, f. 116ᵃ
And ho bere on hym þe belt and bede hit hym swyþe— 1860
And he granted and hym gafe with a goud wylle—
And bisoȝt hym, for hir sake, disceuer hit neuer,
Bot to lelly layne fro hir lorde; þe leude hym acordez
þat neuer wyȝe schulde hit wyt, iwysse, bot þay twayne
      for noȝte; 1865
      He þonkked hir oft ful swyþe,
      Ful þro with hert and þoȝt.

1830 þat] þat þat   1858 Myȝt] myȝ   1863 fro] for

Bi þat on þrynne syþe
Ho hatz kyst þe knyȝt so toȝt.

Thenne lachchez ho hir leue, and leuez hym þere,   1870
For more myrþe of þat mon moȝt ho not gete.
When ho watz gon, Sir Gawayn gerez hym sone,
Rises and riches hym in araye noble,
Lays vp þe luf-lace þe lady hym raȝt,
Hid hit ful holdely, þer he hit eft fonde.   1875
Syþen cheuely to þe chapel choses he þe waye,
Preuély aproched to a prest, and prayed hym þere
þat he wolde lyste his lyf and lern hym better
How his sawle schulde be saued when he schuld seye heþen.
þere he schrof hym schyrly and schewed his mysdedez,   1880
Of þe more and þe mynne, and merci besechez,
And of absolucioun he on þe segge calles;
And he asoyled hym surely and sette hym so clene
As domezday schulde haf ben diȝt on þe morn.
And syþen he mace hym as mery among þe fre ladyes,   1885
With comlych caroles and alle kynnes ioye,
As neuer he did bot þat daye, to þe derk nyȝt,
        with blys.
        Vche mon hade daynté þare
        Of hym, and sayde, 'Iwysse,   1890
        þus myry he watz neuer are,
        Syn he com hider, er þis.'

Now hym lenge in þat lee, þer luf hym bityde!
ȝet is þe lorde on þe launde ledande his gomnes.
He hatz forfaren þis fox þat he folȝed longe;   1895
As he sprent ouer a spenne to spye þe schrewe,
þer as he herd þe howndes þat hasted hym swyþe,   f. 116b
Renaud com richchande þurȝ a roȝe greue,
And alle þe rabel in a res ryȝt at his helez.
þe wyȝe watz war of þe wylde, and warly abides,   1900
And braydez out þe bryȝt bronde, and at þe best castez.
And he schunt for þe scharp, and schulde haf arered;
A rach rapes hym to, ryȝt er he myȝt,
And ryȝt bifore þe hors fete þay fel on hym alle,

1872 ho] he   Gawayn] G   1878 lyste] Burrow; MS. lyfte

And woried me þis wyly wyth a wroth noyse.   1905
þe lorde ly3tez bilyue, and lachez hym sone,
Rased hym ful radly out of þe rach mouþes,
Haldez he3e ouer his hede, halowez faste,
And þer bayen hym mony braþ houndez.
Huntes hy3ed hem þeder with hornez ful mony,   1910
Ay rechatande ary3t til þay þe renk se3en.
Bi þat watz comen his compeyny noble,
Alle þat euer ber bugle blowed at ones,
And alle þise oþer halowed þat hade no hornes;
Hit watz þe myriest mute þat euer men herde,   1915
þe rich rurd þat þer watz raysed for Renaude saule
          with lote.
      Hor houndez þay þer rewarde,
      Her hedez þay fawne and frote,
      And syþen þay tan Reynarde,   skin (v)   1920
      And tyruen of his cote.

And þenne þay helden to home, for hit watz nie3 ny3t,
Strakande ful stoutly in hor store hornez.
þe lorde is ly3t at þe laste at hys lef home,
Fyndez fire vpon flet, þe freke þer-byside,   1925
Sir Gawayn þe gode, þat glad watz withalle,
Among þe ladies for luf he ladde much ioye;
He were a bleaunt of blwe þat bradde to þe erþe,
His surkot semed hym wel þat softe watz forred,
And his hode of þat ilke henged on his schulder,   1930
Blande al of blaunner were boþe al aboute.
He metez me þis godmon inmyddez þe flore,
And al with gomen he hym gret, and goudly he sayde,
'I schal fylle vpon fyrst oure forwardez nouþe,
þat we spedly han spoken, þer spared watz no drynk.'   f. 117ᵃ
þen acoles he þe kny3t and kysses hym þryes,   1936
As sauerly and sadly as he hem sette couþe.
'Bi Kryst,' quoþ þat oþer kny3t, '3e cach much sele
In cheuisaunce of þis chaffer, 3if 3e hade goud chepez.'
'3e, of þe chepe no charg,' quoþ chefly þat oþer,   1940
'As is pertly payed þe chepez þat I a3te.'

1906 lachez] cachez   hym] by   1909 braþ] bray   1919 Her] her her
1920–1 *written as one line*   1936 þe *supplied*

'Mary,' quoþ þat oþer mon, 'myn is bihynde,
For I haf hunted al þis day, and noȝt haf I geten
Bot þis foule fox felle—þe fende haf þe godez!—
And þat is ful pore for to pay for suche prys þinges　　　1945
As ȝe haf þryȝt me here þro, suche þre cosses
　　　　　so gode.'
　　　'Inoȝ,' quoþ Sir Gawayn,
　　　'I þonk yow, bi þe rode',
　　　And how þe fox watz slayn　　　1950
　　　He tolde hym as þay stode.

With merþe and mynstralsye, wyth metez at hor wylle,
þay maden as mery as any men moȝten—
With laȝyng of ladies, with lotez of bordes
Gawayn and þe godemon so glad were þay boþe—　　　1955
Bot if þe douthe had doted, oþer dronken ben oþer.
Boþe þe mon and þe meyny maden mony iapez,
Til þe sesoun watz seȝen þat þay seuer moste;
Burnez to hor bedde behoued at þe laste.
þenne loȝly his leue at þe lorde fyrst　　　1960
Fochchez þis fre mon, and fayre he hym þonkkez:
'Of such a selly soiorne as I haf hade here,
Your honour at þis hyȝe fest, þe hyȝe kyng yow ȝelde!
I ȝef yow me for on of yourez, if yowreself lykez,
For I mot nedes, as ȝe wot, meue to-morne,　　　1965
And ȝe me take sum tolke to teche, as ȝe hyȝt,
þe gate to þe grene chapel, as God wyl me suffer
To dele on Nw ȝerez day þe dome of my wyrdes.'
'In god fayþe,' quoþ þe godmon, 'wyth a goud wylle
Al þat euer I yow hyȝt halde schal I redé.'　　　1970
þer asyngnes he a seruaunt to sett hym in þe waye,
And condue hym by þe downez, þat he no drechch had,　　f. 117ᵇ
For to ferk þurȝ þe fryth and fare at þe gaynest
　　　　　bi greue.
　　　þe lorde Gawayn con þonk,　　　1975
　　　Such worchip he wolde hym weue.
　　　þen at þo ladyez wlonk
　　　þe knyȝt hatz tan his leue.

1962 selly] sellyly　　　1973 ferk] frk

With care and wyth kyssyng he carppez hem tille,
And fele þryuande þonkkez he þrat hom to haue,   1980
And þay ȝelden hym aȝayn ȝeply þat ilk;
þay bikende hym to Kryst with ful colde sykyngez.
Syþen fro þe meyny he menskly departes;
Vche mon þat he mette, he made hem a þonke
For his seruyse and his solace and his sere pyne,   1985
þat þay wyth busynes had ben aboute hym to serue;
And vche segge as soré to seuer with hym þere
As þay hade wonde worþyly with þat wlonk euer.
þen with ledes and lyȝt he watz ladde to his chambre
And blyþely broȝt to his bedde to be at his rest.   1990
Ȝif he ne slepe soundyly say ne dar I,
For he hade muche on þe morn to mynne, ȝif he wolde,
          in þoȝt.
     Let hym lyȝe þere stille,
     He hatz nere þat he soȝt;   1995
     And ȝe wyl a whyle be stylle
     I schal telle yow how þay wroȝt.

IV

NOW neȝez þe Nw Ȝere, and þe nyȝt passez,
   þe day dryuez to þe derk, as Dryȝtyn biddez;
Bot wylde wederez of þe worlde wakned þeroute,   2000
Clowdes kesten kenly þe colde to þe erþe,
Wyth nyȝe innoghe of þe norþe, þe naked to tene;
þe snawe snitered ful snart, þat snayped þe wylde;
þe werbelande wynde wapped fro þe hyȝe,
And drof vche dale ful of dryftes ful grete.   2005
þe leude lystened ful wel þat leȝ in his bedde,
þaȝ he lowkez his liddez, ful lyttel he slepes;
Bi vch kok þat crue he knwe wel þe steuen.
Deliuerly he dressed vp, er þe day sprenged,   f. 118a
For þere watz lyȝt of a laumpe þat lemed in his chambre;   2010
He called to his chamberlayn, þat cofly hym swared,
And bede hym bryng hym his bruny and his blonk sadel;

1981 aȝayn] aȝay   2010 laumpe] laupe

þat oþer ferkez hym vp and fechez hym his wedez,
And grayþez me Sir Gawayn vpon a grett wyse.
Fyrst he clad hym in his cloþez þe colde for to were,   2015
And syþen his oþer harnays, þat holdely watz keped,
Boþe his paunce and his platez, piked ful clene,
þe ryngez rokked of þe roust of his riche bruny;
And al watz fresch as vpon fyrst, and he watz fayn þenne
        to þonk;   2020
    He hade vpon vche pece,
    Wypped ful wel and wlonk;
    þe gayest into Grece,
    þe burne bede bryng his blonk.

Whyle þe wlonkest wedes he warp on hymseluen—   2025
His cote wyth þe conysaunce of þe clere werkez
Ennurned vpon veluet, vertuus stonez
Aboute beten and bounden, enbrauded semez,
And fayre furred withinne wyth fayre pelures—
Ȝet laft he not þe lace, þe ladiez gifte,   2030
þat forgat not Gawayn for gode of hymseluen.
Bi he hade belted þe bronde vpon his balȝe haunchez,
þenn dressed he his drurye double hym aboute,
Swyþe sweþled vmbe his swange swetely þat knyȝt
þe gordel of þe grene silke, þat gay wel bisemed,   2035
Vpon þat ryol red cloþe þat ryche watz to schewe.
Bot wered not þis ilk wyȝe for wele þis gordel,
For pryde of þe pendauntez, þaȝ polyst þay were,
And þaȝ þe glyterande golde glent vpon endez,
Bot for to sauen hymself, when suffer hym byhoued,   2040
To byde bale withoute dabate of bronde hym to were
        oþer knyffe.
    Bi þat þe bolde mon boun
    Wynnez þeroute bilyue,
    Alle þe meyny of renoun   2045
    He þonkkez ofte ful ryue.

Thenne watz Gryngolet grayþe, þat gret watz and huge,   f. 118ᵇ
And hade ben soiourned sauerly and in a siker wyse,
Hym lyst prik for poynt, þat proude hors þenne.

2027 vertuus] s repr. by -us abbr.

þe wyȝe wynnez hym to and wytez on his lyre,   2050
And sayde soberly hymself and by his soth swerez:
'Here is a meyny in þis mote þat on menske þenkkez,
þe mon hem maynteines, ioy mot þay haue;
þe leue lady on lyue luf hir bityde;
ȝif þay for charyté cherysen a gest,   2055
And halden honour in her honde, þe haþel hem ȝelde
þat haldez þe heuen vpon hyȝe, and also yow alle!
And ȝif I myȝt lyf vpon londe lede any quyle,
I schuld rech yow sum rewarde redyly, if I myȝt.'
þenn steppez he into stirop and strydez alofte;   2060
His schalk schewed hym his schelde, on schulder he hit laȝt,
Gordez to Gryngolet with his gilt helez,
And he startez on þe ston, stod he no lenger
       to prraunce.
       His haþel on hors watz þenne,   2065
       þat bere his spere and launce.
       'þis kastel to Kryst I kenne':
       He gef hit ay god chaunce.

The brygge watz brayde doun, and þe brode ȝatez
Vnbarred and born open vpon boþe halue.   2070
þe burne blessed hym bilyue, and þe bredez passed—
Prayses þe porter bifore þe prynce kneled,
Gef hym God and goud day, þat Gawayn he saue—
And went on his way with his wyȝe one,
þat schulde teche hym to tourne to þat tene place   2075
þer þe ruful race he schulde resayue.
þay boȝen bi bonkkez þer boȝez ar bare,
þay clomben bi clyffez þer clengez þe colde.
þe heuen watz vphalt, bot vgly þer-vnder;
Mist muged on þe mor, malt on þe mountez,   2080
Vch hille hade a hatte, a myst-hakel huge.
Brokez byled and breke bi bonkkez aboute,
Schyre schaterande on schorez, þer þay doun schowued.
Wela wylle watz þe way þer þay bi wod schulden,
Til hit watz sone sesoun þat þe sunne ryses   2085
       þat tyde.
       þay were on a hille ful hyȝe,
       þe quyte snaw lay bisyde;

þe burne þat rod hym by
Bede his mayster abide.   2090

'For I haf wonnen yow hider, wyȝe, at þis tyme,
And now nar ȝe not fer fro þat note place
þat ȝe han spied and spuryed so specially after;
Bot I schal say yow for soþe, syþen I yow knowe,
And ȝe ar a lede vpon lyue þat I wel louy,   2095
Wolde ȝe worch bi my wytte, ȝe worþed þe better.
þe place þat ȝe prece to ful perelous is halden;
þer wonez a wyȝe in þat waste, þe worst vpon erþe,
For he is stiffe and sturne, and to strike louies,
And more he is þen any mon vpon myddelerde,   2100
And his body bigger þen þe best fowre
þat ar in Arþurez hous, Hestor, oþer oþer.
He cheuez þat chaunce at þe chapel grene,
þer passes non bi þat place so proude in his armes
þat he ne dyngez hym to deþe with dynt of his honde;   2105
For he is a mon methles, and mercy non vses,
For be hit chorle oþer chaplayn þat bi þe chapel rydes,
Monk oþer masseprest, oþer any mon elles,
Hym þynk as queme hym to quelle as quyk go hymseluen.
Forþy I say þe, as soþe as ȝe in sadel sitte,   2110
Com ȝe þere, ȝe be kylled, may þe knyȝt rede,
Trawe ȝe me þat trwely, þaȝ ȝe had twenty lyues
    to spende.
He hatz wonyd here ful ȝore,
On bent much baret bende,   2115
Aȝayn his dyntez sore
ȝe may not yow defende.

'Forþy, goude Sir Gawayn, let þe gome one,
And gotz away sum oþer gate, vpon Goddez halue!
Cayrez bi sum oþer kyth, þer Kryst mot yow spede,   2120
And I schal hyȝ me hom aȝayn, and hete yow fyrre
þat I schal swere bi God and alle his gode halȝez,   f. 119^b
As help me God and þe halydam, and oþez innoghe,
þat I schal lelly yow layne, and lance neuer tale
þat euer ȝe fondet to fle for freke þat I wyst.'   2125

2105 dyngez] dynnez

'Grant merci', quoþ Gawayn, and gruchyng he sayde: *with displeasure*
'Wel worth þe, wyȝe, þat woldez my gode,
And þat lelly me layne I leue wel þou woldez.
Bot helde þou hit neuer so holde, and I here passed, *loyally*
Founded for ferde for to fle, in fourme þat þou tellez, *in fear*   2130
I were a knyȝt kowarde, I myȝt not be excused.   *xxx - re girdle.*
Bot I wyl to þe chapel, for chaunce þat may falle,
And talk wyth þat ilk tulk þe tale þat me lyste,
Worþe hit wele oþer wo, as þe wyrde lykez
          hit hafe.   2135
        þaȝe he be a sturn knape   *fellow*
          To stiȝtel, and stad with staue, *deal with . standing there*
        Ful wel con Dryȝtyn schape   *but why the trust*
          His seruauntez for to saue.'   *to green girdle*

'Mary!' quoþ þat oþer mon, 'now þou so much spellez,   2140
þat þou wylt þyn awen nye nyme to þyseluen, *harm*   *familiar*
And þe lyst lese þy lyf, þe lette I ne kepe.
Haf here þi helme on þy hede, þi spere in þi honde,
And ryde me doun þis ilk rake bi ȝon rokke syde, *path*
Til þou be broȝt to þe boþem of þe brem valay; *wild*   2145
þenne loke a littel on þe launde, on þi lyfte honde,
And þou schal se in þat slade þe self chapel, *valley*
And þe borelych burne on bent þat hit kepez. *massive*
Now farez wel, on Godez half, Gawayn þe noble!
For alle þe golde vpon grounde I nolde go wyth þe,   2150
Ne bere þe felaȝschip þurȝ þis fryth on fote fyrre.'
Bi þat þe wyȝe in þe wod wendez his brydel,
Hit þe hors with þe helez as harde as he myȝt,
Lepez hym ouer þe launde, and leuez þe knyȝt þere
          al one.   2155
        'Bi Goddez self,' quoþ Gawayn,
          'I wyl nauþer grete ne grone;
        To Goddez wylle I am ful bayn, *obediant.*
          And to hym I haf me tone.' *taken*

Thenne gyrdez he to Gryngolet, and gederez þe rake, *strikes* *follows*
                                                     f.'120ª *path*
Schowez in bi a schore at a schaȝe syde, *makes his way, small wood*   2161
Ridez þurȝ þe roȝe bonk ryȝt to þe dale; *across*

2131 not] mot   2137 and] & &   2150 go] ge

And þenne he wayted hym aboute, and wylde hit hym þoȝt,
And seȝe no syngne of resette bisydez nowhere,
Bot hyȝe bonkkez and brent vpon boþe halue,   2165
And ruȝe knokled knarrez with knorned stonez;
þe skwez of þe scowtes skayned hym þoȝt.
þenne he houed, and wythhylde his hors at þat tyde,
And ofte chaunged his cher þe chapel to seche:
He seȝ non suche in no syde, and selly hym þoȝt,   2170
Saue, a lyttel on a launde, a lawe as hit were;
A balȝ berȝ bi a bonke þe brymme bysyde,
Bi a forȝ of a flode þat ferked þare;
þe borne blubred þerinne as hit boyled hade.
þe knyȝt kachez his caple, and com to þe lawe,   2175
Liȝtez doun luflyly, and at a lynde tachez
þe rayne and his riche with a roȝe braunche.
þenne he boȝez to þe berȝe, aboute hit he walkez,
Debatande with hymself quat hit be myȝt.
Hit hade a hole on þe ende and on ayþer syde,   2180
And ouergrowen with gresse in glodes aywhere,
And al watz holȝ inwith, nobot an olde caue,
Or a creuisse of an olde cragge, he couþe hit noȝt deme
            with spelle.
       'We! Lorde,' quoþ þe gentyle knyȝt,   2185
       'Wheþer þis be þe grene chapelle?
       Here myȝt aboute mydnyȝt
       þe dele his matynnes telle!

'Now iwysse,' quoþ Wowayn, 'wysty is here;
þis oritore is vgly, with erbez ouergrowen;   2190
Wel bisemez þe wyȝe wruxled in grene
Dele here his deuocioun on þe deuelez wyse.
Now I fele hit is þe fende, in my fyue wyttez,
þat hatz stoken me þis steuen to strye me here.
þis is a chapel of meschaunce, þat chekke hit bytyde!   2195
Hit is þe corsedest kyrk þat euer I com inne!'
With heȝe helme on his hede, his launce in his honde,   f. 120b
He romez vp to þe roffe of þe roȝ wonez.

2171 were] we   2177 rayne] first two letters uncertain   2178 þenne]
þē e; n from offset   2179 Debatande] first e from offset   2180 Hit]
h from offset   2182 al from offset   2187 Here] he

þene herde he of þat hyȝe hil, in a harde roche
Biȝonde þe broke, in a bonk, a wonder breme noyse,   *loud/fierce*   2200
Quat! hit clatered in þe clyff, as hit cleue schulde,
As one vpon a gryndelston hade grounden a syþe.
What! hit wharred and whette, as water at a mulne;   *made a grinding noise*
What! hit rusched and ronge, rawþe to here.   *grievous*
þenne 'Bi Godde,' quoþ Gawayn, 'þat gere, as I trowe,   2205
Is rychched at þe reuerence me, renk, to mete   *prepared in honour of me*
          bi rote.   *with ceremony*
      Let God worche! "We loo"—
      Hit helppez me not a mote.
      My lif þaȝ I forgoo,   2210
      Drede dotz me no lote.'   *noise*

Thenne þe knyȝt con calle ful hyȝe:
'Who stiȝtlez in þis sted me steuen to holde?   *is master, to keep the agreed day*
For now is gode Gawayn goande ryȝt here.   *walking*
If any wyȝe oȝt wyl, wynne hider fast,   *come*   2215
Oþer now oþer neuer, his nedez to spede.'
'Abyde', quoþ on on þe bonke abouen ouer his hede,
'And þou schal haf al in hast þat I þe hyȝt ones.'   *promised*
Ȝet he rusched on þat rurde rapely a þrowe,   *went on with that noise quickly for a time*
And wyth quettyng awharf, er he wolde lyȝt;   *turned aside*   2220
And syþen he keuerez bi a cragge, and comez of a hole,   *makes his way*
Whyrlande out of a wro wyth a felle weppen,   *nook*
A denez ax nwe dyȝt, þe dynt with to ȝelde,   *danish axe*
With a borelych bytte bende by þe halme,   *a mighty blade curved back ... line with the shaft*
Fyled in a fylor, fowre fote large—   *sharpened at a whetstone*   2225
Hit watz no lasse bi þat lace þat lemed ful bryȝt—
And þe gome in þe grene gered as fyrst,
Boþe þe lyre and þe leggez, lokkez and berde,   *face*
Saue þat fayre on his fote he foundez on þe erþe,   *courteously*
Sette þe stele to þe stone, and stalked bysyde.   *haft*   2230
When he wan to þe watter, þer he wade nolde,
He hypped ouer on hys ax, and orpedly strydez,   *aggressively*
Bremly broþe on a bent þat brode watz aboute,   *fiercely grim*
          on snawe.
      Sir Gawayn þe knyȝt con mete,   f. 121ª
      He ne lutte hym noþyng lowe;   2236

2205 as] at   2223 with to] wᵗ o

þat oþer sayde, 'Now, sir swete,
Of steuen mon may þe trowe.'

'Gawayn,' quoþ þat grene gome, 'God þe mot loke!
Iwysse þou art welcom, wyȝe, to my place,   2240
And þou hatz tymed þi trauayl as truee mon schulde,
And þou knowez þe couenauntez kest vus bytwene:
At þis tyme twelmonyth þou toke þat þe falled,
And I schulde at þis Nwe ȝere ȝeply þe quyte.
And we ar in þis valay verayly oure one;   2245
Here ar no renkes vs to rydde, rele as vus likez.
Haf þy helme of þy hede, and haf here þy pay.
Busk no more debate þen I þe bede þenne
When þou wypped of my hede at a wap one.'
'Nay, bi God,' quoþ Gawayn, 'þat me gost lante,   2250
I schal gruch þe no grwe for grem þat fallez.
Bot styȝtel þe vpon on strok, and I schal stonde stylle
And warp þe no wernyng to worch as þe lykez,
                    nowhare.'
    He lened with þe nek, and lutte,   2255
    And schewed þat schyre al bare,
    And lette as he noȝt dutte;
    For drede he wolde not dare.

THEN þe gome in þe grene grayþed hym swyþe,
Gederez vp hys grymme tole Gawayn to smyte;   2260
With alle þe bur in his body he ber hit on lofte,
Munt as maȝtyly as marre hym he wolde;
Hade hit dryuen adoun as dreȝ as he atled,
þer hade ben ded of his dynt þat doȝty watz euer.
Bot Gawayn on þat giserne glyfte hym bysyde,   2265
As hit com glydande adoun on glode hym to schende,
And schranke a lytel with þe schulderes for þe scharp yrne.
þat oþer schalk wyth a schunt þe schene wythhaldez,
And þenne repreued he þe prynce with mony prowde wordez:
'þou art not Gawayn,' quoþ þe gome, 'þat is so goud halden, 2270
þat neuer arȝed for no here by hylle ne be vale,
And now þou fles for ferde er þou fele harmez!   f. 121^b
Such cowardise of þat knyȝt cowþe I neuer here.

Nawþer fyked I ne flaȝe, freke, quen þou myntest,
Ne kest no kauelacion in kyngez hous Arthor.   2275
My hede flaȝ to my fote, and ȝet flaȝ I neuer;
And þou, er any harme hent, arȝez in hert;
Wherfore þe better burne me burde be called
    þerfore.'
      Quoþ Gawayn, 'I schunt onez,   2280
      And so wyl I no more;
      Bot þaȝ my hede falle on þe stonez,
      I con not hit restore.

'Bot busk, burne, bi þi fayth, and bryng me to þe poynt.
Dele to me my destiné, and do hit out of honde,   2285
For I schal stonde þe a strok, and start no more
Til þyn ax haue me hitte: haf here my trawþe.'
'Haf at þe þenne!' quoþ þat oþer, and heuez hit alofte,
And waytez as wroþely as he wode were.
He myntez at hym maȝtyly, bot not þe mon rynez,   2290
Withhelde heterly his honde, er hit hurt myȝt.
Gawayn grayþely hit bydez, and glent with no membre,
Bot stode stylle as þe ston, oþer a stubbe auþer
þat raþeled is in roché grounde with rotez a hundreth.
þen muryly efte con he mele, þe mon in þe grene: 2295
'So, now þou hatz þi hert holle, hitte me bihous.
Halde þe now þe hyȝe hode þat Arþur þe raȝt,
And kepe þy kanel at þis kest, ȝif hit keuer may.'
Gawayn ful gryndelly with greme þenne sayde:
'Wy! þresch on, þou þro mon, þou þretez to longe;   2300
I hope þat þi hert arȝe wyth þyn awen seluen.'
'For soþe,' quoþ þat oþer freke, 'so felly þou spekez,
I wyl no lenger on lyte lette þin ernde
    riȝt nowe.'
      þenne tas he hym stryþe to stryke,   2305
      And frounsez boþe lyppe and browe;
      No meruayle þaȝ hym myslyke
      þat hoped of no rescowe.

He lyftes lyȝtly his lome, and let hit doun fayre
With þe barbe of þe bitte bi þe bare nek;   f. 122ª

þaȝ he homered heterly, hurt hym no more ~~~struck fiercely~~ 2311
Bot snyrt hym on þat on syde, þat seuered þe hyde. ~~skin~~
þe scharp schrank to þe flesche þurȝ þe schyre grece, ~~penetrated~~
þat þe schene blod ouer his schulderes schot to þe erþe; ~~shine~~
And quen þe burne seȝ þe blode blenk on þe snawe, ~~sprang~~ 2315
He sprit forth spenne-fote more þen a spere lenþe, ~~with feet together~~ ~~fiercely~~
Hent heterly his helme, and on his hed cast,
Schot with his schulderez his fayre schelde vnder,
Braydez out a bryȝt sworde, and bremely he spekez— ~~angrily~~
Neuer syn þat he watz burne borne of his moder 2320
Watz he neuer in þis worlde wyȝe half so blyþe— ~~man~~
'Blynne, burne, of þy bur, bede me no mo! ~~cease, violence~~ ~~offer~~
I haf a stroke in þis sted withoute stryf hent,
And if þow rechez me any mo, I redyly schal quyte,
And ȝelde ȝederly aȝayn—and þerto ȝe tryst— ~~promptly~~ ~~fiercely~~ 2325
              and foo.
        Bot on stroke here me fallez—
        þe couenaunt schop ryȝt so,
        Fermed in Arþurez hallez—
        And þerfore, hende, now hoo!' ~~stop~~ 2330

The haþel heldet hym fro, and on his ax rested,
Sette þe schaft vpon schore, and to þe scharp lened,
And loked to þe leude þat on þe launde ȝede,
How þat doȝty, dredlez, deruely þer stondez ~~boldly~~
Armed, ful aȝlez: in hert hit hym lykez. ~~fearless (aweless)~~ 2335
þenn he melez muryly wyth a much steuen, ~~voice~~
And wyth a rynkande rurde he to þe renk sayde: ~~ringing voice~~
'Bolde burne, on þis bent be not so gryndel. ~~fierce~~
No mon here vnmanerly þe mysboden habbez, ~~ill used~~
Ne kyd bot as couenaunde at kyngez kort schaped. ~~behaved~~ 2340
I hyȝt þe a strok and þou hit hatz, halde þe wel payed;
I relece þe of þe remnaunt of ryȝtes alle oþer. ~~claims~~
Iif I deliuer had bene, a boffet paraunter ~~nimble~~
I couþe wroþeloker haf waret, to þe haf wroȝt anger. ~~harm~~ ~~more harshly~~
Fyrst I mansed þe muryly with a mynt one, ~~threatened~~ 2345
And roue þe wyth no rof-sore, with ryȝt I þe profered ~~cut~~ ~~gash~~

2329 Fermed in] *Menner, from offset* ferı; *rest illegible*   2337 rynkande]
Napier; MS. rykande   2339 habbez] habbe   2344 anger] *doubtful,*
ger *perhaps legible*

For þe forwarde þat we fest in þe fyrst nyȝt,   f. 122ᵇ
And þou trystyly þe trawþe and trwly me haldez,
Al þe gayne þow me gef, as god mon schulde.
þat oþer munt for þe morne, mon, I þe profered,   2350
þou kyssedes my clere wyf—þe cossez me raȝtez.
For boþe two here I þe bede bot two bare myntes
      boute scaþe.
   Trwe mon trwe restore,
    þenne þar mon drede no waþe.   2355
     At þe þrid þou fayled þore,
     And þerfor þat tappe ta þe.

'For hit is my wede þat þou werez, þat ilke wouen girdel,
Myn owen wyf hit þe weued, I wot wel for soþe.
Now know I wel þy cosses, and þy costes als,   2360
And þe wowyng of my wyf: I wroȝt hit myseluen.
I sende hir to asay þe, and sothly me þynkkez
On þe fautlest freke þat euer on fote ȝede;
As perle bi þe quite pese is of prys more,
So is Gawayn, in god fayth, bi oþer gay knyȝtez.   2365
Bot here yow lakked a lyttel, sir, and lewté yow wonted;
Bot þat watz for no wylyde werke, ne wowyng nauþer,
Bot for ȝe lufed your lyf; þe lasse I yow blame.'
þat oþer stif mon in study stod a gret whyle,
So agreued for greme he gryed withinne;   2370
Alle þe blode of his brest blende in his face,
þat al he schrank for schome þat þe schalk talked.
þe forme worde vpon folde þat þe freke meled:
'Corsed worth cowarddyse and couetyse boþe!
In yow is vylany and vyse þat vertue disstryez.'   2375
þenne he kaȝt to þe knot, and þe kest lawsez,
Brayde broþely þe belt to þe burne seluen:
'Lo! þer þe falssyng, foule mot hit falle!
For care of þy knokke cowardyse me taȝt
To acorde me with couetyse, my kynde to forsake,   2380
þat is larges and lewté þat longez to knyȝtez.
Now am I fawty and falce, and ferde haf ben euer
Of trecherye and vntrawþe: boþe bityde sorȝe
    and care!

I biknowe yow, knyȝt, here stylle,
Al fawty is my fare;   2386
Letez me ouertake your wylle
And efte I schal be ware.'

Thenn loȝe þat oþer leude and luflyly sayde:
'I halde hit hardily hole, þe harme þat I hade.   2390
þou art confessed so clene, beknowen of þy mysses,
And hatz þe penaunce apert of þe poynt of myn egge,
I halde þe polysed of þat plyȝt, and pured as clene
As þou hadez neuer forfeted syþen þou watz fyrst borne;
And I gif þe, sir, þe gurdel þat is golde-hemmed,   2395
For hit is grene as my goune. Sir Gawayn, ȝe maye
þenk vpon þis ilke þrepe, þer þou forth þryngez
Among prynces of prys, and þis a pure token
Of þe chaunce of þe grene chapel at cheualrous knyȝtez.
And ȝe schal in þis Nwe ȝer aȝayn to my wonez,   2400
And we schyn reuel þe remnaunt of þis ryche fest
        ful bene.'
    þer laþed hym fast þe lorde
    And sayde: 'With my wyf, I wene,
    We schal yow wel acorde,   2405
    þat watz your enmy kene.'

'Nay, for soþe,' quoþ þe segge, and sesed hys helme,
And hatz hit of hendely, and þe haþel þonkkez,
'I haf soiorned sadly; sele yow bytyde,
And he ȝelde hit yow ȝare þat ȝarkkez al menskes!   2410
And comaundez me to þat cortays, your comlych fere,
Boþe þat on and þat oþer, myn honoured ladyez,
þat þus hor knyȝt wyth hor kest han koyntly bigyled.
Bot hit is no ferly þaȝ a fole madde,
And þurȝ wyles of wymmen be wonen to sorȝe,   2415
For so watz Adam in erde with one bygyled,
And Salamon with fele sere, and Samson eftsonez—
Dalyda dalt hym hys wyrde—and Dauyth þerafter
Watz blended with Barsabe, þat much bale þoled.
Now þese were wrathed wyth her wyles, hit were a wynne
        huge   2420

2385 catchword I beknowe yow knyȝt   2390 hardily] hardilyly
2396 Sir Gawayn] Sir G:

To luf hom wel, and leue hem not, a leude þat couþe.
For þes wer forne þe freest, þat folȝed alle þe sele
Exellently of alle þyse oþer, vnder heuenryche
          þat mused;
    And alle þay were biwyled   2425
    With wymmen þat þay vsed.
    þaȝ I be now bigyled,
    Me þink me burde be excused.

'Bot your gordel', quoþ Gawayn, 'God yow forȝelde!
þat wyl I welde wyth guod wylle, not for þe wynne golde,   2430
Ne þe saynt, ne þe sylk, ne þe syde pendaundes,
For wele ne for worchyp, ne for þe wlonk werkkez,
Bot in syngne of my surfet I schal se hit ofte,
When I ride in renoun, remorde to myseluen
þe faut and þe fayntyse of þe flesche crabbed,   2435
How tender hit is to entyse teches of fylþe;
And þus, quen pryde schal me pryk for prowes of armes,
þe loke to þis luf-lace schal leþe my hert.
Bot on I wolde yow pray, displeses yow neuer:
Syn ȝe be lorde of þe ȝonder londe þer I haf lent inne   2440
Wyth yow wyth worschyp—þe wyȝe hit yow ȝelde
þat vphaldez þe heuen and on hyȝ sittez—
How norne ȝe yowre ryȝt nome, and þenne no more?'
'þat schal I telle þe trwly,' quoþ þat oþer þenne,
'Bertilak de Hautdesert I hat in þis londe.   2445
þurȝ myȝt of Morgne la Faye, þat in my hous lenges,
And koyntyse of clergye, bi craftes wel lerned,
þe maystrés of Merlyn mony hatz taken—
For ho hatz dalt drwry ful dere sumtyme
With þat conable klerk, þat knowes alle your knyȝtez   2450
          at hame;
    Morgne þe goddes
    þerfore hit is hir name:
    Weldez non so hyȝe hawtesse
    þat ho ne con make ful tame—   2455

'Ho wayned me vpon þis wyse to your wynne halle
For to assay þe surquidré, ȝif hit soth were

þat rennes of þe grete renoun of þe Rounde Table;
Ho wayned me þis wonder your wyttez to reue,
For to haf greued Gaynour and gart hir to dyȝe   f. 124ª
With glopnyng of þat ilke gome þat gostlych speked   2461
With his hede in his honde bifore þe hyȝe table.
þat is ho þat is at home, þe auncian lady;
Ho is euen þyn aunt, Arþurez half-suster,
þe duches doȝter of Tyntagelle, þat dere Vter after   2465
Hade Arþur vpon, þat aþel is nowþe.
þerfore I eþe þe, haþel, to com to þyn aunt,
Make myry in my hous; my meny þe louies,
And I wol þe as wel, wyȝe, bi my faythe,
As any gome vnder God for þy grete trauþe.'   2470
And he nikked hym naye, he nolde bi no wayes.
þay acolen and kyssen and kennen ayþer oþer
To þe prynce of paradise, and parten ryȝt þere
          on coolde;
        Gawayn on blonk ful bene   2475
        To þe kyngez burȝ buskez bolde,
        And þe knyȝt in þe enker-grene
        Whiderwarde-so-euer he wolde.

Wylde wayez in þe worlde Wowen now rydez
On Gryngolet, þat þe grace hade geten of his lyue;   2480
Ofte he herbered in house and ofte al þeroute,
And mony aventure in vale, and venquyst ofte,
þat I ne tyȝt at þis tyme in tale to remene.
þe hurt watz hole þat he hade hent in his nek,
And þe blykkande belt he bere þeraboute   2485
Abelef as a bauderyk bounden bi his syde,
Loken vnder his lyfte arme, þe lace, with a knot,
In tokenyng he watz tane in tech of a faute.
And þus he commes to þe court, knyȝt al in sounde.
þer wakned wele in þat wone when wyst þe grete   2490
þat gode Gawayn watz commen; gayn hit hym þoȝt.
þe kyng kyssez þe knyȝt, and þe whene alce,
And syþen mony syker knyȝt þat soȝt hym to haylce,
Of his fare þat hym frayned; and ferlyly he telles,

2461 glopnyng] gopnyng   — gome] gomen   2467 þyn aunt] þy naunt
2472 and kennen *supplied*   2491 Gawayn] G::

Biknowez alle þe costes of care þat he hade,   2495
þe chaunce of þe chapel, þe chere of þe knyȝt,
þe luf of þe ladi, þe lace at þe last.   f. 124^b
þe nirt in þe nek he naked hem schewed
þat he laȝt for his vnleuté at þe leudes hondes
> for blame.   2500

         He tened quen he schulde telle,
         He groned for gref and grame;
         þe blod in his face con melle,
         When he hit schulde schewe, for schame.

'Lo! lorde,' quoþ þe leude, and þe lace hondeled,   2505
'þis is þe bende of þis blame I bere in my nek,
þis is þe laþe and þe losse þat I laȝt haue
Of couardise and couetyse þat I haf caȝt þare;
þis is þe token of vntrawþe þat I am tan inne,
And I mot nedez hit were wyle I may last;   2510
For mon may hyden his harme, bot vnhap ne may hit,
For þer hit onez is tachched twynne wil hit neuer.'
þe kyng comfortez þe knyȝt, and alle þe court als
Laȝen loude þerat, and luflyly acorden
þat lordes and ladis þat longed to þe Table,   2515
Vche burne of þe broþerhede, a bauderyk schulde haue,
A bende abelef hym aboute of a bryȝt grene,
And þat, for sake of þat segge, in swete to were.
For þat watz acorded þe renoun of þe Rounde Table,
And he honoured þat hit hade euermore after,   2520
As hit is breued in þe best boke of romaunce.
þus in Arthurus day þis aunter bitidde,
þe Brutus bokez þerof beres wyttenesse;
Syþen Brutus, þe bolde burne, boȝed hider fyrst,
After þe segge and þe asaute watz sesed at Troye,   2525
         iwysse,
         Mony aunterez here-biforne
         Haf fallen suche er þis.
         Now þat bere þe croun of þorne,
         He bryng vus to his blysse! AMEN.   2530

HONY SOYT QUI MAL PENCE.

2506 in *supplied*   2511 mon] non

NOTES

1 With this opening, setting the story in the framework of history by reference to Troy, Gollancz compares the beginning of *Winner and Waster* and the end of the alliterative *Morte Arthure*. For a discussion of sources and associations see T. Silverstein, *M.P.* lxii (1964–5), 189–206.

3–5 *Þe tulk*. Madden understood this to mean Aeneas of l. 5, *hit watz* there referring back. Gollancz took it to mean Antenor, on the ground that according to the medieval tradition which began with Dares Phrygius and Dictys Cretensis it was he who took the lead in betraying Troy to the Greeks; *hit watz* would then refer forward. Either construction of *hit watz* is possible; but Madden's view is to be preferred. The poet needed Aeneas for his genealogy, but Antenor was superfluous. Guido de Columnis, in his *Historia Destructionis Troiae* (which is based ultimately on Dares and Dictys and which was the source of most later versions of the story) associated Aeneas with the plot from the first: 'Troyanis igitur existentibus tantis doloribus anxiosis et inclusis in urbe, Anchises cum eius filio Henea, Anthenor etiam cum eius filio Pollidamas consilium inierunt qualiter uitas eorum possent saluas facere ne perderentur a Grecis, et si aliud facere non possent, prodere ciuitatem' (ed. N. E. Griffin (Cambridge, Mass., 1936), p. 218), and singled him out for condemnation by Hecuba: 'Heccuba uero et eius filia Polixena se fuge dederunt. . . . Eis tamen fugientibus obuiauit Heneas. Cui Heccuba . . .: "Ha nequam proditor. . . . Prodidisti patriam tuam et urbem in qua natus fuisti"' (p. 234). According to Guido, Aeneas was tried and exiled by the Greeks for his deceit in concealing from them Polyxena, through whom Achilles lost his life (p. 240).

The legend of Aeneas' treachery did not embarrass writers in English who wished to trace the descent of the Britons from him, through Brutus. Guido's account is closely followed, for example, in *The Gest Hystoriale of the Destruction of Troy* 11832 ff., esp. 11973, 'The traytor with tene, vntristy Eneas'; in the *Scottish Troy Fragments* 830 ff.; and in Lydgate's *Troy Book* iv. 4538 ff., 6316–469. *Trewest* in 4 must mean 'veriest, surest, most real', referring to *tricherie*, for a man who plotted treason could not be called 'most faithful'; *athel* (5) means 'of noble birth' without implication of honourable character. *Tried* (4) Gollancz took as 'probably "distinguished, famous"', adding that the first example in *O.E.D.* of *try* in the legal sense, of a person, is of 1538. But the development of this passage calls for an event, not a general condition such as fame or distinction; and in *Pearl* 707 'when þou arte *tryed*' refers to Judgement Day. It seems right therefore to accept the legal and personal sense here.

6 *prouinces*. The word may seem to depend on Guido's 'Et nonnulle alie

... prouincie' (p. 11); but it is quite common in alliterative poetry, notably some seven times in *Wars Alex.* and three in *Purity*.

7 *west iles*. This must be a general term for western lands, not Britain alone. Cf. *insulae gentium* in Gen. x. 5 of the lands settled by descendants of Japhet. See *O.E.D.* under *isle* sb. 1. b, and note on 12 below.

8 This line evidently goes with what follows, the whole being in the historic present. There is no ground for Gollancz's suspicion of corruption.

11 *Tirius*. MS. *Ticius* occurs nowhere else, and has defied attempts to explain it. Madden suggested that it might 'possibly have been derived from Titus Tatius, king of the Sabines and afterwards colleague of Romulus at Rome'. Tuscany is said by Wace (51–52) to have been ruled by *Turnus*, whom Geoffrey of Monmouth had called 'rex Rutilorum'; and something of this kind could have been corrupted. But Silverstein notes that, though *Tuscus*, the name best suited to the founder of Tuscany, does occur in early commentaries on Virgil, his father is represented as being *Tyrrhenus* (hence the Tyrrhenian Sea), sometimes *Tirrus* or *Tirius*; and this last is very close to our MS. *Ticius* (especially with the form of *r* used by this scribe). Though no existing text likely to have been known to the poet has this form, some manuscripts of Geoffrey report Brutus as coming to the Tyrrhenian Sea (*Tyrrenum equor*)—'Ibi iuxta littora inuenerunt quattuor generationes de exulibus Troie ortas, quæ Antenoris fugam comitate erant' (i. xii)—and Guido speaks of Aeneas 'Tirenum nauigando per pelagus' (p. 109). The emendation thus gives an intelligible form.

12 *Langaberde*. Langobardus was the legendary ancestor of the Langobardi or Lombards. Nennius in *Historia Brittonum*, ch. 17, represents him as a descendant of Japhet, and also as cousin of Brutus the founder of Britain.

13 *Felix Brutus*. According to Nennius, Brutus was a grandson of Aeneas and founder of Britain. Geoffrey makes him great-grandson (son of Silvius, son of Ascanius), and this became the usual form of the legend (Faral iii, pp. 6–11, 74). He is nowhere else called *Felix*, and it seems unlikely that the mere need for an alliterating word would make the poet choose a Latin rather than an English adjective. Silverstein, pursuing Gollancz's observation that Laȝamon uses *sæl* 'fortunate' of Brutus, shows that *felix* was a conventional term for founders of cities and was in fact used of both Aeneas and Antenor. Yet the suggestion for its use here may have been partly graphic—it is curious that the fourteenth-century *Anonymous Short English Metrical Chronicle* (ed. E. Zettl, E.E.T.S. 196 (1935), 11–12), should read

> A muchel man cam fram Troie iwis
> He was icliped *filius* Brutys.

This may be a corruption of the name *Siluius Brutus* which is found in some manuscripts of Nennius; but however it arose, a reading of this

kind in a source may well have prompted *felix*, for the abbreviation for
-*us* resembles some shapes of *x* (see this line in the illustration facing
p. 1).

For the early history of the legend see Bruce, *Evolution*, ii. 51–53.

25 *Bretaygne*. This is usually explained as gen. case without ending. But
alle at this date is not normally followed by *of*, and it is simpler to take
of Bretaygne as qualifying *kynges*—'but of all who dwelt here, kings of
Britain'.

26 *Arthur*. This name is a Welsh form of the Latin *Artorius*. Most of the
Arthurian names found in Middle English are derived immediately from
Old French, though they may ultimately be of Celtic origin; but Arthur
in Old French is called *Artu* (nom. *Artus*). For the historicity of Arthur
see K. H. Jackson in *Arthurian Literature*, ch. 1, and R. Bromwich,
Trioedd, pp. 274–7.

31 *as I in toun herde*. This is doubtless a conventional appeal to authority,
of a kind very common in Middle English; for examples see Oakden,
ii. 387–8. It cannot be taken as evidence for the existence of a source in
which the present story was fully developed. *In toun* means generally
'among men, in company'; see 1049 and note.

35–36 In view especially of Chaucer's 'I am a Southren man, I kan nat
geeste "rum, ram, ruf"', by *lettre*' (*Parson's Prol.* I. 42–43), and of the use
of *loken* ('fastened' rather than 'linked', since it is evidently parallel to
stoken, referring to the story not the letters), it is likely that this passage
relates to the technique of alliterative verse. (There appears to be no
comparable metrical application of *letter* until the sixteenth century.) The
adjective *lel* will then mean 'correct, exact', much as in *Purity* 425, 'Of
þe lenþe of Noe lyf to lay a *lel* date'—though it is often used in ME.
verse as a vague commendatory epithet (e.g. *Parl. Thre Ages* 115). But
in two fifteenth-century Scots passages *lel* as applied to *letteris* must mean
'truthful'; notably 'in letteris leill but lyis' in Henryson's *Age and Youth*,
a poem using alliterative phrases. (See P. J. Frankis, *N. & Q.* ccvi (1961),
329–30.) It may be that this was the meaning intended here: 'embodied
in truthful words'—comparable to 'word oþer fand soðe gebunden' in
Beowulf 870–1. In that case 36 would have to refer to the story, not the
verse technique. The other interpretation appears preferable; but in any
event it would be wrong to understand *lel* as 'loyal' and the passage as
a kind of manifesto by a self-consciously traditionalist poet.

37 *Camylot*. Malory identifies Camelot with Winchester (e.g. *Works*,
p. 92), but he is unique in this; even Caxton in the preface to his edition
of Malory speaks of it as a town in Wales, and there is no agreement on
its possible site. The poet evidently conceived it to be somewhere in the
south of England; see note on 691. In many Arthurian stories the court
is at Carlisle, of which Carduel is a variant.

vpon Krystmasse. Madden notes that the Vulgate *Lancelot* says that
Arthur held court and wore his crown five times a year—Easter, Ascension

alliterative poems. Cf. 2470 and *Morte Arthure* 537, 'The comlyeste of knyghtehode þat vndyre Cryste lyffes'. The earliest appears to be Laȝamon, *Brut* 27977, 'nusten heo under Criste nenne ræd godne'.

54 *first age.* This evidently means the 'springtime' of their lives, the sense in which *prime* was formerly used: see *O.E.D.* under *prime* sb.¹, 8; cf. *Wars Alex.* 657, 'Quen Philip see him sa fers in his first elde', and *Mum and the Sothsegger* (ed. M. Day and R. Steele, E.E.T.S. 199 (1936)) iii. 34, 'her prime age'.

60 'While New Year was so fresh that it was only newly come'. The sense is weak and the line may be corrupt, but no satisfactory emendation has been proposed. Metrically the line is adequate: $Nw(e) \; \mathcal{z}er(e)$ appears to have had level or fluctuating stress, for elsewhere in the poem it alliterates on *n* five times and on *ȝ* five times, and three occurrences do not take part in the alliteration. Here the caesura must come after *ȝep,* so that both cases of *ȝ* are in the first half-line. This arrangement is not rare; cf. 541 (*n, l, l/ n*) and 656 (*f, s, s/ f*).

Though in the Middle Ages the legal and ecclesiastical year began on various dates (in England from the late twelfth century on 25 March, the Annunciation, which continued until 1752), the Roman use of 1 January seems never to have fallen out of popular memory and observance, and the term 'New Year's Day' never meant anything else. Its first recorded use is in Orm; OE. used *gēares dæg*.

65 *nayted.* ON. *neyta*, related to OE. *nēotan*, meant 'use, enjoy', but in ME. it acquired also the sense of 'repeat, recite' as in *St. Erkenwald* 119 (emended), of prayers: 'welneghe al þe nyȝt hade naityd his houres'. Such a meaning best suits *crye* and *neuened*; the word *Nowel* was shouted in celebration.

67 'Cried loudly New Year gifts, and gave them in person'. The giving of presents at New Year is mentioned as early as the twelfth century (e.g. by Jocelin of Brakelond, *Cronica*, ch. 46; ed. H. E. Butler (London, 1949), p. 62) as a custom characteristically English. Precisely in what way these lords and ladies contended for their gifts is not known. Emerson suggested, with great probability, that the gift about which ladies laughed though they had lost, while 'he that won was not wroth', was a kiss (*J.E.G.P.* xxi (1922), 365). Support for this suggestion may be found in *Arden of Feversham*, i. 123–5:

> Alice. Bear him from me these pair of silver dice
>   With which we played for kisses many a time;
>   And when I lost, I won, and so did he.

71 *þe mete tyme.* *O.E.D.* takes this as 'until the fitting time', that is, as long as was fitting. This is unlikely, since preparations for dinner follow at once.

73 *Þe best burne ay abof.* In this description the company do not sit at the Round Table, but as in a hall of the author's own time and with the

Day, Pentecost, All Saints, and Christmas (*Vulgate*, iii. 107). The allitera-tive *Morte Arthure* also opens with a Christmas feast, at Carlisle, which is followed by a challenge on New Year's Day.

39 *rekenly*. The OE. adj. *recen* meant 'ready, prompt', but in ME. the word extended its meaning to become a generally laudatory epithet; e.g. in *Pearl* it is applied to the Pearl, and to a rose, and in *Purity* to the virtuous men who Abraham hopes might be found in Sodom.

þe Rounde Table. There is an account of the founding of the Round Table in Laȝamon's *Brut* (ed. Madden, 22737–957), much expanded from the brief mention in Wace (*Brut* 9747–60). Arthur's guests quarrelled because of the order in which they were placed. Then a 'crafti weorcman' in Cornwall offered to make him a round table so that all should sit equally high. Sixteen hundred men and more could sit at it. But in both the Vulgate *Estoire de Merlin* and in the *Suite du Merlin* (pp. 94–97) Merlin is said to have made the table for Uther, as the third 'holy table' after those of the Last Supper and of Joseph of Arimathea. (Only 150 knights could sit at it.) Uther gave it to King Leodegan, father of Guenever, and she brought it to Arthur as part of her dowry. This is the version followed by Malory (*Works*, pp. 97–98).

43 *caroles*. These were dances accompanied by song. Originally the carole was a simple ring-dance: see the introduction to R. L. Greene, *A Selec-tion of English Carols* (Oxford, 1962). In France the primitive form was elaborated into various intricate types, such as rondel and ballade, as early as the twelfth century. In the fourteenth century caroles were a fashionable form of entertainment on days of festivity; there are descrip-tions in *Sir Launfal* (ed. A. J. Bliss (London, 1960)) 637 ff., in the Chau-cerian *Romaunt of the Rose*, 743 ff., and in the prologue to Chaucer's *Legend of Good Women*.

44 *ful fiften dayes*. So, in the *Suite du Merlin*, after Merlin had told Arthur of his descent a feast was held which lasted 'quinze jours tous pleniers' (p. 173). Cf. *Arthour and Merlin* 3582, 'ful fourtenniȝt'.

46 *glaum ande gle*. MS. *glaumande gle*, as if a pres. part.; but there is no evidence of a verb formed from ON. *glaum-r*, 'merry noise'. *Glaum ande gle* forms a phrase of the common type of alliterating synonyms; cf. *glam and gle* 1652, the common *gamen and gle*, and ON. *glaumr ok gleði*. The copyist evidently confused the conj. *and(e)* with the pres. part. ending, as he did again in 1426.

49 *him*. This is the first of several cases in the poem of *him/hym* as a plural, 'them' (noted by Brett, *M.L.R.* xxii (1927), 455). There are un-doubted examples also in *Pearl* 635, 715 (where most editors emend to *hem*), and in *Purity* and *Patience*, as well as elsewhere in the fourteenth century.

51 *vnder Krystes seluen*. Comparable phrases meaning no more than 'under heaven, on earth' (cf. 56) are frequent in ME., especially in

seating according to rank which the Round Table was designed to avoid (see note on 39). With this passage cf. *Purity* 114–17.

74 *Guenore.* Guenever, Arthur's queen, Gwenhwyvar in Welsh romance. The name probably means 'white phantom'; see R. Bromwich, *Trioedd*, pp. 380–5.

77 *tolouse.* This seems to be the only occurrence of this spelling of the word. It is taken, as by *O.E.D.*, to be a form of *tuly*, which is fairly well recorded; cf. 568, 858. It is probably, like many names of cloths, from a place-name, but on the strength of this one occurrence it cannot confidently be associated with Toulouse. (In *Purity* 1108 *toles of Tolowse* is used of knives.)

tars. A rich and costly stuff used in western Europe in the fourteenth and fifteenth centuries for garments and furnishings. It takes its name from Tharsia, where it was made, and which is situated by *Mandeville's Travels* thus: 'The kyngdom of Cathay marcheth toward the west vnto the kyngdom of Tharse the whiche was on of the kynges þat cam to presente oure lord in Bethleem. . . . And on this half towardes the west is the kyngdom of Turquesten' (ed. Hamelius, p. 169).

81 *discrye.* The text has been altered here. This word has been mostly rewritten in dark ink by a hand using long forms of *s* and *r* different from the main scribe's. A following erasure has been so effective that only traces can be seen under ultra-violet light; the writing seems to have been simply the following line, misplaced.

82 *gray.* This is the conventional epithet for a heroine's eyes in many romances, imitated from French *vair*. See D. S. Brewer, 'The Ideal of Feminine Beauty in Medieval Literature', *M.L.R.* l (1955), 257–69.

86 *childgered.* The general sense of boyish conduct can be deduced from a few occurrences of the related noun. *Child gere* and *childire geris* are in *Wars Alex.* *824 (Dublin MS. only), 1773 (Ashmole; Dublin *gammez*); *childess gæress* in *Ormulum* 8050, 10885, evidently meaning 'childish behaviour'. In Orm's system the spelling *æ* implies a historical long vowel, so that derivation from ON. *gervi* (as e.g. *M.E.D.*) is unacceptable. The word should be equated with that best known in Chaucer, *Knight's Tale*, A. 1531, 'thise loveres in hir queynte geres' (see *O.E.D.* under *gere*), and found several times qualified by *wild* (see *M.E.D.* under *gere* n., 5 (a), (b)). Its origin is obscure; *O.E.D.* compares MDu. *gere, gaer*, 'desire, passion'. See C. A. Luttrell, *N. & Q.* ccvii (1962), 449–50.

87 *lyȝt.* This must be adjectival: 'He liked his life to be gay.' Gollancz's 'easily' does not suit the following clause.

88 *longe.* MS. *lenge*; *o* and *e* are distinct in this manuscript, but confusion between them, due probably to their similarity in the exemplar, is frequent: see the emendations in 438, 697, 946, 1389, 1872. For the 'split infinitive' cf. *to lelly layne* 1863; the construction is at least as old as the second text of Laȝamon.

90 ff. This custom of Arthur's is mentioned in many French romances, including the closely related *Livre de Caradoc* (see p. xvi) as well as Chrétien's *Perceval* which it continues (ed. Hilka, 2822–6 and note). See also *La Queste del Saint Graal* (ed. A. Pauphilet (repr. Paris, 1949), p. 5) and the corresponding passage in Malory (*Works*, p. 855). In all these examples the feast was at Pentecost; cf. Malory's 'Tale of Sir Gareth of Orkeney' (source unknown): 'So evir the kynge had a custom that at the feste of Pentecoste in especiall afore other festys in the yere, he wolde nat go that day to mete unto that he had herde other sawe of a grete mervayle. And for that custom all maner of strange adventures com byfore Arthure, as at that feste before all other festes' (*Works*, p. 293). But the origin of the custom, as Madden noted, is said in the Vulgate *Merlin* to have been a vow made by Arthur on 15 August at the first court after his marriage: 'iou veu a dieu que ia ne serrai al mangier deuant que aucune auenture i sera auenue de quel part ke che soit' (*Vulgate*, ii. 320).

96–99 The meaning appears to be: 'or some man begged him for a trusty knight to join with him in jousting, a man to stake [his] life against another, each to let the other have the better part as fortune would assist them.' *Jopardé*, 'even game', here still means hazard rather than danger; *lay* requires an object, which can only be *lif*. *Lede* can thus hardly be infin. (in any case no suitable sense of the verb is known); it is probably the frequent noun, defined by the infin. *to lay*, in unusual order for the alliteration. Its insertion is comparable to that of *renk* in 2206. These difficult appositional uses seem to be related to the common superfluous vocatives in which these words appear; e.g. *leude* 1109, 1675. It is less likely to be an attributive use of the noun, or an error for a genitive.

104, 107 *in stal(l)e*. This phrase was used in OE. to mean 'standing up', and *on stalle* in this sense occurs in the ME. *Bestiary* (ed. R. Morris in *An Old English Miscellany*, E.E.T.S. 49 (1872)) 661, 663, 671, 679.

107 Arthur's place was in the middle of the long side of the high table, facing the hall. He is shown there in the first of the illustrations to the poem in the manuscript; similarly in *Arthour and Merlin* 6511: 'King Arthour sat, wiþouten fable, Midelest at þe heiʒe table.' Guenever (who stands rather behind Arthur in the illustration) would be on his left (74), with Gawain next to her and then Agravain on Gawain's 'other side'. Bishop Bawdewyn 'began the table', that is, sat in the place of honour on the King's right, with Ywain beside him. The company were served in pairs, as 128 indicates; hence Ywain 'ate with him', i.e. the bishop. So the placing, seen from the hall, was:

Ywain Bawdewyn   Arthur Guenever   Gawain Agravain

This seating plan was correctly explained by Emerson, *S.P.* xxii (1925), 181.

109 *Gawan*. For the other spellings of the name see the index. Those beginning with *W* (*Wawan*, etc.; cf. *Wenore* 945) are due to the Welsh

and French treatments of initial *Gw*. In Welsh initial *g* in certain conditions (the so-called soft mutation) was absent, and the forms without
g were frequent. In Celtic names current in Old French this *g(w)* was
treated like Germanic *w*: in most dialects it appears as *g(u)*, and *Gauvain*
was the normal form of this name. But in some northern French dialects,
and to some extent also in Anglo-Norman, Celtic *(g)w* and Germanic *w*
appeared as *w*. In the *Brut* by Wace, who was born in Jersey and attached
to the court of Henry II of England, Gawain's name is spelt *Walwein* (see
Arnold's edn., index). The forms ending in *-wain*, *-vain* resemble other
Arthurian names such as *Owein/Iwain* and *Agravain*, and some of them
appear in good (twelfth-century) manuscripts of Geoffrey of Monmouth—
Gualguainus, *Galgwainus*, etc. (ed. Griscom, p. 652). But in Welsh texts,
notably in *Culhwch ac Olwen* in the *Mabinogion*, the Arthurian character
corresponding to Gawain is called Gwalchmei ap Gwyar, a name which
had appeared in the triads, and is attested still earlier in Old Breton in
the form *Walcmoei*. The etymology of *Gwalchmei*, and its relation to
Gauvain/Gawain, are disputed. *Gwalch* means 'hawk', but *mei* is uncertain. It is quite possible that the form *Gualguainus* in Geoffrey is a distortion of *Gwalchmei*; many Arthurian names show variations greater
than this. In view of the Breton form it is more likely that the *-vain*
type is an analogical innovation than that the Welsh form has been altered. The earliest Continental form of the name is *Galvagin* (Modena
cathedral relief, twelfth century, probably early); this may have been
influenced by another Celtic name which appears in the latinized shape
Volaginius in Tacitus (*Historiae*, ii. 75). The view adopted here is due
mainly to R. Bromwich, *Trioedd*, pp. 369–75; see also her ch. 5 in
Arthurian Literature, and Loomis in *Arthurian Tradition*, pp. 146–8.

In Middle English the variation of *G-* and *W-* may be due to French
alone; but the regularity of the medial *-w-* in English, contrasted with *-v-* in
French *Gauvain*, is remarkable. It suggests that the name may have come
into English direct from Welsh, as *Arthur* certainly did (see note on 26),
though no such Welsh form is recorded. Forms with *v* in English, notably
Gavin which is still a popular name in the north, are relatively modern.

Gawain is said to have been the son of Lot(h), king of Lothian, Orkeney,
and other Scottish territories. His mother was Arthur's sister, named
Anna by Geoffrey, Belisent in some French romances, Morgawse in
Malory. According to William of Malmesbury (ii. 342) Gawain (*Walwen*)
ruled over Galloway (*Walweitha*).

In early Arthurian tradition both Continental and insular Gawain is
presented as the greatest of Arthur's knights, famed for his courtesy as
well as invincible in battle. (For references see note on 553 and Loomis
in *Arthurian Tradition* as above.) This view of him continued in both
French and English; the best-known expression of his reputation for
courtesy is in Chaucer's *Squire's Tale* (F. 89–97), where the strange knight
greeted the company

> With so heigh reverence and obeisaunce,
> As wel in speche as in his contenaunce,

That Gawayn, with his olde curteisye,
Though he were comen ayeyn out of Fairye,
Ne koude hym nat amende with a word.

For ME. romances which have Gawain as their hero see Wells's *Manual of the Writings in Middle English* (New Haven, 1916), pp. 51 ff.

But another tradition of Gawain was developed in romances in which he was not the central figure: as other heroes became celebrated Gawain's standing was reduced. He retains his courtesy, but is no longer the chaste knight of the tradition represented in this poem, nor so successful in arms. This process can be observed first in French in the *Suite du Merlin*, and it is continued in *Lancelot* and especially the prose *Tristan*. In Middle English this reduced conception of Gawain appears only in narratives founded on these French versions, especially the alliterative *Morte Arthure* and Malory, from whom Tennyson adopted it. See B. J. Whiting, 'Gawain: his Reputation . . .', *Mediaeval Studies*, ix (1947), 189–234.

110 *Agrauayn a la dure mayn*. In Chrétien's *Perceval* Agrevains is 'li orguelleus as dures mains' (ed. Hilka, 8139–40), and in the Middle High German *Parzifal* (dated 1331–6) is 'Agrapens mit der herten hende' (ed. K. Schorbach (Strassburg, 1888); see Hulbert, *Manly Anniversary Studies* (Chicago, 1923), p. 17). Agravain was Gawain's brother, and his character suffered from the same French romancers as Gawain's; they represent him as spying on Lancelot's visits to Guenever because he was jealous of Lancelot's fame and prowess. Sir Degrevant of ME. romance may be identical with Agravain, as Halliwell suggested (*Thornton Romances* (Camden Soc., 1844), p. 289; cf. *Sir Degrevant* (ed. Casson, p. 116)). If so, this embodies the older tradition and is the only surviving romance that makes him its hero.

112 *Bawdewyn*. In the Welsh romances of the *Mabinogion* Arthur has a bishop Bedwini, who is evidently the same person. In the triads too he is 'chief of bishops in Cornwall'. The Celtic name has been assimilated in French romance to the French name *Baudouin*, from Germanic *Baldwini*.

113 *Ywan, Vryn son*. Ywain, son of Urien (Welsh *Owein fab Urien*), well known in Arthurian legend; see especially Chrétien's *Yvain* and the English version *Ywain and Gawain* (ed. A. B. Friedman and N. T. Harrington, E.E.T.S. 254 (1964)). Probably both were historical Welsh kings; see R. Bromwich in *Arthurian Literature*, p. 49, and *Trioedd*, pp. 479–83. According to Taliesin Owein killed Ida, king of Bernicia, who is recorded in the Anglo-Saxon Chronicle as dead in 560. His father Urbgen (Urien) is said by Nennius (ch. 63) to have warred successfully against Ida's son Theoderic, who ruled, Nennius implies, 572–9. Urien's kingdom was Rheged, which was perhaps in Cumberland, though there was another district of the same name in South Wales, including the Gower peninsula and part of Carmarthen. In later legend the southern Rheged was the one assigned to him, for we find him called king of Gorre (Gower) in Malory and elsewhere. In the *Suite du Merlin* Ywain's mother is said to have been Morgain la Fée. If Arthur and he were both historical they could hardly have been contemporaries, as they are represented in the romances; Geoffrey makes Urien Arthur's contemporary.

with hymseluen. That is, beside the bishop; for *hymseluen* meaning 'him' cf. *yourself* 'you' 1522.

114 ff. Compare the very similar description of Belshazzar's feast in *Purity* 1401 ff.

115 *at þe sidbordez.* The medieval hall was like the hall of an Oxford or Cambridge college, with the high table on the dais at one end and rows of tables near the long sides of the hall and parallel with them. These rows were the *sidbordez.*

118 *nakryn.* Almost the same form occurs in *Purity* 1413, *nakeryn noyse.* The nom. pl. is *nakerys* 1016, where the rhyme on *hys* distinguishes the vowel of the ending from that of the other rhyming pair of the wheel, *repayres, þayres.* This, together with the spelling *-y-* in all three forms, suggests that the French etymon was the AN. type **nacarie* rather than the recorded CFr. *nacaire* (cf. *history/histoire*, etc.), though in other ME. texts the form is *naker*, pl. *nakers*, as in Chaucer, *Knight's Tale*, A. 2511. It is not quite certain that this determines the form *nak(e)ryn*, for though in this manuscript the vowel of inflexional syllables is overwhelmingly written *e*, the adjectival ending, OE. *-en*, also appears as *-in/-yn* in *sylkyn* 610, *syluerin* 886. The form *nakryn* is commonly (as by *O.E.D.*) explained as gen. pl., with extension to the French-derived *naker* of the ME. descendant of OE. *-ena* proper to weak nouns and some strong fems.; cf. *Piers Plowman* B. i. 105 *kingene kynge*, and some others. But in the present phrase, and others like it in *Purity* (mainly alliterating, as *fenden folk* 224, *on blonkken bak* 1412, *besten blod* 1446, but also *on folken wyse* 271) and also in *Octovian* (ed. G. Sarrazin (Heilbronn, 1885)) *bestyn kyng* 478, the absence of *-e* suggests that the ending is that of the adj. rather than the gen.—as indeed the sense of *fenden* and *folken* in these examples requires. The meanings of genitive and adjective often come close together, and in some dialects the endings *-ene* and *-en* early became confused—notably in the Katherine Group: see d'Ardenne, *Iuliene*, p. 209, and *M.E.D.* under *besten, fenden(e, folk.*

126-7 'Each knight took ungrudged (*withouten loþe*) what he himself desired.'

132 'A different, very new, noise quickly approached, so that the prince might be allowed to take food.' The approaching noise of the Green Knight's arrival heralded the marvel that Arthur had vowed to wait for; cf. Malory, *Works*, p. 858: 'Now may ye go to youre dyner,' seyde sir Kay unto the kynge, 'for a mervalous adventure have ye sene.'

134 *not* is otiose: 'The sound (of the trumpets) had scarcely ceased for a moment.' Similar constructions are found elsewhere with *uneþe* (as with *hardly* in substandard modern speech; e.g. *Mandeville's Travels* (ed. Hamelius), p. 128: 'noman may vnnethe see but fissch.'

137 *On þe most.* Literally 'one the largest', so 'the very largest'; cf. 1439, 2363. *One* strengthening the superlative was a common ME. construction, and survived to Shakespeare's time; e.g. *Henry VIII*, II. iv. 48: 'one the wisest prince'. See Mustanoja, *Syntax*, pp. 297–9.

140 *etayn.* Elsewhere this word is usually *et(t)en*, in keeping with its derivation from OE. *eoten.* The present form is evidently a re-formation on the model of the French ending -*ain*, for it appears in the mid fifteenth-century *St. Christopher* (ed. C. Horstmann, *Altenglische Legenden* (Heilbronn, 1881), p. 463, l. 788) rhyming with *slayne.*

140–2 'Half a giant on earth I believe he was, but at any rate the biggest of men I declare him to be, and at the same time the shapeliest of stature that could ride.' L. 141 is sometimes rendered, 'I must nevertheless declare him to be a man'; but in this manuscript the verb *most* is only the past, or 2 sg. pres., of *mot*: 'I must' is *I mot*, as 1965, 2510. The meaning of *hope* here, 'suppose, believe', is common especially in the north and north midlands from the fourteenth to the seventeenth century; see again 352, 926, 2301.

144 *Both.* Napier's emendation of MS. *bot* has been challenged (e.g. by Menner, *M.L.N.* xli (1926), 399), but it is essential to the sense because after the concessive *al were* in the previous line there is no place for an adversative. The scribe similarly drops final *h* before an initial *h* in *wit* 113.

149 *fade.* A word of obscure origin found only in northerly texts and nearly always in rhyme. Its meaning, deduced from contexts, is 'bold' or 'hostile', and *M.E.D.* suggests derivation from *fa* 'enemy'.

150 *enker-grene.* This collocation appears again in 2477, but nowhere else. *Enker* does not occur before any other adjective (or adverb), and *M.E.D.* is probably right in treating this group as a compound. *Enker* is otherwise known only in the adv. *enkerly*, in the alliterative *Morte Arthure* and in Scottish texts (see *D.O.S.T.* under *enkrely*), and is evidently derived from the fairly common ON. intensive *einkar.* It may have come to be vaguely associated with OFr. *vert encré*, but cannot have had its meaning 'dark green' (so *O.E.D.*) because the Green Knight's colour is explicitly said to be a bright grass-green (235).

153 *meré.* This is evidently 'merry, fair', OE. *myrige*, not 'honourable, splendid', OE. *mǣre*; cf. 1736, where the decisive spelling *mery mantyle* occurs, as it does again in *Wars Alex.* 2864.

154 *pane.* This was apparently the facing of fur at the edge of the mantle; the word is regularly used with names of furs, especially miniver and ermine. Cf. the following passage from rules for ceremonies at the court of Henry VII: 'Item, on new yerre's day the Kinge ought to were his sircot, his kirtille, and his pane of ermyne; and if his pane be v ermyne depe, a duke shall be but iiij, an erle iij' (*The Antiquarian Repertory*, ed. F. Grose and others (London, 1807), p. 329).

155 *blaunner*. Since this word is most commonly spelt -*nn*-, Kaluza (edn. of *Libeaus Desconus* (Leipzig, 1890), 129 n.) is probably right in deriving it from AN. *blaunc-ner* 'white (and) black', which might well describe ermine. The few occurrences spelt -*mer* (e.g. 856), if not errors, might be due to association with OFr. *mer* 'pure' as in *orm(i)er*.

157 As this line stands in the manuscript the metre is unsatisfactory: if the caesura follows *hose* there is no alliterating sound in the second half-line; if it precedes it the second half-line is too heavy. The emendation adopted is the simplest, for the poet often refers to a colour or material previously mentioned by a phrase of this form without noun—*of þe same* 170, 881 (and with wider application 1640), *of þat ilke* 173, 1930. (This usage later became common in heraldry; see *O.E.D.* under *same* B. 4. d.) A copyist might easily have added *grene* for the sake of clarity, since it has not been mentioned since 151. With this reading the caesura comes between the adjectives and the noun *hose*, but this is not rare— cf. 754, 919.

Heme is of uncertain meaning, evidently the same word as in *hemely halched aboute* 1852. Some such sense as 'suitable, proper' would fit both these passages and a difficult line in the Harley Lyrics, 'þat hem mihte henten ase him were heme' (ed. Brook, 6. 42).

160 *scholes*. Emerson suggested that this means simply 'shoeless' (*M.L.N.* xxxvi (1921), 212; comparing *botelees* in *Piers Plowman*, B. xviii. 11). There is no doubt that he was right. Medieval French and Spanish texts, as well as manuscript illustrations, show that knights riding on peaceful pursuits often wore hose without shoes; see C. Clark, *R.E.S.*, N.S. vi (1955), 174–7, and M. Rigby in the same, vii (1956), 173–4. This is fully in keeping with the unwarlike appearance of the Green Knight emphasized in 203 ff. and especially 271. So, 'and there he rides with no shoes on his feet'.

165 *to tor for to telle*. An alliterative formula; cf. 719, and *Dest. Troy* 8717, *William of Palerne* 1428, 5066, *Cursor Mundi* 14085. Not only *tor* but the whole phrase may be of Scandinavian origin: cf. ON. *tortalið-r* 'difficult to tell', and *Fornmanna sǫgur*, vi (1831), 162: 'sva miklu fé í gulli ok gersimum at torvelt er mǫrkum at telja'. *Tere* is a frequent variant; see *O.E.D.*

167 *gaudi* is unique in this collective sense; it generally means a large ornamented bead.

168 *payttrure*. The usual form of the word is *peitrel*; here another ending has been substituted. Originally the peitrel was a plate of armour protecting the horse's breast; later it became merely ornamental, as it no doubt is here since the knight is unarmed. Cf. 601.

For illustrations of the pendants see the British Museum *Guide to the*

Mediaeval Antiquities (1924), pp. 5, 6. They were usually enamelled with the arms of the owner.

169 *molaynes.* H. L. Savage notes that *moleins pur freins* is glossed in Kelham's *Dictionary of the Norman Language* (1799) (*Philologica: the Malone Anniversary Studies* (Baltimore, 1949), pp. 167–78). He quotes the gloss as 'bits, bosses for bridles', but it is in fact 'bosses, bits for bridles'.

171 *skyrtes.* MS. *sturtes* has been regarded as a form of *start*, OE. *steort* 'tail', which is applied to projections of various kinds. But there is no evidence of its use for any part of a saddle or trappings, and in the corresponding passage describing the arming of Gawain and his horse at 597 ff. the same set of technical terms, *payttrure*, *cropore*, and *arsounez*, is completed by *skyrtez*. This evidently means 'saddle-skirts', the leather flaps of the saddle, to which enamel might well be applied. It is doubtless the word intended here; the form could be *skurtes*, with the alternation of *y* and *u* seen in such words as *girdel* 1829, *gurdel* 2395, but *tu* here is like enough to *ky* to have been written in mistake for it.

186 *capados.* From the picture of the Green Knight's hair and beard trimmed above his elbows it appears that this garment must be a kind of hood with cape attached and closed under the chin. G. L. Hamilton (*M.P.* v (1908), 365–76) compares it with the type called in French *chaperon*, for illustrations of which see J. Evans, *Dress in Medieval France*, pls. 21, 31. The origin of the word, and why it is called 'king's', are not certainly known; Hamilton thinks it developed from *Cappadocia*, this type of hood, worn under the helmet (as in 572), having earlier been made of Cappadocian leather; but this does not suit the occasional forms containing *u*, especially *cappe de huse* in Russell's *Boke of Nurture* (ed. Furnivall in E.E.T.S. 32, p. 178, l. 909) where it rhymes with *vse* and *excuse*. Such forms are presumably altered.

209 'A cruel axe to describe in words, if anyone could.'

210 The manuscript order, 'þe hede of an elnȝerde þe large lenkþe hade', does not give satisfactory sense or metre, but the transposition of *hede* and *lenkþe* removes both difficulties. For similar transposition see 785, 1719, and *Pearl* 529.

211 *grayn.* This is evidently ON. *grein* 'branch', but its application here is uncertain. The only closely comparable use in ME. is *Kyng Alisaunder* (ed. G. V. Smithers, E.E.T.S. 227, 237 (1947–53)) 6527, of the horn of a rhinoceros: 'þe horne is sharp als a swerd Boþe by þe *greyne* and atte ord.' Here *greyne* evidently refers to the edge, in distinction from the point. In the present passage 'edge' will not do since it is specified at the end of 212; *O.E.D.*'s 'blade' seems most likely. The 'head' includes both blade and back; the blade could be of green steel and beaten gold, and the cutting edge, the *bit* or *egge*, polished bright by grinding. The parts can thus be sufficiently distinguished, and *grayn* takes its place with *hede* and *bit* as a substantial element. *Grayn* has been taken to mean 'spike' (as still by *M.E.D.*), but it seems unlikely that only a spike would be of green steel and gold and not the blade itself.

214 *Þe stele*. This is OE. *stela* 'shaft', distinct from *stele* 'steel' in 211. This passage has been variously interpreted; the simplest way is to regard *stele* as parallel to the earlier items in the description, and the second half of the line as relative: 'the shaft of a stout staff by which the grim knight gripped it'.

224 *word þat he warp*. Cf. 1423. This is a very old phrase in alliterative use. It occurs in Old English poetry: *Elene* 770, 'word aweorpan'; *Gnomic Verses (Maxims* I) 189, 'oft hy wordum toweorpa ð'; and in Old Norse (though it is no longer alliterative except in the past pl.): e.g. *Vafþrúðnismál* 7:

> Hvat's þat manna es í mínum sal
> verpumk orði á?

and *Atlamál* 43 ('urpusk á orðum'), and several times in prose. It was evidently a common Germanic phrase. It is frequent in ME., e.g. in *St. Katherine* (ed. E. Einenkel, E.E.T.S. 80 (1884)) 643, 1325, *Owl and Nightingale* 45, *Dest. Troy* thirty times, and other poems including *Patience*, *Purity*, and *St. Erkenwald*; see Oakden, ii. 308.

229 Comparison with 304 shows that *hym* is the plural pron. (see note on 49), and that the meaning is 'rolled them up and down' (Napier).

237 *þat þer stod* must refer to men standing about in the hall, retainers and servants, who went forward to see what the Green Knight would do. The nobles at the table remained still and silent (242–3). In 246–7 *al* and *sum* are best taken as adverbs: 'I think it was not entirely owing to fear, but partly out of courtesy.'

257 *won*. The ME. sense 'abode' apparently derives from ON. *ván* 'hope, expectation', in such uses as *konungs var þangat ván*, 'there was expectation of the king's being there' passing into 'the king was in residence there'. Cf. also ON. *allir vánir* 'all the places where one may expect to find a thing or person' (agreeing with the ME. pl. use as 685), and modern Norwegian *von* 'haunts of game'. The development was assisted by association and alliteration, as here, with *wunien*, *wonen* 'dwell', but rhymes in careful texts show absence of final -*e* and stem vowel $\bar{a}$, $\bar{o}$. Texts that distinguish OE. *o*, *a* before nasal consonants (as *o*) from OE. and ON. $\bar{a}$ (as *a*) invariably have the form *wane(s)*.

267 *in fere*. Probably 'in company', i.e. with a company of fighting men. It is remarkable that in *Rauf Coilȝear* 702 the phrase is used of a knight fighting alone; having been long applied to the company of fighting men it had come to mean generally 'in martial fashion', which may be the sense here. In the phrase *in feir of war* quoted as a parallel by P. G. Thomas (*Eng. Studien*, xlvii (1913), 311–13) *feir* is a different word, from OFr. *afaire*; see *D.O.S.T.* under *fere* n.[4]

286 *brayn* occurs again as adj. and adv., evidently meaning 'furious(ly)', in Wyntoun and Douglas (see *D.O.S.T.*); its origin is not certain. It is usually taken (as by *M.E.D.* and *D.O.S.T.*) to be an abbreviation of *braynwod* (see 1461 and note), but such abbreviation is hard to parallel. T. A. Knott (*M.L.N.* xxx (1915), 105) compares the later *brainish*, for which see *O.E.D.*

288 *giserne.* The gisarm was strictly a kind of bill or halberd, having a long handle with an axe-blade and also a spike or knife-like blade in line with the shaft. The word is evidently used loosely here as a mere synonym for *ax* (208, 289); it does not suit either the description at 208 ff. or the illustrations in the manuscript. It is used equally loosely in 2265 for the Green Knight's other axe, which in 2223 was described as a 'Danish axe'. The word was probably taken from a French source: it is a *jusarme* that the *vilain* carries in *La Mule sans Frein* (see p. xvii).

296 *barlay.* This word is probably to be identified with *barley* of modern English dialects, used as a cry to claim a temporary truce in games or to stake a claim to some desirable object; see I. and P. Opie, *The Lore and Language of Schoolchildren* (Oxford, 1959), pp. 135, 146–9. The sense 'truce' does not fit the situation here; perhaps it means '(when I claim) my turn'. The origin of the word is obscure; none of the suggested etymologies is satisfactory.

298 *A twelmonyth and a day.* This period was common in legal agreements, to ensure the completion of the term of a year; see *O.E.D.* under *year* 6. b. The use of it thus continues the technical legal tone of *quit-clayme* 293. But it was also common in romantic compacts, e.g. Malory, *Works*, p. 866: 'I woll make here a vow that to-morne, withoute longer abydynge, I shall laboure in the queste of the Sankgreall, and that I shall holde me oute a twelve-month and a day or more if nede be.'

304 *runischly.* Cf. *runisch* adj. 457. The word is obscure, in ME. peculiar to alliterative verse. It occurs again in this manuscript in *Purity* 1545 and *Patience* 191, and as *renischche, renyschly* in *Purity* 96, 1724, as well as four times in *Wars Alex.*, notably in a passage resembling the present one in other ways also (4930–1):

> þe renke within þe redell þan raxsils his armes,
> Rymed him full renyschly & rekind þir wordis.

The contexts are not decisive as to its central meaning; 'rough, fierce' suits some, 'strange' others. John Ray, in his *Proverbs* (2nd edn. 1691) gives among 'North Country words' '*Rennish*; Furious, passionate'. The alternation *u/e* points to earlier *ēo*; cf. ON. *hrjónn* 'rough' and OE. *hrēoh, hrēow*. *Roynyshe* in *St. Erkenwald* 52 is probably the same word (at the date of the manuscript *oy* and *u* vary in some words); but *roi(g)nous* in *Romaunt of the Rose* 988, 6190, *Piers Plowman* B. xx. 82, etc., and later *roinish*, both meaning 'scurvy, coarse', are of Romance origin and apparently not connected.

307 *coȝed.* This verb seems to have denoted a wider range of vocal sounds than modern *cough.* Cf. Chaucer, *Miller's Tale,* A. 3697–8:

> And softe he cougheth with a semy soun,
> 'What do ye, hony-comb, sweete Alisoun?'—

words which can hardly have been 'coughed'. In the present passage a cough is too discreet a sound for so fierce a character as the Green Knight—a scornful cry, almost a crow, would suit better. The direct ancestor of the word does not occur in OE., but the frequentative *cohhetan* appears once, in *Judith* 270, where it describes the noise made by Assyrian troops outside Holofernes' tent as they try to wake him: 'ongunnon cohhetan, cirman hlude'. This must mean rather 'cry out, shout' (so C. T. Onions in Sweet's *Anglo-Saxon Reader,* 10th edn. (Oxford, 1946)) —the variation with *cirman,* which is used of birds, implies a continuous outcry. (Variant forms such as *cowed* in some ME. texts suggest possible association with *cou,* a variant of 'chough'.)

308 *rimed hym.* The sense 'drew himself up' is supported by the passage in *Wars Alex.* quoted in the note on 304.

319 *wroth as wynde.* A frequent simile; Onions (*N. & Q.* cxlvi (1924), 244) quotes eight examples.

327 *bayþen.* ON. *beiða* meant 'ask, request', but the ME. verb only 'inquire' in *St. Erkenwald* and 'grant, consent' elsewhere (*M.E.D.*). ON. *beina* meant 'forward (a request)', and appears in the phrase 'bayne me my bone' in *Siege of Jerusalem* 181; the similarly alliterative phrase with *bayþen,* as here, may occur again in the *Harley Lyrics* (ed. Brook, 3. 35), 'Crist þat bayþeþ me mi bone', but the manuscript there reads *bayeþ* and might equally well be emended to *bayneþ.*

331 *þat* is relative, 'who intended'; so 'intending to strike with it'.

337 *to drynk.* From late OE. to the seventeenth century the infin. of verbs of eating and drinking was often used with ellipsis of the object, and came to function as a noun.

350 *to take hit to yourseluen* depends on *not semly* 348.

351–2 'many so bold . . . that I think nobody on earth readier in courage'. *Haȝer* is the only Scandinavian adoption in ME. which appears to retain the inflexional *-r* of the nom. sg. masc.—a form reproducing only the stem *hag-* would be normal. The anomaly is doubtless due to analogical re-formation of *hag-r* after the example of *fagr* 'fair', in which the *r* is part of the stem. The tendency to associate *hagr* and *fagr* is seen in modern Icelandic, which has the abstract noun *hegrð* (instead of **hegð*) on the analogy of *fegrð* 'fairness'.

353 *bodyes.* This use of *body* in the general sense of 'man, person' is common in ME. and gives rise to the pronominal *anybody, nobody,* etc. A related use with a defining possessive adj. functions as an equivalent of a pronoun with *self,* as *mi bodé* 357; cf. Chaucer, *Man of Law's Tale*

Epilogue, B. 1185: 'My joly body schal a tale telle'; *Quatrefoil of Love* 33: 'Scho blyssede his body with buke and with belle'; *Sir Eglamour* (ed. F. E. Richardson, E.E.T.S. 256 (1965)), 94–95: Lincoln MS. 'In dedis of armes, be God on lyue, ʒour body es worthe oþir fyue', Cotton MS. 'ʒe ar counted worth oþur fyue'; Malory, *Works*, p. 308: 'my body and this thirty knyghtes'. See Mustanoja, *Syntax*, pp. 148–9, and note on 1237 below.

355 '(There would be) the least loss in my life', i.e. 'My life would be the smallest loss.'

356 *Bot* 'only' doubles the force of *only* later in the line: 'I am only to be praised inasmuch as you are my uncle.'

359 *foldez*. This might formally be imper. pl. (see p. 147); but that would seem too abrupt an address to the king at this point and it is better taken as 3 sg. pres. indic., intrans. as the verb is in 499, with a sense close to that of *falles* in 358.

360 *rych* is usually taken to be infin. meaning 'decide', but this does not give good sense: why should deciding involve blame? Nor does the verb *rich* elsewhere mean 'decide'—see *O.E.D.* under *rich* v.². The word is evidently the adj., following its noun as in the same phrase *cort ryche* 347, and similarly *þis burn rych* 20, *þe sale riche* 243, *þis douþe ryche* 397; a good specimen of the familiar stylistic device of repeating a set pattern of words in a particular position in the line. The sense is, 'Even if I speak improperly, let all this noble court be free from blame.'

372 'Take care that you deal one stroke; and if you manage him rightly, I readily believe that you will survive the blow that he is to offer you afterwards.'

384 *wyth no wyʒ ellez*. Gollancz observes that this cannot mean that Gawain will bring no supporters with him, since the terms of the challenge require him to take the return blow alone. The best suggestion is Napier's, that *wyth* means 'at the hands of'—Gawain will take the blow from the Green Knight and no-one else.

406 ff. The antithesis here is between 406–9 on the one hand and 410–11 on the other; *smartly I þe teche* is a variant of *I þe telle trwly*.

409 *frayst my fare*. Gollancz suggests, 'call and ask how I am getting on'. But though this suits *Wars Alex.* 2019 it is by no means the only sense of the phrase. More suitable to the present situation is that exemplified in *Quatrefoil of Love* 378 ff.:

> When grett fyres and grym are graythede in oure gate . . .
> We seeke after socoure on euerylke a syde . . .
> When we hafe *frayste of þat fare* felde es our pride.

This must mean 'when we have experienced that'; cf. *Prick of Conscience* (ed. R. Morris (Phil. Soc., 1863)) 1358: 'Many men þe world here fraystes, Bot he es noght wyse þat þarin traistes.' So rather 'try my behaviour', 'see what I will do'.

412 *slokes*. The word is obscure. The most likely etymon appears to be ON. *slokna* 'go out' (of fire), with meaning generalized to 'stop', perhaps partly by association with *slake* which is itself used of the cessation of sound in 244. The ending is probably imper. pl., in which *-es* is well attested in this text (see p. 147). Gollancz objects that the Green Knight and Gawain use the sg. to each other; but the Green Knight is not addressing Gawain, who has not been speaking—he is breaking off his own speech. *Slokes* looks like a general exclamation, 'enough!', not addressed to a particular person and so susceptible of having a pl. ending.

413–15 Rhymes of this kind, between a single word and a phrase comprising preposition (occasionally verb) and pronoun, are found e.g. in Chaucer, *Canterbury Tales, Prol.* 671–2, *Miller's Tale*, A. 3699–700, 3709–10, *Troilus* I. 4–5, II. 989–91; Gower, *Confessio Amantis* II. 2015–16, III. 99–100, 891–2; Hoccleve, *Regement of Princes* 1966–7, *La Male Regle* 126–8; also earlier, as in *Owl and Nightingale* 545–6, 1671–2.

426 *broun*. This word is commonly applied to metal in the Middle Ages, evidently meaning 'shining'. It is used mainly of steel, but in *Pearl* 990 *burnist broun* is applied to gold. The use is ancient: cf. OE. *brūnecg* in *Beowulf* 1546, *Maldon* 163, OHG. *brūn* similarly, and OFr. *brunir*, whence *burnish*. See note on 618.

435 Cf. 2060, and *Wars Alex.* 778: 'Stridis into stele-bowe, stertis apon loft.'

443 'By the time his words were uttered', i.e. before he spoke.

451–2 Gollancz says that *to fotte a dunt* should mean to strike, not receive, a blow, comparing *Pearl* 1158. But there is no difficulty in taking it as parallel to *foch þe such wages* 396. The phrase *disserued þou habbez* has usually been punctuated as a parenthesis, but it is better regarded as the beginning of a sentence completed in the next line, 'You have deserved to be repaid.' Though *ȝelde* earlier, and still normally, took a dative of person, by this date indirect objects were beginning to be admitted as subjects of passive constructions with such verbs as *pay, please, quit*, and the extension to *ȝelde* would be easy.

476–7 *gaynly* 'appositely' draws attention to the word-play in the following line. 'Heng vp þyn ax' is meant literally, but figuratively as well—'Have done with this business.' The expression is proverbial: e.g. *Owl and Nightingale* 658, Robert of Gloucester's *Chronicle* (ed. W. A. Wright, Rolls ser. (1887)) ii. 11771; see also Brett, *M.L.R.* xiv (1919), 7, and *The Oxford Dictionary of English Proverbs* (2nd edn. 1948) under *Hang up one's hatchet*.

480 *tytel*. Best understood in the legal sense of 'that which justifies or substantiates a claim (*O.E.D.* under *title*, 6); so 'to describe the marvellous event with its genuine authority', the axe on the wall certifying the truth of the story. Cf. 626. *to telle* depends on *myȝt* in the previous line; when an auxiliary is followed by two infinitives the second is preceded by *to*—see *Pearl*, ed. Gordon, note on 1073.

483 *as derrest my3t falle* is best compared with 890: 'as might befit the most noble' (Napier).

492 *3elpyng*. 'Words of challenge' were one of the things Arthur hoped to hear at 96–99.

493 *hym* is plural, referring to the courtiers, who had earlier had no marvels to relate but now have more than enough—'Though when they sat down they lacked words, now they are well supplied with serious matter, their hands crammed full.' This makes all the pronouns in 493–4 refer to the same *þay*. (Arthur himself had not 'lacked words'—he was *talkkande* at 108.)

500 ff. On this famous passage on the changing seasons, a skilful and subtle development of a medieval convention, see D. A. Pearsall, *M.L.R.* l (1955), 129–34, and T. Silverstein in *Toronto University Quarterly*, xxxiii (1963–4), 258–78. Silverstein observes that 'þa3 þe ende be heuy' (496) recalls Prov. xiv. 13, 'extrema gaudii luctus occupat', and 'þe forme to þe fyniment . . .' (499) echoes a passage in the *Distichs of Cato*.

520 *To bide* depends on *wela wynne*, etc., 518—the plant grows up from the seed (*þeroute*) 'to enjoy a delightful glance of the bright sun'.

521 *hym*. Gollancz rightly equates this with *hym* in the next line, i.e. the plant of 518: 'But then autumn hastens on and encourages it at once, warns it to ripen for fear of the winter.' For *harden* in this sense cf. 1428.

526 *lancen*. In the manuscript *n* and *u* are usually indistinguishable, so that this could be read *laucen*. Gollancz does read it so, seeking to keep apart *laucen* 'loosen', from ON. *lauss*, and *launcen* 'prick, spur, ride', from AN. *launcer*. It is true that most French words containing *a* before *n* and another consonant have *aun* in this manuscript, as *chaunce*, *daunsed*, *haunche*, and also that a verb 'loosen' exists in the author's vocabulary, spelt *lausen* 1784, *lawsez* 2376. But the *aun* spellings are not without exception—*gra(u)nt* and *tra(u)nt* have both—and it is unlikely that the distinction was systematically made. Both clear cases of 'loosen' are transitive; and in several passages, including this one and 1212, *lancen* gives more appropriate sense.

531 *no fage*. For the emendation see C. T. Onions in *T.L.S.* 16 August and 20 September 1923, where evidence for the phrase in ME. is collected; also *M.E.D.* under *fage*. Onions notes that *as þe worlde askez* is a conventional phrase in ME. meaning 'as the world requires', occurring e.g. in the alliterative *Morte Arthure* 2187 and *Piers Plowman* B. Prol. 19. For other uses of the same pattern see R. A. Waldron, *Speculum* xxxii (1957), 797.

536 *Al-hal-day*. All Saints' Day, 1 November. Arthur regularly held his court then (see note on 37), and Gawain might reasonably wait for so important an occasion before setting out.

546 *cost*. This derives from ON. *kǫstr*, etymologically 'choice' but with a range of senses including 'condition'. Here 'terms' suits best: 'You know the terms of this affair; I do not want to speak to you of the difficulties of it, except for a small point.' Gawain, with his customary modesty, does not wish to trouble Arthur except that he must take his leave, as 548 specifies.

551 *Errik*. The name is Celtic, in Breton *Guerec*, but probably influenced in form by English *Eric* from ON. *Eirikr*. This is Erec son of Lac who is the hero of Chrétien's *Erec et Énide* (see note on 553), identical with Arrake fitz Lake in *The Awntyrs off Arthure*.

552 *Doddinaual de Sauage*. Properly *Dodinal* or *Dodinel li Sauvage*, 'the wild' (so called, according to the Vulgate *Merlin*, because he liked hunting in wild forests). *Þe duk of Clarence*, named Galeshin, was according to *Merlin* cousin, according to *Lancelot* brother, of Sir Dodinel.

553 *Launcelot*. Lancelot du Lac, son of King Ban of Benwick. His fame as an Arthurian knight (whatever his ultimate origins in legend—see Loomis, *Arthurian Tradition*, ch. xxvi) comes from France. He is first mentioned by Chrétien in *Erec et Énide* (ed. M. Roques (Paris, 1952)) 1671–4:

> Devant toz les boens chevaliers
> doit estre Gauvains li premiers,
> li seconz Erec, li filz Lac,
> et li tierz Lancelot del Lac.

Later, in *Le Chevalier de la Charrette*, Lancelot is the chief knight of Arthur's court, and he now appears also as Guenever's lover. But Lancelot is not Chrétien's creation: there is evidence of an earlier French poem about him which is now lost but which was used by Ulrich von Zatzikhoven (see p. xviii).

Lyonel was son of King Bohort of Gannes and Lancelot's cousin.

Lucan was the royal butler, usually called *li bottellier*, in Malory *Sir Lucan the Butlere* or *de Butler*.

554 *Boos*. Probably identical with Boso in Geoffrey of Monmouth. He is later called *Boors* or *Bors*, as in Malory.

Byduer. Bedwyr in the Welsh triads, with Cei the earliest of Arthur's knights. He is the same as the Bedivere, brother of Lucan, who in Malory and his source is the sole survivor of Arthur's last battle with Modred on the Camlan. In Geoffrey (where he is butler) he and Kai are killed in Arthur's great victory over the Romans.

555 *Mador de la Port*. This is Mador's usual style in French romance and in Malory; presumably he was taken to be Arthur's chief porter. He does not appear in Welsh.

558 *derue*. The manuscript may be read either thus or *derne*. But 'painful' is better here than 'private'; for though at 541 the courtiers conceal their misgivings, after 550, when Gawain has spoken of his departure, the tone changes and his words at 563–5 show that he knew what they felt.

564 *dere* could be either 'dear, pleasant', OE. *dēore*, or 'fierce, cruel', OE. *dēor*. The latter, as a synonym of *derf*, is possible; and, though not elsewhere in *Gawain*, is part of the poet's vocabulary: it occurs in *Purity* 214. But the former, making an inclusive phrase of a common type ('young and old', etc.) is more likely: 'What can one do but face whatever Fate may send, whether painful or pleasant?' Gollancz usefully compares 1507 'druryes greme and grace'.

568 *tulé*. For *tuly*; cf. note on 77. Inventories show that it was of a deep red colour.

570 ff. With this description of the arming of Gawain compare the arming of Arthur in the alliterative *Morte Arthure* 902 ff., and in Manning's *Chronicle* (ed. Furnivall, Rolls ser. (1887)), i. 10025-54; cf. also the arming of the Trojan lords in Lydgate's *Troy Book*, iii. 44-108 (quoted by Sir Walter Scott in the notes to his edn. of *Sir Tristrem*, p. 269, but attributed to 'Clariodes'), and of the Black Prince in *Winner and Waster* 111-18. Gawain's gear, especially in the elaboration of the *payttrure* and the *couertor*, suggests the latter part of the fourteenth century; cf. note on 1739.

572 *closed aloft*. Presumably 'fastened at the neck'; cf. 186 and note.

574 *sabatounz*. Steel shoes consisting of a toe-cap and plates, introduced early in the fourteenth century. The word is first used in English by Manning in his *Chronicle* about 1330 translating Wace's *cauces de fer* (i. 10026), though in Wace's time foot armour would have been of mail. *O.E.D.* describes sabatons as 'broad-toed', but Brett observed that medieval evidence does not support this (*M.L.R.* xxii (1927), 453-4). The effigy of the Black Prince in Canterbury Cathedral shows sabatons ending in long 'pikes' (see for example *Medieval England*, pl. 52 and pp. 323-4; Kelly and Schwabe, p. 67). Since the Black Prince died in 1376 his equipment is likely to be of the type familiar to the *Gawain* poet. Broad-toed armour shoes were in fact not usual until the early sixteenth century.

    segge fotez. The absence of *-s* in the gen. *segge* is presumably to avoid repetition of the *-es* ending (OE. *secges*). In *fotez* the older *-en*, *-e* of the dat. pl. (OE. *fōtum*) has been replaced by the *-es* of most nom.–acc. pls.; contrast *on his fote* 2229, etc. *Fotes* occurs also in *Ancrene Wisse* in *under hire fotes* f. 45a. 9, beside *under hire uet* 13, 16, where MS. Nero has *uoten* and *uet* and MS. Titus *fet* in all three. But it is not confined to the west midlands: *on his fotes* occurs in *King Horn* (MS. Laud 108, ed. J. Hall (Oxford, 1901)) 521, and *fotes* as acc. in *Wars Alex.* 4851.

596 *conueyed*. They escorted him to the mounting stage in the castle court.

597 *Gryngolet*. Gollancz thought that this name belonged originally to the boat of the mythical hero Wade (*Saga-book of the Viking Society*, v

(1906), 104). But the earliest authority for Gringalet as the name of Wade's boat is Speght in his edition of Chaucer, 1598, whereas the word is widely applied to Gawain's horse from Chrétien's time onwards—e.g. *Erec et Énide* 3935, *Chevalier à l'Épée* 226 (in both apparently as a common noun, *le gringalet*). The name is probably of Celtic origin. Gwalchmei's horse appears in a single Welsh triad as Kein Caled, but this may be an alteration of an earlier form. The French *Guingalet*, *Gringalet* (the latter with intrusive *r*, as often in the French treatment of Celtic or Germanic *w* (cf. variants such as *Giflet*, *Gryfflet*; *Guiromelant*, *Grimolans*)) suggest a name beginning (*g*)*w*, probably Welsh **Gwyngalet* 'white-hard'. See R. Bromwich, *Trioedd*, pp. ciii–cvii, 104, 106.

602 *couertor*. The rich cloth covering of the horse. It often reached almost to the ground; cf. *Awntyrs off Arthure* 386: 'His stede with sandelle of Trise [*read* Tarse] was trapput to the hele.' A good illustration is the picture of Sir Geoffrey Luttrell in the Luttrell Psalter f. 202^v, reproduced as frontispiece to the British Museum facsimile of the manuscript (ed. E. G. Millar, 1932) and often elsewhere.

603 *ryche golde naylez* defines *al*: 'all set on a red background were splendid gold nails'.

606 ff. *stapled*, etc. Staples were used to strengthen the helmet, especially at joints; the name was also given to the hooks by which other armour was attached to the helmet. Inside the helmet was padding (*stoffed wythinne*) to take the shock of blows; outside it, as part of the fastening of the *auentayle*, was the *horson* (*vrysoun*), an ornamental band of silk (609–13); see G. L. Hamilton, *M.P.* v (1908), 371. The *auentail* (also called *camail*) was 'a tippet of mail attached by staples to the bascinet to protect the throat and neck, and falling to the shoulders. It is distinctive of military equipment of the XIVth century, its place being taken in the next century by a plate gorget and bevor' (Sir James Mann, *Wallace Collection Catalogues. European Arms and Armour* (1962), I. xxxv. See also Hamilton, *M.P.* iii (1905) 541–6; B. White, *Neophilologus* xxxvii (1953), 113–14). Around the upper part of the helmet was the *cercle* (615), a gold band studded with gems; this rich form of *cercle* is characteristic of the later Middle Ages; cf. *Awntyrs off Arthure* 381, *Morte Arthure* 908–9. For illustrations of armour see especially the Wallace Collection Catalogue quoted above, and Kelly–Schwabe, p. 63.

611–12 *peruyng*. This is evidently a spelling of *pervink* 'periwinkle', *-ng* for *-nk* being the reverse of the type seen in *ȝonke þynk* 1526. This form of the word, though usually with final *-e*, is recorded from late OE. to Lydgate. The periwinkle is a common feature of medieval manuscript decoration, its trailing stems providing very suitable forms for foliated borders; it is clearly recognizable by its opposed leaves and five-petalled blue flowers. Birds, including parrots and doves, are still more frequent in such borders, variously set on or among the foliage. This type of design was as appropriate for embroidery as for manuscript illumination.

It was used even on metal-work, as described in *Purity* 1464–6 where the lids of gold cups were

> al bolled abof with braunches and leues,
> Pyes and papeiayes purtrayed with-inne,
> As þay prudly hade piked of pomgarnades;

and similarly 1482–4. (On the use of similar designs in all the arts see especially Joan Evans, *English Art 1307–1461* (Oxford, 1949), pp. 43–44.) In the present line *bitwene* is most simply taken as the preposition, postponed as it often is, e.g. 1060; but it might possibly be an adverb in the manner of *Awntyrs off Arthure* 510: 'Trayfolede with trayfoles, and trewluffes bytwene'. Periwinkle appears also in other kinds of decoration— in *Wars Alex.* 4541 Ercules has a hat adorned with flowers 'Of palme and of peruy[n]k and othire proud blossoms', and in *Romaunt of the Rose* 901–4 on the God of Love's robe,

> Ther lakkide no flour to my dome
> Ne nought so mych as flour of brome
> Ne violete ne eke pervynke
> Ne flour noon that man can on thynke.

The word has hitherto been read *pernyng* (as *O.E.D.*), and usually taken as pres. part. of a verb formed by metathesis from *prene* 'preen'. But there are many objections to this. The sense is inappropriate—the birds in manuscripts are nearly always drawn merely sitting, or occasionally flying —and syntax and form are abnormal—*preen* is transitive or reflexive, metathesis of *r* does not occur with a long vowel, and -*yng* in the pres. part., though it appears in this text, is rare. See *N. & Q.* ccxi (1966), 448–51.

Trulofez are usually believed to be 'true lover's knots'. This may be right, but such devices are rare except in tapestries and the reference is probably rather to the flower so called, *Paris quadrifolia* or Herb Paris (see *O.E.D.* under *true-love*, 4). Cf. especially *Emaré* 125, 149: 'Portrayed þey wer wyth trewe-loue-flour', in a passage resembling the present in other ways also, notably 118 'Seuen wynter hyt was yn makynge' compared with 613 here. In *Degrevant* 1496–1500 popinjays and trueloves appear together on bed-hangings, trueloves with jewels in *Awntyrs* 354, *Parl. Thre Ages* 120, *Rauf Coilȝear* 473, and trueloves as armorial bearings in *Degrevant* C. 471.

618 *broun*. This may perhaps mean only 'shining', as the term is used of metal; see note on 426. But this would be redundant, and since medieval lapidaries regularly mention brown diamonds it seems more likely that these are what is meant; e.g. 'þe diamaundes þat commen oute of ynde ben cleped þe males, & arne broun of colour & of violet'(*English Mediaeval Lapidaries*, ed. J. Evans and M. S. Serjeantson, E.E.T.S. 190 (1933), p. 30).

620 *pentangel*. As Madden remarks, though Gawain's arms are described in many romances they nowhere embody the pentangle. The romances assign him a shield 'de sinople [i.e. green] a un aigle d'or' or with a lion or gryphon. The word *pentangle* appears only in English, first here and not again until Browne's *Pseudodoxia Epidemica* of 1646, 'They are afraid of the pentangle of Solomon.' In medieval Latin the figure was named *pentaculum* (whence French *pentacle*) or *pentalpha*, and it was later called *pentagonon* and *pentagram(ma)*—the last, together with the German *Drudenfuss*, prominent in Goethe's *Faust*. *Pentangle* is evidently a blend of *pentacle* and *angle*. The figure is said to have been used by the Pythagoreans as a symbol of health, and also by the neo-Platonists and Gnostics to signify perfection; but it was known to the Jews as well, thus coming to be called 'Solomon's seal', and is obviously related to the similar figure, the hexagram, in which two equilateral triangles interlock to form a six-pointed star—this, inscribed in a circle, was eventually adopted as the symbol of Judaism (the *Magen David*, 'Shield of David'). The pentangle was long used as a magic sign, believed to give power over evil spirits. Its use in this way was condemned by Christian writers, such as the Jesuit Athanasius Kircher in his *Arithmologia* (Rome, 1665), p. 216: 'voces horrendae vna mixtis sacris nominibus, nodo quem Salomonis vocant, adnexo . . .'; but it had much earlier come to be adapted to Christian symbolism, the five points sometimes being connected with the five letters of the name Jesus, or the five wounds; it appears as an ornament in manuscripts (see Loomis, *J.E.G.P.* xlii (1943), 168) and on churches (e.g. the fourteenth-century church of Adderbury in Oxfordshire). Nothing like the symbolism attributed to it here is known anywhere else, and there is no evidence whatever for its being called 'the endless knot' in spite of the poet's 'oueral' (630). The absence of record in English is doubtless accidental, for he could hardly have expected his audience to follow his description of the figure if they had never seen it; cf. also 'wyth þe peple' (664). The only medieval English interest known in the figure is mathematical: Thomas Bradwardine (archbishop of Canterbury 1349) describes it in *Geometria Speculativa* (printed Paris 1530, p. 4, with figures). See further J. R. Hulbert, *M.P.* xiii (1915–16), 721–30; R. H. Green, *ELH* xxix (1962), 129–35; J. A. Burrow, *Reading*, pp. 187–9.

624 *in tent*. This has previously been printed as one word and glossed as the adj. 'intent'. But this adj. is not otherwise recorded until 1606, there is a clear space after *in* in the manuscript, and the noun *tent* is well evidenced, especially in the north, in the sense 'purpose': e.g. *Cursor Mundi* 14288: 'Mari was in anoþer tent.' See *O.E.D.* under tent sb.².

630 *endeles knot*. So called because its interlacing lines are joined so as to be continuous, and if followed out they bring the tracer back to the starting point, as described in 657–62; see the diagram p. 96.

632 *in fyue and sere fyue syþez*: 'in five ways, and five times in each way'. Gawain is virtuous in five ways, and in each way with reference to five things, viz. the five wits, the five fingers, the five wounds, the five joys, and five 'social virtues'. Each of these groups is symbolized by a side of the pentangle.

636 *nwe*. The point of this is not clear. The author has said that the pentangle was familiar, and has not hinted that Gawain had ever borne any other arms. It is probably no more than 'newly painted'.

640 *fyue wyttez*. This phrase is early used of the five senses, as *Cursor Mundi* 17015-18:

> Til bodi haf tint his wittes fiue
> þe saul wil noght þar fra.
> Hering, sight, smelling and fele,
> cheuing, er wittes five.

R. W. Ackerman has observed that it was conventionally used in manuals of confession, and more widely in contexts relating to confession and penitence (*Anglia* lxxvi (1958), 254-65). But it does not follow that this is relevant here; the point is simply that Gawain did not sin through indulgence in the pleasures of the senses. The phrase was extensively used where confession and penitence were not in question—e.g. the allegory of *Ancrene Wisse*, 'þe heorte wardeins beoð þe fif wittes' (ed. Tolkien, f. 12b), and of *Sawles Warde*, where 'þe monnes fif wittes' are the servants of Wit, the master of the house (*Early ME. Verse and Prose*, ed. J. A. W. Bennett and G. V. Smithers (Oxford, 1966), p. 248).

641 *fyue fyngres*. The five fingers were sometimes allegorized as five virtues (R. H. Green, *ELH* xxix (1962), 134), but can hardly be so here since this would partly repeat 651-5. No special significance is apparent. The only particular applications of 'five fingers' in ME. are to the fingers of the Devil; see *M.E.D.* under *finger*, 3.

642 *þe fyue woundez*. The five wounds of Christ (in hands, feet, and side) are a very frequent subject of medieval meditation and devotional writing. There is a notable link with the five wits in a prayer in *Ancrene Wisse*: 'for þe ilke fif wunden þe þu on hire [sc. the Cross] bleddest, heal mi blodi sawle of alle þe sunnen þet ha is wið iwundet þurh mine fif wittes' (ed. Tolkien, f. 7a). See further D. Gray, *N. & Q.* ccviii (1963), 50-51, 82-89, 127-34, 163-8, and references there.

645-6 'His steadfast resolution rested, above all else, on the fact that he drew all his fortitude from the five joys . . .'. MS. *forsnes* is irregularly compounded, but in view of two later occurrences quoted by *O.E.D.* and *D.O.S.T.* we should keep it rather than emend to *fersnes*. In any case 'fortitude' is a more likely virtue than fierceness to be inspired by the five joys. But MS. *fong* is probably an error for *feng*, which is the usual form of the past of *fonge* in this manuscript.

Þe fyue joyez are often celebrated in medieval literature. Usually they were the joys of Our Lady in the Annunciation, the Nativity, the Resurrection, the Ascension, and the Assumption, though this list is variable. For ME. poems, and a prose prayer, on the theme see Wells's *Manual*, p. 536. There is a beautiful description of the joy of the Nativity in *Purity* 1073-88. The five joys sometimes appear in the same texts as the five wounds; e.g. a lyric on 'þe vif blyssen' includes the lines: 'He make vs clene and bryhte | for his wundes fyue' (C. Brown, *English Lyrics of the XIIIth Century* (Oxford, 1932), no. 41, 23-24).

Thus three of these groups of five had been common in devotional use long before the date of this poem, and to some extent associated.

649 *inore*. This was formerly read *more*, which does not give the required sense; but there appears to be a clear distinction between the first minim (which is slightly longer) and the next two. The spelling with single instead of double *n* is easy to parallel, e.g. *wonen* 2415.

hir ymage. This is modelled upon the image of the Virgin associated with Arthur. Nennius (ch. 56) relates that Arthur bore the image on his shoulders in his eighth battle against the Saxons. William of Malmesbury (1. 8) says he had it sewn on his armour at the battle of Mount Badon. Geoffrey of Monmouth (IX. iv) says that he had on his shoulders his shield named Pridwen, 'in quo imago sancte marie dei genitricis inpicta ipsum in memoriam ipsius sepissime reuocabat'. The first account of it in English is Laȝamon's:

> He heng an his sweore ænne sceld deore;
> his nome wes on Bruttisc Pridwen ihaten;
> þer wes innen igrauen mid rede golde stauen
> an onlicnes deore of Drihtenes moder.

(*Selections*, ed. Brook, 2839–42). Manning has a similar rendering in his *Chronicle*, 10045–50. See also the quotations in Gollancz's note.

652–4 Despite the importance given to this group of virtues by their climactic position, they do not seem to have been chosen by the poet with especially close regard to the adventure which follows, or to the particular qualities for which Gawain is later praised. The emphasis at the end of the poem is almost all on faithfulness to one's pledged word (2348, 2381); this is also given the leading place as the total significance of the pentangle (626); yet here it is *pité* that 'passez alle poyntez', though at the same time Gawain practises *fraunchyse* and *felaȝschyp* 'forbe al þyng'. It looks as if these qualifying phrases, as well as the associations of the pairs of virtues, were determined more by form than meaning. Gollancz suggests that the poet may have had in mind the 'baronage of Love' in the *Roman de la Rose* (11211 ff.), which includes *Fraunchise, Pité, Largesce, Cortoisie*, and *Compaignie*, the last of which is equivalent to *felaȝschyp*. In itself this is possible, for he certainly knew the *Roman*; but it is not apposite in the context and he could easily have assembled these qualities without it. Nor does the 'baronage' include the equivalent of *clannes*, which in ME. meant not simply 'chastity' but 'sinlessness, innocence' generally—it glosses *honestas, mundicia, puritas, sinceritas* (*Catholicon Anglicum*, ed. S. J. H. Herrtage (Camden Soc., 1882)). *Cortaysye* was a word of great range and power at this time, embracing 'chivalrous' conduct of all kinds from courtly politeness to compassion and nobility of mind, and extending to divine grace, as in the *Ayenbite of Inwyt* (ed. Morris, E.E.T.S. 23, revd. P. Gradon (1965)), p. 97: 'Nou loke þe greate cortaysie of oure zuete maystre Iesu crist'; similarly in Wyclif, in *Piers Plowman*, and most strikingly in *Pearl* 432 ff. It is significantly associated with *clannes* in *Purity* 12–13. *Pité* at this time, and in this poet, could mean either 'pity' or 'piety', and Gollancz prefers the latter. But Gawain's piety has been fully shown in 642–50, and further emphasis on it would be otiose. 'Pity', in the wide sense of 'compassion', is surely what is meant.

656 'Now all these five groups, in truth, were fastened upon this knight, and each one joined to another so that none had an end; and were fixed upon five points that were never wanting; nor did they come together on any side, or come apart either, without end at any corner that I find anywhere, wherever the tracing began or came to an end.' The author's

ingenuity in thus expounding the indivisibility, yet distinctness, of Gawain's qualities may fairly be thought greater than the conviction it carries. The positive social virtues of the last group (651 ff.) may well be so linked, but there is obvious incompatibility between it and the preceding two groups, in which the 'fives' are the established devotional objects of the five wounds and the five joys to which single qualities of Gawain are related.

660 *I oquere fynde.* The reading is tentative, for the scribe's intention is not clear. The manuscript is usually read *jquere*, but the first letter has not the usual shape of *j*, and there is a curved mark over the *u*. Madden emended to *aiquere*, but this means 'everywhere' and is inappropriate after 'without'; the form of 'anywhere' is *auwhare* in *Purity* 30, but could also be *owhere* (cf. *nowhere* 2164, and the alternatives *oþer*, *auþer* 'either'), and the *o* might have been dropped before the similar bow of *q*.

674 ff. Cf. the similar lament in *Le Chevalier à l'Épée* 160–3:

> 'Ahi', fet li uns, 'tant mar fus,
> Biaus chevaliers, genz et adrois!
> Certes il ne fu mie drois
> Que fussiez bleciez ne laidiz.'

681 *angardez pryde.* These two words are associated again in *Winner and Waster* 267 and *Dest. Troy* 9745, though the syntactical relations are different. *Angard of pride* in *Dest. Troy* suggests a sense 'excess' for *angard*, and this is supported by numerous uses of the adv. *angardly* in the same poem, e.g. 5113: 'angert vs all angardly sore'. How this sense

arose from the normal OFr. meaning of *angarde*, which is 'vanguard', is
not clear. See Brett, *M.L.R.* viii (1913), 160–2.

691 ff. The general direction of Gawain's itinerary is clear: since he
rode into North Wales, and came 'þurȝ þe ryalme of Logres', a southern
site of Camelot is to be inferred (see note on 37). His route through
North Wales to Wirral presents difficulties. According to 698 he rode
east, keeping the isles of Anglesey (Anglesey proper, Holy Island, Puffin
Island, etc.) on his left. Then he crossed 'the fords by the headlands,
over at the Holy Head'. It is not apparent which fords and headlands are
meant, or if the Holy Head was one of these promontories or a place further
on. But it seems likely that Gawain was following a known route, since
the author speaks of '*the* fords by *the* headlands' and expects his audience
to know them. The usual route in the Middle Ages can be inferred from
the *Itinerarium Kambriae* of Giraldus Cambrensis, and the invasion of
Henry II in 1135. Giraldus tells how he travelled east along the north
coast of Wales, crossing the rivers Conwy and Clwyd where they flow into
the sea, thence through St. Asaph to Basingwerk (near Holywell), thence
along the coast of the estuary of the Dee, crossing the Dee below Chester
(*Opera*, ed. J. F. Dimock, Rolls ser. vi (1868), pp. 136–9). 'The fords by
the headlands' may refer to the crossing of the Conwy and Clwyd, both
of which flow into the sea with promontories on either side. On the left
bank of the Clwyd near the mouth is a place still called Forydd, 'ford'.
The Holy Head is where Gawain passed into Wirral, and so would
be somewhere on the Dee between Chester and the estuary. No such
place is known there now, nor is there any record of a Holy Head other
than Holyhead in Anglesey, which is obviously excluded by 698.

The possibility that the author's geography is inaccurate must also be
considered. But he writes as if he knew these places, and it is the only
part of the journey he chooses to specify by place-names. He knew that
Anglesey comprised several islands, and that Wirral was a wilderness.
It seems preferable to accept that he knew North Wales and Cheshire,
and that his 'Holy Head' was a place which is no longer known by that
name.

A more adventurous interpretation is proposed by J. McN. Dodgson
in *Early English and Norse Studies presented to Hugh Smith* (London,
1963), 19–25. He envisages a crossing at the very mouth of the Dee
estuary, at the 'forelands', the Point of Air in Flintshire and the north-
west corner of the Wirral peninsula near West Kirby. This would
normally be impracticable, but there was a legend, preserved in a life of
St. Werburgh of Chester (1513) of a miraculous crossing 'like as to
Moises deuided the redde see' by the constable of Chester in the early
twelfth century. On this reading Holy Head would mean West Kirby,
by association of such forms as *Kerkeby* with *Kaerkeby*, a variant of
Caer Gybi, the Welsh name of Holyhead in Anglesey. Though this view is
highly ingenious and in many ways attractive, the poet might be expected
to have made more of so legendary a crossing.

Gollancz's suggestion that 'Holy Head' refers to the severed head of

E

St. Winifred, whose story 'would make a natural appeal to Gawain', is altogether too fanciful; the poet gives no hint that Gawain went that way because of a special interest in heads chopped off and replaced.

691 *Logres*. Welsh *Lloegyr*, approximately England south of the Humber. Geoffrey (II. i) says that it was named after Locrine, eldest son of Brutus, who after his father's death ruled the middle part of the island.

701 *þe wyldrenesse of Wyrale*. Wirral was made into a forest by Ranulph le Meschin ('the young'), fourth earl of Chester (d. *c.* 1129), and remained wild as late as the sixteenth century (G. Ormerod, *History of the County Palatine and City of Chester*, revd. T. Helsby (London, 1882), ii. 353–4). H. L. Savage gives evidence of the concern caused to the authorities in the fourteenth century by criminals who resorted there (*M.L.N.* xlvi (1931), 455–7).

702 *God oþer gome wyth goud hert*. This is a variant of the conventional 'God and good men' (for which see C. T. Onions, *T.L.S.* 13 August 1931, p. 621, and E. S. Olszewska, 'Alliterative Phrases in the *Ormulum*: Some Norse Parallels', *English and Medieval Studies presented to J. R. R. Tolkien* (London, 1962), p. 125). It is consequently the subject of the sentence. A. C. Cawley first published this interpretation in his edition, but Onions had independently proposed it privately.

709 ff. Clearly Gawain rides a long way after he lands in Wirral. Madden suggested that the forest of 741 ff. is Inglewood Forest in Cumberland, the traditional setting of Arthurian adventures. Attempts to identify the castle and the 'Green Chapel' are probably vain; Hautdesert is likely to have been as imaginary as Camelot.

715 *warþe*. For the meaning 'ford' see P. Haworth, *N. & Q.* ccxii (1967), 171–2.

723 *anelede*. This seems to derive from OFr. *aneler*, Lat. *anhēlare*, 'breathe', hence 'aspire'. In English the only examples of comparable date are in Wyntoun's *Chronicle* (early fifteenth century); e.g. 'Constantynys sonnys thre That anelyd to that ryawte' (see *D.O.S.T.*). This has clearly lost all association with literal panting; presumably the use here has done so equally, and is to be taken as 'pursued'.

734 *caryeȝ*. Elsewhere in this manuscript the form is *cayr-*; but in several texts *carien* undoubtedly appears in the sense of *cayren*, and there was evidently genuine confusion between the two verbs in the fifteenth century. See T. A. Knott, *M.L.N.* xxx (1915), 106–7; C. A. Luttrell, *Neophilologus* xxxix (1955), 209; *M.E.D.* under *carien*, 5.

762 This was a common formula of prayer, though usually in the order *Kryst cros*, etc. The order *Cros Kryst* is not an error, for it occurs also in *The Boke of Curtasye* 144 (a north-western text like *Gawain*); see *The Babees Book*, p. 303. It is probably modelled on OFr. *crois Crist*; cf. M. Welsh *croes crist* (Black Book of Carmarthen, ed. J. G. Evans (Pwllheli, 1906), p. 82. 2).

774 *Gilyan*. It is St. Julian the Hospitaller who is thanked by Gawain—
he was the patron and protector of travellers, 'qui ab itinerantibus pro
inveniendo bono hospitio invocatur' (*Legenda Aurea*). Knights errant
in French romance commonly invoke him, and so also in Chaucer's
House of Fame 1022: 'Seynt Julyan, loo, bon hostel!' His legend is told in
the *Legenda Aurea*, xxx; in ME. in *The Early South-English Legendary*
(ed. C. Horstmann, E.E.T.S. 87 (1887)), pp. 256–60, and *The South
English Legendary* (ed. C. d'Evelyn and A. J. Mill, E.E.T.S. 235 (1956)),
pp. 32–37; and in Middle Scots in *Barbour's Legendensammlung* (ed.
Horstmann (Heilbronn, 1881)), pp. 218–29.

777 *gerdez*. This emendation rests on the analogy of 2062 and 2160.
The copyist's error was in mistaking the position of the abbreviation for
er in his exemplar.

778 þe *chef gate* is the main approach road; þe ȝatez 782 are the castle
gates. This text distinguishes regularly between *gate* and ȝate.

785 As the text stands in the manuscript the relative þat on blonk houed
is separated from its apparent antecedent *burne*, and also breaks awkwardly into the sentence which runs on from *bonk* to *of* þe . . . *dich*.
It is likely that a scribe transposed the very similar words *blonk* and *bonk*.
'He remained on his horse, which came to a halt on the bank of the
deep double ditch.' Cf. note on 210.

790 Similarly in *Purity* 1458–9 the 'aþel vessel' brought out at Belshazzar's feast comprised cups

as casteles arayed,
Enbaned vnder batelment wyth bantelles quoynt.

Enbaned must mean 'provided with *bantels*', the architectural feature
described in *Pearl* 992 f., where they are set in the form of steps at the
foot of the city wall. Here they are horizontal courses of masonry set
near the top of the wall, projecting outwards under the battlements. See
Gordon's note on *Pearl* 992, *M.Æ.* ii (1933), 184 f., and Brett, *M.L.R.*
xxii (1927), 456.

791 *bitwene* here means 'at intervals' (of space), as again 795. This sense,
not recorded in dictionaries (even *M.E.D.*), is related to the use with
ferre which *M.E.D.* quotes from *Isumbras* 169; cf. *Morte Arthure* 934:
'Festenez theire faire stedez o ferrom bytwenne.'

792 *loupe*. For loop-holes with shutters cf. the passage quoted in *O.E.D.*
under *loop* sb.[2] from Gregory's *Chronicle* (*c.* 1470): 'They hadde . . .
loupys with schyttyng wyndowys to schute owte at.'

794 ff. Such elaborate castles with numerous ornamental pinnacles and
chimneys rising from 'bastel' roofs began to appear in the latter half of
the fourteenth century. The poet is evidently describing the architectural
fashion of his own time.

796–800 Cf. *Purity* 1461–3.

802 Cf. *Purity* 1407–8, where the 'logges' placed over the dishes of food were

on lofte coruen,
Pared out of paper and poynted of golde.

It is evidently the elaboration of the castle workmanship that the simile is meant to emphasize; there is no suggestion that it was insubstantial.

815 The MS. line is obviously defective in metre and sense. Gollancz suggests supplying ӡare & com, but ӡerne suits the poet's usage better.

822 *quel.* An unstressed form of *whil*, very occasionally found elsewhere; cf. *tel* 1564 for *til*.

835 *welde* is normally transitive. Gollancz emends it here to *wone*, in the light of 814, holding that the scribe may have picked it up from 837 (which in our manuscript he writes opposite the present line). This may be right; but the assumption of a run-on line gives satisfactory grammar, and run-on lines do occur—e.g. 648, 773.

839 *Per* is often used in ME. to introduce a wish of this kind, in a way that cannot be reproduced in modern English. For typical examples in Chaucer see Robinson's note on *Knight's Tale*, A. 2815.

845 In *Awntyrs off Arthure* 357 Arthur also has a 'beueren berde'.

847 Similarly in *Wars Alex.* 4922 the sun-god has 'fell face as þe fire'.

849 'to hold a lordship over good lieges'. The phrase *in lee* is obscure; it may mean 'in tranquillity, in peace' (*O.E.D.*); or 'in hall', an alliterative variant of *in mote, on flet*; or 'as protector (of)', similar to *hlēo* in OE. verse for 'lord'. The second seems most likely; cf. 1893.

864 ff. The passage is difficult, perhaps slightly corrupt (there are numerous obvious errors in this part of the manuscript—see the footnotes), and much disputed. For a summary of opinions see Savage, *Gawain-Poet*, pp. 176–90. The following seems possible: 'As soon as he took one and was clothed in it, (one) that fitted him well with flowing skirts, the very spring it almost seemed to each man from his appearance, all his limbs under it all in glowing and delightful colours . . . .' Gawain put on a bright-coloured robe, under which appeared his limbs clad in closer-fitting garments of various colours; cf. 152 ff., 1928–31.

879 *bleeaunt.* Here a rich fabric, but in 1928 applied to a garment. The etymology and sense-development are uncertain. The form *bliaut* was used in French as early as the twelfth century for a long over-tunic, worn by both sexes (see especially J. Evans, *Dress in Medieval France*, pp. 5 ff. and pls. 7, 10); it does not seem to have been used for a fabric as well. In AN. the ending was replaced by *-ant, -aunt* proper to the pres. part. (e.g. *bliaunt* in the AN. *Bevis of Hampton* 738, 745), perhaps in part because *u* and *n* were indistinguishable in most manuscripts. The form with *n* appears also in Welsh and MLG., but HG. and Icelandic have that without *n*. ME. usually has the -*n*- type, but the other also occurs, e.g. *blyot* in *Parl. Thre Ages* 482.

We cannot tell how far the shape of the *bleaunt* in fourteenth-century England preserved that of the twelfth-century French *bliaut*. J. L. Nevinson, in *Medieval England* ch. ix, writes: 'As might be expected, there are archaisms in *Sir Gawain and the Green Knight* such as the trailing *bliaut* worn indoors with a surcoat and a hood hanging on the shoulder' (p. 308). Yet from his attitude to armour and architecture the poet seems unlikely to have intended archaism in costume. It may be that the word had acquired a more general sense of 'robe', which it might easily do from the use of the cloth for mantles, as here; cf. also *Sir Tristrem* 410: 'In o robe . . . of a blihand broun.'

884 In the Middle Ages the tables were usually not fixed, but consisted of boards on trestles which after meals were taken away and often hung on the walls of the hall.

893 *sawes so sleʒe*. MS. *sleʒez* is clearly wrong, and the original may have had *sawsez so sleʒe*.

896 *As hende*. A common adverbial phrase meaning in effect 'courteously', found also with def. art. as in 1104; for other examples see B. D. H. Miller, *N. & Q.* ccvi (1961), 378–9. Here it is usually taken with the preceding sentence, but that awkwardly repeats the earlier *hendely*. *Hende* is often vocative (see glossary), and this seems most suitable here— 'Of your courtesy'. It is true that the bob most frequently goes with what precedes, but not invariably, e.g. 1100.

897 *þis penaunce*. When Gawain calls the dinner of fish a feast because it is cooked in so many ways, they remind him that Christmas Eve is a fast day; later he will do better. John Russell's *Boke of Nurture* describes a similarly elaborate fish dinner, fish *sewes*, and sauces for fish; see *The Babees Book*, pp. 166–8, 171–5.

901 ff. 'Then tactful questions and inquiries were discreetly made of the prince about himself, in answer to which he courteously avowed that he was a member of the court ruled by the noble and gracious Arthur alone . . . .'

908 The lord of the castle is evidently not present at this point—he greets Gawain by name only at 937. His rejoicing here is therefore not dramatically correct. He must have recognized Gawain when he arrived (835); but if suspense is to be maintained by his behaving as if he had not met him before, his satisfaction should be public and assumed, not private and apparently surprised.

916 ff. On Gawain's reputation see note on 109.

929 *niyʒt*. This spelling occurs elsewhere in the manuscript; see *Pearl*, ed. Gordon, 630 and note.

939 The failure of alliteration in the second half-line implies corruption.

944 *of alle oþer* goes with *fayrest*—'she was fairest of all'. This illogical use of *other* is not uncommon in ME.; cf. *Dest. Troy* 39 *derrist of other* 'more worthy than all others'. It appears sporadically in modern use; *O.E.D.* gives examples under *other* adj., pron. B. 5. b.

945 *Wenore*. For the form see note on 109. Guenever in romances is the standard of beauty, and the expression 'fairer than Guenever' was no doubt conventional. In 'The Lady of the Fountain' Cynon says of maidens that they are 'lovelier than Gwenhwyfar' (*Mabinogion*, ed. Jones and Jones, p. 157). Geoffrey (IX. ix) says of Guenever, 'tocius insule mulieres pulcritudine superabat', and the Vulgate *Merlin*, 'ce estoit la plus bele feme qui fust en toute bertaigne au tans de lors' (ii. 157). See also 81 ff. of this poem.

946 Mrs. Wright observed that MS. *he* must be an error for *ho* or else a use of the form *he* for 'she'; Gawain does not leave his seat until the lord gives him permission to do so at 971 (*J.E.G.P.* xxxiv (1935), 173). For the same emendation see 1872.

955–6 The syntax, as often in this cumulative style, is ambiguous. On general grounds it is likely that what shone so white was the lady's 'breast and bright throat' rather than her kerchiefs, for the contrast is between the displayed beauties of the young woman and the all but covered ugliness of the old one, not between the qualities of their linen. Accordingly *displayed* is past tense pl., with subject *kerchofes*, and 956 is a relative clause—absence of an expressed subject relative is good syntax at this date; e.g. Chaucer, *Canterbury Tales*, Prol. 529: 'With hym ther was a Plowman was his brother.'

958 *chalkquyte*. Onions's emendation (*N. & Q.* cxlvi (1924), 245) is necessary to the alliteration; cf. 798. *M.E.D.* records seven other occurrences of this compound, including *Degrevant* 1506 'chalk-whyȝth as the *mylk*'.

960 *toreted*. The manuscript has *toret*, with a longer space than usual before the following ampersand. OFr. *to(u)ret* was an embroidered edge of a headdress. Godefroy quotes from the *Danse macabre* (1486):

> Dames, ployez vos gorgerettes,
> Il n'est plus temps de vous farder,
> Voz *toretz*, fronteaulx, et bavetes
> Ne vous porroient icy aider.

See also Evans, *Dress in Medieval France*, p. 57, and the 'trellised' *touret* in pl. 55. This word is evidently in place in this context, and an adjective formed from it seems most likely to have been intended.

965 *for Gode*. The rhyme shows that this is not *for gode* 'for good'; *gode* with tense *ō* (sometimes spelt *goud*—see p. 133 and glossary) would not rhyme with *brode* with slack *ō*, whereas in this group of poems a short vowel may rhyme with a long one of the same quality: e.g. *nyme* 993: *tyme*, *þise* 1103: *ryse*, *vpon* in *Pearl* 208: *ston*. Alternatively, *brod* may have

shortened its vowel, as later rhymes (notably in Milton) indicate; see
E. J. Dobson, *English Pronunciation* 1500–1700 (Oxford, 1957), § 33. The
sense here is not 'by God' but rather 'before God (this is true)'.

967 *balʒ*. MS. *bay* is not intelligible here; Brett's suggestion that it is the
first element of *bay window* (*M.L.R.* viii (1913), 162–3) is unsuitable
because that originally denotes the interior opening, not the exterior
bulge. A copyist could misread *lʒ* as *y*. See 2032, and for the alliterative
association of *balʒ* and *brode* cf. *Wars Alex.* 4923, *Parl. Thre Ages* 112.

968–9 'Sweeter to taste was she whom she was leading'; *lyk* has not the
modern sense 'lick' but rather 'taste'; cf. *Purity* 1521 'So long likked þise
lordes þise lykores swete.'

975 'They ask him for (his) acquaintance', that is, 'desire to be acquainted
with him'. For this sense of *callen of* cf. 1882.

977 In *Wars Alex.* 353 'takis him betwene þam twa' is used of the queen
taking Anectanabus aside. With the use here cf. *Shrewsbury Fragments* (in
E.E.T.S. E.S. civ (1909)) C. 27 'Ful tenely toke him hom betwen'.

979 Cf. *Morte Arthure* 235: 'Thane spyces vnsparyly þay spendyde
thereaftyre.' Here *spycez* must mean spiced cakes or the like, since the
wine comes in the next line. (So W. P. Ker, reported by Mrs. Wright,
J.E.G.P. xxxiv (1935), 345.)

984 *wayned*. Though MS. *u* and *n* are usually indistinguishable, the letter
here looks more like *n*. The verb *wayne* generally means 'send, bring',
but the etymological sense 'move' could develop to a figurative 'urge,
challenge'.

992 Possibly, as Hulbert and Knott suggest (*M.L.N.* xxx (1915), 106),
knyʒt should be read, as more likely than *lord* to give rise to the MS.
error *kyng*; but *lord* is more than thirty times applied to Bertilak, and
alliteration rather than internal rhyme is normal in the wheel. That *kyng*
is an error, and not a mysterious vestige of a mythological analogue,
cannot be doubted in the light of the poet's words everywhere else.

1002 The metrical pause falls between *by* and *lent*; *by* thus following
its case is accented. This word-order, frequent with many prepositions
in OE. prose as well as verse, is still common in ME. verse but rare in
prose.

1003 ff. 'Gawain and the fair lady sat together right in the middle (of the
high table), where the food fittingly came and then (was served) through
the whole hall as best became the company. When every man had been
promptly served according to his rank, there was (such) food . . . .' *Bi* is
a conjunction as in 1169, 2032.

1006 *grome* in late ME. became confused with *gome* 'man', which it
eventually replaced; cf. modern *bridegroom*, OE. *brýdguma*. Here *grome*
probably means 'man', though it could be 'servant' as in 1127.

1008–9 '(such) that it would be very difficult for me to tell of it, even if perhaps I took pains to describe it in detail'. *And* has its common ME. meaning 'if'.

1014 *pat*. MS. *&*. A correlative to *such* 1011 is required, and the ampersand seems to have been miswritten for *þᵗ*; so again 1032, 1386.

1022 Gollancz appears to be right in deducing that a line has been omitted after this. St. John's Day is 27 December, and the feasting goes on very late (1025–7). Guests who mean to leave in the morning take leave of the host before going to bed, but Gawain is induced to stay longer. The others duly leave very early (1126 ff.) and the same morning the host goes hunting. But the hunts and the three temptations occupy the last three days of the year (1965–8), and this agrees with Gawain's statement in 1066 that he has only three days left. 28 December is therefore not accounted for, and since the author is attentive to dates this is unlikely to be an oversight.

1028 *stronge*. The meaning is plainly 'not belonging to the household', so that the word is a form of 'strange'. The use of *o* in this position in French words (obscurely related to the common *au*) is mainly southern and most frequent in *Ayenbite*, but it is sporadic elsewhere (see *Sir Gawain and the Carl of Carlisle*, ed. Kurvinen, note on 9). *Stronge* appears again in *Purity* 1494, so that it was evidently part of this scribe's repertory.

1032 *wayued*. This verb is hard to distinguish from *wayne*; see note on 984. Early editions here read *wayned*, and Gollancz still does so; but cf. 1976 'Such worchip he wolde hym weue', where *weue*, rhyming *leue*, is from OE. *wǣfan* influenced in sense by the probably cognate ON. *veifa*. The two forms *wayue* and *weue* interchange in ME.; cf. the phrase in 1743 *wayuez vp a wyndow*, beside *William of Palerne* 2978 *weued vp a window*; *Purity* 453 *wafte he vpon his wyndowe*; Laȝamon (ed. Madden) 19003 *wefden up* 'opened'.

1038 *heȝe kyng*. Here and in 1963 this is treated as a compound, alliterating on *h*, as OE. *hēahcyning* (Emerson, *J.E.G.P.* xxi (1922), 379).

1045 'that he could not by any means'.

1049 *toun*. Here in the general sense 'habitation of men', a further extension of the use in 31. This idiom in speaking of time and seasons is very old. In OE. examples are: *Menologium* 8 'se kalend us cymeð to tune', 138 'scriþ Weodmonað on tun', and several other times in that poem; *Byrhtferth's Manual* (ed. S. J. Crawford, E.E.T.S. 177 (1929)), p. 54, 6 'þa monðas gan on tun', beside 23–24 'cymð se monð to mannum'; cf. *Beowulf* 1134 'in geardas'. In ME. compare: Laȝamon (ed. Madden) 24196 'Averil eode of tune', and similarly 24242, where the older MS. has *to londe* for *to tune*; also the Harley lyric 'Lenten ys come wiþ loue to toune' (ed. Brook, no. 11). Thus the line means, 'Before the holy days (Christmas week) had wholly passed'.

1053 *I ne wot in worlde.* The insertion of *ne* is required by the sense, and is always found in this common alliterative formula; cf. *Pearl* 65, *Dest. Troy* 12903, *William of Palerne* 314, 478, etc. It appears also in Icelandic: *Völsungs Rímur* (ed. F. Jonsson, *Fernir Fornislenskir Rímnaflokkar* (1896), p. 43) i. 12 'Vissa eg ei í veröldu fyrr væri stærri halla.'

1067 This idiom (which *O.E.D.*, under *me* 7. d, records only from 1812) appears to be a more colloquial variant of that with the pronoun in the nom., as in 1826, and *Pearl* 386, 'And I a man al mornyf mate'. The latter is not uncommon in the fifteenth century; e.g. Malory, *Works*, p. 826: 'to kepe my counsell and ye nat hurte thereby'. (In the present line it might be possible to explain *me* as dat. and *fayn* used with the construction of *lef*, but this does not seem to occur elsewhere.)

1068–78 The inconsistent use of *þe* and *yow* in these lines is remarkable, especially *ʒe* and *þyn* together in 1071; see pp. 144–5.

1074 *in spenne* is evidently a tag like *in stedde* 439, with a vague sense such as 'there'. *Spenne* is probably the same word as *spene* in *Wars Alex.* 4162 *on þe spene*, where it seems to mean '(piece of) land'. It is probably also the same as in 1709 and 1896, both in the phrase *ouer a spenne*. There it must be some kind of fence, and derivation from ON. *spenni* 'clasp' is likely; from this, 'piece of land enclosed by a fence' might develop. See A. H. Smith, *English Place-Name Elements*, ii. 136–7.

1108 'Good sir, let us exchange—answer honestly—whichever, sir, may fall to our lot, worthless or better.'

1112 Indefinite, as *quo laytes þe soþe* 355: 'if anyone will bring us the drink (with which to seal the bargain)'; cf. 1409. *þis* is idiomatic in referring to something well known or customary.

1117 *stemed* is evidently the same verb as *stemmed* 230, though used rather vaguely of absence of motion instead of cessation from it. The clearest indication of its meaning is *Purity* 905, 'loke ʒe stemme no stepe, bot strechez on faste'. *O.E.D.* puts the two *Gawain* cases under a separate verb, *stem* v.[1] 'to debate with oneself'; but this suits less well.

1129 Both *trussen* and *males* were the everyday terms: 'pack their bags'.

1139 There are descriptions of the hunting and 'undoing' of deer resembling those which follow here in several other English romances; cf. especially *Parl. Thre Ages* 1–99; *Awntyrs off Arthure* 33–65; *Sir Tristrem* 441–526; *Ipomadon*, A. 587–686, B. 366–416. See also *Summer Sunday* 1–30, and Chaucer, *Book of the Duchess* 344–86. The following passages may have been suggested to the poet by some incident in a French romance such as that in *Le Chevalier à l'Épée* where Gawain's host goes to 'view his woods' (372–5):

> Li ostes dist apres mengier
> Qu'il vialt aler ses bois veoir,
> Et si rova Gauvain seoir
> Et deduire o la damoisele.

But Loomis traces the 'huntsman host' back to Welsh Legend (*Wales*, ch. vi).

1140 *kenel*. All the hounds were in one large kennel, which would be 'of x. fadmys of lengthe and v. of brede, if þere be many houndes' (*Master of Game*, ch. xx and pl. xxii).

1141 *þre bare mote*. The mote was a long note. The fourteenth-century horn had only one note, and different calls were made by combining notes of different length. The names given in the hunting treatises are

        mote   trut   trororout   trorororout⁻

Three motes were blown at the uncoupling (unleashing) of the hounds. For *mote* without inflexion cf. *Book of the Duchess* 375–7.

> The mayster-hunte anoon, fot-hot,
> With a gret horn blew thre mot
> At the uncouplynge of hys houndes.

1142 *braches*. The same kind of hounds as *rachchez* 1362 etc., scenting hounds hunting in a pack. They were small hounds, in build resembling modern beagles. They were to be used as *taysours* (note on 1150 ff.). Twiti says, 'Touz ceaus (bestes) qe sunt enchacés sunt˜meüz de lymer; et touz ceaus enquillez sunt trovez de brachez' (ed. Tilander, ll. 21–22); that is, all animals that are 'enchased' are moved by a 'limer', and all that are 'hunted up' (the method used here) are found by braches. The braches are now unleashed, and those said to be unleashed in 1147 are doubtless the greyhounds.

1143 'And they whipped in and turned back [the hounds] that strayed away on other scents.'

1144 The context might seem to require this to be understood as 'hunting hounds', not men; but elsewhere in the poem, and in medieval use at large, the word is always used of men, and it is best to accept this here also; 'a hundreth' is presumably a hyperbolical term for any large number.

1150 Cf. *Master of Game* xxiii: 'This word "quest" is a terme of hert hunters bi younde þe see, and is as mooch to say as whan an hunter goþ to fynde of an hert and to herborowe hym'—*herborowe* means 'track to the lair'. But *quest* was also used of the peculiar cry of hounds on scenting or viewing game; see *O.E.D.* under *quest* 6. b, and *Master of Game* xiv: '. . . rennynge houndes, þe whiche moste renne alle þe day questynge and makyng gret melody in her langage and seiyng gret vilany and chydyng þe beste þat þei enchace.'

1150 ff. The hunt is like that described in *Master of Game* xxxvi, 'whan þe Kyng wil hunt in foreste or in parke for þe hert with bowes, grey-houndes, and stable' (*stablye* 1153). Men and hounds were stationed at various points around the area in which the game was to be hunted. Light greyhounds and other *taysours* (hounds for putting up and driving game) were slipped, and as they drove the deer the *stablye*, or beaters belonging to the ring of stations, directed their course to where the lord and his party stood ready to shoot them. The men of the *stablye* also tried to strike down the deer if they came close enough, and at any of the stations there might be some larger greyhounds ('receivers') to pull the deer down. The stations where special preparations were made to kill the deer constituted the *resayt* (1168).

1156–7 The close season of the hart (stag) and buck—the male of the red and fallow deer respectively—was from 14 September to 24 June. Hinds and does—the females of the same two species (cf. *Ipomadon* B. 389 'herte and hynde, buk and doo')—were hunted from 14 September to 2 February (*Master of Game*, appendix under 'Seasons of Hunting'). There is some uncertainty whether *meue* or *mene* should be read in 1157. *Meue* is the technical term for starting a stag (cf. the pp. *meüz* in Twiti, note on 1142, and *meved* in *Master of Game*), and seems the likelier word to be used here. There was also in French a verb *mener* 'to chase hard' (Cotgrave's *Dictionary*, 1611), derived from *menée*, the name of a hunting call used as a signal that the deer was in full flight; see Tilander, *Essais*, pp. 9 ff., 39. Twiti (94–95) says it was blown only to the stag, the boar, and the wolf.

1158 ff. The noise, confusion, and slaughter of this scene, and the terror of the mass of hunted animals, make unacceptable any suggestion of a symbolic parallel between it and the simultaneous quiet pursuit in the castle bedroom.

1162 *hedez* must apply to the arrows, not the deer; a hind or doe has not a broad head, and stags and bucks are expressly excluded.

1167 ff. 'Whatever animal escaped the men who were shooting was pulled down and slaughtered at the receiving stations, by the time they had been driven from the high ground and down to the waters; the men at the lower stations were so skilled, the greyhounds so huge that they seized them at once and pulled them down right there, as fast as men could look.'

1168 Something has evidently been lost in the second half-line, which is metrically incomplete; perhaps *ryȝt* after *rent*. (The stress must be on the first syllable of *resayt*; see p. 151.)

1169 *taysed*. A technical term for driving game; see *The Noble Arte*, p. 246.

þe wattrez. According to the hunting treatises a hunted stag usually made for a river. Cf. *Boke of St. Albans* sig. e vij (Tilander pp. 50–52):

> For .ii. cawses the hert desirith to the Ryuer. & note wele theis termys foloyng descende & oder

> > Oon cause for the Ryuer descende he is ay
> > And so is he to the water when he takith the way
> > Why callist thow hym .descende. mayster I the pray
> > Fot he payris of is myght the sooth I the say

A nother is to the water whi he gooth other whyle
The howndes that hym sewen to founde to begyle.

The cunning stag would come out of the water by the same way as he
went in: *Master of Game* iii: 'and he shal ruse aȝein þe same waye þat he
come, a bowe shoot or more, and þan he shal ruse out of þe way.'

1170–1 The *þat*-clause is evidently consecutive, not relative, and the
absence of a pronoun subject for *geten* is idiomatic in OE. and ME.

1174 *abloy*. An AN. variant of OFr. *esbloi*, pp. of *esbloir*, modern *éblouir*
(E. M. Wright, *M.L.R.* xviii (1923), 86): 'the lord, carried away with
joy, often galloped and dismounted.'

1183 '(He heard) a little noise at his door, and (heard it) stealthily open.'
The emendation *dernly* for MS. *derfly* assumes that the copyist took *n*
as *u* and substituted the alternative *f*; for the sense cf. 1188. The recorded
uses of *derf* imply boldness or vigour, unsuitable here. *Vpon* is infin.
depending on *herde*. For the spelling with *v* cf. *vpon* adj. 'open', *Pearl* 198,
Purity 318, 453.

1224 *þat oþer half* apparently means that she will tuck him up in the
bedclothes on the side opposite to that on which she is sitting; cf. 1211.

1237 This line has commonly been understood as if each word bore its
modern meaning—'You are welcome to my body.' Since so crude an
offer is ill suited to this early stage of the lady's courtship of Gawain (the
situation is further advanced at 1496), critics have found it hard to account
for. For example Gollancz says: 'The lady's bluntness in coming to the
point testifies to her inexperience in such a role.' But *cors*, in addition
to its literal sense of 'body' (alive or dead), was used idiomatically with
possessive adjectives to mean 'person', as in effect the equivalent of
a personal pronoun. The idiom was very common in French; e.g.
Chrétien, *Yvain* 3798 'autretant l'aim come mon cors', where *mon cors*
means 'myself'; *Raoul de Cambrai* 1413 'Ja Damerdieu ne puist ton cors
aidier.' It was imitated in English, sometimes with *body* in place of *cors*—
see note on 353—sometimes retaining *cors*: Chaucer, Introd. to *Pardoner's
Tale*, C. 304 'I pray to God so save thy gentil cors'; *Purity* 683 'þat I ne
dyscouered to his corse my counseyl so dere'. (See *M.E.D.* under *cors* 3
(a) for further examples.) The quotation from *Purity* shows that this poet
knew the idiom. In the present passage, therefore, *my cors* can certainly
mean 'me'. As for *welcum* (*to*), its semantic history is inadequately docu-
mented. *O.E.D.*, though it records the sense 'freely permitted or allowed,
cordially invited', gives only the construction with infin. (as e.g. in
Gawain 814) and fails to notice the familiar modern use with noun or
pronoun object. Where 'welcome to' appears in *Gawain*, as it does twice
(252 'welcum iwys to þis place', and similarly 2240), the meaning is the
simple literal one. The other common use of the phrase applies to the
person who is pleased, as *Canterbury Tales*, Prol. 762 'Ye been to me right
welcome', *William of Palerne* 3148 'ȝe ben welcom to me, bi Crist þat me
made.' There is one medieval example resembling the other application,

in *Castle of Perseverance* (*Macro Plays*, ed. Furnivall, E.E.T.S. E.S. xci (1904) 589; new edn. M. Eccles, no. 262 (1969) 585)—Mundus greets Mankind: 'Welcum, syr, semly in syth! þou art welcum to worthy wede', and goes on to promise him wealth and luxury: 'with my seruyse I schal þe foster and fede . . . To þi cors schal knele kayser and knyth.' Yet this is not exactly the modern use; Mundus says not that Mankind is free to help himself to rich garments, etc., but that he has done well to come where they are available. It appears, therefore, that *welcum to* should not be interpreted in the sense which occurs first to a modern reader, but in that exemplified by Chaucer's Host; that is, the line means 'You are welcome to me', 'I am glad to have you here.' It is true that the following line 'to choose your own course (of action)', 'do as you like', implies what the other interpretation would make explicit; but it does so in a reasonably discreet tone, in keeping with the courtly atmosphere of what has gone before. Further, Gawain's reply is appropriate to a speech of friendly welcome rather than a blunt proposal of adultery: 'In good faith, that seems to me very agreeable, though I am not now such a man as you speak of. I am unworthy to attain to such honour as you describe.'

1238–40 *of fyne force* is a conventional term which long remained in legal use. Blount's *Law Dictionary* (1670) remarks: 'seems to signifie an absolute necessity or constraint, not avoidable'. It is thus quite distinct from 'constrayne wyth strenkþe' 1496. 'It behoves me of necessity to be your servant, and I shall be.' To complete the sense of *schale* the subject 'I' must be supplied from *me behouez*; the infin. *be* is present in the preceding clause, so that the passages quoted by Brett in comparison (given in Gollancz's note) are not strictly apposite. The *-e* of *schale* is no doubt merely scribal, the rhyme being on an infin. without ending as it commonly is; see p. 145.

1250 *hit were littel daynté*. 'It would show little good breeding.'

1252 For *þe* here inconsistent with *your* in the next line cf. 1272 and 1275, and note on 1068–78.

1255 *garysoun oþer golde*. Cf. *golde ne garysoun* 1837, a variant of *gold and gersum*, a common alliterative formula in ME.: often in Laȝamon, also *St. Marherete* (ed. F. M. Mack, E.E.T.S. 193 (1934) 6. 15), *Rauf Coilȝear* 936, and other examples in *M.E.D.* under *gersum(e* 1 (c). The phrase is of Scandinavian origin; cf. *Eddica Minora* (ed. A. Heusler and W. Ranisch, 1903) IV. 6, 16, XV. 10 *gull ok gǫrsimar* (etc.); *Vǫlundarkviða* 19 *gull rautt ok gǫrsimar*; *Bosa Rímur* (ed. O. L. Jiriczek, 1894) VI. 51 *gull og silfr og gersemar*, VII. 76; and elsewhere in Icelandic prose as well as verse, cf. note on 165. In *Gawain* the ON. loan *gersum* has been replaced by the French *garysoun*; an intermediate stage appears in *Awntyrs off Arthure* 664, *gersone and golde*. OFr. *garison* meant 'defence, protection', then 'possessions', and this evidently became associated with *gersum*.

1263–7 Satisfactory sense cannot be made of this passage as it stands. It is evidently corrupt, but no fully convincing emendations have yet been proposed. 1265 could perhaps mean 'and others take their line of action very much from other people', but—admitting this strained sense for *fongen hor dedeȝ*—this does not suit what follows, and would require a stronger stress on the two occurrences of *oþer* than the alliteration on *f* suggests. It seems best to take *fongen* (with Ker) as past part., parallel to *founden* in the line above; but *hor dedeȝ* then needs a preposition (unless it is wholly corrupt for some quite different word such as *honourez*). In 1266 MS. *nysen* cannot intelligibly be derived from *nice* 'foolish'. It could be read *uysen* 'devise' (so Menner, *M.L.R.* xix (1924), 206–8), but this does not give sense either. It may be a haplographic error for *nys euen*, which suits what Gawain is likely to have said. If these suggestions are adopted the passage means: 'My lady,' said the man good-humouredly, 'may Mary repay you, for I have found in you a noble generosity, and received much else from other people by their actions; but the honour that they assign to me, since my desert is not equal to it, is to the honour of yourself, who can behave no otherwise than well.'

wel connez. The usual idiom is *connen god*, 'to know how to behave, to have good sense'; for many examples see *M.E.D.* under *connen* 6 (c). Here *wel* apparently takes the place of *god*, with the same force.

1281 'The lady behaved as though she loved him greatly.' Napier preferred to retain MS. *a*, as a reduced form of *ho* 'she', though parallels do not seem to occur. But *lyk* requires a correlative. The idiom does not usually include *lyk*, but a conjunction is indispensable; cf. *let as* 1189, 1201, 2257, and the ON. idiom (the origin of the ME. one) *láta sem*. Here *lyk as* answers to OE. *gelíce swá*.

1283–5 If 1284 were taken, as it sometimes is, as part of the lady's thought, it would imply that she knew that Gawain was obliged to face the blow from the Green Knight. The story as presented has given her no opportunity to know this, so that it would be a serious flaw in the handling of the plot. Morris in his edition, followed by Gollancz, emended 1283: 'þaȝ ho were burde bryȝtest, þe burne . . .', which gives good sense; but it is hard to see how the MS. reading might have arisen from such an original. The punctuation in the text is an attempt, not very satisfactory, to preserve the manuscript and yet not spoil the suspense. 1283 is elliptical—' "Even if I were the most beautiful of ladies", the lady thought (still he would resist).' *Þe* at the beginning of 1284 demands a correlative, and this can only be *for (lur)*, etc.—'The less amorousness he brought with him because of the harm he was looking for without delay, the blow that was to strike him down, and had of necessity to be done.' For this use of *lode* 'journey' cf. Orm 3455: 'habbenn wiþþ himm o lade'.

1298 The syntax is loose; perhaps *And* at the beginning of the line should be emended to *Þat*: 'in whose person courtliness is so entirely embodied'.

1304 *fire* is probably for *firre* 'further': 'I shall kiss at your command, and more, as is the duty of a knight lest he displease you.'

1320 *barayne*. Cf. *Master of Game* iii: 'As of þe hyndes some bene bareyn, and some be þat bere calfes; of þise þat bene bareyn here sesoun bygynneþ whan þe sesoun of þe hert failleþ, and lasteþ to lenton.' See note on 1156–7.

1324 *querré*. Used here of the collection of killed deer. Originally it was the reward of offal given to the hounds, called *cuirée* because fed to them on a hide, as described in 1359. Twiti says: 'e les chiens serrunt rewardez del cool e de la bowaylles e de la faie, e il serra mangé sur le quir. E pur ceo est il apelee quyrreye' (157–9). Essentially the same is said in *Boke of St. Albans* sig. f iiij.

1325 *þe best*. The nobles and gentry made it a point of honour to be skilled in breaking up deer. So Tristram gained honour at the court of King Mark, and when the Duke of Calabria's daughter from her pavilion saw Ipomadon 'dight the venison' she 'thoght in hyr herte than That he was come of gentill men' (*Ipomadon* B. 409–10). The numerous other accounts of cutting up deer, in both romances and hunting treatises in French and English, all describe the anatomy of a stag. But here the animals are hinds, so that Gollancz's reference (his note on 1331) to the 'coddis' mentioned in *St. Albans* is not apposite. On this passage see J. D. Bruce, *Eng. Studien*, xxxii (1903), 23–36.

1328 *þe asay*. For a fuller account see *St. Albans* sig. f iij (Tilander 543 ff.). The position of the assay and the method of trial are described in *The Noble Arte*, pp. 133–4. This is said by Gascoigne to be a specifically English practice, not described in his French original: 'The chiefe huntsman (kneeling, if it be to a Prince) doth holde the Deare by the forefoote, whiles the Prince or chief cut a slit drawn alongst the brysket of the deare, somewhat lower than the brysket towards the belly. This is done to see the goodnesse of the flesh, and howe thicke it is.'

1329 'Two fingers (breadth of fat) they found in the poorest of them all.'

1330 ff. The *erber* is the gullet. Bruce quotes the *Jewell for Gentrie* (1614): '. . . begin first to make the arbor which is the conduit which leadeth into the stomacke, guts and bag, and must be made fast and close by a round knot'. So in *La Chace dou Cerf* (13th cent., ed. Tilander, 1960) 359–63:

> Et les espaules autresi
> Dois lever aprés, ce te di.
> La souzgorge aprés en levez,
> L'erbiere et le josier [windpipe] coupez
> Et l'erbiere dever nouer.

The gullet was evidently scraped (*schaued* 1331) free of the flesh adhering to it, and tied to prevent the escape of the contents of the stomach. It was not removed until after the carcase was skinned.

1333 *bowelez* is the form of the word in 1609. MS. *balez* is evidently a negligent repetition of the preceding *bale*. The form **baulez* previously suggested is unsuitable because, though *au/aw* varies with *ou/ow* in some English words (see p. 135) it is not a spelling for Fr. *ou* representing /u:/.

1334 'deftly, so as not to loosen the ligature of the knot'—that is, the knot securing the *erber* as in the quotations in the note on 1330. This use of *for* 'to prevent or guard against' is frequent. This interpretation, which best suits the narrative, and the emendation of *&* to *þe*, are due to Gollancz. For *lere* early editors read *bere*; Gollancz printed *lere* as an emendation, but this appears to be in fact the MS. reading. The word is well attested from the fourteenth century onwards; see *O.E.D.* under *lear*².

1336 *guttez.* This may mean some of the upper viscera, not the bowels; but it probably simply repeats what has been described before.

1337–8 Cf. *Noble Arte*, pp. 134–5: 'We vse some ceremonie in taking out the shoulder. . . . Then with his shoulder knyfe he cuts an hole betweene the legge and the brysket, and there puts in his knife, and looseneth the shoulder from the syde . . . vntill he haue quyte taken out the shoulder, and yet lefte the skynne of the syde fayre and whole.'

1342 *avanters.* Part of the numbles in the fore-part of the deer; cf. *St. Albans* sig. e vij^v:

>   Oon croke of the Nomblis lyth euermoore
>   Vnder the throote bolle of the beest be foore
>   That callid is auauncers.

1345 *Euenden.* As Gollancz remarks, *-den* can hardly be a true form of 'down', as *O.E.D.* takes it to be. Rather than emend it is better to accept Emerson's interpretation of the word as the past of *euenen* (*J.E.G.P.* xxi (1922), 386).

1347 *þat* is contrasted with the first *hit* (the carcase) in 1346, meaning what they have cut away from the carcase.

1355 *corbeles fee.* Cf. *Noble Arte*, p. 135: 'There is a litle gristle which is vpon the spoone of the brysket [i.e. at the end of the breast-bone] which we call the Rauens bone, bycause it is cast vp to the Crowes or Rauens whiche attende hunters'; also *St. Albans*, 'That is corbyns fee: at the deeth he will be.' It was thrown into the branches of a tree (*kest in a greue*), as the *Chace dou Cerf* says: 'L'os corbin mie n'obliés, Haut sur un arbre le metez.'

1358 *Vche freke for his fee.* Each man had some portion as his perquisite. The man who killed a deer marked it, and later claimed the hide as his fee. The man who 'undid' the deer had the left shoulder, and sometimes the head. The right shoulder went by custom to the forester, the neck to the hunters. The numbles, haunches, and sides belonged to the lord (*Master of Game, St. Albans*).

1362 *prys.* The call blown when the deer had been taken (OFr. *prise* 'capture'). Twiti says: 'Quant le cerf est pris vous devez corneer quatre mootz.' *The Master of Game* (xxxiv) says that the chief personage of the hunt should then blow four motes, wait for a short interval—less than half an Ave Maria—then blow four motes a little longer than the first four. Then all the rest would blow: 'Trut, trut, trororow, trororow', followed by four motes. They would continue blowing thus all the way home; cf. 1364.

1377 *to governs þe tayles* in this construction, not, as it might appear, the preceding *hym*, which would require the stress to be on the preposition (cf. 292). Cf. Chaucer, *Nun's Priest's Tale*, B. 4139 'I shal myself to herbes techen yow.'

 tayles. The tail was left on the carcase; cf. *St. Albans* sig. f iii:

> Then fleeth thessame wyse all that oder syde
> Bot let the tayll of the beest still ther oon byde.

1393–4 'It may be such [i.e. from such a source] that it is the better gain of the two, if you would tell me where you won this same wealth by your own abilities'—an oblique indication that the lord knew it was from his wife.

1396 'Since you have received what is due to you, you are not entitled to expect any more.' This is one of the numerous places in which the bob looks as if it were an afterthought, changing the original construction; cf. 338, 1074, 1553, 2135. MS. *trawe ȝe non oþer* would be a complete and idiomatic imperative sentence, just as *frayst me no more* in the previous line is. Interpretation of *frayst* as infin., with 1396 a parenthesis, is strained. For a similar though not identical inelegance at the bob see 2325–6.

1406 *Wat.* Emendation of MS. *þat* seems justified by the frequency of 'what' in phrases of this shape. The error must be due to mere negligence, for in the fourteenth century the OE. *wynn* had long ceased to be used and *w* did not resemble *þ*. Gollancz suggests that the scribe transposed the two halves of this line, for two alliterating sounds fall in the second half and only one in the first; but this may have been acceptable—there are many irregularities of alliteration in the poem.

1412 ff. There are similar descriptions of boar-hunting in other romances, notably *Avowynge of Arther* st. iii–xvii; *Garin le Loherain* (ed. P. Paris, ii (Paris, 1835), pp. 225–30; ed. J. E. Vallerie (Ann Arbor, 1947), §§ c–cii); the First Continuation of Chrétien's *Perceval*, 11975–12006; *Guy of Warwick* (fifteenth-century version, ed. J. Zupitza, E.E.T.S. E.S. xxv–vi (1875–6)) 6417–60.

1419 Cf. *Noble Arte*, p. 151: '[Bores] lie moste commonly in the strongest holdes of Thornes and thicke Bushes.'

1422 *rehayted.* The huntsman would call the names of the hounds that first gave tongue on the scent, and urge the others to come up. Cf. note on 1699–1700.

1427 *rocherez.* Mrs. Wright observed that in northern dialects *rocher* means 'a steep rocky bank', which gives good sense here (*Eng. Studien*, xxxvi (1906), 218). It appears to be distinguished in use from *rokk(e)*; see glossary.

1436 *blodhoundez.* These are the 'limers', larger hounds than the raches, led on a *liam* or leash to the place where they are to work. They are described by Gaston Phoebus (of whose *Livre de la Chace* the *Master of Game* is largely a translation) as large black-and-tan hounds of a build and shape of head resembling modern bloodhounds. The large 'rennyng hound' in *Master of Game* xiv, which is 'right good for þe wilde boor but not good for þe hert' is probably the same dog used in a pack. The use of the limer to find a boar is well described in *Garin le Loherain* (see note on 1412 ff.).

1438 *soȝt* is best taken as intrans., and *ouerþwert* as a prep. governing *seggez*: 'through the (line of) men'. For the action cf. 1589, and for the scene *Garin* (ed. Vallerie) 10326–8:

> Se gist li pors dedenz .i. grant rochier.
> Cant il entent l'abai du lïemier
> Encontrement s'est li senglers dreciez.

1440 The second half-line in the MS. lacks alliteration. Brett suggested supplying *sengler* 'boar that has left the herd' (*M.L.R.* viii (1913), 163), and Gollancz took this further, substituting *synglere* for *wiȝt*. But the sense is still not good, partly because *fro* (itself an emendation) must be given the extended meaning 'away from'. The construction calls for a verb instead of *wiȝt*, with *þat* a relative pronoun. The likeliest verb is *siȝe, seȝe,* 'fall' then 'go' (*O.E.D.* under *sye* v.¹), which occurs in 1879 and 1958, and has a weak past tense *sey(i)t* in *Dest. Troy* 2512, 3398, 6644. The substitution of *wiȝt* might have been due to a scribe's failure to recognize this word (perhaps *siȝet* in an earlier copy): in *Wars Alex.* 1388, 1481, and 2182 forms of *seȝe* in the Ashmole MS. are altered to *soght* in the Dublin MS. The phrase *for olde* means 'because of age' (so Gollancz), a common ME. idiom best known in Chaucer's *Knight's Tale*, A. 2142, 'col-blak for olde' (on which see Robinson's note and Mustanoja, *Syntax*, p. 381). The line then means, 'which had long since gone from the herd because of his age'. Cf. Twiti: 'quant il est de quatre annees il doit partyr hors de la soundre par age. Et quant il est party hors de la soundre qe il va soul, par cel encheson est il appele sengler.'

1442 *grymme.* This word can be pieced together from what remains in its place and the offset on the opposite page. Of *ful* the *f* is fairly clear. This and *sparred* 1444 are due to Menner, *M.L.N.* xli (1926), 398.

  gronyed. This word, applied to the boar's savage grunts, is from OFr. *grognir*, possibly blended with OE. *grunian.* This verb in ME. is confused with *grone* from OE. *grānian*; cf. *Master of Game* vi: 'And for no strooke ne for wounde þat men doon to hym [he] playnneth nat ne crieþ not, bot whan he renneth vpon þe men þen he manesseth strongly gronyng'; also *Avowynge of Arther* xii: 'So grisly he gronus', rhyming *stonis* 'stones'.

1446 *rechated.* Originally the recheat was used to call the hounds back from a false scent; later, as here, to call them to the hunters or to urge them on. Twiti gives different calls for different types of hunt. One is 'trout trout trourourout' twice, followed by 'trourourout' thrice (104–5).

1451 *mute.* A pack of hounds; in *St. Albans*, a list of terms for 'The Compaynys of beestys and fowlys', following the 'Boke of Huntyng', distinguishes a 'mute of houndes' and 'a kenell of Rachis'. (But since the same list includes such items as 'an vncredibilite of Cocoldis' and 'a Gagle of women'—and 'a worship of writeris'—it is not necessarily to be strictly respected.) Of the number that made a *mute* the French treatise *Roy Modus* says: 'Muete de chiens est quant il y a douze chiens courans et un limier; et se mains en y a, elle n'est pas dite muete, et se plus en y a, miex vaut' (ed. G. Tilander, S.A.T.F. (1932), ch. 3, 77–80).

1452 *of* is partitive, 'some of'.

1456 *scheldez.* Cf. *Master of Game* vi: 'þei [boars] han an hard skyn and stronge flessh, and specially vppon þe shuldire, that is called þe sheeld.'

1461 *braynwod.* A frequent compound from *William of Palerne* to the mid-fifteenth century; see *M.E.D.* under *brain* 4 (b) and *D.O.S.T.* for additional Scottish examples.

1463 The only alliteration in the second half-line falls on *on*, which led Emerson to take it as an adv., and interpret *lyte* as the pron.: 'few drew on' (*J.E.G.P.* xxi (1922)). But this gives less good sense and abnormal order—in such a construction *on* would immediately precede the verb; *on lyte* certainly occurs, as a phrase of related meaning, in 2303—though alliterating on *l*.

1467 *schafted.* *O.E.D.*, recording this as the unique occurrence, must be right in suggesting the meaning 'set'. This does not imply that the sun set at this point; it is a summary statement, filled in by the following passage at 1561 ff. An exactly similar anticipation of the end of the day appears in the deer-hunt, where 1176–7 'drof þat day wyth joy Thus to þe derk nyȝt' is followed at 1319 by the long account of the cutting up of the deer. A verb *schaft* must presumably have acquired the sense 'set' from a literal meaning such as 'send out long low beams'. See p. 131.

1493 *deuayed.* This reading of the manuscript, rather than *denayed*, is supported by *de vaye* (so written, with *v* not *u*) 1497—though the alliteration is different (Brett, *M.L.R.* x (1915), 194–5). These are the only examples of the word recorded in *M.E.D.*

1495 *mere* is here taken as a spelling of *mery*; cf. 1263 *þe myry mon*. But it might be *mere* 'beautiful, fair' from OE. *mǣre*; cf. *þis mai mere* 'this fair maid' rhyming with *chere* 'face' in *Annot and John* (*Harley Lyrics*, ed. Brook, no. 3), 9.

1508 ff. The general intention of these lines is clear enough, but the construction is inconsequent and no simple assumption of a lost line (as by Gollancz) will make it logical: 1512–19 are a digression in thought, but 1520 still does not simply resume the sentence broken off at 1511. There may be some corruption, but it is possible that the anacoluthon was intended to reproduce the occasional incoherence of colloquial language.

In 1512–13 the meaning is: 'to select from the whole code of knightly conduct, the thing most praised is the observance of true love, the learning of the knightly profession.' Both here and in 1541 *armes* must have this generalized sense, for the lore and practice of fighting are not in question; the point is that courtly love is the kind of scholarship to be expected of knights.

1514 'To describe the endeavour of true knights, it is the inscribed title and text of their deeds, how . . . .' The deeds of knights are compared to those in a book of romance: service of love is both its title and its text.

1526 *ȝonke þynk.* The unvoicing of the final consonant is characteristic of west-midland dialect: 'a young thing'. Cf. *rynk* 'ring' 1817, 1827.

1543 *or* here means 'than'. It is originally the same word as ME. *or, ar* 'before'; see *O.E.D.* under *or* adv.¹, C. 2, 3.

1550 *woȝe.* This has generally been taken as the noun descended from OE. *wōh* 'wrong', which is possible in view of *faut* and *euel* in the next two lines. But by this date *wogh* apparently meant 'harm, injury' rather than 'sin'; and the second half-line does not really fit any of these interpretations. *Woȝe* may equally well be the infin. 'woo', OE. *wōgian*; cf. *wowyng* 2361, with the common alternation of *ȝ* and *w*. This makes the following clause intelligible—she tried to induce him to make advances, though she did not really desire his love but tempted him with an ulterior motive.

1558 *ruþes hym.* The sense seems to be 'bestirs himself'. The verb occurs only here and *Purity* 895, 1208, where it is used of rousing people from sleep. The etymology is obscure; it may be ON. *hryðja* 'shake' (cf. MHG. *rütten*), traces of which are seen in ON. (*h*)*ryðja* 'toss' and 'clear out', a blend of more than one original word.

1561–5 'But the lord dashed over the countryside many a time, pursues his ferocious boar, that rushes over the slopes and bit asunder the backs of the best of his hounds where he stood at bay, till bowmen broke it [i.e. the bay] and made him move further out despite his resistance.'

1566 *felle* is for *fele* 'many' rather than 'cruel, deadly' (OFr. *fel*). For other such spellings see p. 137.

1573 ff. 'Of him then were wearied all the men so bold who stood about him, of harassing him from a distance, but none dared approach him because of the danger'; *irked* (impersonal) here has two constructions, first with *with hym* and then with the infin. *to nye.*

1581 *kachande* 'urging on'. OFr. *cach(i)er* and *chacier* were dialectal variants, both derived from Lat. **captiare* and meaning 'pursue, chase, hunt'. The sense 'catch, seize' of *cach* was developed in England through association with native *lacche*, and *chacier* was also adopted as *chase*. But in ME. the older sense of *cache*, 'urge on, drive', is often found as well; both appear in *Gawain* (see glossary).

1593 For the killing of a wild boar with a sword cf. Arthur in *Avowynge* *of Arther* xvi, after his spear is broken; he thrusts his sword in at the neck just as the lord does. In *Master of Game* Baillie-Grohman (pl. xlvii) illustrates swords with broad point, of *c.* 1500, for boar-hunting. He quotes Gaston Phoebus as saying that to kill a boar with the sword when the animal was not 'held' by hounds was 'a fairer thing and more noble' than to kill him with the spear.

1595 ʒedoun. For this colloquially assimilated form cf. *puddoun* 'put down' twice in a letter of Agnes Paston's of *c.* 1451 (Clarendon edn. (1958), no. 16). A similar form may lie behind *sweʒe doun* 1796. Napier emended to ʒed ouer, but this gives the wrong sense because 1599 shows that the boar remained in the water.

1603 *brachetes.* The etymologically correct form of the sg. is *brachet*. The pl. in French was *brachetz, brachez*; but when in late AN. *tz* or *z* became in sound simple *s* this form was taken to be pl. and a new sg. *brach* was formed—the usual type in this poem; see glossary.

1605 *wodcraftez.* Cf. *Master of Game* xxxiv (though of deer): 'If þe lord wol haue þe deer vndoon he þat he biddeþ, as biforun is saide, shuld vndo hym þe moost wodmanly and clenly þat he can; and wondre[þ] ʒe not þat y say woodmanly, for it is a poynt þat longeþ to a woodmannys craft; and þough it be wel sittyng to an hunter for to cun don it, neuer þe latter it longeþ moor to wodemannys craft þan to hunters.'

1607 Cf. *Avowynge of Arther* xvii: 'The hed of that hardy He sette on a stake.'

1610 *rewardez.* This is the correct technical term, as the hunting treatises show; e.g. *The Craft of Venery* (ed. Tilander), 120–4: 'When the borre is takyn, he schall be undo all hearid, and yf he be undo as it is ryʒt he schall have xxxii hasteletts. And ʒe schall ʒyve to youre houndez the bowels broyled with bred, and that is clepid reward, for it is not ete on non [h]ide [*MS.* side]; for as much as is eten on the [h]ide schall be callid quyrrye, and that other is called reward.'

1612 *hastlettez.* Etymologically this word means 'pieces of roast meat', but it came to be applied especially to edible entrails of the pig. From the use of *hatz out* this seems to be the sense here; but Twiti gave it a much wider application: 'Il y ad deus menuz hastiletz que serrount pris de les deus quisses dedeinz, pus yl y ad la teste, pus le coler, pus le espaules e les costez, pus les filetz, pus les haunches e le qoer e le pomoun e lez pestles e la eschine, que serra copee en quatre, e les gambouns. Et quant il est tut apparaillé, il avera xxxii hastiletz del sengler par dreit' (178–83). Cf. *Craft of Venery* in preceding note.

1613 *hem* must refer to the *cheldez*, the two sides of the carcase.

1623 MS. *laʒed* requires an excessively awkward parenthesis. The emendation has the further advantage that *myry* is treated in the normal way as adj.—it is not used adverbially elsewhere in this manuscript.

1634 *let lodly þerat*, 'expressed horror at it'. Gawain exclaimed at the ugly and dangerous appearance of the boar, admiring the lord's prowess in killing such an animal.

1647 *drowe* looks like a past tense, but from the sequence must be present: 'You will soon be rich if you do such business.' The rhyme, as *lawe* shows, must have been on /aw/; *knowe* is an alternative to *knawe*, and *drowe* has been so spelt to conform to it.

1648 *trestes alofte*. It is not necessary to insert *on* before *trestes*; *alofte* is a preposition, 'upon', postponed. Cf. *þeralofte* 569, and another example in *M.E.D.* (*O.E.D.* quotes first from 1509.)

1655 *coundutes of Krystmasse and carolez*. The OFr. *condut*, Med. Lat. *conductus*, was evidently in origin a motet sung while the priest was proceeding to the altar; but the word came to be applied to a part-song, and was associated with Christmas as early as *The Owl and the Nightingale* (481–3). On *carolez* see note on 43. But here they are apparently performed without dancing; for other examples of this see R. L. Greene, *Selection of English Carols*, pp. 28–30. The same collocation of 'coundythes and carolles' appears in *Parl. Thre Ages* 254.

1657 *oure*. This use of 'our' (as in 'our hero') is not noticed by *O.E.D.* until the seventeenth century.

1659 *wyth stille stollen countenaunce*, 'with looks of favour stealthily concealed'.

1660 *with hymseluen* must mean 'within himself, in his mind', not 'angry *at* himself'—for which he had no cause. So again 2301.

1661–3 The exact sense is doubtful, partly because the precise significance of two words, *nurne* and *towrast*, is uncertain. *Nurne* occurs five times in *Gawain*, and elsewhere only in *Purity* and *St. Erkenwald* (each three times). The contexts do not reveal a firm central meaning; several suggest 'say, mention', but at 1823 it must be essentially 'offer'. Here the antithesis of *nurne aȝaynez* and *nurture* requires the phrase to mean 're-fuse, repel' or the like. *Towrast* is likely to be past part. of a verb *towrest* (cf. *wrast* 1482), meaning 'twisted'; but its application is obscure—perhaps only 'against his inclination'.

1671 *to schulde*, 'had to go to', with common omission of infin. of verb of motion.

1680 'Now "third time turn out best" remember in the morning.' They were to exchange their day's gain for the third time next day, but for the present they may forget it and think only of entertainment. *Þrid tyme þrowe best* is a proverb quoted also in *Seven Sages* (Cotton–Rawlinson version, ed. K. Campbell (Boston, 1907)) 2062: 'Men sais þe thrid time thrawes best.' An approximate modern equivalent is 'third time pays for all'.

1699 ff. Descriptions of fox-hunting are rare in medieval romance. There is a brief one in Laȝamon (ed. Madden, 20839–70) introduced as a simile of Arthur's pursuit of Childric. But they have their place in the hunting treatises; e.g. _Master of Game_ viii and pl. x; _Craft of Venery_ 141-65. _St. Albans_, distinguishing 'beasts of venery' (hart, hare, boar, and wolf) from 'beasts of the chase' has (sig. e j):

> I shall yow tell which be beestys of enchace.
> Oon of theym is the Bucke, a nother is the Doo,
> The Fox and the Martron and the wilde Roo.

1699-1700 'Some hounds hit on the scent where the fox waited; they trail often from one side to another, in the practice of their wiles.' The hounds, finding that the fox's trail was involved by his doubling, often cast to one side to find a loop of it which would lead to a clear trail. That the subject of _traylez_ is the hounds and not the fox is indicated not only by _her_ 'their', but also by the description of fox-hunting in _The Craft of Venery_: 'Syre hunter, hou schalt thou seche the fox?' 'Y schall blow at the furst iij motez, and afturward y schall let myn houndez out of coupull, and y schall sey "so howʒe" iij tymes al in hyʒe, and sey nouʒt "sta houʒe", that is to sey "sta ho"; and afturward trayle aftur, "cha ha ha hoe". And afturward y schall seye "sa howʒe, hue, amys, so ho hue, ho syre, hoe!" And yf eny hounde trayle of hym and hathe a name as Richere or Bemounde, ʒe schull seye, "Oyez, a Bemounde! Dons, oyez, huy, a luy est, dount a luy est! avaunt a Bemound, avaunt! ho syre, ho ho ho!" and draw all ʒoure houndez to hym.' This use of _trail_ v. is not recorded in _O.E.D._ until 1590.

1700 MS. _a trayteres_ is probably corrupt, but might possibly represent OFr. _al tretour, a tretours_ (rare), 'in a detour'. For the emendation _a traueres_ cf. _Purity_ 1473 'So trayled & tryfled a trauerce wer alle'.

1701 _kenet_. Cf. _Master of Game_ xiv: 'There ben also rennyng houndes some lasse and some moor. And þe lasse byn clepid kenettis, and þes houndes rennen wel to al maner game, and þei serven for al game. Men clepin hem heirers [i.e. harriers].'

1703-4 The reference of the prons. _his_ and _he_ is uncertain. It seems better to take them as meaning the fox, so that all the pronouns from 1703 to the end of the stanza have the same reference; but good sense can be made also by taking the first two to mean the kennet, with the change of reference at the semicolon in 1704. See Savage, _M.L.N._ xliv (1929), 249-50.

1709 _spenne_. See note on 1074.

1710 _strothe_. From place-name evidence this is seen to mean 'a piece of marshy land overgrown with brushwood'. See Smith, _Elements_ ii, under _storð_ and _strōd_; Ekwall, _Concise Oxford Dict. of English Place-Names_ (4th edn., 1960), p. 451; _Pearl_, ed. Gordon, note on 115.

1714 _graye_. Apparently greyhounds (though these are not etymologically 'grey'—see _O.E.D._), which were leashed in threes (Savage, _P.M.L.A._ xlvi (1931), 175).

1719 ff. Cf. *Master of Game* viii: 'The huntynge for þe foxe is faire for þe good crie of þe houndis þat folowen hym so nye and wiþ so good a wille. Alway þei sente of hym for he fleþ by þik spoies [thickets], and also for he stinkeþ euermore'; and similarly *Noble Arte* ch. 67.

list vpon lif. MS. *lif vpon list* will hardly yield sense, and the transposition is particularly easy owing to the similarity of *s* and *f*; for other apparent instances of this scribal weakness see note on 210. Though in this phrase the usual form of the noun is *lyue*, the uninflected *lyf* occurs after other prepositions.

1726 *titleres.* These are the hounds kept at hunting stations or relays to be slipped as the fox ran past. *Title*, a variant of OFr. *ti(l)tre*, is defined in Godefroy's *Dictionnaire*: 'relai placé au milieu d'un bois, où l'on pose les chiens pour qu'ils puissent mieux poursuivre la bête au moment où elle passe'. Tilander (*Essais*, p. 104) quotes Deschamps (*Œuvres*, iv (S.A.T.F., 1884), 320):

> De courre aux chiens n'ay nulle joye
> D'estre au title est nommez musart,

and Cotgrave's *Dictionary* (1611) under *tiltre*: 'a brace of dogs layed in a place to be let slip at a Deere as he passeth by'.

1729 *lad hem bi lagmon.* The only known parallel is 'Hit [*sc.* lust] ledys ȝou be lagmon' in the fifteenth-century Shropshire poet Audelay (ed. E. K. Whiting, E.E.T.S. 184 (1931), p. 232, l. 114). *Lagman* was used in western dialects for the last of a line of reapers. The picture intended is evidently of the lord and his company strung out after the fox—'at his heels'. See Menner, *P.Q.* x (1931), 163–8.

1730 *myd-ouer-vnder.* O.E.D. quotes only two examples of this compound, one translating Lat. *meridiem*. But *undern* had a wide range of application: in *Pearl* 513 it means the third hour (Matt. xx), but it was also used in the fourteenth and fifteenth centuries for midday. *Over* in this compound must mean 'after'. *Midovernoon* occurs several times in ME. meaning 'the middle of the afternoon', and that would be the best sense here, fitting the poet's treatment of the other hunts as well as this one. That it must have been afternoon before the fox was caught appears from 1922. There is no ceremony this time: the fox is quickly skinned and the party makes for home because night is approaching.

1733 The use of *luf* is difficult to reconcile with the lady's true motive—she was Gawain's 'enmy kene' (2406). Perhaps the author meant to mislead hearers unfamiliar with the story.

1738 This line has probably suffered in transmission; the position of *goud* after its noun is pointlessly abnormal and metrically awkward. Gollancz's suggestion that *hwez* is a distortion of a word from OE. *húfe* 'head-covering' is attractive, but it would involve a greater change of form than he allows and is not in fact supported by the passage in *Purity* which he adduces.

1739 *tressour*. This word is applied to various types of band or ribbon confining the hair, but here is evidently a net or fret having jewels set at the intersections; see the illustration in the frontispiece. A lady in *Awntyrs off Arthure* 369 has a similar headdress: 'Her fax in fyne perré was fretted in folde', and the lady Mildore in *Sir Degrevant* 651–2: 'With topyes [i.e. topazes] [hur] trechoure Ouertrased that tyde' (on which see Casson's note in his edn.). Though this kind of head-dress was, as Madden observed, characteristic of the reigns of Richard II and Henry IV, it was long in use and in French the word is much earlier; so in *Romaunt of the Rose* 568–9,

> And with a riche gold tresour
> Hir heed was tressed queyntly,

the original has *treceor*.

1743 *wayuez vp*. See note on 1032.

1750 'Sunk in the deep torpor of dreams that noble knight was muttering like a man troubled by many grievous thoughts of how . . .'.

1752 An infin. dependent on *schulde* has obviously been omitted by the copyist; *dele hym* is supplied on the analogy of 2418. *þat day* refers forward to the *when*-clause in the next line.

1755 Some editors keep the manuscript reading, but it is unsatisfactory because unless *þat comly* refers to the lady there is nothing for Gawain to answer. It would be easy for *com* to be dropped after *comly*.

1768–9 The syntax is inconsequent and the metre of 1769 irregular. Even if *stod* is taken as subjunctive—whether a development or a scribal alteration of *stode* 'would have stood'—the tense sequence fails because *mynne* can only be present subj. Gollancz emends to *con mynne*, making both verbs indicative. The thought is livelier, even if the grammar is unorthodox, if *stod* is taken as indic. but *mynne* kept as subj.—'There *was* in fact great danger, if Mary should not take care of her knight.' Hulbert and Knott (*M.L.N.* xxx (1915), 107) reject the interpretation of MS. *mare* as a form of 'Mary', largely on the ground that 'the interference of the Virgin would spoil the whole crucial part of the test, and seems inconceivable from such an artist as our poet'. The point is well made; but their own interpretation requires too much straining of language to be acceptable.

1782 *lemman*. Though there are exceptions, this word was generally already derogatory; cf. Chaucer's *Manciple's Tale*, H. 217–20:

> the gentile, in estaat above,
> She shal be cleped his lady, as in love;
> And for that oother is a povre womman,
> She shal be cleped his wenche or his lemman.

1786 *for alle þe lufez vpon lyue*. The lady refers to the practice of swearing by God's love, Christ's love, etc., and includes all these oaths in one—

'for all the loves there are, do not conceal the truth'. The expression occurs in OFr.; e.g. *Perlesvaus* (ed. Nitze) 423: 'Je vos requier seur totes amors.'

1811 'Every man must act according to his circumstances—do not resent it or be pained by it.'

1814 *þat lufsum vnder lyne.* 'That lovely one under linen' is a kind of kenning for 'that lovely lady'. There were many such conventional phrases describing persons as 'fair under garment'. This same one occurs in *Sir Tristrem* 1202, 2816; *Eger and Grime* (in the Percy Folio MS., ed. J. W. Hales and F. J. Furnivall (London, 1867)) 251; and, applied to lords, in *Emaré* 864. Some of the parallel phrases are: 'worthy under wede', 'semely under serke', *Emaré* 250, 501; 'geynest under gore', 'brihtest under bys', *Harley Lyrics* (ed. Brook) 4. 37, 5. 38; 'comelye under kell', *The Green Knight* (Percy Folio) 255.

1832–3 *schaped* is best derived from *chape*, a metal mount or trimming. *M.E.D.* quotes some examples of the noun spelt *schape*, and cf. *schere* for *chere* 334. The adj. appears in Chaucer, *Canterbury Tales, Prol.* 366: 'Hir knyves were chaped noght with bras, But al with silver.' For *brayden* used of gold cf. especially *Purity* 1481 'brayden of golde', and for *beten* of gold applied to fabric *Beues of Hamtoun* (ed. E. Kölbing, E.E.T.S. E.S. xlvi (1885)) 1159: 'þe broider is of tuli selk, Beten abouten wiþ rede gold.'

1836 *nay* 'said . . . not' is the past tense of *nie*, unrecorded in the present, but from the stressed stem *ni-* of OFr. *neier*. The past is formed on the analogy of *lie/lay*. It occurs again in *Purity* 805: 'And þay nay þat þay nolde neȝ no howsez' (Napier). Elsewhere the verb is *nay*, past *nayed* (see *O.E.D.*).

1853 *haþel vnder heuen.* Cf. OE. 'hæleð under heofonum', as *Beowulf* 52, *Solomon and Saturn* (ed. Menner (New York, 1941)) 60. Probably the ME. phrase descends from this; it occurs again in *Wars Alex.* 4937.

1859 *þulged.* Though this form occurs nowhere else, derivation from O.E. *ge-þyldgian* (so *O.E.D.*, but with reserve) is like that of *mynged* 1422 from *myndgian*. *Ming* is quite common, and rhymes with *sing* etc.; its *-ng* must therefore represent /ŋg/. For the development see d'Ardenne, *Iuliene*, glossary under *studgi* and p. 167.

1862 *disceuer.* The spelling with *c* before *e* may suggest that the word could be 'dissever' rather than 'discover'. But 'dissever' would have to be followed by *from*, and there are several other records of *disceuer* 'discover' in ME. (*M.E.D.* under *discoveren*); this gives better sense here. It is noteworthy that the lady does not impose the condition of secrecy until Gawain has accepted the girdle.

1878 *lyste.* So read by J. A. Burrow (*Reading*, p. 105) instead of *lyfte* of earlier editors. But, though Knott remarked in discussing 1719 that MS. *ft* and *st* are indistinguishable (*M.L.N.* xxx (1915), 102), this is not in fact so: they are usually quite distinct, *st* being ligatured but *ft* written separately (cf. e.g. *ft* twice in 369 with *st* twice in 391); and the present form is clearly *lyfte*. Nevertheless Burrow, comparing 'to hyre hys lyff' in Malory (*Works*, p. 896. 20) and also (privately) 'to hiere . . . thi lif' in Gower, *Confessio Amantis* iv. 1789, is right in saying that *lyste* gives the required sense, and the reading is justified as an emendation.

1881 *þe more and þe mynne*. 'The greater and the smaller, every one', a common alliterative tag in ME. It occurs, e.g., in *Piers Plowman* C. iv. 399; *York Mystery Plays* (ed. L. Toulmin-Smith (Oxford, 1885)) 41. 28; *Le Bone Florence of Rome* (ed. W. Viëtor (Marburg, 1893)) 549; *Emaré* 915; *Minor Poems of the Vernon MS.* (ed. Furnivall, E.E.T.S. 117 (1901)) 725. 7, 743. 99; *Liber Cure Cocorum* (ed. R. Morris (Phil. Soc., 1862)) 8. 18; *King Hart* (in *Maitland Folio MS.*, ed. W. A. Craigie, S.T.S. 1919) 68. It is accommodated to English from Scandinavian; cf. *Vǫluspá* i:

> Hljóðs biðk allar helgar kindir,
> Meiri ok minni mǫgu Heimdallar.

'For a hearing I pray all divine beings and the sons of Heimdall greater and lesser.' Also *Fornmanna sǫgur* vi. 250: 'eigi neytti hann matar meira né minna.'

1882 On this passage Gollancz remarks: 'Though the poet does not notice it, Gawain makes a sacrilegious confession.' This is unacceptable. A poet so concerned with Gawain's piety and attention to religious observances could not fail to 'notice' sacrilege. His insistence on the completeness of the confession and absolution—'schrof hym schyrly', 'sette hym so clene'—leaves no room for such an interpretation; nor would a man of Gawain's devotion, if he had been tempted by the fear of death to abuse the sacrament of confession, feel merrier than he ever had in his life. His joy is depicted as consequent on the absolution, which means that the absolution was valid. The poet evidently did not regard the retention of the girdle as one of Gawain's 'mysdedez, þe more and þe mynne', which required to be confessed.

1932 *godmon*. This is presumably to be understood as the compound meaning 'master of the house', as 1029 etc. (always divided in the manuscript). Though the alliteration here is on *m* (alone of all the occurrences), compounds often alliterate on the second element (see p. 151).

1941 *chepez*. This word does not alliterate, and moreover is plural though the verb is singular. It is evidently an error of the copyist, picked up from 1939. In this type of error the original need not have resembled the mistaken form; but it might have been *porchaz* or *porchez* 'gain', with *por-* abbreviated.

1946 The end of the first half-line is with *þro*, which should therefore be construed with *þryʒt*, not with *þre cosses*: 'such precious things as you have pressed warmly upon me here, such three kisses so good'.

1962 *selly*. MS. *sellyly*; there are adverbs in the text ending in *-lyly*, but an adjective could not do so. Cf. similar dittography in 2390. The lack of an alliterating *s* in the second half-line no doubt implies corruption.

1964 'I will give you myself for one of your men.' Here ȝef is used for the sake of alliteration though the usual forms of the verb 'give' in these poems have g-. The same variation for alliterative convenience is found in *Wars Alex.*; see Skeat's glossary. But the sentence is hardly idiomatic, and is probably corrupt in some way.

1975 'Gawain thanked the lord.'

1979 The elaborate leave-taking was required by good breeding. The attention given to manners is characteristic of French romance; cf. the leave-taking of Perceval in Gerbert de Montreuil's continuation of Chrétien's *Perceval* (ed. M. Williams (Paris, 1922)) 1159–85.

1999 *þe day dryuez to þe derk.* Not 'the day passes on to darkness', for it is the passing of night that is in question. *Day* here means the dawn, and *dryuez to* means 'makes way towards, against'; cf. 222. So 'Daylight comes up on the darkness.'

2004 *wapped.* Onions noted a similar use of this word in Lancashire records: *Liverpool Town Books* (ed. J. A. Twemlow (Liverpool, 1918)), i. 292: 'the snowe dryvyng and wappyng to and froe'.

2008 'By every cock that crowed he was reminded of the appointed hour.'

2018 'The rings of his rich coat of mail cleansed of rust'. Chain armour was rolled (*rokked*) to rub the rust off; cf. Laȝamon (ed. Madden) 22287 'heo ruokeden burnen', for which the later MS. has 'hii rollede wepne'.

2022 *wypped*, 'wiped, polished'. For the spelling with double *p* see p. 137; there was evidently a sporadic shortening of the vowel in this word, for *-pp-* is written in other northerly texts also; e.g. *Cursor Mundi* 17683.

2023 'The handsomest (from here) to Greece'; cf. *Pearl* 231 'No gladder gome heþen into Grece.'

2027 *Enmurned.* This reading leaves the first half-line with only one alliterating word, and Gollancz may be right in regarding it as a scribal substitute for *enuirened* or the like; but there are numerous lines with single alliteration, and since adequate sense is given by *ennurned* it is here retained.

2035 *þat gay wel bisemed* is best understood as a relative clause: 'which well suited that handsome man'; cf. note on 955–6.

It is noteworthy (but not always noticed) that Gawain wears the girdle over his surcoat, in full view, not concealed under his armour as might have been expected. He had taken leave of his host the night before, and knew he would not meet him again before leaving.

2072 'He praised the porter, who was kneeling before the prince [sc. Gawain].'

2073 *gef hym God* has been understood (in previous edns. of this book and in *M.E.D.* under *God* 8 (b)) as 'commended him to God'. But this requires a harsh change of construction at *goud day*, which must be the direct object of *gef*. The line seems rather to be an elliptical and distorted, perhaps idiomatic, way of saying 'gave him (as farewell) *good day* and *God save you*'—i.e. *God* is direct object as well as *goud day*. Cf. *Cursor Mundi* 8068: 'And gaf þam Godd and als god dai' (J. A. Burrow). *Good day* at this date commonly meant 'goodbye'.

2079 'The clouds were high, but it was threatening under them.' Gollancz treats *vp-halt* as past part. of *vp-halde(n)*; but no other case of such a weak form appears to be known—*halden* or *holden* is the regular participle in all the poems of this manuscript. *Halt* must be a syncopated form of *halet*, so 'drawn up'.

2092 *note*, 'noted', originally the past part. of the ME. verb from OFr. *noter*. Weak verbs with stems ending in a dental frequently do not take an inflexional ending in the past part. in this dialect.

2102 *Hestor*. This form at first sight looks like a mistake for Hector, and it is doubtless the Trojan Hector who is intended. But Hestor appears to be a genuine variant, occurring in several French romances including the Vulgate *Merlin* and the *Suite du Merlin*.

2111 *may þe knyʒt rede*, 'if the knight may have his will'. But this is inconsistent with the complete certainty with which the guide predicts Gawain's death, and Sisam's interpretation, '(I) may þe, knyʒt, rede', 'I can advise you, sir knight', has much to commend it (*Fourteenth Century Verse and Prose*, v. 43 n.).

2123 *As help me . . . þe halydam*. This probably originated as a formula in serious oaths taken on some specific holy thing, especially a relic; this would account for *þe*. The article appears in OE. ('on þam haligdome swerian'), but not always; cf. *Peterborough Chron.* 1131: 'aðes swor on halidom'. The closest parallel is More, *A Dyaloge* (1529; *Works*, 1557, p. 237): 'My lordes all, as helpe me God and halidome, maister doctour here sayd. . . .' Here, though these are the words of a witness, the oath is casual.

2136–7 'Though he is a grim fellow to deal with, and armed with a club'. So savage a character might be expected to carry a club; cf. the description of the black man on the mound, armed with a club, in 'The Lady of the Fountain' (*Mabinogion*, tr. Jones and Jones, p. 158). There may be a suggestion that a club would be a suitable weapon for the Green Knight in 384, 'wyth what weppen so þou wylt'.

2167 'The clouds seemed to him to be grazed by the crags.'

2173 *forʒ*. This has been taken (as by *M.E.D.* under *fors*) as the first appearance in English of *force* 'waterfall'. But though *ʒ* is often used for apparently voiceless *-s* in unstressed final syllables, as *berdlez* 280, it is not elsewhere used with this value after *r* in a stressed syllable; cf. *arʒe*, *berʒ(e)*, *burʒ(e)*, *sorʒe*, *þurʒ(e)*. The word is therefore presumably OE. *furh* 'furrow', used in the sense of watercourse. This also suits the scene better than 'waterfall', which would not be in place at the bottom of a valley. (See Emerson, *J.E.G.P.* xxi (1922), 405 and xxvi (1927), 257.)

2177 *his riche.* Apparently 'his noble [steed]'. The line is awkward and may contain a corruption of something like *and hit riched to* 'drew it to'; cf. *Dest. Troy* 2370:

> And raght to my reyne, richet o lenght,
> Bound vp my blonke to a bogh euyn.

Also 1231 'ricchis his reynys', 6693 'Ector richit his reyne'.

2195 *þat chekke hit bytyde,* 'which destruction befall'; *þat . . . hit* is equivalent to 'which'. *Chekke* originally referred to the checkmate at chess.

2198 *roffe.* The correct reading is due to Gollancz.

2199 The existing analogous romances leave out the whetting, except in the account of Lancelot's adventures in *Perlesvaus* where there is a bare mention of it.

2205 ff. *þat gere,* etc. Perhaps: 'That contrivance, as I believe, is prepared in honour of meeting me as a knight in customary form.' The passage seems to be corrupt, and there are several matters of doubt: *at þe reuerence* is a common phrase, but normally is followed by *of* or preceded by a genitive; the reference and construction of *renk* are not clear; *bi rote* does not occur elsewhere in a sense that seems appropriate here.

2208 *Let God worche.* The common idiom was 'Let God (i)worth', e.g. in Langland and Trevisa; see *O.E.D.* under *worth* v.[1] B. 4 and *iworth* 6. But 'work' is also adequately evidenced (*O.E.D.* under *work* v. 21. b), especially *Hali Meiðhad* (ed. A. F. Colborn (Copenhagen, 1940)) 120–1: 'Ne þearf þu bute wilnin. & leote godd wurchen. haue trust on his help.' The manuscript here has clearly *c* not *t*. So: 'Let God do his will. (To say) "Alas!" helps me not a bit; though I lose my life no noise shall make me afraid.'

2216 *Oþer now oþer neuer.* Probably already a set phrase. *O.E.D.* quotes it first from 1560, but Sir John Paston used it in 1475.

2219 'Yet he went on with the noise urgently for a time, and turned away (to continue) with his whetting before he would come down.'

2223 *denez ax.* Properly not the same weapon as the guisarm, as the Green Knight's axe is called in 288 (see note) and 2265. The Danish axe was the ordinary long-bladed battle-axe, which had no spike as the guisarm had. It was so called, and in OFr. *hache danoise*, because it was a favourite weapon of the Vikings who raided England and France.

þe dynt with to ʒelde, 'to return the blow with'—the usual ME. order in such constructions.

2226 *bi þat lace,* '(measured) by that thong'; cf. 217–20.

2230 The Green Knight used the handle of the axe as a staff as he walked; *stele* is 'shaft' as in 214 (see note). *Stalked* evidently means 'stalked (with long strides)', though this sense is not otherwise found until the sixteenth century (*O.E.D.*); the early meaning was 'go stealthily', and the change may be due to association with the noun *stalk*.

2274–6 These lines are evidently closely dependent on the source. They are very near even to the reproof given to Lancelot in the similar episode in *Perlesvaus* (see p. xvii): 'Sire chevalier, aussi ne fist mie mon frere que vos oceïstes, ainz tint le chef et le col tout coi. Autresi vos covient il faire.'

2275 *in kyngez hous Arthor*. In ME., when two nouns in apposition are in the genitive case usually only the first of them takes the inflexional ending. It may be either the title, as here, or the name, as *Iulienes heast þe empereur* in *Ancrene Wisse* (*Early Middle English Verse and Prose* (Oxford, 1966), XVIII. 65).

2290 *rynez*. Since *n* and *u* are indistinguishable in the manuscript, it is uncertain whether this verb is *ryne* 'touch' (OE. *hrīnan*) or *ryue* 'cleave' (ON. *rífa*) as in 1341. The latter has been supported by reference to *roue* 2346; but the position there is different, after the blow which has indeed cut Gawain, and should not determine the choice here. The sense of *ryne* is more appropriate to the context.

2297 *hode*. Gollancz is evidently right in taking this not as the headgear 'hood' (OE. *hōd*), as earlier editors understood it, but as the 'order' of knighthood (OE. *hād*). A hood is not high, nor is there any word of Arthur's having given one to Gawain. Accordingly *halde*, and *kepe* 2298, are not imperatives but 3 sg. subjunctives, and *keuer* means 'manage, succeed' as in 804: 'Let the exalted order that Arthur conferred on you now preserve you, and save your neck at this stroke, if it can.'

2316 *spenne-fote*. *O.E.D.* has 'with feet close together', deriving *spenne* from ON. *spenna* v., 'clasp'; see *spenet* and *spenne* in glossary, and note on 1074. J. H. Smith (*M.L.N.* xlix (1934), 462–3) shows that jumping with the feet together is standard practice in the broad jump, and cites French parallels with *ioint les piez* and the like. Yet similar words meaning 'kick' exist in continental Germanic languages—MDu. *spinnevoeten*, LG. *spinne-foten*, mod. Frisian *spinfoetsje*—which it would seem can hardly be unconnected, though no relation is apparent.

2318 Gawain had his shield slung on his back, and by a movement of his shoulders swung it under his arm to the front.

2326 *foo*, 'fiercely', is parallel with *ȝederly* above.

2332 *schore*. Used in the general sense 'ground', as *stone* in the similar line 2230.

2345–6 'I threatened you in sport with a single feinted blow, and did not rend you with a gash—with justice I made you the offer ...' (R. W. King, *R.E.S.* v (1929), 451).

2361 *þe wowyng of my wyf.* 'Subjective' gen.: 'my wife's wooing of you'.

2367 *wylyde werke.* *O.E.D.* under *wild* 7.b takes *wylyde* as a spelling of 'wild', in the frequent sense 'licentious'; see further E. S. Olszewska, *N. & Q.* ccxi (1966), 451–2. But 'wild' is nowhere else so spelt, and the proposed sense would give a weak anticlimax with *wowyng*. *Wylyde* seems rather to be an adj. formed on *wile* 'skill' with the common suffix *-ede*. *Werke* is best understood by comparison with 1817 'red golde werkez', 2026 'þe clere werkez', and especially 2432 'þe wlonk werkkez', which is applied to the girdle in a somewhat similar way. So: 'That was not for any excellent piece of workmanship, or for love-making either.'

2374 *couetyse.* The word seems inappropriate. But the definition of avarice, in medieval treatises on the sins, was very wide; e.g. *Ancrene Wisse* (ed. Tolkien) f. 56b. 3–5: 'Edhalden cwide, fundles, oðer lane, oðer þerwið mis-fearen, nis hit spece of ȝisceunge [avarice] & anes cunnes þeofðe?' Though the girdle had been given to Gawain, so that he had certainly not wrongfully acquired it, his failure to exchange it for the Green Knight's winnings might be held to be a branch of 'couetyse'.

2387 'Let me win your good will.'

2399 Owing to the difficulty of rendering *at* in this line Sisam (*Fourteenth-Century Verse and Prose*, v. 331 and note) emends to '*at* the grene chapel *of*'. But this does not give very good sense, for the 'token' should surely be *of* the adventure rather than the knights. It is possible to understand the manuscript thus: 'This will be an excellent token of the adventure of the Green Chapel in the dwellings (*or* company) of chivalrous knights.' This use of *at* is common with the names or designations of particular persons, but difficult to parallel with more general terms; cf. Malory, *Works*, 1136. 3–5: 'hit shall be well undirstonde, bothe at the kynge and the quene and with all men of worship.' See *M.E.D.* under *at* 2b.

2416–19 This list of names is a homiletic commonplace; see R. W. King, *M.L.R.* xxix (1934), 435–6.

2444 *þat oþer.* To provide alliteration in the second half-line this must be pronounced *þe toþer*; contrast 110 and 2412.

2445 *Bertilak de Hautdesert.* This reading of the name is due to Gollancz. Early editors printed *Bernlak*, but Hulbert observed that it was either *Bertilak* or *Bercilak*, and preferred the latter (*Manly Anniversary Studies*, p. 12). Gollancz thought the doubtful letter was *t* rather than *c*, and he appears to be right. This form of the name fits the other occurrences of what is apparently the same name, *Bertolais* in the OFr. Vulgate cycle (*Bertolais* is nom.; the acc. was *Bertolai*, earlier *-lac*) and *Bertelak* in the ME. translation of *Merlin* (ed. H. B. Wheatley, E.E.T.S. 10, 21 (2nd edn., 1875, 1877)). None of the knights bearing the name (which is apparently of Celtic origin) can be identified with the Green Knight. The name *Hautdesert* has been held to refer to the Green Chapel, and to mean 'high hermitage' because *disert* in Celtic languages had acquired the special sense 'hermitage'. But a specialized Celtic meaning is very unlikely to appear in so characteristically French a compound as *Haut-desert*. *Desert* is an extremely common element in French place-names, and it always means 'deserted or solitary place, waste land'; see A. Dauzat and Ch. Rostaing, *Dictionnaire étymologique des noms de lieux en France* (1963). Further, since the 'chapel' was at the bottom of a valley it could not well be called 'high', and it was not a hermitage. The name evidently applies to the castle, from which, rather than from the obscure mound, the lord would take his name.

2446 The sentence beginning here is probably incompletely presented by the manuscript; but some kind of sense can be made of it by assuming the long parenthesis marked off by the dashes in 2448–55.

2448 *Merlyn.* The famous wizard of Arthur's court. He fell in love with Morgan, who induced him to teach her his magic arts (see next note). Merlin is first mentioned by Geoffrey of Monmouth in the *Prophetiae Merlini* incorporated in his *Historia Regum Britanniae* (c. 1135), and in the poem *Vita Merlini* (Faral, iii. 306–52). In medieval Welsh a number of poems of prophetic content are ascribed to Myrddin, who is represented as living in sixth-century Britain. This tradition was taken up by Geoffrey and grafted on to Nennius's account of a youth named Ambrosius who prophesied to Vortigern. He calls him Merlinus Ambrosius, associates him with Arthur, and makes him a wizard. For summaries and references see *Arthurian Literature*, and R. Bromwich, *Trioedd*, pp. 469–74.

2452 *Morgne þe goddes.* Morgan is called 'goddess' by Giraldus Cambrensis in *Speculum Ecclesiæ*, dist. ii, cap. 9: 'Propter hoc enim fabulosi Britones et eorum cantores fingere solebant quod *dea* quædam phantastica, scilicet et Morganis dicta, corpus Arthuri in insulam detulit Avalloniam ad ejus vulnera sanandum' (*Opera*, ed. J. S. Brewer, Rolls ser. iv (1873), p. 49). A Paris manuscript of the Vulgate *Lancelot*, not used by Sommer for his edition, records that she is called 'Morgain la déesse'; the passage is printed in Jonckbloet's *Roman van Lancelot* ii (1849), lxix: 'Il fu voirs que Morgains . . . sot moult d'enchantement et de charoies sor totes fames; et por la grant entente qu'ele i mist en lessa-ele et guerpi la covine des genz et conversoit et jor et nuit ès granz forez parfondes et fontainnes, si que maintes genz, dont il i avoit moult de foles par tot le païs, ne disoient mie que ce fust fame, mès il l'apeloient Morgain-la-déesse.' The term 'goddess' is consistent with Geoffrey of Monmouth's account in the *Vita Merlini* of *Morgen*, the chief of nine sisters who preside over the 'insula pomorum que fortunata vocatur' to which Arthur is brought to be healed after his last battle. (*Morgen* means 'sea-born'.) The derivation of Morgain from the Irish *Morrigan*, which has often been suggested, is evidently unacceptable; see especially J. Vendryes, *Études Celtiques*, vi (1953–4), 365. See R. Bromwich, *Trioedd*, pp. 461–3; and for another view Loomis, 'Morgain la Fée and the Celtic goddesses', *Speculum* xx (1945), 183–203, repr. in *Wales*, pp. 105–30.

2460 The cause of Morgan's hatred of Guenever is given in the Vulgate *Lancelot* and in *Le Livre d'Artus* (ed. Sommer, iv. 124, vii. 135). Morgan had an intrigue with a knight named Guiomar, which was discovered and revealed by the queen. Morgan had to leave the court, and joined Merlin: 'tant chevalcha amont et aual quele troua Merlin que elle amoit par amors. Et il li moustra quanque elle sauoit dencantement.' To annoy Guenever and the knights of the Round Table she built a chapel in a valley, from which no one who entered could escape who had been faithless in love. Several of Arthur's knights were imprisoned, but were released by Lancelot. It is perhaps the story of Morgan's chapel that suggested the introduction of Morgan into this poem. Madden pointed out that a passage in the *Prophecies of Merlin* shows her as a figure similar to that in 951 ff.: 'Ha, dame,' fait Morgain, 'vous m'avez honnye, car l'on cuidoit que je fusse de jeune aage, et ilz ont veu ma chair nue et ridée, et mes mamelles pendans, et aussi la peau de mon ventre, dont la nouvelle sera comptée en maint lieu.' 'Morgain,' fait la Dame d'Avallon, 'je scay certainement que par maintes fois avez esté en vostre lict toute nue avec maint beau chevalier.' 'En nom Dieu,' fait Morgain, 'se je y ay esté, aussi me suys-je baignée, et oings tous mes membres, dont les chevaliers les troverent toutes fresches et dures.'

Morgan's aged appearance, while her half-brother Arthur is described as still a youth (86 ff.) is accounted for by a passage in the *Suite du Merlin* p. 166: 'Et sans faille elle fu bele damoisiele jusques a celui terme que elle commencha aprendre des enchantemens et des charroies; mais puis que li anemis fu dedens li mis, et elle fu aspiree et de luxure et de dyable, elle pierdi si otreement sa biauté que trop devint laide, ne puis ne fu nus qui a bele le tenist, s'il ne fu enchantés.'

2464 The story of Uther and Igern is first told by Geoffrey of Monmouth (*Historia* VIII. xix). Arthur's father is called Uther also in the earliest Welsh poems, in manuscripts of the end of the twelfth century.

2467 *þyn aunt*. Since the alliteration is vocalic, the scribe's division *þy naunt* evidently misrepresents the poet (Savage, *M.L.N.* lix (1944), 349).

2480 The antecedent of *þat* is *Wowen*.

2494 ff. It was usual for knights in Arthurian romances to relate their adventures to Arthur. In the *Suite du Merlin*, Merlin advises Arthur to make each knight swear before setting out on a quest that he will report it faithfully on his return.

2511 'For a man may hide his (spiritual) harm, but cannot unfasten (get rid of) it.' The scribe often makes mistakes in the number of minims (e.g. 629, 865, 1037), and the emendation is essential to sense. (See S. O. Andrew, *R.E.S.* vi (1930), 182; L. M. Perry, *M.L.R.* xxxii (1937), 80–81.) For a similar figurative use of *happe* v. see 655. *Vnhap* has usually been taken as a noun and *hit* as a verb—'unless misfortune may befall', i.e. 'without misfortune ensuing'—but apart from the awkwardness of the superfluous *ne*, and the abnormal use of *may* in such a function, this meaning does not suit the context. It is not the danger of ignoring the past, but the impossibility of doing so, that is Gawain's point.

2514 ff. This decision has sometimes been taken as an indication that the poem was composed with reference to some order of knighthood. Some orders had collars which were worn much as Gawain wore the lace (2485–6). The legend at the end of the poem *Hony soyt qui mal pence* is the motto of the order of the Garter, but neither that order nor any other, so far as is now known, wore a green sash. In *The Green Knight*, the later romance based on *Gawain*, the lace is white and is said to be the origin of the collar worn by the knights of the Bath. No adequate evidence has yet been found that a reference of this kind was intended in *Gawain*.

2523 *Brutus bokez*. This term might be applied to any chronicles or romances of British times, not necessarily devoted to the legendary history of Brutus. In the romance of *Arthour and Merlin* the French source is called 'þe Br(o)ut' (3486, 3675, etc.), though the story of Brutus was not told in it. In Welsh, *brud* is still used meaning generally 'chronicle'.

ADDITIONAL NOTE

1467 *schafted*. Mrs. U. Dronke draws attention to a related phrase in the last stanza of *Peblis to the Play* (printed in *The Maitland Folio Manuscript*, vol. i, ed. W. A. Craigie, S.T.S. II. 7 (1919), p. 183):

> Be þat the sone wes settand schaftis
> And neir done wes þe day . . . . .

APPENDIX

LANGUAGE

SPELLING AND SOUNDS

MOST of the spelling in this manuscript is characteristic of the late fourteenth century. In dealing with medieval spelling two general considerations are important:

(i) Though spelling was far from fixed many conventions were already established, and the letters or letter-groups cannot be treated as if they were modern phonetic symbols. One spelling may be used for what must have been more than one phoneme, and one phoneme may be represented by more than one spelling. The neglect by the scribe of this manuscript to observe a strict relation between spelling and sound can be seen in rhymes such as *Gawan: frayn* 487–9; *blowe: inno3e* 512–14; *3ede: leude* 1122–4 (cf. *lude* 133 etc.); *knyffe: bilyue* 2042–4.

(ii) Such unsystematic spellings need not arise only from partial interference by a scribe with an original that was regular. Autograph manuscripts often contain inconsistent spellings: even so relatively regular a text as the *Ayenbite of Inwyt* (B.M. MS. Arundel 57) has some variations. Such a practice as the present scribe's use of *qu* as well as *wh* for the descendant of OE. *hw* (the sound represented being simply /w/, as alliteration shows—see below) need by no means indicate that the scribe was more northerly than the author. The group *qu* may easily have come to serve merely as an alternative symbol for /w/ in the author's own spelling. The obviously related spelling *qw* was certainly so used in the fifteenth century, when, for example, Clement and William Paston the younger both used *qw* and *w* interchangeably, and William even spelt 'was' *qwas*.

VOWELS

Unstressed syllables

The value of final -*e* in this manuscript cannot be determined with confidence (except where it stands for etymological -*i* or OFr. -*é*). The scribe writes -*e* very often, sometimes even -*ee* as *eldee* 844, *trwee* 1274; and in many places it can be justified historically, e.g. in many nouns and adjectives ending in a vowel (or an inflexion containing a vowel) in OE. or OFr., as *erthe* 4, *grene* 150, *age* 54. But in many other places it is not etymologically correct, as *burȝe* 9, *burne* 73, *loude* 64, *laye* 30; and it is also very often omitted from forms where it could have been justified both etymologically and metrically, as *wroȝt* 3, *gray* 82, *say* 84. From these latter two groups it appears that the scribe treated -*e* as an optional feature of spelling, without grammatical or phonetic force.[1] A number of rhymes further show that a historical -*e* was not pronounced: *fayn* (adj. pl.) *840* : *Gawayn*; *payne* (infin.) *1042* : *Gawayn*; *graunte* (infin.) *1841* : *seruaunt*; *myȝt* (pa. t.) *201* : *lyȝt*.[2] On the other hand, the rhymes *sope* 415 : *to þe* and *wape* 2355 : *ta þe* demand pronunciation as two syllables. In view of the strength of the other evidence it seems most likely that these are conventional archaistic pronunciations and that in general -*e* was no longer sounded. But it may well have been used optionally in particular places—as for emphasis, or before a pause, or at the end of a line—which we cannot determine from the written page.

Etymological /i/ in final unstressed position is often written *e*, which is marked in the edited text with an acute accent: *bodé* 357, *meré* 153, *Maré* 1769. The vowel of unstressed syllables ending in a consonant is usually written *e*, but occasionally represented in other ways: *auenturus* 491, *etayn* 140, *lentoun* 502, and the group of French words discussed on p. 143. The -*us* ending is common in west-midland texts, but is so rare in this manuscript that it can have no local significance. The other cases look more like alterations of the ending than mere spelling confusion; see the note to 140.

Stressed syllables

The vowel symbols do not regularly distinguish length, except that historical /u:/ is represented by *ou/ow* as *toun*, *now*, whereas /u/ is spelt *u* (initially *v*), as *ful*, *purȝ*, *vp*, or *o*, mainly next to minim letters as *com* 347 beside *cum* 1073, but also elsewhere as *borȝ* 2, *bot* 30. The spelling *god* represents both 'God' and 'good', but in a few places 'good' is written *good* (129, 381) or *goud* (668, 702); the latter may indicate raising of the vowel, but it may be only a device to distinguish the tense /o:/ from the slack vowel in such words as *brode*, *home*. Other doubling of letters to show vowel length is sporadic, as *foo*, *fee*, *lee*. The letter *u* represents, in addition to /u/, a sound derived from French /y/, spelt *u*, in words like *duk*, *endured*, *pure*, and apparently a similar sound in some English words which had /y(:)/, spelt *y*, in West Saxon, as *burde*, *fust*, *lur*, as well as *bur* from ON. (In a few words *u* is used for the reflex of

---

[1] His indifference to this, and to other details of spelling, is well shown by his treatment of *Pearl* 865, which he copied twice: first as catchword on f. 50^b and then as the first line on f. 51. He wrote first *leste les þow leue my tale farā*; then *lestles þ^u leue my talle farande*.

[2] Further examples are given by M. Borroff, pp. 156–7.

earlier /i/: *hult* 1594, *wruxled* 2191, *rudelez* (from OFr.) 857.) But the reflex of OE. /y(:)/ is far more often represented by the letter *y*, sometimes in words spelt also with *u*, as *bylde* beside *bult*, *dynt* beside *dunt*, and also in others, as *fyre*, *gyld*, *kynde*, *kysse*; and occasionally by *e*, as *meryly* beside *muryly*. The scribe, or the author, cannot have intended words spelt in two ways to be pronounced differently except when rhyme required an alternative, and one or other of the forms is evidently conventional. Unrounding of the sound to /i(:)/ in some words is shown by rhymes, as *wynne* 15 : *perinne*, *pryde* 587 : *tyde*. Further, in some words *u* alternates with *w(e)*, as *drury* 1517, *drwry* 2449; *sute* 191, *swete* 180, 2518. Here the vowel derives from French *u*, as it does also in *grwe*, *remwe*, and *swez* 1562, but *u(e)* also alternates with *w(e)* to represent the reflex of OE. *ēow* in *truly*, *trw(e)ly*, and *crue*, *knwe* 2008; and *we* alternates with *ewe* in *nwe*, *newe*; *hwe*, *hewe* 'colour'; and *hewe*, *hwen* 'cut'. Moreover, *ewe* but not *we* is used for OE. *ēaw* and *ǣw*, as *schewe*, *lewed*. Though there are no rhymes between the reflexes of French *u* and OE. *ēow* it is likely that the sounds had fallen together in /iu/. But in view of such variations in the use of letters it is not possible to be sure of the meaning of *u* as the reflex of OE. *eo* in lengthening position in *burne*, *rurde*; cf. *boerne* for OE. *burne* 1570. Since *u* is used for the reflex of OE. *y* predominantly in the neighbourhood of labials and *r* in *burde*, etc., it is likely that it is intended to represent a rounded vowel, which could be favoured by this environment, and the same general considerations apply to these words; but it need not imply raising to the high front position.

The letter *y* is very frequent as an alternative to *i*, without distinction of length. A redundant *i* is occasionally added to it, as *iwyis* 264; in *niy3t* 929 this may imply lengthening—it is probably not a mere error, since it occurs in three other places in the manuscript (see Gordon, *Pearl*, 630 note). *Y* is doubled in *myyn* 1067; cf. *iisse* 732.

OE. *a* before a nasal consonant not in a lengthening group varies with *o* in some words, as *can* 340, *con* 230, even when presumably lengthened in an originally open syllable as *game* 365, 1314, *gomen* 273; *name* 400, *nome* 10; *schame* 2504, *schome* 2372. At 365 and 2504 the rhyme with (French) *blame*, and at 1314 with *dame*, shows that the vowel is unrounded. A few words always have *a*, as *schrank(e)* (four times), but in many *o* is regular: *mon*, *mony*, *blonk*, *ponk*, *wlonk*. (*Blonk* in fourteenth-century alliterative poems nearly always has *o* even in texts which otherwise have *a* before nasals, as *Wars Alex.*) Before nasals in lengthening groups there is some variation: *hande* 458, 1203 (rhyming *la3ande*—this pres. part. ending seldom has *o*, though there are some cases in *Dest. Troy*), but *honde* 206 etc. Before *-ng* the spelling is regularly *o*: *longe*, *song*, *stronge*; but the rhyme at 32–36 is with *tonge*, OE. *tunge*. Before other lengthening groups the usual spelling is *o* as *colde* (*coolde* 2474), *olde*, but *halde* strongly predominates over *holde*.

OE. and ON. *ā*, *á* are usually spelt *o*, and rhymes show rounding in *brode*, *lode* 967-9 : *Gode*; *lote* 639, 1917 : *cote*. But a few spellings with *a* also appear, equally confirmed by rhyme in *wape* 2355 : *scape*. In *hame* 1534 : *schame*, *game* and 2451 : *name*, *tame* the sound is not quite certain owing to the varying treatment of OE. *a* in this position (see the preceding paragraph).

No distinction is made in spelling between theoretically tense and slack *ē*. OE. *ǣ¹* (Anglian *ē*) rhymes on tense *ē* in *were* 320: *lere*; *slepes* 1686: *kepes*. OE. *ǣ²* before *n* rhymes on tense *ē* in *clene* 146: *grene*. Tense *ē* before *ȝ* is often spelt *e*, as *deȝe* 996, *heȝe* 281, *neȝ* 929, but raising to /iː/ is shown in *dyȝe* 2460, *flyȝe* 524, *hyghe*, *hyȝe* 137, 1138, and this is proved by the rhymes *syȝe* 83 : *discrye*, *yȝe* 228: *studie*.

The vowel shortened from OE. *ēa* and *ǣ²* is spelt *a* in *grattest* (vowel from OE. *grēattra), *hadet*, *walt* (from *welde*), *clanly*; shortening of *ǣ¹* is also *a* in *brad*.

OE. *ā* in combinations (with *w* or back *g*) which gave /aːw/ in early ME. is spelt variously *ow* and *aw*, as *knowen* 1272, *knawen* 348, but the rhyme of *knowe*, *drowe*, and *lawe* at 1643-7 shows that the *o* spelling conceals an unrounded pronunciation, /aːw/ having fallen in with /aw/ (*drowe* = OE. *dragen*); cf. *bawe* 435, 1564 (OE. *boga*), and *dawed* 1805 (from **dog-*). *Trawe*, *trawpe* show a similar development from OE. *ēow* with shift of stress (though *trwe*, *trwly*, etc. consistently differ).

In some words etymological /i/ is spelt *e*: *clenge* regularly (three times), *schemered* 772, *smeten* 1763, *steropes* 170. This appears to be a direct lowering of *i* which became common in the fifteenth century, and in some cases was favoured by a following nasal before another consonant or by a following *r*. Thus regular *renk* may also belong here, though its *e* may be from ON.; and *mery* 497, *meryly* 740, as well.

A few spellings show the late fourteenth-century change of *er* to *ar*: *start* regularly (five times), and perhaps *charre*(*s*), *marre*, *ȝarrande*.

CONSONANTS

The letters *ȝ* and *þ* are frequent.

ȝ represents:

(i) the voiced front spirant or semivowel /j/, mainly initially as *ȝe*, *ȝif*, *ȝonge*, also in *aȝayn*; *y* is strongly preferred in *yow*, *your*, *yowre*, but is rare elsewhere. After *ē*, *ȝ* presumably once expressed the terminal element of the diphthong arising from the vocalization of the consonant in words like *deȝe*; but if the raising of this vowel was regularly carried out the group *eȝ* would come to represent /iː/, as *yȝ* did in *yȝe* etc., as shown by the rhymes at 83, 228, 245, and notably *hyȝe*

2087: *by*, as well as by spellings such as *fayryȝe* 240. Medially and finally *gh* is an occasional alternative spelling: *negh(e)* 1054, 1836, *segh* 1632, *hyghe* 844.

(ii) the voiceless front fricative before *t*, mainly from OE. *-ht* but sometimes from ON. *-ğð*: *myȝt*, *riȝt*, *sleȝt*. This is the regular spelling of such words.

(iii) the sound /w/ derived from OE. and ON. back voiced fricative *g* (/ɣ/): *folȝe*, *saȝe*, *boȝed* 481, etc. The pronunciation /w/ is shown by frequent spelling of the sound with *w*, as *bawe-*, *lawe* (confirmed by rhyme 1643), sometimes beside spellings of the same word with *ȝ* as *drawen* 1233, *draȝez* 1031; by the use of *ȝ* for etymological *w*, as *broȝez* 305 compared with *browe* 2306; and by rhymes such as *innoȝe* 514: *blowe*. *gh* is sometimes used for the same sound, as *innoghe* 730, *loghe* 1373, *oghe* 1526, *roghe* 1608; cf. the rhyme in *Pearl* 612 of *inoghe* with *rescoghe*, which in *Gawain* is *rescowe* 2308.

(iv) the voiceless back fricative in words with OE. *-ht* after back vowels, or final *h*: *aȝt*, *oȝt*, *puȝt*; *flaȝ*, *þaȝ*; and probably *-hh-* in the parts of *laȝe*. *gh* is an occasional alternative, as *laght* 127.

The scribe's form of *z* is identical with that of *ȝ*. (This leads to a few difficulties of identification; see the note on *forȝ* 2173.) He uses *z* freely —though often in patches—as an alternative to final *-s* in nominal and verbal inflexions, as *brondez*, *settez*. Here it may represent the voiced consonant; but it cannot be proved to do so, for it occurs equally in the suffixes *-less* and *-ness* in which voicing is unlikely: *berdlez*, *hedlez*, *fautlez* 640 beside *fautles* 1761; *lipernez*. A peculiarity of this scribe is his use of *-tz* as the usual ending of the monosyllabic verbs *dotz*, *gotz*, *hatz*, *watz* (and *saytz*, *totz* in *Pearl*), beside occasional *-s* as *dos* 1308, *gos* 935, *was* 169; simple *-z* is not used in these words. This apparently derives from the Old French use of *z* and *tz* to represent the sound /ts/; e.g. the plural of *brachet* was *brachets*, spelt *brachez* or *brachetz*. In French this /ts/ was simplified to /s/ (generally in the thirteenth century, earlier in the north), so that *tz* could be used to represent this sound. (Cf. *fitz* and modern *fils*.) In *Zefirus* the sound must be /z/.

Þ is almost regularly used initially, except that *Th* appears at the beginning of 18 stanzas—e.g. lines 107, 232, 417—including the decorated capitals at 491, 619, 2259. Medially and finally *th* is a frequent alternative.

To represent the sound descended from OE. *hw-* the principal spelling is *wh*, occasionally *w* (*wyle* 60, *wich* 918, *were* 1459); but *qu* is also very frequent. It sometimes appears beside *wh* in the same line and even in the same word—*whyle*, *quyl* 1235; but in a few patches it is the prevailing or exclusive form; e.g. between 1186 and 1205 there are six words of this type and all are spelt *qu*. Such spellings, and others like them such as *quh* (which is mainly Scottish), *qw*, and *qh* are widespread in northerly areas as far south as Norfolk (see e.g. the English Place-Name Society volumes on Cumberland, Derbyshire, and Yorkshire (North, East, and West Ridings)), and appear even in London quite early in the fifteenth century. They must have arisen in dialects in which the sounds of OE. *hw* and *cw* (and French *qu*) had fallen together (cf. J. Wright, *English Dialect Grammar*, § 241), and in some poems, notably *Dest. Troy* and *Wars Alex.*, the reflexes of these two sounds alliterate with each other. But in *Gawain* they do not. OE. *hw* alliterates with *w*, as 224, 398, 1573, even when it is spelt *qu*, as 255, 257, 1186, 1227; and OE. *cw* and French *qu* alliterate either with /kw/ as 1150, 1324, 2109, or with /k/ as 469, 578, 975. Since *h* alliterates with vowels commonly, and voiceless with voiced sounds occasionally, it might be supposed that /hw/ could similarly alliterate with /w/. But if any distinction existed it is likely that there would be some lines alliterating throughout on /hw/, as there are on /h/; and there are none. In three places the convention is reversed and *wh* stands for *qu*—*whene* 'queen' 74, 2492, *whyssynes* 'cushions' 877. Related to the development of *hw* to *w* is that of *squ* to *sw*, confirmed by alliteration in *sware* 138 but spelt also in *swyerez* 824.

For the sound of OE. *sc*, /ʃ/, the regular spelling is *sch*. The French *ch* is represented by the same spelling in *schere* 334, and *cheldez* 1611 suggests that the two sounds had to some extent fallen together in the scribe's usage. Cf. also *schaped* 1832, *cheryche* 946, *Englych* 629.

For /v/, according to the usual ME. practice, *u* is normally used medially and *v* initially (as for the vowel *u* also); but *u* occasionally appears initially, as *uerayly* 161, *uyage* 535. Sometimes this sound is represented by *w*: *wowche* 1391, *schowen* 1454. This is a feature common in northern and Scottish spelling. *Awenture* 29 may be rather a spelling of the by-form *aunter*.

For the sound /k/ the distribution of *k* and *c* is approximately as in modern English (*k* before front vowels and *n*, *c* before back vowels, *l*, and *r*) but *c* occasionally occurs before *e* as *cemmed* 188, *disceuer* 1862.

As in modern spelling *g* is used for the stop in *get*, *gold* as well as the affricate in *gemme*, *gentyle*, where it varies with *i* or *j*. OE. *cg* is represented by *g(g)e*, *gg* in *bryg(g)e*, *rygge*, *segg(e)*, etc., but the same spelling serves for the stop in *big(g)e* 9, 20, *leg(g)e* 575, 2228, *lygez* 1179.

Some consonants etymologically single are written with double letters, as *stedde* 439, *walle* 1403, *felle* 1566. The simplest explanation is that the vowels of these words had for some reason been shortened, and that with the loss of -*e* these spellings were equivalent to *sted*, *wal*, *fel*; cf. the rhyme *pikke* 175: *quik*. But double consonants must in any case have been already simplified, and a few spellings show this: *biges* 9, *were* 271, *inore* 649, *wonen* 1365.

Voiced consonants when final are unvoiced: *hadet*, *bront* 588, *ʒonke pynk* 1526, etc. Usually the conventional spelling is retained, so that for instance -*d* is written though the sound had become /t/. Since *d* could have this value when final, it could be used also to express original final -*t*, as *neked*; similarly *ng* for *nk* in *peruyng* 611.

VOCABULARY

The total number of different words in *Gawain*, excluding the fifty-five proper names, is approximately 2,650. (The number is approximate because it is uncertain whether some collocations should be treated as compounds or not, and whether some inflexional forms should be counted separately.) Over a thousand of these words have no ancestors in Old English. A few are of obscure origin; of those with identifiable etymology some 250 are Scandinavian and about 750 French (including those compounded with English suffixes). The French element is thus very much stronger numerically than the Scandinavian, though the greater familiarity of many of the French words in modern English makes them less conspicuous than their numbers might suggest.

A crude count of this kind says little about the literary quality of the blend. Many of the words originally foreign had come to be so commonly used in English that they cannot have appeared at all unusual to readers in any part of the country. Such of the Scandinavian words as *alofte*, *anger*, *brenne*, *call*, *cast*, *deʒe*, *dreme*, *felaʒe*, *fro*, *gere*, *hap*, *hit*, *knif*, *lawe*, *lowe*, *myre*, *rayse*, *skille*, *take*, *wyndow*, *wrang* were widespread in Middle English (several of them recorded already in OE.), and were often used, for example, by Chaucer. Of the French words many were equally indispensable, the ordinary words for the concepts they express —such as *age*, *cacche*, *chaunce*, *ese*, *fayþ*, *gay*, *honour*, *joy*, *passe*, *pes*, *saue*, *serue*, *vse*, *werre*. Words of this kind appear inevitably in any substantial work of the late fourteenth century, and should be left out of account in assessing the stylistic effect of 'Romance vocabulary'.

But the number of Scandinavian words in *Gawain* that do contribute a particular quality is unusually high. These range from words which are commonplace today but had evidently not yet been accepted into general use at the date of the poem—notably *ille*, which Chaucer uses only in the northern dialect of the *Reeve's Tale*, or *ugly* which he uses only once—to some which have always been very limited in currency, such as *snart*, *strothe*, or the apparently unique *skayned*. Though the strength of this Scandinavian element suggests that such words were frequent in the author's spoken language, a few of them were evidently brought into the poem by the needs of alliteration. Some Norse words had initial sounds that were not common in native English words, so that if one was used it called for others to alliterate with it: following *skete* 19 we find *skyfted* instead of the etymologically English *schyfte*. A different type of special association goes back to alliterative use in ON.: *mynne* 'less' is found in ME. only in the alliterative phrase *more and mynne* (1881 n.), a partial anglicizing of ON. *meiri ok minni*. Such direct reminiscences of Scandinavian literary tradition are not frequent in this poem; for other examples see the notes to 165, 1053, 1255. (Contrast the frequency of adoption in *Ormulum*, shown in E. S. Olszewska's article mentioned in the note to 702.) Alliterative requirements more generally no doubt led to the preservation in ME. of Norse words which could provide synonyms for commonly needed terms: *tulk* is added to the inherited stock of words for 'man', *caple* to those for 'horse', *carp* to the verbs of speaking, *cayre* to those of going. Some of these words have diverged remarkably from their original senses—ON. *tulkr* meant 'spokesman', ON. *karpa* 'boast'. Change of sense with less generalization than in these cases is seen in *on lyte* 'in delay', ON. *hlíta* 'trust'; *neked* 'little', ON. *nekkvat* 'something'.

Despite the extensive use of Scandinavian words in *Gawain*, few of the common 'grammatical' words (pronouns, conjunctions, prepositions) are of Scandinavian origin—fewer than in most texts of the north and north midlands. There are only these: *þay* pron., which is regular; *þayr(es)* poss. adj. and pron. (three times; the usual word is the English *her, hor*); *þoȝ, þof* (twice; usually English *þaȝ*). The ending *-ande* of the pres. part. probably derives mainly from Scandinavian *-andi*, though there are possible contributing features in OE. (see Gordon, *Pearl*, p. 99 n.).

Scandinavian words form the most important element in the body of words identifiable as characteristic of texts written in the north and north midlands; see R. Kaiser, *Zur Geographie des mittelenglischen Wortschatzes* (Palaestra 205, 1937), pp. 154–68. Kaiser lists over 130 typically northern words in *Gawain*, and emphasizes that a number of them are otherwise recorded only in texts from the extreme north.

But words characteristic of, and often confined to, alliterative poetry in ME. are by no means all Scandinavian. The most conspicuous exceptions are the well-known group of synonyms for 'man' which supplement the ordinary *mon, kniȝt, noble, prince*—*burn, freke, gome, hathel, lede, renk, schalk, segge, wyȝe*. Of these *renk*, though it may be directly from ON., has a close cognate in OE. *rinc*; all the others descend from OE. (*hathel* evidently a blend of *hæleþ* and *æþele*), and all the OE. words are found either exclusively or predominantly in poetry. For discussion of the distribution and connotations of these words see especially M. Borroff, and Oakden, vol. ii.

No other group forms so compact an example of the persistence of technical tradition in alliterative verse; but a similarly remarkable range of alliterating initials may be seen in some of the verbs extended beyond their common uses to a more or less generalized sense of 'go', 'move': *boȝe* 481, *cach* 1794, *cheue* 63, *chose* 451, *do* (refl.) 1308, *dresse* 1415, *driue* 222, *found* 267, *glyde* 748, *hale* 136, *helde* 221, *loute* 833, *ricche* (refl.) 8, *schowue* 2161, *sech* 1052, *tourne* 2075, *þryng* 2397. Every one of these bears the alliteration.

Words of French origin, though several of them have been adapted to the kind of alliterative use exemplified in the preceding paragraph, naturally lack the traditional associations of much of the native vocabulary. Those which go beyond the commonplace are so freely used that the author must have been entirely at home in educated, sophisticated society. In addition to French-influenced syntax such as *cros Kryst* (see 762 n.) he sometimes used whole French phrases such as *bone hostel* 776, *beau sir* 1222, as well as the commoner *ma fay* 1495. Many of the French terms are technical, of armour, architecture, dress, household arrangements and etiquette, and the chase; many others are abstract terms of philosophy, morality, and religion: *bewté, bobbaunce, bonchef, bounté, charyté, concience, cortaysye, couardise*; verbs and other words also come within this more or less intellectual range: *acorde, debate, enclyne, graunte, jugge, pitosly, sertayn, specially, vilanous*. The great majority of such words are amply recorded from other writers of the late fourteenth century or earlier, and the poet does not seem to have been much inclined to neologism; but there are some words which are first recorded here—*achaufe, acole, anelede, deprece* 'subdue' (also in *Pearl*), *fyniment, flosche, hawtesse, sauerly, talenttyf, werbelande*—and a few others which are not recorded anywhere else—*abelef* (though Chaucer has *embelif* in the *Astrolabe*), *abloy, deprece* 'release', *devaye, enfoubled, joyfnes*.

ETYMOLOGICAL NOTES ON FOREIGN WORDS

Scandinavian

ON. forms are given in the glossary in the normalized spelling of thirteenth-century Icelandic usual in grammars and dictionaries, except for a few words evidently adopted in East Norse form, as *gres(se)*. In some words an earlier state of Norse than normal Icelandic is required to account for the ME. forms. *Derf/derue* must derive from **dearf-*, *mek-* from **mēuk-*, earlier forms with falling diphthongs (like those of OE.) which changed to the rising diphthongs of Icel. *djarf-r, mjúk-r*. (ON. *ēu* is treated in the same way as OE. *ēo*, similarly developing before /j/ to /iː/ as *dryȝe*.) *Wand* must derive from **wandur*, in which the *a* before *u* in the next syllable developed to *ǫ* in Icel. *vǫnd-r*. As in the same word ON. *w* before a vowel became Icel. *v*, but before *r* it was lost, as *rang-r* from **wrang-*, whence ME. (already late OE.) *wrang*. *Bonk(e)* must derive from **banke*, which by assimilation became Icel. *bakki*; *renk*, if it is indeed from ON., is in the same relation to Icel. *rekk-r*. *Þoȝ* must derive from **þŏh*, which with loss of *-h* became Icel. *þó*.

The sounds of ON. were generally treated in ME. in the same way as the similar sounds of OE.; e.g. /a:/ was rounded to /ɔ:/ as *broþe*. A few sounds had no OE. equivalents, notably /au/, which is kept in ME. as *glaum*, *lausen*.

ON. initial *g* and *k*, and *gg* in other positions, remained stops, in contrast to OE. *g* and *c* before front vowels, and *cg*. Thus *gif* 288 is from ON., *ȝef* 1964 from OE.; and *agayn*, *kyrk* have ON. consonants. But since the spelling *gge* could represent either the stop or the affricate (see p. 137), it is not certain whether forms like *brygge*, *rygge* denote one or the other; since the descendant of the OE. 3rd sg. of *licgan* would be, and indeed is, *lys* (1469), the variant *lygez* 1179 evidently derives from ON. *liggja*.

ON. endings are seldom adopted into ME. The reflexive *-sk* of the middle voice survives in the verb *busk*, though not as an ending; this reflexive *-sk* was usually dropped, as *þryue* from *þrífask*. The adverbial comparative *-r* survives in *helder*. Strong masc. nouns and the nom. sg. masc. of adjectives ended in *-r* in ON., but it was the stem of the word that was adopted in ME. so that this *-r* does not appear. In words such as *anger*, from ON. *angr*, the *-r* is part of the stem, not an ending.

French

The French forms in the text are in some cases distinct from those of Central French:

1. Merging of *ai* and *e* is ancient in central and western dialects, hence *plesaunt*, *ese* for OFr. *plaisant*, *aise*, but in the west *ei* (which became *oi* in CFr.) also merged with *ai*, *e*: *des*, CFr. *deis*, *dois*. In *fay*, *fayþ* (earlier *fei*, *feiþ*) the diphthong remained in Anglo-Norman and followed the same development as ME./ei/ in *wey*, *way*, etc. Between vowels in hiatus a glide developed in AN. (and NEFr.), as *deve(i)er*, *fe(i)e*, and the resulting diphthong fell in with *ai* in the same way: *devaye*, *faye*. *Ryal* is an unexplained special development (common in fourteenth-century English) of *reial*, CFr. later *roial*. Where *oi* is found in this text, as *voyde*, it is original and not from earlier *ei*.

2. Merging of *ie* with *e* (from *a*) is characteristic of the west: *feersly*, CFr. *fiers*; *maner(e)*, CFr. *maniere*.

3. Merging of *üi* with *ü* occurs in NFr. and sporadically in CFr. It appears in ME. as *u*, *eu*, *ew*, etc. (= /iu/), and also as *i* especially before vowels: *sute*, *swete*, CFr. *suite*; *ny(ȝ)e*, CFr. *ennui*; *disstrye*, CFr. *destruire*.

4. Northern (or Picard) *ca-* occurs beside CFr. *cha-*: *cache*, CFr. *chacier*, cf. *chasyng* 1143. Similarly *likkerwys* = CFr. *lecherous*, with anglicized suffix.

5. NFr. *w-* appears beside CFr. *g(u)-*: *werre*, CFr. *guerre*; *Wawain* beside *Gawain*.

The following features are characteristic of Anglo-Norman:

6. *aun, aum* for *an, am*: *chaunce, countenaunce, erraunt*; *graunte* beside *grante, traunte* beside *trante*; **laumpe*, beside *chambre*.

7. Close *o* was represented by *o, u* in twelfth-century French, and later also by *ou*, but this digraph was not admitted before *n, m* in Continental spelling. In Anglo-Norman it was: *vrysoun, countenaunce*.

8. Pretonic *e* in hiatus was early lost in *chaunce*, CFr. *cheance* and *gra(u)nte*, early AN. *graanter*. The *gr-* in this word, for CFr. *cr-* in *creanter*, is confined to AN. and a few very closely related western manuscripts. Intertonic *e* before *r* was lost more commonly than in CFr.: *drury*, CFr. *druerie*; *coprounes*, CFr. *couperon*.

9. Preconsonantal *s* was lost before nasals and liquids: *blame*, CFr. *blasme*; *melly*, CFr. *meslee*; *abelef*, CFr. *a beslif*.

10. The second element of *au* was lost in the syllable *sauv-*, *sauf-*: *sauage*, CFr. *sauvage*; *sanap* (= *sauve-nape*); *saf*, CFr. *sauf*. The *v* in *aventure* was vocalized, giving *aunter*, in some forms with shift of stress (see below).

11. The spelling *ngn* in *syngne* is typical of Continental spelling in the thirteenth and fourteenth centuries; but *ly, ny* for palatals in *fylyolez*, *gronye* is insular.

12. Prefixes are occasionally confused: *abloy* for CFr. *esbloi*; *aumail* for CFr. *esmail*; and often dropped altogether; *chekke*, CFr. *eschec*; *dut*, CFr. *deduit*; *bate*, CFr. *debat*.

It should be borne in mind that many of these changes were taking place at an early date on the Continent also, only are more clearly represented in AN. and ME. than in standard Continental manuscripts, for example (8) and (9); while other differences are merely graphic, as (7) and (11). The AN. underlying the adoptions is thus only an advanced form of French, with a few western and northern features some of which have also been accepted by later standard French.

When French words were taken into ME. the principal accent was eventually shifted to the root syllable. Throughout the ME. period words of French origin could be stressed in either the French or the English way, but in *Gawain* they are nearly always stressed like native English words. French stress is used only for the sake of rhyme, as *uyage* 535: *wage*, *prayere* 759: *sere*. The shift of stress caused the vowels of final syllables to be weakened, and a few suffixes consequently were confused. When the endings *-ain*, *-oun* lost their distinctiveness they could be used in place of original *-en*, as *etayn*, OE. *eoten*, or *lentoun*, OE. *lencten*. This does not seem to have been wholly, or always, a mere matter of spelling; see the note to 140. The French endings *-ure*, *-ere* were similarly confused: *cropure*, *papure*, *salure* for AN. *cropere*, *papere*, *salere*.

French nouns and adjectives were generally adopted in the form of the accusative singular, i.e. without ending; but not *feers* (*feersly* in this text), which has the *-s* of the nom. sg. masc. Of verbs it was the stem that was adopted. In some verbs there was a strong and a weak form according to the position of the stress. In ME. the strong form, as in the present sg., was usually adopted, but sometimes the weak form, as in 1 and 2 pl. Of some verbs there are double forms in ME., as *byle*, *keuer*, *meue* from the strong stem, *boyle*, *kouer*, *moue* from the weak. French verbs in *Gawain* are inflected according to the English weak conjugation, except *nie*, pa. t. *nay*, on the analogy of *lie*, *lay*.

INFLEXIONS

Not many inflexions are confirmed by rhymes, so that those which appear may be the scribe's rather than the author's. Though *-e* is very often written in words of most grammatical categories, the scribe's erratic practice, the imprecision of the metre, and the author's inconsistent use of it in rhyme (see pp. 132–3) make it impossible to say how essential a part this was of the inflexional system of the original language.

NOUNS

The *-e* of the OE. neut. dative survives after a preposition in *for soþe* 415, attested by rhyme.

The gen. sg. of all types of noun usually ends in *-es*, *-ez*: *kynges* 100, *corbeles* 1355, *Arthurez* 29. A few forms without *-s* occur: *fole* 459 (OE. *folan*), *segge* 574 (before *fotez*), *hors* 1904, *duches* 2465; a similar endingless form appears in the pl. *rach* 1907. In groups like *heuen-quene* 647 an earlier gen. merges into the attributive use of an uninflected noun; cf. *trweluf craftes* 1527.

The plural of most nouns ends in *-es*, *-ez*, very rarely *-us* as *auenturus* 491 (in 95, as in the gen. *Arthurus* 2522, the *-us* is expressed by an abbreviation), but *aunterez* 2527. Words of French origin ending in *-r* or *-n* occasionally have only *-s*, *-z*: *cowters* 583, *trystors* 1146, *arsounz* 171, *botounz* 220. A fossilized OE. fem. pl. (*-a*, *-e*) survives in *halue* 2070, 2165; probably *hond* 494 represents OE. *handa*, though it might possibly be meant as distributive sg. OE. neut. pls. without ending are continued in *der(e)* 1151, 1157, etc., *þyng(e)* 652, 1080 (beside *þingez* 645, etc.). *Child* has pl. *childer*. The weak pl. is regular in *yȝen* (but *yȝe* 228), and the gen. pl. ending *-ena* leaves a trace in *nakryn* 118 (see note). After numerals forms without *-s* appear in *myle* 770, *mote* 1141, *dame* 1316. The only pls. with mutated vowel are *breþer*, *men* (*menne* 466), and *fete* which happens to occur only after prepositions (even in *vnder fete* 859), and has the alternative *fote* from OE. *fotum* in a few places and the analogical *fotez* once (574).

ADJECTIVES

Plural forms are not regularly distinguishable because of the uncertainty about *-e*, and the rhyme at 840 shows *fayn* there to have been uninflected. A distinction is probably to be seen in *innogh* sg. 404 compared with *innoȝe* pl. 514 (rhyming *blowe*), *innowe* 1401. Weak forms after demonstratives are not safely identifiable, and are sometimes probably excluded by the metre, as *stif* 322, *bolde* 2043, *quyte* 2088; on the other hand 1177 would be improved by reading **derke*. The gen. pl. survives only in the intensive *alder-*, *alþer-*. Adjectives ending in *-li(ch)* form their compar. and superl. in *-lok(k)er*, *-lok(k)est*, which descend from the late OE. development *-lucor*, *-lucost* of earlier *-licor* (adverbial), *-licost*.

In the syntax of adjectives a noteworthy feature is the author's use of them in the function of nouns, not only in the pl., as *bolde* 'bold men' but also in the sg., both of persons, as *þat gay* 970, *þe hende* 827, and of objects as *þe naked* 423, *þe schyre* 1331.

PRONOUNS

The forms of the first and second persons are mostly unremarkable. The possessive adjs. *my/myn*, *þy/þyn* are used before consonants and vowels respectively, and *myn* and *þyn* are the disjunctive forms. In 2 pl. the disjunctive is *yowrez*. In the acc.–dat. of the 1 pl. the scribe wrote *vs* at 2246, but elsewhere *v* and the abbreviation usually meaning *-us*, though he can hardly have intended a form with long vowel throughout (see introductory note on text).

In the second person the pl. *ȝe, yow*, etc., is generally used in addressing one person regarded as socially superior, as by Gawain to Arthur (343 ff.), by the castle porter to Gawain (814), by the guide also in the first part of the dialogue (2091–125 except 2110), but not the latter part (2140 ff.); also as a matter of courtesy between equals, as by Gawain to the lady and to Bertilak (not to the guide), and by Bertilak as host, in contrast to *þou, þe* of the Green Knight's rougher manner, both to the King and to Gawain, and their hostile return of the same forms. In the scene at the Green Chapel the Green Knight begins with *þou*, but changes to *ȝe* with his change of attitude at 2366, though he reverts to *þou* for a sentence at 2391–6. Gawain follows with *ȝe* at 2385, though not 2379. Though the general lines are clear, there is some inconsistency. Bertilak uses *þou* at 1674–9, and in 2444–70 he changes from *þou* to *ȝè* and back again in a friendly speech which might have been expected to call for the plural throughout. There is a similar mixture at 1068–71. In view of these variations too much cannot be made of the lady's occasional *þou* to Gawain (1272, 1746, 1799), or Gawain's response at 1802. (Chaucer's usage in *Troilus and Criseyde* in any case shows that, at a comparable level of society, the plural was normal even between lovers.)

In 3 sg. the normal fem. nom. is *ho*, but *scho* occurs five times (three of them close together at 1550–6). The pl. nom. is always *þay*; poss. *þayr* appears twice and *þayres* once, but the usual forms are *her, hor*. In acc.–dat. there are no forms with *þ-*; *hem, hom* are usual, but there are six cases of *him/hym* also.

As in ME. generally the ordinary personal pronouns serve as reflexives. Pronouns compounded with *-self, -seluen* are not necessarily reflexive, but may refer to anyone prominent in the speaker's mind; see 113 note. Personal pronouns after prepositions often bear reduced stress, the prep. being accented; this is clear in *tó þe* 413, and probable in *to me* 359, 1828, *on me* 1277, *wyth þe* 2150.

Of demonstratives, the pl. of *þat* is usually *þo*, twice *þose*; the pl. of *þis* is *þis, þise/þyse, þese*.

VERBS

Infin. Most forms are written with *-e*, but many without ending. Rhymes show that no ending was pronounced in many words, even when it was written: e.g. *fyȝt* 278, *say* 300, *roun* 362, *frayn* 489, *strayne* 176, *payne* 1042. A small number of forms in *-en* occur, not in rhyme: e.g. *byden* 374, *seruen* 827, *chepen* 1271, *lyþen* 1719, *sauen* 2040; and *-ne* occasionally in monosyllables, as *bene* 141 and *sene* (in rhyme) 712. Verbs with stems ending in an unstressed syllable regularly appear without ending: e.g. *neuen* 58, *fulsun* 99, *sadel* 1128. *Fayly* has its *-y* from OFr. *faillir*; OE. verbs of the second weak class happen not to occur in infin., though their *i/y* appears in a few other forms: see glossary under *luf, wone*.

Indic. pres. The first sg. is mostly written *-e*, but quite commonly without it: e.g. *haf* 263, *know* 325, 400, *ask* 545. The second and third sg. both end in *-(e)s, -(e)z, -tz*: e.g. *habbes* 327, *fles* 2272, *faylez* 278, *spekez* 2302, *hatz* 2296; *biges* 9, *laȝes* 316, *settez* 14, *dos* 1308, *gotz* 375; *-is* is rare: *ricchis* 8. *Me þink* 348, etc., shows confusion of the historically correct 3 sg. with the first pers. implied by the sense, and this apparently gives rise to the anomalous *hym þynk* 2109; cf. the regular *me þinkkez* 1793, etc.

The pl. ends predominantly in -(e)n: e.g. *holden* 28, *tellen* 272, *sytten* 351, *sayn* 1050, *han* 23 (*hauen* 1255), *arn* 280, *ben* 1646. But there are numerous forms in -e: e.g. *knowe* 546, *calle* 1421, *prece* 2097, and some with no ending: e.g. *kest* 1484, *cach* 1938, *haf* often as 919, 1093, *ar* 207, etc., and endingless forms are shown by rhyme in *expoun* 1506, *rewarde* 1918. There are also occasional northern pls. in -es, -ez: *folʒes* 1164, *beres* 2523, *weldez* 1542, *traylez* 1700; *dares* 315 and *desyres* 1257 are doubtful because the subject is *al* which is sometimes treated as sg., 'everyone'; *hatz* 17, 19 is doubtful because it could agree with each of the separate items of the compound subject; *hyʒes* 1351 is confirmed by rhyme, yet is abnormal because the -s ending is not usual in northern texts when the subject pronoun immediately precedes as it does here.

Indic. past

Strong. In the sg. there is no ending, or occasionally -e: *stek* 152, *stod* 322, *droʒ* 335, *gef* 370, *come* 116 (but *com* rhyming *nome* 807), *sate* 339, *loʒe* 2389. The 2 sg. has no distinctive ending: *gef* 2349, *toke* 2243.

In the pl. -en is usual: e.g. *runnen* 66, *rungen* 195, *seten* 242, *ʒolden* 820, *founden* 1704; but some forms have -e, as *woke* 1025, *fonde* 1329, *bede* 1437, *breke* 2082, and others have no ending—mainly historically sg. forms applied to the pl., as *drof* 1151, *ran* 1420, the analogical *foʒt* 874, and *brek* 1333, and perhaps *blw* 1362 beside *blwe* 1141.

Weak. The 1 and 3 sg. often end in -de, -te, as *herde* 31, *hade* 145, *bende* 305, *bledde* 441, *grypte* 214, *lyfte* 369, *sette* 422; but -ed is very much commoner: e.g. *semed* 73, *liked*, *louied* 87, *bisied* 89, *meued* 90, *loued* 126. Many others are written without -e: *wroʒt* 3, *lut* 418, *layd* 419, *raʒt* 432, *soʒt* 1995, *myʒt* 201, the last two in rhyme.

The 2 sg. usually ends in -des, -tes (-z): *kyssedes*, *raʒtez* 2351; but *myntest* 2274, *fayled* 2356.

The pl. often ends in -den, -ten: *bredden*, *lofden* 21, *wroʒten* 22, *wenten* 72, etc.; but oftener in -ed: *justed* 42, *kayred* 43, *woned* 50, *wakned* 119, etc. Some forms end in -t, as *bult* 25, *went* 1143, attested by rhyme in *kest* 1147, *hent* 1597.

Subjunctive. Except for the common *be* and *were*, forms are distinctive only in 2 and 3 sg. pres., both of which usually end in -e: e.g. *craue* 277, *telle* 380; *lepe* 292, *arʒe* 2301, though there are some forms without ending, as *lymp* 1109, *worth* 2374. Many other forms in situations requiring a subjunctive are not formally different from variants of the indicative: *swap* 1108, *drowe* 1647, *loued* 1281, *helde* 2129, *had* often.

The subjunctive is not always used in places where it would be historically proper; cf. the use in the same conditional sentence of indic. *holdez* and subj. *be*, 285-6.

Imperative. The sg. has no ending, or *-e*: *let* 414, *com* 456, *heng* 477, *ta* 413; *loke* 448, *chose* 451, *ryde* 2144.

The pl. ends in *-(e)s*, *-ez*, or *-e*: *dos* 1533, probably *slokes* 412, *techez* 1533, *letez* 2387, *comaundez* 2411, *layne* 1786, *make* 2468.

Pres. participle. Usually *-and(e)*: *saylande* 865, *laȝande* 1207, *farand* 101, *fannand* 181. Two in *-yng*: *sykyng* 753, *gruchyng* 2126.

Past participle. Strong verbs of all classes usually have *-(e)n*: *driuen* 558, *chosen* 778, *bounden* 192, *stollen* 1659, *cummen* 62, *spoken* 1935, *taken* 2448, *fallen* 23; *tan* 490, *borne* 752, *sene* 197, *ben* 36. A few lose the *-n*: *funde* 396, *fonge* 1315, *biholde* 1842—the last two in rhyme.

Weak verbs have *-(e)d(e)*, *-t*: *sesed* 1, *layde* 156, *wont* 17, *lost* 69.

Preterite-presents. Schal and *may* are 2 sg. as well as 1 and 3: 374, 389; 409, 411. They are used in the pl. as well, beside the variants *schyn* 2401, *mowe* 1397. *Con* twice has the unusual pl. *connez*, with northern *-ez* as in ordinary verbs.

The pl. of *be* is usually *ar(n)*, occasionally *be(n)*, the latter with future sense 1646, 2111.

In comparison with OE. the strong verbs have undergone many analogical changes. Most important of these is the levelling of the vowel *e* (OAnglian *ē*) of the past pl. of the fourth and fifth classes into the past sg.; see the glossary under *bere, swere; breke, gete, gif, heue, se, sitte, speke, stoken.* Exceptions are *gafe* 1861, *forȝate* 1472, *forgat* 2031, past sg. forms which preserve the historical vowel. A few verbs have levelled the sg. into the pl.: *drof* 1151, *ran* 1420. Some strong verbs have changed their conjugation, as **steke* IV (from V), *swere* IV (from VI), *heue* IV or V (from VI). Some strong verbs have also a weak past tense or past part.; see the glossary under *blowe, falle, fle, fonge, laȝe, louke, ryse, schape, speke.* Others, originally strong, are here conjugated weak, as *boȝe, loute, slepe*; but *were*, originally weak, has acquired an alternative strong past *were* on the analogy of *bere*.

METRE

Gawain is composed in stanzas consisting of unrhymed alliterative lines followed by five short rhymed lines. The number of unrhymed lines varies from 12 (lines 20–31) to 37 (lines 928–64), and there are 101 stanzas. There is no quatrain arrangement of the unrhymed lines such as occurs, at least in part, in *Purity, Patience, St. Erkenwald, The Siege of Jerusalem,* and *The Wars of Alexander.*

The Long Alliterative Lines

The metrical unit is the single long line, which has no necessary formal link with the lines preceding and following it. Its structure depends on the distribution of what may be called strong and weak elements of the line as it is read—the syllables which are stressed and unstressed, traditionally named 'lifts' and 'dips'. A single stressed syllable constitutes a lift, but there is no fixed limit to the number of successive unstressed syllables that may compose a dip. The long line is divided by a natural pause, or caesura, into two half-lines each of which normally contains two lifts. The order in which lifts and dips fall varies considerably, but in the second half-line variations are fewer, and the dips often shorter, than in the first.

There are four principal rhythmic types:

A, falling: 11a   Tírius to Túskan
                            496b   háf ȝe no wónder

B, rising: 46a   such gláum ande glé
                            858b   of túly and társ

C, 'clashing' (i.e. with no dip between the lifts):
                            51a   þe most kýd knýȝtez
                            52b   þat euer líf háden

BA, rising-falling (very common):
                            20a   ande quen þis Brétayn watz bígged
                            40b   and réchles mérþes.

A number of second half-lines as they appear in the manuscript have only a single dip, usually between two lifts. In this pattern certain words tend to recur: 294 *stif on þis flet*, 568b *tyȝt ouer þe flet*; 672 *syked in hert*, 2277 *arȝez in hert*; 769 *pyned ful þik*, 795 *trochet ful þik*, 801 *clambred so þik*; 38 *ledez of the best*, 889 *sesounde of þe best*, 1000 *drest of þe best*. Sometimes the dip precedes two lifts: 10 *as hit now hat* (for the form cf. 253 *Arthour I hat*). Since the scribe can be seen to have written *-e* often where it was not historically in place, he may well have omitted it equally unhistorically; and the restoration of earlier forms would give these half-lines the usual two dips. Then *Arthour I hat[te]*, with the *-e* sounded, would have the same pattern as 381 *Gawan I hatte*. This would bring these line-endings nearer to the movement of the majority of lines, for there is a strong predominance of 'feminine endings' in *Gawain* as in most alliterative poems. But there is no doubt that in several important poems, which in other respects have a good deal in common with *Gawain*, half-lines of the same shape as *Arthour I hat* were accepted; no doubt a shortened type had arisen owing to the loss of the earlier endings. Examples are: *Wars Alex.* 2447 *bredid for noȝt*, 4398 *sesys his liȝt*, 5307 *festid his siȝt*; *Dest. Troy* 459 *lemond as gold*, 473 *blessid were I*, 490 *chosen þere way*, 846 *dose hym to goo.* Such rhythms are conspicuous in Dunbar's *The Tua Mariit Wemen*, as 22 *schyning full bricht*, 33 *fynest of smell*, 61 *joyis ane maik.* There is no reason except the frequency of feminine endings to deny the authenticity of this pattern in *Gawain*; and since the frequency of feminine endings does not amount to universality (cf. for example 380, 497, 571, 644) it is an insufficient reason. Such half-lines may therefore be classified as a subdivision of A, as they historically are, or as a compromise between A and B.

Some poets, of whom the author of *Gawain* was one, often used three lifts in the first half-line—though the third need not be of exactly the same prominence as the other two. These may be classified thus:

A, falling: (i) with lifts all separated by dips:

26 áy watz Árthur þe héndest

(ii) with two lifts clashing:

76 smál séndal bisídes

B, rising: (i) 209 a spétos spárþe to expóun

(ii) 2 þe bórȝ bríttened and brént

BA, rising-falling:

(i) 655 were hárder hápped on þat háþel

(ii) 1693 were bóun búsked on hor blónkkez

In the (ii) types (with lifts clashing) there is a slight rhythmic pause in place of an unstressed element. Usually the lifts so placed are the first and second.

There is no fixed rhythmical relation between the first and second half-lines, but they are knit together into a single whole by means of alliterating sounds, of which at least one must obviously fall in each half. These alliterating sounds nearly always begin stressed syllables. The commonest pattern has two alliterating sounds in the first half-line and one in the second, with the latter (as in OE.) normally on the first of the two lifts in that half-line. Typical examples in *Gawain* are:

3 þe *t*ulk þat þe *t*rammes   of *t*resoun þer wroȝt

28 þat a *s*elly in *s*iȝt   *s*umme men hit holden

51 þe most *k*yd *k*nyȝtez   vnder *K*rystes seluen.

Occasionally there is only one alliterating sound in the first half-line, which may fall on either lift:

650 þat quen he *b*lusched þerto   his *b*elde neuer payred

1372 thenne comaunded þe lorde in þat *s*ale   to *s*amen alle þe meny

1497 ȝif any were so *v*ilanous   þat yow de*v*aye wolde.

In some half-lines there appears to be a single alliteration on a full lift, but a less prominent word with the same initial sound may have been felt to contribute to the unity of the long line:

25 *b*ot of álle þat here *b*últ   of *B*rétaygne kýnges.

In the second half-line the alliteration usually falls on the first lift but sometimes on the second, as in 161, 263, 1193, 1654, 2131, etc. Occasionally no alliteration at all appears in the second half-line; this is probably always due to corruption of the text. Corruption is clear in 236, 343, 958, 971, 1030, 1208, 1440, 1906; probable also in 1941 (see notes).

The common use of three lifts, all alliterating, in the first half-line is exemplified in the two opening lines of the poem. By a further extension, every lift in the line may alliterate:

2077 þay *b*oȝen bi *b*onkkez   þer *b*oȝez ar *b*are

þay *c*lomben bi *c*lyffez   þer *c*lengez þe *c*olde.

So also 179, 1254. This may occur even when there are three lifts in the first half:

87 his *l*if *l*iked hym *l*yȝt   he *l*ouied þe *l*asse.

So also 2080, 2082.

In addition to these simple extensions of alliteration, other variations of pattern are made by the use of two alliterating sounds in one line; sometimes alternate, as 377, 906, 1223, 1331; sometimes chiastic, as 335, 544, 1402, 2165. (It is likely enough that some of these are accidental.)

In a few lines a second alliteration of this kind does not span the caesura, but yet adds something to the unity of the line:

60 wyle *N*w ȝer watz so ȝep   þat hit watz *n*we cummen.

So also 541, 656. In 1962 the two words beginning with *s* are separated by the caesura from the two beginning with *h*, which can hardly have been acceptable.

In the details of alliteration there are various licences:

Words beginning with *h* very commonly alliterate with words beginning with a vowel, as 5, 26, 136, 789, 1242. (It is clear that initial *h* in stressed words of Germanic origin was pronounced, from such combinations as 59 *a here*, 743, 1144 *a hundreth*, 1257 *my honde*, 2276 *my hede*; if the *h* had not been pronounced the forms *an*, *myn* would have been used.)

A voiceless consonant is sometimes made to alliterate with the corresponding voiced consonant: *ch* with *j* in 86, *s* with *z* in 517, *f* with *v* in 1375, 1391. *Sch* also alliterates with *ch* in 1081.

Sometimes the alliteration falls on an unstressed syllable, such as a verbal prefix (b*iginez* 112, 1571, contrasted with *begynne* 495, 1340; prefixes in French words also vary, as r*ehersed* 392, d*isserued* 452, but *rehayted* 1422, *displese* 1304). It may fall on an unaccented preposition (987), even if it begins with an unstressed syllable (1693); an unstressed element of an adverb (1741); an auxiliary verb (1943, 2053); a pronoun (2325). In recitation such syllables were probably given an artificial stress. Lines of this sort, however, may sometimes be suspected of having suffered slightly in transmission; at 112, for instance, it is possible that the author wrote *þe bord biginez*, for in addition to alliterating well this is the usual form of the idiom (cf. *Canterbury Tales, Prol.* 52).

The alliteration may fall on the second element of a compound word, even a French noun as unusual as *sourquydrye* 311 (contrast 2457); *Crysten*mas 985 (all other occurrences on *k*); *daylyȝt* 1137, 1180; *quere*fore 1294, *where*-so 395; etc.

As noticed above (p. 137), *wh* (OE. *hw*) alliterates with *w*, which is obscured by the frequent spelling *qu*. In 1518 the alliteration on *v*, and in 1391 on *f*, is obscured by the spelling of *v* as *w*.

A group of consonants is often treated as a unit in alliteration, though it need not be. Thus *gr* 1006, *sl* 729, 1182, *sn* 2003 are repeated in alliteration, whereas elsewhere the first consonant only is repeated (920–1, 2147, 2312). Each of the groups *sp*, *st*, *sk* as a rule alliterates only with the same group, as 158, 570, 979, 2167. (At 209 the sound of *sp* contained in *expoun* alliterates.) *Sch* is not a 'group' since the spelling represents a single consonantal sound. It therefore naturally alliterates with itself, as 160, 317, 424–5, etc.; yet in some lines it is linked with *s*, as 956, 1593, and perhaps 205, 431, etc.

Thus, though the general structure of these lines is similar to that of OE. verse, from which the principles must have descended through an unbroken oral tradition, there are numerous important differences. In ME. the rhythm is purely accentual, and lifts need not fall on syllables that are long as well as stressed; stress is much less regularly associated with grammatical function; the OE. types (D and E) which depend on secondary stress do not appear; alliteration is richer, and this allows freer use of unstressed syllables without weakening the cohesion of the line—half-lines of only four syllables, frequent in *Beowulf*, are rare in *Gawain*.

The Rhymed Lines

The first short line of the group of rhymed lines in each stanza has been called (by nineteenth-century prosodists) the 'bob', and the remaining four the 'wheel'. The bob contains a single stressed syllable preceded by one or sometimes two unstressed, and rhymes with the second and fourth lines of the wheel. A striking feature of the bob in *Gawain* is that it seldom adds anything essential to the meaning, and is often distinctly redundant; e.g. 32, 198, 318, 1203. It is possible that this element of the stanza was an afterthought of the author's, and that the bobs were added after the poem was complete, with a few adjustments. (No other poem has exactly the same stanza structure.) However that may be, despite the placing of the bobs at the side of the long lines (see p. xi) they were not added to the present manuscript later than the poem as a whole, for they are in the same hand and ink as the rest.

Each line of the wheel contains three stresses, usually separated by one or two unstressed syllables. Normally the line begins with an unstressed syllable, so that the rhythm is predominantly rising; but there are some 'headless' lines, e.g. 84, 249, 275, and some with feminine endings, e.g. 33, 414, 1417. If the final -*e* were to be regularly pronounced where it is historical there would be a great many feminine endings; but many lines certainly end on a stressed syllable—e.g. 276, 298, 487, 616, 666, 807—so that feminine endings cannot be essential. In two places -*e* must have been pronounced (see p. 133), but since the number of lines in which it must have been silent is much greater, these are evidently to be regarded as exceptional.

The 'clash of stress' which is common in the unrhymed alliterative half-lines is found in 2452 *Mórgne þe góddés*, and also in 35, 736, 1177, 2136. Usually two, sometimes all, of the stressed syllables in each line alliterate, but the alliteration is not regular.

SELECT BIBLIOGRAPHY

MANUSCRIPT

Pearl, Cleanness, Patience, and Sir Gawain reproduced in facsimile from MS. Cotton Nero A. x with Introduction by Sir I. Gollancz, E.E.T.S. 162, 1923.

EDITIONS

Syr Gawayne, ed. Sir F. Madden, Bannatyne Club, 1839.
Sir Gawayne and The Green Knight, ed. R. Morris, E.E.T.S. 4, 1864, revd. Sir I. Gollancz 1897 and 1912.
Sir Gawain and The Green Knight, ed. J. R. R. Tolkien and E. V. Gordon, Oxford, 1925.
Sir Gawain and The Green Knight, ed. Sir I. Gollancz with introductory essays by M. Day and M. S. Serjeantson, E.E.T.S. 210, 1940.
Sire Gauvain et le Chevalier Vert, ed. E. Pons, Paris, 1946.
Pearl and Sir Gawain and the Green Knight, ed. A. C. Cawley, Everyman's Library 346, 1962. (Spelling partly modernized.)
Other modernized editions have no independent textual value.

EDITIONS OF THE OTHER POEMS IN THE MANUSCRIPT

Early English Alliterative Poems, ed. R. Morris, E.E.T.S. 1, 1864, revd. 1869.
Pearl, ed. Sir I. Gollancz, London, 1891, revd. 1897; new edn., 1921.
The Pearl, ed. C. G. Osgood, Boston, 1906.
The Pearl, ed. S. P. Chase and others, Boston, 1932.
Pearl, ed. E. V. Gordon, Oxford, 1953.
The Pearl, ed. Sister M. V. Hillmann, New York, 1961.
Pearl, ed. Cawley 1962, as above.
Purity, ed. R. J. Menner, New Haven, 1920.
Cleanness, ed. Sir I. Gollancz, London, Part I, 1921, Part II, 1933.
Patience, ed. H. Bateson, Manchester, 1912, 2nd edn., 1918.
Patience, ed. Sir I. Gollancz, London, 1913, 2nd edn., 1924.

In MS. Harley 2250, but sometimes attributed to the same author:
St. Erkenwald, ed. C. Horstmann in *Altenglische Legenden, Neue Folge*, Heilbronn, 1881; ed. Sir I. Gollancz, London, 1922; ed. H. L. Savage, New Haven, 1926.

LANGUAGE AND METRE

M. Borroff, *Sir Gawain and the Green Knight. A Stylistic and Metrical Study*, New Haven, 1962.
B. Kottler and A. M. Markman, *A Concordance to Five Middle English Poems*, Pittsburgh, 1966.

J. C. McLaughlin, *A Graphemic-Phonemic Study of a Middle English Manuscript (Cotton Nero A. x)*, The Hague, 1963.

T. F. Mustanoja, *A Middle English Syntax*, Part I, Helsinki, 1960.

J. P. Oakden, *Alliterative Poetry in Middle English*, Manchester, vol. i, 1930, vol. ii, 1935.

A. H. Smith, *English Place-Name Elements*, E.P.N.S. 25, 26, 1956. See also Gordon's edition of *Pearl*.

CRITICISM

L. D. Benson, *Art and Tradition in Sir Gawain and the Green Knight*, New Brunswick, N.J., 1965.

J. A. Burrow, *A Reading of Sir Gawain and the Green Knight*, London, 1965.

H. L. Savage, *The Gawain-Poet. Studies in his Personality and Background*, Chapel Hill, 1956.

Sir Gawain and Pearl. Critical Essays, ed. R. J. Blanch, Bloomington and London, 1966.

LITERARY HISTORY AND ANALOGUES

Arthurian Literature in the Middle Ages. A Collaborative History, ed. R. S. Loomis, Oxford, 1959. (Ch. 39, on *Gawain*, by L. H. Loomis.)

J. D. Bruce, *The Evolution of Arthurian Romance*, 2nd edn., Göttingen and Baltimore, 1928.

E. Faral, *La Légende Arthurienne*, Paris, 1929.

G. L. Kittredge, *A Study of Gawain and the Green Knight*, Cambridge, Mass., 1916.

R. S. Loomis, *Arthurian Tradition and Chrétien de Troyes*, New York, 1949; *Celtic Myth and Arthurian Romance*, New York, 1927; *The Development of Arthurian Romance*, London, 1963; *Wales and the Arthurian Legend*, Cardiff, 1956.

Texts

'Bricriu's Feast'. *Fled Bricrend*, ed. and trans. G. Henderson, Irish Texts Soc. ii, 1899 (pp. 97–101, 117–29).

Caradoc, Le Livre de, in *Continuations of the Old French Perceval*, ed. W. Roach and R. H. Ivy, Jr., Philadelphia, 1949–55 (i. 89–97; ii. 209–19; iii. 141–56).

Le Chevalier à l'Épée, ed. E. C. Armstrong, Baltimore, 1900.

Chrétien de Troyes, *Perceval*, ed. A. Hilka, Halle, 1932.

Diu Crône, ed. G. F. Scholl, Stuttgart, 1852.

Sir Gawain and the Carl of Carlisle, ed. A. Kurvinen, Helsinki, 1951.

Geoffrey of Monmouth, *Historia Regum Britanniae*, ed. A. Griscom, London, 1929; also in Faral, vol. iii. Translated as *A History of the Kings of Britain* by S. Evans, 1903; revd. C. W. Dunn, Everyman's Library, 1958.

Hunbaut, ed. J. Sturzinger and H. Breuer, Dresden, 1914.

Lanzelet, trans. and ed. K. G. T. Webster and R. S. Loomis, New York, 1951.

The Mabinogion, trans. G. Jones and T. Jones, Everyman's Library, 1949.

La Mule sans Frein, or *La Damoisele à la Mule*, ed. B. Orlowski, Paris, 1911; ed. R. T. Hill, Baltimore, 1911.

Nennius, *Historia Brittonum* in *La Légende Arthurienne*, ed. Faral, vol. iii.

Perlesvaus. Le Haut Livre du Graal, P., ed. W. A. Nitze and T. A. Jenkins, Chicago, 1932–7.

Suite du Merlin. Merlin, roman en prose du XIIIe siècle, ed. G. Paris and J. Ulrich, S.A.T.F., 1886.

Trioedd Ynys Prydein. The Welsh Triads, ed. R. Bromwich, Cardiff, 1961.

The Vulgate Version of the Arthurian Romances, ed. H. O. Sommer, Washington, D.C., 1908–13.

Wace, *Roman de Brut*, ed. I. Arnold, S.A.T.F., 1938–40.

William of Malmesbury, *de Gestis Regum Anglorum*, ed. W. Stubbs, Rolls ser., 1887–9.

Yder. Der Iderroman, ed. H. Gelzer, Dresden, 1913.

THE HISTORICAL SETTING

Medieval England, ed. A. L. Poole, new edn., Oxford, 1958. (Chapters on architecture, costume, armour, etc.)

J. Evans, *Dress in Medieval France*, Oxford, 1952.

F. H. Kelly and R. Schwabe, *A Short History of Costume and Armour chiefly in England* 1066–1800, London, 1931.

La Chace dou Cerf, ed. G. Tilander, Stockholm, 1960.

La Vénerie de Twiti (with *The Craft of Venery*), ed. G. Tilander, Uppsala, 1956. (Also in *The Art of Hunting*, ed. Sir H. Dryden, 1844, revd. A. Dryden, Northampton, 1908.)

The Master of Game (by Edward, second Duke of York, written 1406–13), ed. W. A. and F. Baillie-Grohman, Edinburgh, 1904; modernized edn., London, 1909.

The Boke of Saint Albans (1486), ed. in facsimile W. Blades, London, 1901; the hunting section ed. Tilander as *Julians Barnes Boke of Huntyng*, Karlshamn, 1964.

The Noble Arte of Venerie or Hunting by George Gascoigne, 1575, repr. Oxford, 1908. [Formerly ascribed to Turbervile, but see J. Robertson, *M.L.R.* xxxvii (1942), 484–5, and C. T. and R. Prouty in *Joseph Quincy Adams Memorial Studies*, Washington, 1948, pp. 639–64, esp. p. 650.]

G. Tilander, *Essais d'étymologie cynégétique*, Lund, 1953.

EDITIONS OF TEXTS QUOTED MORE THAN ONCE IN THE NOTES

Ancrene Wisse, ed. J. R. R. Tolkien, E.E.T.S. 249, 1962.

Arthour and Merlin, ed. E. Kölbing, Leipzig, 1890.

The Avowynge of King Arther, ed. J. Robson in *Three Metrical Romances*, Camden Soc., 1842.

The Awntyrs off Arthure in *Scottish Alliterative Poems*, ed. F. J. Amours, S.T.S., 1897.

The Babees Book (*Early English Meals and Manners*), ed. F. J. Furnivall, E.E.T.S. 32, 1868.

Laȝamon, *Brut*, ed. Sir F. Madden, London, 1847; ed. G. L. Brook and R. F. Leslie, vol. i, E.E.T.S. 250, 1963; *Selections*, ed. Brook, Oxford, 1963.

Chaucer, *Works*, ed. F. N. Robinson, 2nd edn., Boston, 1957.

Cursor Mundi, ed. R. Morris, E.E.T.S. 57 etc., 1874–92.

Sir Degrevant, ed. L. F. Casson, E.E.T.S. 221, 1949.

Dest. Troy. The Gest Hystoriale of the Destruction of Troy, ed. G. A. Panton and D. Donaldson, E.E.T.S. 39, 56, 1869–74.

Emaré, ed. E. Rickert, E.E.T.S. e.s. xcix, 1908.

The Harley Lyrics, ed. G. L. Brook, 2nd edn., Manchester, 1956.

Ipomadon (three versions), ed. E. Kölbing, Breslau, 1889.

Iuliene, ed. S. T. R. O. d'Ardenne, Liège, 1936, reissued as E.E.T.S. 248, 1961.

Lydgate, *Troy Book*, ed. H. Bergen, E.E.T.S. e.s. xcvii etc., 1906–20.

Malory, *Works*, ed. E. Vinaver, Oxford, 1947; 2nd edn., 1967.

Mandeville's Travels, ed. P. Hamelius, E.E.T.S. 153–4, 1916.

Morte Arthure, ed. E. Björkman, Heidelberg, 1915.

The Ormulum, ed. R. M. White, Oxford, 1852, revd. R. Holt, 1878.

The Owl and the Nightingale, ed. E. G. Stanley, London, 1960.

The Parlement of the Thre Ages, ed. M. Y. Offord, E.E.T.S. 246, 1959.

Piers Plowman, ed. W. W. Skeat, Oxford, 1886.

The Quatrefoil of Love, ed. Sir I. Gollancz and M. Weale, E.E.T.S. 195, 1934.

Rauf Coilȝear in *Scottish Alliterative Poems*, ed. Amours.

Romaunt of the Rose, ed. M. Kaluza, Part I, Chaucer Soc., 1891.

Scottish Troy Fragments in *Barbour's Legendensammlung*, ed. C. Horstmann, Heilbronn, vol. ii, 1882.

The Siege of Jerusalem, ed. E. Kölbing and M. Day, E.E.T.S. 188, 1931.

Summer Sunday in *Historical Poems of the XIVth and XVth Centuries*, ed. R. H. Robbins, New York, 1959, no. 38.

Sir Tristrem, ed. G. P. McNeill, S.T.S., 1886.

Wars Alex. The Wars of Alexander, ed. W. W. Skeat, E.E.T.S. e.s. xlvii, 1886.

William of Palerne, ed. W. W. Skeat, E.E.T.S. e.s. i, 1867.

Winner and Waster, ed. Sir I. Gollancz, London 1920; revd. M. Day 1931.

ABBREVIATIONS

D.O.S.T.   *Dictionary of the Older Scottish Tongue,* ed. W. A. Craigie
        and A. J. Aitken, Chicago, 1931– .
E.D.D.   *English Dialect Dictionary,* ed. J. Wright.
E.E.T.S. Early English Text Society.
E.P.N.S. English Place-Name Society.
J.E.G.P. *Journal of English and Germanic Philology.*
M.Æ.   *Medium Ævum.*
M.E.D.   *Middle English Dictionary,* ed. H. Kurath, S. M. Kuhn, and
        J. Reidy, Ann Arbor, 1952–
M.L.N.   *Modern Language Notes.*
M.L.R.   *Modern Language Review.*
M.P.   *Modern Philology.*
N. & Q.   *Notes and Queries.*
O.E.D.   *Oxford English Dictionary.*
P.M.L.A. *Publications of the Modern Language Association of America.*
P.Q.   *Philological Quarterly.*
R.E.S.   *Review of English Studies.*
S.A.T.F. Societé des Anciens Textes Français.
S.P.   *Studies in Philology.*
S.T.S.   Scottish Text Society.
T.L.S.   *The Times Literary Supplement.*

GLOSSARY

In the Glossary completeness is aimed at. Intentional exceptions are: (i) references to common forms or uses have been much curtailed (marked *etc.*); (ii) variation between ȝ, *gh*; *i, y*; *th, þ*; *u, v*; and final *-es, -ez*, has often been disregarded; (iii) the inflected forms of nouns, adjectives, and weak verbs have only exceptionally been recorded (for their normal forms see pp. 143–7).

Etymologies. These are given as an aid in interpreting spellings, fixing meanings, and differentiating words of diverse origin and similar appearance. Though extremely brief, they are not solely repetitions of common material; several are here (often very tentatively) suggested for the first time, e.g. *burde, misy, rupe, schynder, wone.* For the better illustration of the forms of the text, the Old French forms cited are largely Anglo-Norman (usually without specification), the Old English forms Anglian. The marking of long vowels has not been attempted in Old French. In Old English the long vowels are marked as in *ān*; uncertain quantity or probable shortening in the Old English period is marked as in ARE, *ǣr*; vowels lengthened in Old English (e.g., before *ld*) are marked as in BOLD, *báld*, when the forms of the text point to, or allow of the possibility of, this lengthening. On the forms cited from Old Norse see pp. 140–1; long vowels are marked as in *ár*.

Arrangement. In Glossary and Index of Names (i) ȝ has a separate alphabetical place immediately after ġ; (ii) þ has a separate place immediately after **t,** and here also is included rare initial **th**; (iii) the MS. distinction between initial **u, v,** and **i, j** has not been observed—only **v** and **i** are used; (iv) initially **y** has its usual place, but medially and finally it will be found in the alphabetical place of **i.**

ABBREVIATIONS USED IN THE GLOSSARY

AN.	Anglo-Norman.
cf.	in etymologies indicates uncertain or indirect relation.
CFr.	Central French.
Dan., ODan.	Danish, Old Danish.
Du., MDu.	Dutch, Middle Dutch.
E., ME., OE.	English, Middle English, Old English.
Fr., OFr., ONFr.	French, Old French, Northern dialects of Old French.
Fris., OFris.	Modern Frisian dialects, Old Frisian.
from	is prefixed to etymologies when the word illustrated has an additional suffix or prefix not present in the etymon.
G.	German.
Gmc.	Germanic.
Goth.	Gothic.
HG., MHG., OHG.	High German, Middle High German, Old High German.
Icel.	Modern Icelandic.
infl.	influenced; influence.
L., Med.L.	Latin, Medieval Latin.
LG., MLG.	Low German, Middle Low German.
n.	see note.
Norw.	Modern Norwegian dialects.
Nth., ONth.	Northumbrian dialect of Old English.
OIr.	Old Irish.
OMerc.	Mercian dialect of Old English.
ON.	Old Norse, especially Old Icelandic.
OProv.	Old Provençal.
OS.	Old Saxon (Old Low German).
prec.	preceding word.
red.	reduction; reduced.
rel.	related.
Swed., OSwed.	Swedish, Old Swedish.
*	is prefixed to forms theoretically reconstructed, and to references to emendations.
+	between elements shows that a compound or derivative is first recorded in Middle English.

GLOSSARY

A

a *interj.* ah 1746.

a *indef. art.* a, one, any, some 76, 208, 2421, etc.; (*with materials*) 571, 573, 879; **an** (*before vowels*) 27, 1808, etc. [OE. *ān*.]

abataylment *n.* battlement 790. [From OFr. *abataill(i)er*, to fortify.]

a-belef *adv.* obliquely, slantwise 2486, 2517. [OFr. *à be(s)lif*.]

abide *v. intr.* to stop, 2090; *imper.* wait! 2217; *trans.* await 1900; endure 1754. [OE. *abidan*.]

abloy *adj.* carried away (with joy) 1174 n. [OFr. *e(s)bloi*, pp.]

abode *n.* stop, stay 687. [Rel. to ABIDE.]

abof, aboue(n) *adv.* above 2217; thereover, upon it 153, 166, 856; in a higher seat 73; in the highest place 112; *prep.* above 184, 478, 765. [OE. *abufan*.]

about(t)e *adv.* about, round about 75, 217, 600, 949, 1427, 2233, etc.; *ben a.*, to be diligent 1986 (cf. PERABOUTE); *prep.* (round) about, around 164, 189, 2187, (*after its case*) 351, 2517, etc.; concerning 68. [OE. *abūtan*.]

absolucioun *n.* absolution 1882. [OFr. *absolucio(u)n*.]

achaufed *pa. t.* warmed 883. [OFr. *eschaufer*.]

acheue *v.* to gain, accomplish 1081, 1107; *acheue to*, make one's way to, reach 1838, 1857. [OFr. *achever*.]

acole *v.* to embrace 1936, 2472. [OFr. *acoler*.]

acorde *n.* agreement 1384. [OFr. *acorde*.]

acorde *v.* to reconcile 2405; *refl.* consent 1863; associate (with) 2380; *pp.* accorded, granted 2519; *intr.* to agree, resolve 2514; *a. wyth*, match (in colour) 602; *a. to*, befit 631; *a. of*, agree to 1408. [OFr. *acorder*.]

adoun *adv.* down 254, 505, 2266, etc.; downwards 2263. [OE. *of-dūne*.]

afyaunce *n.* trust 642. [OFr. *afia(u)nce*.]

aft(t)er *prep.* after, behind, in pursuit of 501, 516, 1188, (*after its case*)1165, 1742, etc.; for 1215, 2093; along 218; *adv.* afterwards 255, 374, 1518, etc.; after the same fashion 171; along 1608. [OE. *æfter*.]

after *conj.* after 2525. [Reduced from OE. *æfter þam þe*.]

agayn *adv.* in return 386, 1638. [ON. *i gegn*, OE. *ongegn*; cf. AȝAYN.]

age *n.* age; *in her first age*, in the flower of their youth 54. [OFr. *ĕage, aage*.]

aghlich *adj.* terrible 136. [ON. *agi* + OE. *-lic*; cf. OE. *egeslic*.]

agreued (*for*) *pp.* weighed down, overcome (with) 2370. [OFr. *agreuer*.]

aȝayn *adv.* back, in return, again 530, 1217, 1459, 2400, etc.; *prep.* against 2116. [OE. *ongegn*.]

aȝaynez *prep.* (*after its case*) towards, to meet 971; against 1661. [Prec. + *adv. -es*.]

aȝlez *adj.* without fear 2335. [ON. *agi* + OE. *-lēas*.]

aȝt(e). See OGHE.

ay *adv.* always, ever 26, 167, 562, etc.; in each case 73, 128, 190. [ON. *ei*.]

ayled *pp.* troubled 438. [OE. *eglan*.]

ayquere *adv.* everywhere 599, 629, 800, 952, 959, 1521; **aywhere** 745, 2181. [OE. *æghwær*.]

ayþer *adj.* each (of two), both 1356, 2180; *as pron.* *1357; *ayþer . . . oþer*, each (the) other 841, 939, 1307, 2472. [OE. *ægþer*.]

alce. See ALS(E).

alder *adj. compar.* older 948; elder 972, 1317. [OE. *ældra*.]

alder-, alþer- *intensive prefix in* **alder-truest, alþer-grattest,** truest, greatest, of all 1486, 1441. [OE. *alra*, gen. pl.]

alderes *n. pl.* princes, kings 95. [OE. (verse) *aldor*.]

algate *adv.* at any rate 141. [Cf. ON. *alla gǫtu*, all along, always.]

G

Al-hal-day *n.* All Saints' Day (1 Nov.) 536. [OE. *alra hálgena dæg.*]

alyue *adj.* living 1269. [OE. *on life.*]

al(le) *adj.* all 7, 39, 50, 54, 1943, etc.; *pron.* all, everything 48, 604, 836, etc.; all (the people), they (them) all 242, 315, 1234, 1578, etc. [OE. *al(l).*]

al(le) *adv.* entirely, quite, everywhere 75, 246, 831, 1608, 1662, etc.; *al peroute*, without any shelter 2481; (*expletive*) moreover 1349; *introd. concessive clause with subj. and inversion*=although 143. [OE. *al(l).*]

aloft(e) *adv.* up, above, at the top 194, 572, 981, 1125, 1818, 2288; on horseback 435, 2060; *as prep.* (*after its noun*) on 1648. [ON. *á loft.*] See LOFT(E).

alosed *pp.* praised 1512. [OFr. *aloser.*]

als(e) *adv.* as 1067; also, as well 270, 1224, 1627, 2360, etc.; **alce** 2492. [Reduced from next.]

also *adv.* also, as well 90, 1155, 2057. [OE. *al-swā.*]

alper-grattest. See ALDER-.

aluisch *adj.* elvish 681. [From OE. *ælf.*]

alway *adv.* always 1482. [OE. *alne weg.*]

am *1 sg. pres.* am 354, 624, 2509, etc. [OE. *eam, am.*]

amende *v. intr.* to improve 898. [OFr. *amender.*]

among *prep.* among 101, 466, 473, etc. [OE. *on mong.*]

amount (*to*) *v.* to amount to, mean 1197. [OFr. *amo(u)nter.*]

anamayld *pp.* enamelled 169. [OFr. *enamaill(i)er.*]

and *conj.* and 354, 566, 1319, 1402; **ande** 20, *46, 151, 270, 308, 323, 756, 788, *1426, 1668; *elsewhere abbrev. in MS., as* 1, 2277; if 1009, 1245, 1271, 1393, 1509, 1647, 1966, 1996, 2129; *and zet*, even if 1009. [OE. *and.*]

anelede *pa. t.* pursued 723 n. [OFr. *aneler.*]

angardez *n. gen. as adj.* excessive, arrogant 681 n. [OFr. *angarde.*]

anger *n.* harm *2344. [ON. *angr.*]

any, ani *adj.* any (whatsoever), some 24, 257, 337, 2470, etc.; *pron.* anyone, any (people) 285, 300, 333, 1497; **anyskynnez** of any kind 1539 (OE. **æniges cynnes*). [OE. *æniɡ.*]

anious *adj.* troublesome 535. [OFr. *anoio(u)s.*]

answare *v.* to answer 241, *1044, *1262; **onsware** 275, 386. [OE. *an(d)swarian.*]

apende *v.* to belong 623, 913. [OFr. *apendre.*]

apere *v.* to appear 911. [OFr. *aper-*, accented stem of *apareir.*]

apert *adj.* evident, plain 154, 2392. [OFr. *apert.*]

apparayl *n.* gear, adornment 601. [OFr. *apareil.*]

aproched *pa. t.* approached 1877. [OFr. *aproch(i)er.*]

aquoyntaunce *n.* acquaintance 975. [OFr. *acointa(u)nce.*]

aray(e) *n.* array, dress 163, 1873. [OFr. *arei.*]

arayed, arayde *pp.* prepared, dressed 1130, 1134; constructed 783. [OFr. *areier.*]

are *adv.* before 239, 1632, 1891. [OE. *ǽr*, late Nth. *ar*; ON. *ár.*]

arered *pp.* retreated, drawn back 1902. [OFr. *arerer.*]

ar(e)wes *n. pl.* arrows 1160, 1455. [OE. *ar(e)we.*]

arʒe *adj.* afraid 241. [OE. *earg.*]

arʒe *v.* to be terrified, quail 1463, 2271, 2277, 2301. [OE. *eargian.*]

aryʒt, oryʒt *adv.* fittingly, in the right fashion 40, 1911. [OE. *on riht, ariht.*]

arme *n.* arm 185, 582, 841, 1305, 2487, etc. [OE. *earm.*]

armed *pp.* armed 2335. [OFr. *armer.*]

armes, -ez *n. pl.* arms, armour 204, 281, 567, 590, 2104; knightly warfare 95, 2437; the knightly profession 1513, 1541; heraldic arms 631. [OFr. *armes.*]

ar(n) *pres. pl.* are 207, 280, 1094, etc.; **are** 1226. [OE. *aron.*]

arounde *adv.* at the edges 1833. [*a-* (OE. *on*)+ROUNDE *adj.*]

arsoun(e)z *n. pl.* saddle-bows 171, 602. [OFr. *arso(u)n.*]

art *n.* art 1543. [OFr. *art.*]

art *2 sg. pres.* art, are 675, 2240, 2270, 2391. [OE. *eart.*]

as *conj.* (even) as, like, in the way that 49, 73, 149, 182, 199, 388, 847, etc.; as far as 193; so as 1033; as if, as though 201, 244, 1202, *1281, etc.; according as 99, 1811, etc.; as (one who), (as) being 321, 638, 896 n., 1104; *with oaths*, so 256, 2123; while, when 703, 995, 1592, etc.; since 324, 1547, 1941; see PERE. [Reduced from ALS.]

as *adv.* (just) as 611, 1021, 1425, etc.; *correl. with* AS *conj.* as 437, 2393, etc.; see AS-TIT, AS-SWYÞE. [As prec.]

asay *n.* 'assay' 1328 n. [AN.; OFr. *essai.*]

ascryed *pa. t.* shouted 1153. [OFr. *escrier.*]

asyngne *v.* to assign 1971. [OFr. *asign(i)er.*]

ask(e) *v.* to ask (for), request 273, 393, 756, 1691, etc.; *absol.* require 530, 1327. [OE. *āxian.*]

askez *n. pl.* ashes 2. [ON. *aska*; OE. *ascan*, pl.]

askyng *n.* request 323, 349. [OE. *ācsung.*]

asoyled *pa. t.* absolved 1883. [OFr. *asouldre, asoill-.*]

aspye *v.* to discover 1199. [OFr. *espier.*]

as(s)ay *v.* to make trial of, put to the proof 2362, 2457. [OFr. *essayer.*]

as(s)aute *n.* assault 1, 2525. [OFr. *as(s)aut.*]

as-swyþe *adv.* at once 1400. [AS + SWYÞE.]

as-tit, as-tyt *adv.* at once 31; in a moment 1210. [AS + TITE *adv.*]

at(e) *prep.* at 1, 264, 464, 836, 2249, etc.; to 929, 1671; in 467, 557; of, from 359, 391, 646, 1977, etc.; according to 1006, 1546; with 2399, *watz hym ate*, was with him 1474; after *hunt* 1340; *adv.* at 1727. [OE. *æt.*]

atyred *pp.* attired 1760. [OFr. *atir(i)er.*]

at(t)le *v.* to intend 27, 2263. [ON. *ætla.*]

atwaped *pa. t.* escaped 1167. [OE. *æt-* away + WAPPE.]

athel, aþel *adj.* noble, glorious splendid 5, 171, 241, 904, 1654, 2466. [OE. *æþele.*]

avanters *n. pl.* part of the numbles of the deer 1342 n. [AN. *avanter*, from *avant.*]

aue *n.* the Ave Maria, 'Hail Mary' 757.

auen. See OWEN.

auentayle *n.* mail neck-guard on helmet, 608 n. [OFr. *aventaille.*]

auenture, aventure, awenture *n.* adventure, marvellous event 29, 250, 489, 2482; **auenturus** *pl.* 95, 491. [OFr. *aventure.*]

auenturus *adj.* perilous 93. [OFr. *aventuro(u)s, -us.*]

auinant *adj.* pleasant 806. [OFr. *avenant.*]

auyse, awyse *v.* to devise 45, 1389; to behold, contemplate 771. [OFr. *aviser.*]

aumayl *n.* enamel 236. [AN. *a(u)mail*, OFr. *esmail.*]

auncian *adj.* old, aged 1001, 2463; *as sb.* 948. [OFr. *a(u)ncien.*]

aune 10. See OWEN.

aunt *n.* aunt 2464, *2467. [OFr. *a(u)nte.*]

aunter *n.* adventure, strange event 27, 2522, 2527. [As AUENTURE, but an older and more popular adoption.]

auntered *pp.* ventured, risked 1516. [OFr. *aventurer.*]

auter *n.* altar 593. [OFr. *auter.*]

auþer. See OÞER *conj.*

away *adv.* away 1718, 2119. [OE. *on weg.*]

awen. See OWEN.

awharf *pa. t.* turned aside 2220. [OE. *ahweorfan.*]

ax(e) *n.* axe 208, 330, 2223. [OF. *æx.*]

B

bade. See BIDE.

bay(e) *n.* baying of hounds about an animal making a stand: *byde (at) þe baye*, turn, stand at bay 1450, 1582; the defensive position of the animal: *bode in his bay*, stood at bay 1564. [OFr. *(a)bai.*]

baye *v.* to bay, bark 1142, 1362; bay at 1603, 1909. [OFr. *baier.*]

bayn *adj.* obedient 1092, 2158. [ON. *þeinn*, direct.]

bayst *pa. t.* was dismayed 376. [AN. (*a*)*baiss*-, OFr. *esbaïr, esbaïss*-.]

baybe(n) *v.* to grant 327 n.; agree 1404; consent 1840. [ON. *beiða*, see note.]

bak *n.* back 143, 1563; *at his bak*, behind him 1571. [OE. *bæc*.]

bak-bon *n.* backbone 1352. [Prec. + OE. *bān*.]

baken *pp.* baked 891. [OE. *bacan*.]

bald(e)ly *adv.* boldly, vigorously 376, 1362. [OE. *baldlice*.] See BOLD.

bale *n.* destruction, death 2041; misery 2419. [OE. *balu*.]

balé *n.* belly 1333. [OE. *bæl(i)g*.]

balȝ(e) *adj.* swelling with round smooth surface *967 n., 2032, 2172. [OE. *balg*; Ekwall, *Pl.-N. Lancs.*, p. 7.]

bande *n.* band 192. [OFr. *bande*.]

baner *n.* banner (hung on trumpet) 117. [OFr. *ban(i)ere*.]

barayne *adj.* barren, without fawn 1320. [OFr. *baraigne*.]

barbe *n.* barb (of arrow) 1457; cutting edge (of axe) 2310. [OFr. *barbe*, beard, barb.]

barbican *n.* outwork, outer fortification of a castle 793. [OFr. *barbacane*.]

bare *adj.* bare, naked, exposed 207, 746, 955, 961, etc.; without armour 290; mere 2352; downright, actual 277; *þre bare mote*, three single notes 1141; *adv.* without qualification, completely 465; barely 1066. [OE. *bær*.]

barely *adv.* unconditionally, without fail 548. [OE. *bærlice*.]

baret *n.* strife, fighting 21, 353, 2115; trouble, sorrow 752. [OFr. *barat*.]

bargayn *n.* bargain, agreement 1112. [OFr. *bargaine*.]

barlay *adv.* (?) in my turn 296 n. [Not known.]

barred *pp.* barred, marked with parallel stripes 159, 600. [From next.]

barres *n. pl.* transverse bars adorning belt 162. [OFr. *barre*.]

bastel *n.* tower of castle; *bastel rouez*, roofs of towers 799. [OFr. *bastille* (recorded later than in English).]

batayl *n.* fight 277. [OFr. *bataille*.]

bate *n.* strife, fighting 1461. [Shortened from DEBAT.]

baþed *pp.* steeped 1361. [OE. *baþian*.]

bauderyk *n.* baldric 621, 2486, 2516. [Cf. OFr. *baudrei*, MHG. *balderich*.]

bawemen *n. pl.* bowmen, archers 1564. [OE. *boga* + *mann*.]

be-. See also BI-, BY-.

be *prep.* by 1788, 2271; according to, in 1216; *be twenty*, twenty at a time 1739. [OE. *be*.] See BI.

be *v.* to be 1071, 1240, 1393, 2179, etc.; *lettez be*, cease from 1840; **to bene** 141 (OE. *to bēonne*); **be(n)** *future 2 pl.* will be 1646, 2111; **be** *imper.* 1211, 2338; **be** *subj. pres. sg.* (may) be 272, 286, 448, 1242, 2107, etc.; *wheþer this be?* can this be? 2186; **be(n)** *pl.* 497, 2440, etc.; **ben(e)** *pp.* been 613, 677, 1956, 2343, etc. [OE. *bēon*.]

beau *adj.* fair; *beau sir* = OFr. *beau sire* 1222.

becom *v.* to become 1279; **bycommes, bicumes** is fitting (for) 471, 1491; **becom** (*to*) *pa. t. sg.* came, got (to) 460; **bicome** *pl.* became 6. [OE. *be-cuman*.]

bed(de) *n.* bed 994, 1122, 1191, 1232, 1413, etc. [OE. *bedd*.]

bedde. See BID(DE).

beddyng *n.* bedclothes, trappings of bed 853. [OE. *bedding*.]

bede *v.* to offer 374, 382, 2322; **bede** *pa. t.* 1824, 1834, 1860, 2248, 2352; **bade**, commanded 1437 (*pl.*), 2012, 2024 (*with active infin.*), 2090; see BIDDE. [OE. *bēodan*, already confused with *biddan*.]

bed-syde *n.* bedside 1193. [Earlier *beddes side*; see SIDE.]

belde *n.* courage 650. [OE. *béldo*.]

bele *adj.* fair, gracious 1034; see BEAU. [OFr. *bele*, fem.]

bellez *n. pl.* bells 195. [OE. *belle*.]

belt *n.* belt 162, 1860, 2377, 2485. [OE. *belt*.]

belted *pp.* girt on 2032. [From prec.]

bemez *n. pl.* rays 1819. [OE. *bēam*.]

bench(e) *n.* bench 280, 344; *vpon bench*, at table 337, 351. [OE. *benc*.]

bende *n.* band 2506, 2517. [OE. *bend*.]

bende *pa. t.* bent; wrinkled (brows) 305; *pp.* in *b. by*, curved back in line with 2224; *hatz much baret b.*, has directed (brought about) much strife 2115. [OE. *béndan*.]

bene *adj.* pleasing, fair 2475; *adv.* pleasantly 2402. [(?) OFr. *b(i)en*, adv.]

bent *n.* grassy ground, field 2233, 2338; bank 1599; (*vp)on bent*, on the (hunting) field 1465; (of battle) 353, 2115; on the ground, there 2148. [A special use of *bent*, grass; OE. *beonet*.]

bent-felde *n.* the hunting field 1136. [Prec. + FELD.]

ber *n.* beer 129. [OE. *bēor*.]

berd(e) *n.* beard 182, 306, 334, 845, 2228. [OE. *béard*.]

berdlez *n.* beardless 280. [OE. *beard-lēas*.]

bere *v.* to bear, carry, wear, lift 265, 637, 1616, 1913, 2066, 2261; have, possess 1229; cast (light) 1819; *b. felaȝschip*, accompany 2151; **beres** *pres. pl.* bear (witness) 2523; **ber(e)** *pa. t.* 637, 2066, etc.; *bere on hym*, pressed on him 1860; **born(e)** *pp.* born 752, 996, 2320, 2394; *b. open*, laid open 2070. [OE. *beran*.]

berez *n. pl.* bears 722. [OE. *bera*.]

berȝe(e) *n.* mound 2172, 2178. [OE. *be(o)rg*.]

beseche *v.* to beg, implore 341, 753, 776, 1881; **bisoȝt** *pa. t.* 96, 1834, 1862. [OE. *be-* + *sēcan*.]

best *adj. superl.* best, noblest 73, 78, 259, 1563, 2101, etc.; *þe best*, the best man 1645; those of highest rank 550, 1325; *the b. thing to do* 1216; *wyth þe b.*, among the b., as well as any 986; *of þe b.*, from among the b. there were, (those) of the b. quality 38, 863, 880, 1145; in the b. manner 889, 1000. *adv.* best 73, 1005, 1680. [OE. *betst*.]

best *n.* beast 1359, 1377, 1436, 1603, 1631, 1901. [OFr. *beste*.]

beten *pa. t. pl.* beat 1437; *pp.* set (with stones, gold), embroidered 78, 1833, 2028. [OE. *bēatan*.]

bette *pp.* kindled 1368. [OE. *bētan*.]

better *adj. compar.* better, more valiant 353, 793, 2278; *as sb.*, something better 1109; *þe better* 1393 n.; *adv.* better 680, 1220, 1276, 1782, 1878 (see LERNE); *þe better*, the better (off), better, more 410, 1035, 1084, 2096. [OE. *betera, bet(t)ra*, adj.]

beuerage *n.* beverage, drink 1112, 1409. [OFr. *bevrage*.]

beuer-hwed *adj.* beaver-coloured, reddish brown 845. [OE. *beofor* + *-hiwede*.]

bewté *n.* beauty 1273. [OFr. *beauté*.]

bi, by *prep.* (*sometimes after its case*) by, beside, along, over, according to, etc. 20, 67, 214, 734, 1002 n., 1296, 1344, 2104, 2120, 2364, etc.; on (occasions) 41; near 1574; towards 2310; measured by 2226; (in oaths) 323, 1110, 1644, etc.; *conj.* by the time that 1169; when 1006, 2032. **bi þat** *adv.* by that time 597, 1868; thereupon 2152; *conj.* by the time that 443, 928, 1137, 1321, 1365, 1412; when 1678, 1912, 2043. [OE. *bǐ*].

bicause of *prep.* because of, for 1843. [BI + CAUSE.]

bicom(m)e, bicume. See BECOM.

bid(de), bedde (1374) *v.* to ask, request 1089; exhort, command 344, 370, 1374, 1603, 1999; **bede** *pa. t.*, see BEDE; **boden** (form due to BEDE) *pp.* asked 327. [OE. *biddan*.]

bide, byde(n) *v. trans.* to wait for 376, 520, 2292; stand (and face), withstand 290, 374, 1450, 2041; *intr.* wait, stay, stand firm 1092, 1366, 1582, 1585; **bode** *pa. t.* 785, 1564; **bade** *pa. t.* 1699. [OE. *bidan*.]

bye *v.* to buy 79. [OE. *bycgan*.]

bifalle, befalle *v.* to happen 382, 1776. [OE. *be-fallan*.]

bifor(n)e *prep.* before 1126, 1675; in front, ahead, in presence of 108, 347, 368, 1616, etc., (*after its case*) 123, 694, 716, 1704; above 914; in preference to 1275, 1781; **before, byfor(n)e** etc., *adv.* in front 422, 1741; previously 1405, 1577. [OE. *be-foran*.] See HERE.

big *adj.* strong 554; **bigger** *compar.* 2101; **bigly** *adv.* mightily 1141, 1162, 1584. [Uncertain.]

big(g)e *v.* settle, found 20; build 9. [ON. *byggva*.]

bigyle *v.* beguile, deceive 2413, 2416, 2427. [OE. *be-*+OFr. *guiler*.]

bigyn(n)e, begynne *v. intr.* to begin 1340, 1571, 1606; *trans.* 495; found 11; *biginez þe table*, has the place of honour 112; **bygan** *pa. t.* 661. [OE. *be-ginnan*.]

bigog *interj.* 390, corruption of *bi God.*

bigrauen *pp.* engraved, carved 216. [OE. *be-grafan*.]

biȝonde *prep.* across, beyond 2200. [OE. *be-geóndan*.]

byȝt *n.* fork (of the legs) 1341 (forelegs), 1349 (hind legs). [OE. *byht*.]

bihynde *adv.* behind 607, 1350; at the back 1741; inferior 1942. [OE. *be-hindan*.]

byholde, beholde *v.* to see, behold 232, 250, 1187; **behelde** *pa. t.* 794; **bihalden, -holde** *pp.* beholden, obliged 1842; in duty bound 1547. [OE. *be-háldan*, hold, behold.]

bihoue, by-, be- *v. impers.* to behove; as in *me bihoues*, I am obliged, (in duty) bound to, must 324, 456, 1065, 1068, 1216, 1239, etc.; *bihoues*, (he) is to 1754; **bihous** *pres. sg.* 2296; **bihoued** *pa. t.* 1771, 2040; **byhode** 717; *burnes behoued to*, it was time for folk to go in 1959. [OE. *be-hófian*.]

bikenne *v.* to commend 1307; **bikende** *pa. t.* 596, 1982. [OE. *be-*+KENNE.]

biknowe *v.* to acknowledge, confess 2385, 2495; **beknew** *pa. t.* 903; **beknowen** *pp.* cleared by confession 2391. [Cf. OE. *be-cnāwan*, know.]

bylde *v.* to build 509; **bult** *pa. t.* dwelt 25. [OE. **byldan*, in *pp. gebyld*.]

byled. See BOYLE.

biliue, bylyue *adv.* quickly 132, 1128, 1136, 1171, etc. [OE. **be life*.]

bynde *v.* to bind 1211; **bounden** *pp.* 192, 2486; bound, trimmed, adorned (with attached ornament) 573, 600, 609, 2028. [OE. *bindan*.]

bischop *n.* bishop 112. [OE. *biscop*.]

bisemez *v. impers.* it is fitting (for), becomes 1612, 2191; **bisemed** *pa. t.* (it) suited 622, 2035. [OE. *be*+SEME.]

bisyde *prep.* (*after its case*) beside 109, 1030, 1657, 1777 (see LAY) 2172; *hym b.* sideways 2265; *adv.* alongside, hard by, round about 1083, 1582, 2088, 2230. **bisides, bisydez** *adv.* at the sides, round about 76, 856, 2164. [OE. *be sidan*, at the side; see SIDE.]

bisied, bysily, bisinesse. See BUSY, BUSYLY, BUSYNES.

bisoȝt. See BESECHE.

bit(te), bytte *n.* blade, cutting edge 212, 426, 2224, 2310. [ON. *bit*.]

bite *v.* to bite 1598; *bite (of, on)*, cut into, pierce 426, 1162, 1457; **bot(e)** *pa. t.* 426, 1162, 1563. [OE. *bitan*.]

bityde *v.* to happen, befall 1406; *pres. subj.* 1893, 2195, etc.; **bitidde** *pa. t.* 2522. [OE. *be-*+TYDE.]

bytoknyng *n.* sign; *in b. of*, as a symbol of 626. [OE. **bitācnung*.]

bitwene *prep.* between 977, 1316, 1768, (*after its case*) 611, 1060, 2242, etc.; *adv.* at intervals 791, 795. [OE. *be-twēon(an)*.]

biwyled *pp.* deluded 2425. [OE. *be-*+*wiglian*.]

blake *adj.* black 958, 961. [OE. *blǣc*.]

blame *n.* blame 361, 1779; fault, 1488, 2506; *for b.*, as a rebuke 2500. [OFr. *bla(s)me*.]

blame *v.* to blame 2368. [OFr. *bla(s)mer*.]

blande *n.* mingling; *in blande*, (mingled) together 1205. [ON. *í bland*.]

blande *pp.* (*prob. wk.*) adorned 1931. [ON. *blanda*, str. and wk.]

blasoun *n.* shield 828. [OFr. *blaso(u)n*.]

blaste *n.* blast 784, 1148. [OE. *blǣst*.]

blaunner *n.* a fur, perhaps ermine 155 n., 573, **856*, 1931. [AN. **blaunc-ner*.]

blawyng *n.* blowing 1601. [OE. *blā-wung*.]

ble(e)aunt *n.* a rich stuff 879 n.; a mantle made of it 1928. [OFr. *bliaut*, AN. *bliaunt*.]

blede *v.* to bleed 441, 1163. [OE. *blēdan.*]

blenche *v.* to start back, swerve 1715. [OE. *blencan*, deceive.]

blende, blent *pp.* mingled 1361, 1610; *pa. t.* streamed together 2371 (cf. 2503). [OE. *ge-bléndan.*]

blended *pp.* deluded 2419. [OE. *bléndan*, to blind.]

blenk(e) *v.* to gleam 799, 2315. [ON. *blekkja*, older **blenkja.*]

blered *pp.* bleared 963. [Cf. OE. *a-blered, blere*, bald.]

blesse *v.* to call a blessing upon, wish well to 1296; *refl.* cross oneself 2071; **blessyng** *n.* blessing 370. [OE. *blētsian, blětsung.*]

blykke *v.* to shine, gleam 429, 2485; **blycande** *pres. p.* 305. [OE. *blican; blician.*]

blynne (*of*) *v.* to cease (from) 2322. [OE. *blinnan.*]

blysful *adj.* delightful 520. [From next.]

blys(se) *n.* happiness, joy 18, 825, 1368, 2530, etc. [OE. *bliss.*]

blyþe *adj.* merry, glad 922, 1273, 1398, 2321, etc.; bright, gay 155, 162; *adv.* 1684; **blyþely** *adv.* gaily, merrily 1311, 1834; pleasantly 1990. [OE. *bliþe, bliþelice.*]

blod(e) *n.* blood 89, 317, 2315, etc.; kinship 357; mettle 286. [OE. *blōd.*]

blod-houndez *n. pl.* bloodhounds 1436. [Prec.+OE. *húnd.*]

blonk *n.* horse, steed 434, 785, 1581, 2012, 2024, 2475; *pl.* **blonkkez** 1128, 1693. [OE. (verse) *blanca.*]

blossumez *n. pl.* blossoms 512. [OE. *blŏsma.*]

blowe *v.*[1] to bloom 512. [OE. *blŏwan.*]

blowe *v.*[2] to blow 1465; **blw(e)** *pa. t.* 1141, 1362; **blowed** 1913. [OE. *blāwan, blēow.*]

blubred *pa. t.* bubbled 2174. [Echoic.]

blunder *n.* turmoil, trouble 18. [From ME. *blundren*, daze, be dazed, rel. to *blind.* Cf. ON. *blunda*, Norw. *blundra*, doze.]

blusch *n.* gleam 520. [From next.]

blusche *v.* to glance, look 650, 793; **blusschande** *pres. p.* gleaming 1819. [OE. *blyscan.*]

blwe *n.* blue (stuff) 1928. [OFr. *bleu.*]

blwe *pa. t.* See BLOWE *v.*[2]

bobbaunce *n.* pomp, pride 9. [OFr. *boba(u)nce.*]

bobbe *n.* cluster 206. [Unknown.]

bode *n.* command 852; offer 1824. [OE. *bod.*]

bode(n). See BIDE, BID(DE).

bodi, body *n.* body 143, 966, etc.; *pl.* men 353; **bodé** in *my b.* myself 357. [OE. *bodig.*]

boerne; boffet. See BORNE; BUFFET.

boȝe *v.* to turn, go 344, 434, etc.; **boȝed** *pa. t.* 481, 1189, etc.; **boȝen** *pres.* or *pa. t. pl.* 2077; *boȝe fro* (*of*), leave 344, 1220. [OE. *būgan*, str.]

boȝez *n. pl.* boughs, branches 765, 2077. [OE. *bŏg.*]

boyle, byle *v.* to boil, bubble, 2082, 2174. [OFr. *boillir.*]

bok(e) *n.* book 690, 2521, 2523. [OE. *bŏc.*]

bold(e) *adj.* bold, valiant 272, 286, 1465, 2338, etc.; *as sb.* bold men 21, 351; *adv.* boldly, quickly (?) 2476. [OE. *báld, bálde* (instanter).]

bole *n.* tree-trunk 766. [ON. *bolr.*]

bolne *v.* to swell 512. [ON. *bolgna.*]

bonchef *n.* happiness 1764. [OFr. *bonch(i)ef.*]

bone *adj.*: *bone hostel*, a good lodging 776. [OFr. *bon hostel.*]

bone *n.* request, boon 327. [ON. *bón.*]

bones, -ez *n. pl.* bones 424, 1344. [OE. *bān.*]

bonk(e) *n.* hill-side, slope 710, 1571, 2172, etc.; **bonkkes, -ez** *pl.* 14, 1562, etc.; *bi bonk*, on the slopes, 511; shore, bank 700, 785. [ON. *bakki*, older **banke.*]

bor *n.* boar 722, 1441, 1448, 1590, 1606, 1616. [OE. *bār.*]

borde *n.*[1] table 481. [OE. *bord.*]

borde *n.*[2] band, embroidered strip 159, 610. [OE. *borda.*]

bordez. See BOURDE.

borelych *adj.* strong, massive 766, 2148, 2224. [Cf. OE. *borlice*, excellently.]

borȝ(e). See BURȜ(E).

borne, boerne *n.* stream 731, 1570, 2174. [OE. *búrne.*]

borne; bornyst. See BERE; BURNYST.

bost *n.* outcry, clamour 1448. [Not known.]

bot *adv.* only, but 30, 280, 356, 701, 1050, 1795, etc.; *bot oure one,* alone by ourselves, 1230. [OE. *būtan.*] See BOUTE.

bot *conj.* (i) except, other than, but 357, 547, 565, 763, 1054 (see NOLDE) 1553, 1887, etc.; *noȝt bot,* only 1267, 1833 (see NOBOT); *no more bot* no more than 2312; (ii) unless 716, 1210, 1300; *bot if,* unless 1782, 1956; (iii) but, however, yet 25, 85, 141, 2511 n., etc. [OE. *būtan, būte.*]

bot(e). See BITE.

botounz *n. pl.* buttons, bosses 220. [OFr. *bo(u)to(u)n.*]

boþe, both(e) *adj. and pron.* both 111, 192, 371, 582, 2352, etc.; either 2070, 2165; *adv.* as well, too 129, 155, 1580, etc.; both 18, *144, etc. [ON. *báðir.*]

boþem *n.* bottom 2145. [OE. *botm,* *boþm* (still NWM.).]

boun *adj.* ready 852, 1311, 1693; dressed 2043; *boun to,* bound, setting out for 548. [ON. *búinn, bún-.*]

bounté *n.* worth, virtue 357, 1519. [OFr. *bo(u)nté.*]

bourde, borde *n.* jest 1212, 1409, 1954. [OFr. *bo(u)rde.*]

bourded *pa. t.* jested 1217; **bourdyng** *n.* jesting 1404. [OFr. *bo(u)rder.*]

boure *n.* bedroom 853; ladies' bower 1519. [OE. *būr.*]

bout(e) *prep.* without 361, 1285, 1444, 2353. [OE. *būtan.*]

boweles *n. pl.* bowels, intestines *1333, 1609. [OFr. *bo(u)el.*]

brace *n. collective,* pair of arm-pieces 582. [OFr. *brace.*]

braches, -ez *n. pl.* hounds 1142 n., 1563, 1610; **brachetes** 1603 n. [OFr. *brachet.*]

brad *pp.* grilled 891. [OE. *brǣdan, brēdan.*]

bradde *pa. t. intr.* reached 1928. [OE. *brǣdan,* from *brād.*]

brayde *v.* to draw, pull 1584, 1609, 1901, 2319; swing 621; **brayd(e)** *pa. t.* pulled 1339; flung 2377; twisted, 440; spurted (*intr.*) 429; **brayde** *pp.* pulled 2069; **brayden, brawden** linked 580; embroidered 177, 220, set 1833. [OE. *bregdan,* pp. *brogden, bregden.*]

brayen *v.* to bray, cry out 1163. [OFr. *braire.*]

brayn *n.* brain 89. [OE. *brægn.*]

brayn *adj.* (?) mad 286 n. [?Shortened from adjs. such as next.]

braynwod *adj.* frenzied 1461, 1580. [OE. *bræg(e)n+wōd.*]

braþ. See BROPE.

braunch(e) *n.* branch 265, 2177. [OFr. *bra(u)nche.*]

brawden. See BRAYDE.

brawen, brawne *n.* (boar's) flesh 1611; *such a b. of a best,* such a quantity of flesh on any boar 1631. [OFr. *brao(u)n.*]

bred *n.* bread 891, 1361, 1610. [OE. *brēad.*]

bredden *pa. t. pl.* bred, were produced, multiplied 21. [OE. *brēdan.*]

bredez *n. pl.* planks 2071. [OE. *bred.*]

brek, breke(n) *pa. t.* broke, cut open 1333; broke down, overcame 1564; *intr.* burst forth, was uttered 1764; foamed 2082. [OE. *brecan.*]

brem(e) *adj.* brave, stout 1155; fierce 1142, *1441, 1580; wild 2145; loud 1601, 2200; *adv.* stoutly 781; **bremlych** *adv.* gloriously 509; **brem(e)ly** fiercely 1598, 2233, 2319; quickly 779. [OE. *brēme,* adj. and adv.]

brenne *v.* to burn 832, 875; *trans.* broil 1609; **brent** *pp.* 2; **brende** refined (by fire), bright (gold) 195 (cf. ON. *brent gull*). [ON. *brenna.*]

brent *adj.* steep 2165. [Cf. OE. *brant,* ON. *brettr,* older *brent-.*]

bresed *adj.* bristling 305. [Not known.]

brest *n.* breast 143, 182, 955, 1339, 1741, 2371. [OE. *brēost.*]

breþer *n. pl.* brothers-in-arms 39. [ON. *brœðr,* OMerc. *broeþre,* pl.]

breue *v.* to write down 2521; declare 465, 1393, 1488; announce (presence of game) by giving tongue 1436. [Med.L. *breviāre,* OE. *gebrēfan.*]

bryddes, -ez *n. pl.* birds 166, 509, 610, 746. [OE. *bridd*, young bird.]

brydel *n.* bridle 177, 434, 600, 1131, 2152. [OE. *brīdel*.]

bryg(g)e *n.* drawbridge 781, 821, 2069; *gen.* 779. [OE. *brycg*.]

bryȝt *adj. and adv.* bright 117, 129, 212, 269, 2226, 2517, etc.; pure white 155, 573, 856, 955; *compar.* 236; *superl.* fairest 1283. [OE. *berht*.]

brymme *n.* water's edge 2172. [Uncertain; cf. MHG. *brem* border.]

bryné. See BRUNY.

bryng *v.* to bring 825, 925, 1112, 2024, 2530 (*subj.*), etc.; **broȝt** *pa. t. and pp.* 337 (*with infin. as object*), 779, 853, 1120, 1519, 1990, 2145, etc. [OE. *bringan*.]

brit(t)en *v.* to break up, destroy 2, 680; cut (up) 1339, 1611. [OE. *brytnian*.]

brod(e) *adj.* broad, wide 14, 845, 1162, 2233, etc.; long 212; *adv.* with wide-open eyes 446. [OE. *brād*; *brāde*, adv.]

broȝez; broȝt. See BROWE; BRING.

broke *n.* stream 2082, 2200. [OE. *brōc*.]

bronde *n.* brand; piece of burnt wood 2; sword 561, 828, 1901, 2032, 2041; **bront** 588, 1584. [OE. *bránd*, *brónd*.]

broþe *adj.* fierce, grim 2233; **braþ** *1909; **broþely** *adv.* 2377. [ON. *brādr*, *brādliga*.]

broþerhede *n.* brotherhood 2516. [OE. *brōþor* + suffix *-hede* rel. to OE. *-hād*.]

broun *adj.* brown 618 n., 879; *as sb.* brown hide (of deer) 1162; bright, shining 426. [OE. *brūn*.]

browe *n.* brow, forehead 1457, 2306; *pl.* **broȝes, -ez** eyebrows 305, 961. [OE. *brū*.]

bruny *n.* mail-shirt 861, 2012, 2018; **bryné** 580. [ON. *brynja*, OFr. *brunie*.]

brusten *pp.* broken 1166. [ON. *bresta*; OE. *berstan*.]

buffet, boffet *n.* blow 382, 1754, 2343. [OFr. *buffet*.]

bugle *n.* bugle 1136, 1141, 1465, 1913. [OFr. *bugle*.]

bukkez *n. pl.* bucks 1155. [OE. *bucca*.]

bulk *n.* (headless) trunk *440. [ON. *búlki*, heap, cargo.]

bullez *n. pl.* wild bulls 722. [Cf. ODan. *bul*; OE. *bula*, *bulluc*.]

bult. See BYLDE.

bur *n.* onslaught, blow 290, 374, 548; strength 2261; violence 2322. [ON. *byrr*, a following wind.]

burde *n.* maiden, damsel 613, 752, 942, 1373, etc.; lady 961, 1283, etc. [OE. *byrde*, embroideress; cf. *byrdistre*, and ON. *byrða*.]

burde *pa. t. subj. impers.*; *me burde*, I ought to 2278, 2428. [OE. *gebyrian*.]

burȝ(e), borȝ(e) *n.* castle, city 2, 9, 259, 550, 843, 1034, 1092, 2476. [OE. *burg*.]

burn(e), buurne (825) *n.* warrior, knight, man 20, 73, 259, 272, 1582, 2320, etc.; *voc.* sir (knight) 1071, 2284, 2322. [OE. *béorn*.]

burnyst, bornyst *pp.* polished 212, 582. [OFr. *brunir*, *burnir*, *burniss-*.]

burþe *n.* birth 922. [OE. *ge-byrd*, *byrþ-*.]

busy *v. intr.* to be busy, bestir oneself 1066; **bisied**, *pa. t. trans.* stirred 89. [OE. *bysigian*.]

busyly, bysily *adv.* earnestly, eagerly 68, 1824. [From OE. *bysig*.]

busynes *n.* solicitude 1986; **bisinesse** importunity 1840. [OE. *bysignes*.]

busk *n.* bush 182, 1437. [ODan. *buske*.]

busk(ke) *v. intr.* to get ready, array, dress 1220, 1693; *intr.* make haste (to) 509, 1136, 1411, 1448, 2284, 2476; **busken** *vp*, hasten 1128; *trans.* make 2248. [ON. *búask*, refl.]

buttokez *n. pl.* buttocks 967. [Obscure.]

C

cace, case *n.* chance 907; occurrence 1196; circumstances, affair 546; *to vche a cace*, to everything she chanced to say 1262. [OFr. *cas*.]

cach(che), kach *v.* to catch; **caȝt, kaȝt** *pa. t.* 643, 1011, 1118; *pp.* 1225, 2508. To chase, urge on 1581,

cach (*cont.*)

2175; catch, seize 368, 434, 1225, 1906 (MS.); take 133, 1118, 1305; receive, get 643, 1011, 1938; acquire 2508; ca3t vp, raised 1185; *intr.* in ka3t to, laid hold of 2376; *cach*, hasten, go 1794. [ONFr. *cach(i)er*, infl. by LACH(CHE).]

cacheres, *n. pl.* huntsmen 1139. [ONFr. *cach(i)ere* nom.]

cayre, kayre *v.* to ride 43, 1048, 1670, 2120. [ON. *keyra.*]

cakled *pp.* cackled 1412. [Cf. Dan. *kagle.*]

calle, kalle *v. intr.* to call (out), shout 807, 2212, etc.; *c. on,* call to 1701, 1743; *c. of,* crave, beg for 975, 1882; cry out (of hounds) 1421; *trans.* to call, name 456, 664, 964, 2278, etc.; summon, call 1127, 1140, 1666, etc. [ON. *kalla,* OE. (late) *ceallian.*]

can. See CON *auxil.*

capados *n.* a kind of hood 186 n., 572. [(?) OFr. *Capadoce,* Cappadocia.]

caple *n.* horse 2175. [Cf. ON. *kapall.*]

care *n.* sorrow, grief 557, 1254, 1979, 2384; trouble 2495; *care of,* anxiety concerning 2379. [OE. *caru.*]

care *v.* to grieve for 674; be concerned (for) 750, 1773. [OE. *carian.*]

carye *v.* ride 734 n. [AN. *carier.*] See CAYRE.

carnelez *n. pl.* embrasures in the battlements 801. [ONFr. *carnel.*]

carole *n.* dance and song combined 43, 473, 1026, 1655, 1886. [OFr. *carole.*]

carp *n.* talk, conversation 307, 1013; **karp** mention 704. [ON. *karp,* bragging.]

carp(p)e, karp *v.* to speak, say 263, 360, 377, 1088, 1221, 1979; converse 696, 1225. [ON. *karpa,* brag.]

case. See CACE.

cast, kest *n.* stroke 2298; trick 2413; (?)fastening 2376; *pl.* speech, utterances 1295. [ON. *kast.*]

cast, kest *v.*; **cast, kest** *pa. t.* 228, 1649, 2317, etc.; *pp.* 64, 878, etc. To cast, throw, put 621, 878, 1355, 1484, etc.; lift 1192; *kest . . . to,* cast

(his eye) on 228; *of k.,* cast off 1147; to utter 64; offer, make 2242, 2275; *intr. or absol.* aim 1901; cast about in mind, ponder 1855; *c. vnto,* speak to, address 249. [ON. *kasta.*]

castel *n.* castle 767, 801 (*attrib.*), 1366; **kastel** 2067. [ONFr. *castel.*]

caue *n.* cave 2182. [OFr. *cave.*]

cauelaciounz. See KAUELACION.

cause *n.* cause; *at þis c.,* for this reason 648. [OFr. *cause.*]

cemmed *pp.* combed 188. [OE. *cemban.*]

cercle *n.* circlet 615 n. [OFr. *cercle.*]

chace *n.* hunt 1416, 1604. [OFr. *chace.*]

chaffer *n.* trade 1647; merchandise 1939. [OE. *cēap+faru;* cf. ON. *kaupfǫr.*]

chalk-whyt, -quyte *adj.* white as chalk 798, *958. [OE. *cealc+hwit.*]

chamber, chambre *n.* private sitting-room or bedroom 48, 833, 978, 1402, 1742 (*attrib.*), etc. [OFr. *chambre.*]

chamberlayn *n.* chamberlain, groom of the chamber 1310, 2011. [OFr. *chamberlain.*]

chapel(le), chapayle *n.* (private) chapel 63, 451, *705, 1070, 1876, 2186, etc. [OFr. *chapele.*]

chaplayn *n.* priest serving a chapel *930, 2107. [OFr. *chapelain.*]

charcole *n.* charcoal 875. [OE. *col,* first element uncertain.]

charg *n.* importance; *no charg,* it does not matter 1940. [OFr. *charge.*]

charge *v.* to put on 863; charge, enjoin 451. [OFr. *charg(i)er.*]

chargeaunt *adj.* onerous, toilsome 1604. [OFr. *chargea(u)nt.*]

charyté *n.* charity, kindliness 2055. [OFr. *charité.*]

charre *v. trans.* to turn back 1143; take 850; *intr.* return 1678. [OE. *cerran, cærran.*]

charres *n. pl.* affairs, business 1674. [OE. *cerr, cærr.*]

chasyng *n.* chasing 1143 n. [From OFr. *chac(i)er.*]

chastysed *pa. t.* rebuked 1143. [OFr. (rare) *chastiser.*]

chaunce *n.* chance, fortune 1406, 2068; adventure 1081, 1838, 2399,

2496; *cheuez þat ch.*, brings it to pass
2103; *for ch.*, in spite of anything
2132. [OFr. *ch(e)a(u)nce.*]

chauncely *adv.* by chance 778. [From
prec.]

chaunge *v.* to exchange 1107, 1406,
1678; turn 711, 2169 (see CHER(E));
change 863. [OFr. *cha(u)ng(i)er.*]

chaunsel *n.* chancel 946. [OFr.
cha(u)ncel.]

chauntré *n.* singing of mass 63.
[OFr. *cha(u)nterie.*]

chef *adj.* chief, principal 1512, 1604;
main (road) 778; **chefly** *adv.* particularly 978; quickly *850, *883,
1940; **cheuely** 1876. [OFr. *ch(i)ef.*]

cheyer *n.* chair 875. [OFr. *chaiere.*]

cheke *n.* cheek 953, 1204. [OE. *cē(a)c.*]

chek(k)e *n.* checkmate; ill luck 2195;
fortune 1107 (gain), 1857. [OFr.
esch(i)ec.]

cheldez. See SCHELDE.

chemné *n.* fireplace 875, 978, 1667;
chymné 1030, 1402; **chymnees**
pl. chimneys 798. [OFr. *cheminée.*]

chepe *n.* trade; price 1940; *pl.* goods
(got in trade) 1941 n.; *hade goud
chepez*, had good bargains 1939.
[OE. *cēap.*]

chepen *v.* to bargain 1271. [OE.
cēapian.]

cher(e), schere *n.* (expression of)
face 334; *chaunge ch.* turn this way
and that 711, 2169; demeanour,
behaviour 1759, 2496; *made gret ch.*,
behaved graciously 1259; *bele ch.*,
gracious company 1034; mood,
frame of mind 883; *mad ay god
ch.*, remained cheerful 562; *with ch.*,
merrily 1745. [OFr. *ch(i)ere.*]

cheryche *v.* to treat kindly; salute
graciously 946; **cherysen** *pres. pl.*
receive kindly, entertain 2055. [OFr.
cherir, cheriss-.]

ches. See CHOSE.

cheualry *n.* knighthood, knightly
conduct 1512. [OFr. *chevalerie.*]

cheualrous *adj.* chivalrous 2399.
[OFr. *chevalero(u)s.*]

cheue *v.* to acquire, get 1271, 1390;
bring about 2103; *intr.* come (to an
end) 63; *cheue to*, make your way
to 1674. [OFr. *chevir* and *achever.*]

cheuely. See CHEF.

cheuisaunce, cheuicaunce *n.* winnings, gain 1390, 1406, 1678; *ch. of*,
obtaining 1939. [OFr. *chevis-
sa(u)nce.*]

chylde *n.* child 647; **chylder** *pl.* 280.
[OE. *cild*, pl. *cildru.*]

child-gered *adj.* boyish, merry 86 n.
[Prec.+*gere*, mood; cf. MDu.
gere, gaer.]

chymbled *pp.* bound, wrapped up
958. [Cf. ON. *kimbla.*]

chymne(es). See CHEMNÉ.

chyne *n.* chine, backbone 1354.
[OFr. *eschine.*]

chyn(ne) *n.* chin 958, 1204. [OE. *cinn.*]

chorle *n.* man (of low birth) 2107.
[OE. *ceorl.*]

chose *v.* to choose, select 863, 1271,
1310; *to chose of*, conspicuous among
1512; pick out, perceive 798; *chose
þe waye (gate)*, take one's way, go
930, 1876; *hence intr.* make one's
way, go 451, 778, 946; *subj.* (that)
you go 451; **ches** *pa. t. sg.* 798,
946; **chosen** *pl.* 930; **chosen** *pp.*
chosen 1275; undertaken 1838;
made his way 778. [OE. *cēosan.*]

clad *pa. t.* clothed, dressed 2015; *pp.*
covered 885. [OE. (rare) *clæþan*, pa.
t. *clǽdde.*]

clayme *v.* to claim 1490. [OFr.
clamer, 3 sg. *claime.*]

clamberande *pres. p.* clustering
1722; **clambred** *pp.* 801. [ON.
klambra.]

clanly *adv.* clean; without omission
393. [OE. *clǽn-lice.*] See CLENE.

clannes *n.* purity, freedom from sin
653. [OE. *clǽn-nes.*]

clatered *pa. t.* clattered, re-echoed
2201; *pp.* fallen clattering down
1722; **claterande** *pres. p.* splashing
731. [Cf. OE. *clatrung.*]

clene *adj.* clean, pure 885, 1013, 1883,
2393; bright 158, 161; elegant,
fair 146, 154, 163, 854; *adv.* clean,
2391; bright 576, 2017; neatly 792;
completely 1298. [OE. *clǽne.*]

clenge *v.* to cling (to the earth)
1694, 2078; *c. adoun*, shrink down
(into the earth) 505. [OE. *clingan.*]

clepe *v.* to call 1310. [OE. *cleopian.*]

cler(e) *adj.* clear, bright, fair 631, 854, 942, 1181, 1747, 2351, etc.; *as sb.*, fair lady 1489; *adv.* in *cler quyt*, pure white 885. [OFr. *cler*.]

clergye *n.* learning; magical lore 2447. [OFr. *clergie*.]

clerk *n.* clerk, priest 64; **klerk** sage, wizard 2450. [OE. *cler(i)c*; OFr. *clerc*.]

cleue *v. intr.* to split 2201. [OE. *clēofan*, trans.]

clyff(e), klyf(fe) *n.* cliff, (high) rock 713, 1166, 1431, 1722, 2078, 2201. [OE. *clif*.]

cloyster *n.* enclosure, wall 804. [OFr. *cloistre*.]

clomben *pa. t. pl.* climbed 2078. [OE. *climban*, pa. t. pl. *clumbon*.]

close *v.* to close, fasten 572 n., 1742; enclose, cover 186, 578; *pp.* contained 1298; *closed fro*, free from 1013. [From OFr. *clos*, n.]

closet *n.* closed pew in the castle chapel for the lord and his family 934, 942. [OFr. *closet*.]

cloþe *n.* cloth 2036; table-cloth 885; *on clothe*, on the table 125; **cloþes, -ez** *pl.* clothes 2015; coverings (for chair) 876; bedclothes 1184; table-cloths 1649. [OE. *clāþ*.]

cloudez *n. pl.* clouds 505, 727; **clowdes** 1696, 2001. [Cf. OE. *clūd*, mass of earth or rock.]

clusteres *n. pl.* clusters 1739. [OE. *cluster*.]

cnokez 2 *sg.* knock, deal a blow 414. [OE. *cnocian*.]

cofly *adv.* promptly 2011.[OE. *cāf-līce*.]

coȝed *pa. t.* cried out, shouted 307 n. [OE. *cohhetan*.]

coynt, coyntly(ch). See KOYNT.

coke *n.* cock 1412; **kok** 2008. [OE. *cocc*.]

colde *adj.* cold 727, 731, 818, 1732, 1844 (see HOT), etc.; sad 1982; **coolde** the cold (snowy) ground 2474; **colde** *n.* (the) cold 505, 747, 2001, 2015, 2078. [OE. *cāld*, n. and adj.]

colen *v.* to cool; assuage, relieve 1254. [OE. *cōlian*, intr.]

colour *n.* colour 1059; complexion 944. [OFr. *colo(u)r*.]

com(me), cum *v.* to come, arrive 347, 594, 1073, 1476, etc.; *com ȝe*, if you go 2111; **com(e)** *pa. t.* 116, 502, 1004, *1755, etc.; **com(en)** *pl.* 556, 824; *c. to*, entered into 1855; **com-(m)en** *pp.* 907, 2491, etc., **cum-(m)en** 60, 62, 533. [OE. *cuman*.]

comaunded, cumaunde *v.* to bid, command 366, 850, 1372; order 992; **comaundez** *imper.* commend 2411. [OFr. *co(u)ma(u)nder*.]

comaundement *n.* orders, bidding 1303, 1501. [OFr. *coma(u)ndement*.]

comended *pa. t.* commended, praised 1629. [OFr. *com(m)ender*.]

comfort *n.* solace, pleasure 1011, 1221, 1254. [OFr. *confort*.]

comfort *v.* to comfort 2513; solace, amuse 1099. [OFr. *conforter*.]

comly, cumly *adj.* fair, beautiful, noble 934, 1366, 1732; **comlych** 469, 539, 1366, 2411, etc.; *quasi-sb.* fair knight 674; fair lady 1755; **comloker** *compar.* 869; **comlokest** *superl.* 53, 767, 1520; *quasi-sb.* fairest lady 81; **comly(che)** *adv.* fittingly, graciously 648, 1307, 1629, 1794; **comlyly** 360, 974, etc. [OE. *cȳmlic, cȳmlīce*, infl. by assoc. with ME. *becomen*.]

commen, -es, cummen. See COM.

companyny(e), companye *n.* company 556, companionship 1011; (her) company 1099; (polite) society 1483; **compeyny** retinue 1912. [OFr. *compai(g)nie*.]

compas *n.* measurement; proportion 944. [OFr. *compas*.]

compast *pa. t.* pondered 1196. [OFr. *compasser*.]

con *v.*[1] I know how to, can 2283; 3 *sg.* 2138, 2455; **connez** 2 *pl.* 1267 n., 1483; **couth, couþe, cowþe** *pa. t.* could 45, 1125, 1299, 1486, 1937, 2273, etc.; knew their craft 1139. [OE. *can, cūþe*.]

con *v.*[2] *auxil. with infin. as equiv. of pa. t.* did 230, 275, 362, 1598, 1666, etc.; **can** 340, 1042. [Prec. confused with ME. *gan*, did.]

conable *adj.* fitting, excellent 2450. [Reduction (Northern) of OFr. *covenable*.]

concience *n.* conscience; mind 1196. [OFr. *conscience*.]

confessed *pp.* in *c. clene*, made clean by confession 2391. [OFr. *confesser*.]

conysaunce *n.* cognisance, badge 2026. [OFr. *conissa(u)nce*.]

connez. See CON.

conquestes *n. pl.* conquests 311. [OFr. *conqueste*.]

constrayne *v.* to compel, force 1496. [OFr. *constreindre, constreign-*.]

contray *n.* region 713; *bi. c.*, over the land 734. [OFr. *contrée*.]

conueyed *pa. t.* escorted 596 n. [OFr. *conveier*.]

coolde. See COLDE.

coprounes *n. pl.* ornamental tops 797. [OFr. *co(u)pero(u)n*.]

corbel *n.* raven 1355 n. [OFr. *corbel*.]

corner *n.* corner 1185. [OFr. *cor-n(i)er*.]

cors *n.*[1] body; *mi c.* me 1237 n. [OFr. *cors*.]

cors *n.*[2] course (at dinner) 116; **cource** 135. [OFr. *co(u)rs*.]

corsed *pp. and adj.* cursed 2374; **corsedest** *superl.* 2196. [OE. *cŭrsian*, from OIr. *cúrsagim*.]

corsour *n.* courser (horse) 1583. [OFr. *corsier*, with altered suffix.]

co(u)rt *n.* court, members of noble household 43, 360, 400, 903, etc.; **ko(u)rt** 1048, 2340; *to cort*, home 1099. [OFr. *co(u)rt*.]

cortays(e) *adj.* chivalrous, courteous, gracious 276, 469, 539, 1013, 1511, 1525; *quasi-sb.* gracious lady 2411. **cortaysly** *adv.* courteously, graciously 775, 903. [OFr. *co(u)rteis*.]

cortaysy(e) *n.* courtesy, (manners and virtues of) chivalry 247, 263, 653, 1298, 1491, 1773. [OFr. *co(u)rteisie*.]

cort-ferez *n. pl.* companions at court 594. [OFr. *co(u)rt*+OE. *fēra*.]

cortyn *n.* curtain, bed-hanging (*see frontis.*) 854, 1185, 1192, 1732; **cortayn** 1476. [OFr. *co(u)rtine*.]

cortyned *pp.* curtained 1181. [From prec.]

coruon *pp.* carved 797. [OE. *ceorfan*, pp. *corfen*.]

cosyn *n.* cousin; kinsman 372. [OFr. *co(u)sin*.]

cosse *n.* kiss 1300, 1946, 2351, 2360. [OE. *coss*.] See KYSSE.

cost *n.* nature, quality 944, 1272, 1849, 2360; terms 546; *pl.* manners, ways, disposition 1483; condition, plight 750; *c. of care*, hardships 2495. [Late OE. *cost* from ON. *kostr*.]

costez *3 sg.* coasts, passes by the side of 1696. [From OFr. *coste*, n.; cf. AN. *costeier*.]

cote *n.* coat (skin) 1921; tunic 152, 335; coat-armour (see next) 637, 2026. [OFr. *cote*.]

cote-armure *n.* coat armour, a vest of rich stuff, embroidered with heraldic devices, worn over the armour 586. [Prec.+OFr. *armeüre*.]

coþe *pa. t. sg.* quoth, said 776; **quoþ* 256, 309, 1779, etc. [OE. *cwæþ*.]

couardise *n.* cowardice 2508; **cowardise** 2273; **coward(d)yse** 2374, 2379. [OFr. *couardise*.]

couenaunt, couenaunde *n.* agreement, compact 393, 1384, 2328, 2340; *pl.* terms of compact 1123, 1408, 1642, 2242. [OFr. *covena(u)nt*.]

couerto(u)r *n.* coverlet 855, 1181; horse-cloth, trapper 602 n. [OFr. *co(u)verto(u)r*.]

couetyse *n.* covetousness 2374, 2380, 2508. [OFr. *coveitise*.]

coundue *v.* to conduct 1972. [OFr. *co(u)nduire*.]

coundutes *n. pl.* 'conductus'; *c. of Krystmasse*, Christmas carols 1655 n. [OFr. *co(u)nduite*.]

counse(y)l *n.* counsel 682; *to your c.*, to advise you 347. [OFr. *co(u)nseil*.]

counseyl *v.* to advise, counsel 557. [OFr. *co(u)nseill(i)er*.]

countenaunce *n.* bearing; expression of face 335; custom 100; favour, looks of favour 1490, 1539, 1659. [OFr. *co(u)ntena(u)nce*.]

couples *n. pl.* leashes 1147. [OFr. *co(u)ple*.]

cource; court. See CORS *n.*[2]; CORT.

couþ(e), cowþe. See CON.

couþe *adj.* evident, plain to see 1490. [OE. *cūþ*.]

couþly *adv.* familiarly 937. [OE. *cūþ-līce*.]

coward(d)yse etc. See COUARDISE.

cowpled *pa. t.* coupled, leashed together (in pairs) 1139. [OFr. *co(u)pler.*] See COUPLES.

cowters *n. pl.* elbow-pieces (of armour) 583. [OFr. **co(u)t(i)ere* from *co(u)te* elbow.]

crabbed *adj.* crabbed; unconvivial 502; perverse 2435. [Obscure.]

craft *n.* skill (in an art or pursuit) 1380; affairs, doings 471; *pl.* (magic) crafts 2447; (skilful) ways, dealings 1527; pursuits 1688. [OE. *cræft.*]

crafty *adj.* skilfully made 572. [OE. *cræftig.*]

craftyly *adv.* ingeniously 797. [OE. *cræftig-lice.*]

cragge *n.* crag 1430, 2183, 2221. [M.Welsh **crag*; cf. M.Breton *cragg.*]

crakkande *pres. p.* echoing, ringing 1166; **crakkyng** *n.* (sudden) blaring 116. [OE. *cracian.*]

craþayn *n.* churl, boor 1773. [Obscure.]

craue *v.* to claim 1384; ask for 277 (*subj.*), 283; crave, beg (for) 812, 1300, 1670. [OE. *crafian,* demand.]

crede *n.* creed 643, 758. [OE. *crēda.*]

creped *pa. t.* crept 1192. [OE. *crēopan,* str.]

cresped *pp.* curled 188. [OFr. *crespe*; OE. *cirpsian,* v.]

crest *n.* mountain-top 731. [OFr. *creste.*]

creuisse *n.* fissure 2183. [OFr. **creveīz.*]

cry(e) *n.* shouting 64; **kry** 1166; cry (for help), appeal 775. [OFr. *cri.*]

crye, cri(e) *v.* to shout, call 1088, 1445; lament 760; *kryes þerof,* gives tongue at it (the line of scent) 1701. [OFr. *crier.*]

Crystenmas(se) *n.* Christmas 502; *quasi-adj.* 985; **Krystmasse** 37, 1655; **Crystemas** 283; **Cristmasse, Crystmasse** 471, 683; *þat Krystmasse,* those Chr. festivities 907; *Krystmasse euen,* Christmas Eve 734. [OE. *cristen,* adj.+ *mæsse*; cf. OE. (late) *crist-mæsse.*]

croys *n.* cross 643. [OFr. *crois.*]

croked *adj.* crooked; *were neuer croked,* never went astray, never failed 653. [From ON. *krókr,* n.]

cropure, cropore *n.* crupper 168, 602. [OFr. *crop(i)ere,* with altered suffix.]

cros *n.* cross 762 n. [ON. *kross,* from OIr. *cros.*]

croun *n.* crown 364; *þat bere þe c. of þorne,* Christ 2529; crown of the head 419, 616. [OFr. *co(u)ro(u)ne*; cf. ON. *krúna.*]

crowen *pp.* crowed **1412; **crue** *pa. t.* 2008. [OE. *crāwan.*]

cum, cum-. See COM, COM-.

curious *adj.* skilfully made, of elaborate design 855. [OFr. *curio(u)s.*]

D

dabate 2041. See DEBATE *n.*

day(e) *n.* day 44, 61, 1022, 1075, etc.; (life) time 2522; daylight 1126, 1999, etc.; *vpon d.,* by day 47; *in daye,* ever 80; *dayez,* in the day 1072. [OE. *dæg.*]

daylyeden. See DALY.

dayly3t *n.* daylight 1137, 1365. [DAY+LY3T; cf. OE. *dæges liht.*]

daynté, dayntye *n.* courtesy, courteous treatment 1250, 1662; honour 1266; *hade d. of,* felt regard for, admired 1889; *pl.* delights, dainties 121, 483, 998, 1401. [OFr. *deint(i)é.*]

daynté *adj.* delightful 1253. [Attrib. use of prec.]

dale *n.* (bottom of) valley 1151, 2005, 2162. [OE. *dæl.*]

daly *v.* to trifle, make (courtly) love 1253; **daylyeden** *pa. t. pl.* 1114. [OFr. *dalier.*]

dalyaunce *n.* courtly conversation 1012, 1529. [OFr. **dalia(u)nce.*]

dalt(en). See DELE.

dame *n.* lady 470; *pl.* 1316. [OFr. *dame.*]

dar *pres. t.* dare 287, 300, 1991; **durst** *pa. t.* 1493, 1575. [OE. *dearr, dorste.*]

dare *v.* to cower 315, 2258. [OE. *darian.*]

daunsed *pa. t.* danced 1026; **daunsyng** *n.* 47. [OFr. *da(u)ncer.*]

dawed *pa. t. subj.* would be worth 1805. [OE. *dugan.*]

debate, dabate *n.* resistance 1754, 2041, 2248. [OFr. *debat.*]

debate *v.* to debate, dispute 68; **debatande** *pres. p.* deliberating 2179. [OFr. *debatre.*]

debonerté *n.* courtesy 1273. [OFr. *deboneret(i)é*, from phrase *de bon(e) aire.*]

dece, des *n.* raised platform, dais (on which high table stood) 61, 75, 114, 222, 250, 445, 478, 1000. [OFr. *deis.*]

ded *adj.* dead; slain 725, 2264. [OE. *dēad.*]

dede *n.* deed, act 1047, 1089, 1265 n., 1629; task 1327; occupation 1468; affair 1662. [OE. *dēd.*]

defence *n.* defence; *with d.* defensively 1282. [OFr. *defense.*]

defende *v.* to defend 1551, 2117; *pp.* forbidden 1156. [OFr. *defendre.*]

degré *n.* rank 1006. [OFr. *degré.*]

deȝe *v.* to die 996, 1163; **dyȝe** 2460. [ON. *deyja.*]

dele 2188. See DEUEL.

dele *v.* to deal, mete out 295, 397, 1266, *1752, 2285; (blows) 560; give 1805; perform 2192; partake of, receive 1968; **dalt(en)** *pa. t.* and *pp.* 452, 1114, 2418, 2449; (?)conversed 1668; *d. with*, behaved to 1662. See DRURY, VNTYȜTEL. [OE. *dǣlan.*]

delful, dulful *adj.* grievous 560, 1517. [From DOEL.]

deliuer *adj.* nimble 2343; **deliuerly** *adv.* quickly 2009. [OFr. *de(s)livre.*]

delyuer *v.* to assign 851; *pp.* dealt with, over 1414. [OFr. *de(s)livrer.*]

demay *imper. refl.* be perturbed 470; **dismayd** *(for) pp.* dismayed (at) 336. [OFr. *de(s)maier.*]

deme *v.* to judge, consider 240, 246, 1529; think fit, determine 1082, 1089, 1668; tell, say 1322, 2183. [OE. *dēman.*]

denez *adj.* Danish 2223 n. [OE. *denisc;* OFr. *daneis.*]

dep(e) *adj.* deep, profound 741, 786, 1159, 1748; *adv.* 787. [OE. *dēop; dēope,* adv.]

depaynt(ed) *pp.* painted 620; depicted 649. [OFr. *depeindre,* 3 sg. pres. and pp. *depeint.*]

departe *v.* to separate 1335; *intr.* part 1983; **departyng** *n.* parting 1798. [OFr. *departir.*]

deprece *v.*[1] to subjugate 6; **deprese** press, importune 1770. [OFr. *depresser.*]

deprece *v.*[2] to release 1219. [OFr. *de(s)presser,* free from pressure; *de(s)priser,* free from prison.]

der(e) *n. pl.* deer 1151, 1157, 1322, 1324. [OE. *dēor.*]

dere *adj.* costly, precious 75, 121, 193, 571; pleasant 47, 564 n., 1012, 1026, 2449; beloved, dear 470, 754; noble 2465; festal 92, 1047; *as sb.* dear 1492, 1798; noble 678, 928 (Gawain dining alone). **derrest** *superl.* noblest 445, 483. [OE. *dēore;* compar. *dēorra.*]

dered *pa. t.* afflicted, hurt 1460. [OE. *derian.*]

derely *adv.* splendidly 1559; pleasantly 1253; courteously 817, 1031; neatly 1327; deeply 1842. [OE. *dēorlīce.*]

derf, derue *adj.* doughty 1000, 1492; stout, 1233; grievous, severe 558, 564, 1047. [ON. *djarfr,* bold, infl. by sense of OE. *deorfan, derfan.*]

derk *adj.* dark 1177, 1887; *n.* dark(ness) 1999. [OE. *de(o)rc.*]

derne *adj.* private 1012; **dernly** *adv.* stealthily *1183 (MS. *derf-*), 1188. [OE. *derne, dernlīce.*]

deruely *adv.* boldly 2334. [ON. *djarfliga.*]

derworþly, *adv.* sumptuously 114. [OE. *dēorwurþlīce.*]

des. See DECE.

deserue, disserue *v.* to deserve 452, 1779, 1803. [OFr. *deservir.*]

desyre *v.* to desire 1257. [OFr. *desirer.*]

destiné *n.* fate, destiny 564, 996, 1752, 2285. [OFr. *destinée.*]

deþe, dethe *n.* death 1600, 2105. [OE. *dēaþ.*]

deuaye *v.* to deny, refuse 1493, 1497. [OFr. *deve(i)er.*]

deue *v.* to stun, to strike down 1286. [OE. *dēafian.*]

deuel, dele *n.* Devil 2188, 2192. [OE. *dēofol.*]

deuys *n.* in *a deuys* = OFr. *a devis*, at one's desire, perfect 617. [OFr. *devis*.]

deuise *v.* to relate 92. [OFr. *deviser*.]

deuocioun *n.* devotions 2192. [OFr. *devocio(u)n*.]

dewe *n.* dew 519. [OE. *dēaw*.]

diamauntez *n. pl.* diamonds 617. [OFr. *diamant*.]

dich *n.* ditch, moat 766, 786, 1709. [OE. *dīc*.]

dy3e. See DE3E.

di3t, dy3t *v.* to appoint; *d. me þe dom*, adjudge me the right 295; *d. hym*, went 994; *pp.* set 114; appointed 678, 1884; dressed 1689; prepared 1559; made 2223. [OE. *dihtan*.]

dille *adj.* foolish, stupid 1529. [OE. *dylle, rel. to *dol*.]

dyn *n.* noise, merrymaking 47, 1159, 1183, 1308. [OE. *dyne*.]

diner *n.* dinner (the chief meal of the day, begun about 2 o'clock) 928, 1559. [OFr. *di(s)ner*.]

dyngez *pres. t.* smites *2105. [ON. *dengja*, wk.]

dyngne *adj.* worthy 1316. [OFr. *digne*.]

dynt *n.* blow 202, 1460, 2264, etc.; **dunt(e)** 452, 1286. [OE. *dynt*.]

disceuer, discouer *v.* to uncover, reveal 418, 1862. [OFr. *descovrir*, 3 *sg. descuevre*.]

disches *n. pl.* dishes 122, 128. [OE. *disc*.]

discrye *v.* to behold 81. [OFr. *descrire*, variant of *descrivre*.]

disert *n.* desert, merit 1266. [OFr. *desert*.]

dismayd 336. See DEMAY.

displayed *pa. t.* displayed, left uncovered 955. [OFr. *despleier*.]

displese *v.* to displease 1304; *impers. subj.* let it displease 1839; *imper. pl. refl.* take offence 2439. [OFr. *desplaisir, -plesir*.]

dispoyled *pp.* stripped 860. [OFr. *despoill(i)er*.]

disport *n.* entertainment 1292. [OFr. *desport*.]

disserue See DESERUE.

disstrye *v.* to destroy 2375. [OFr. *destruire*.]

dit *pp.* closed, locked 1233. [OE. *dyttan*.]

do *v.* to do 1089, etc.; **dos, dotz** *3 sg.* 1308, 2211; *imper. pl.* 1533; **did(de)** *pa. t.* 998, 1327, etc.; **don(e)** *pp.* 478, 928, etc. To do, perform, make 565, 1082, etc.; *do me*, afford me 1798; *dotz me drede*, makes me afraid 2211; *didden hem vndo*, had them cut up 1327; to put, set 478; *do way*, cease from 1492; *dos hir*, goes 1308; *dos come!* 1533; *pp.* over 928, 1365. [OE. *dōn*.]

doel *n.* lament 558. [OFr. *doel*.]

doggez *n. pl.* dogs 1600. [OE. (late) *docga*.]

do3ter *n.* daughter 2465. [OE. *dohtor*.]

do3ty *adj.,* doughty, brave 2264; *as sb.* hero 2334. [OE. *dohtig*.] See DU3TY.

dok *n.* tail 193. [Cf. Icel. *dokkur*.]

dole *n.* part 719. [OE. *dāl*.]

dom(e) *n.* judgement, doom 295, 1216, 1968. [OE. *dōm*.]

domezday *n.* doomsday 1884. [OE. *dōmes dæg*.]

donkande *pres. p.* moistening 519. [Cf. ON. *dǫkk*, pool; Swed. dial. *dänka*, to moisten.]

dor(e) *n.* door 136, 1140, 1183, 1233, 1308, 1742. [OE. *duru, dor*.]

do(e)s *n. pl.* does 1159, 1322. [OE. *dā*.]

doser *n.* wall-tapestry (behind table) 478. [OFr. *doss(i)er*.]

dote *v.* to lose one's wits 1956; **doted** *pp.* dazed 1151. [Cf. MDu. *doten*.]

double *adj.* double (-channelled) 786. **doub(b)le** *adv.* double 2033; with twice the usual amount 61, 483. [OFr. *do(u)ble*.]

double-felde *adv.* with twice the usual amount 890. [Prec.+OE. *-féld*, *pp.*; cf. *þriféldan*, etc.]

doun *adv.* down 368, 817, 2309, etc.; *prep.* 1595 n., 2144. [OE. *of dūne, adūne*.]

dounez, downez *n. pl.* hills 695, 1972. [OE. *dūn*.]

doute *n.* fear 246; *had doute*, was afraid 442. [OFr. *do(u)te*.]

douteles *adv.* doubtless 725. [DOUTE +OE. *-lēas*.]

douth(e) *n.* (assembled) company 61, 397, 1365, 1415, 1956. [OE. *duguþ.*]

dowelle *v.* to remain 566, 1075, 1082. [OE. *dwellan.*]

draȝe *v.* to draw, lead 1031; **drowe** *pres. subj.* carry on (trade) 1647; **droȝ(en)** *pa. t.* drew 335; closed 1188; *intr.* withdrew 1463; **drawen** *pp.* 1233. [OE. *dragan.*]

draȝt *n.* drawbridge 817. [OE. *dræht;* ON. *dráttr,* older **draht-.*]

draueled *pa. t.* muttered (in sleep) 1750. [Cf. ON. *drafl,* tattle; *drafa,* to talk nonsense.]

drechch *n.* delay 1972. [Stem of OE. *dreccan,* trouble.]

drede *v.* to fear 2355; *intr.* be afraid 2211. [OE. *drǣdan.*]

drede *n.* fear 315, 2258. [From prec.]

dredles *adj.* fearless 2334. [From prec.]

dreȝ, dryȝe *adj.* unmoved 335; enduring 724; incessant 1460; heavy 1750; *as sb.* in *dragez on d.,* holds back 1031; *adv.* forcibly 2263; **dreȝly** *adv.* unceasingly 1026. [ON. *drjúgr,* older **dréug-.*]

dreme *n.* dreaming 1750. [ON. *draumr,* dream: OE. *drēam,* music.]

dreped *pp.* slain, killed 725. [OE. *drepan,* smite; ON. *drepa,* kill.]

dres(se) *v.* to arrange, array 75, 1000, 2033; turn, direct 445; *dresses hym vpon grounde,* takes his stand 417; *dres me to,* proceed to 474; *intr.* to prepare 566; go, repair to 1415; *dressed vp,* got up 2009. [OFr. *drec(i)er.*]

dryftes *n. pl.* (snow)drifts 2005. [ON. *drift.*]

dryȝe *adj.* See DREȜ.

dryȝe *v.* to endure 560; *d. vnder,* withstand, survive 202. [OE. *drē(o)gan.*]

Dryȝtyn *n.* God 724, 996, 1548, 1999, 2138. [OE. *dryhten.*]

drynk *n.* drink 497, 1684, 1935. [OE. *drinc.*]

drynk *v.* to drink 337; **dronken** *pa. t. pl.* 1025, 1114, 1668; *pp.* as *adj.* drunk 1956. [OE. *drincan.*]

dryue *v.* to drive; **drof** *pa. t.* 786, 1151, etc.; **dryuen, driuen** *pp.*

558, 1047, etc. *Trans.* to drive, strike 389, 523, 1047, 1159, 2005; pass (the day) 1176, 1468; to make 558, 1020; *drof to,* hemmed in, enclosed 786; *intr.* come, make one's way 121, 222; rush, run 1151; hurtle 2263; *dryuez to,* comes up on, follows on, 1999 n. [OE. *drīfan.*]

droȝ(en). See DRAȜE.

droȝt *n.* drought 523. [OE. *drūgoþ, *drŭhþ-.*]

dronken. See DRYNK.

dropez *3 sg.* drops 519. [OE. *dropian.*]

droupyng, drowping *n.* torpor, troubled sleep 1748, 1750. [ON. *drúpa,* v.]

drowe. See DRAȜE.

drury(e), drwry *n.* love 1507, 1517, 1805; love-token 2033; *dalt. d.,* had love-dealings 2449. [OFr. *druerie.*]

dubbed *pp.* adorned 75, 193; arrayed 571. [OFr. *ado(u)ber, aduber.*]

dublet *n.* doublet, jacket 571. [OFr. *do(u)blet, dublet.*]

duches *n.* duchess 2465 (*gen.*). [OFr. *duchesse.*]

duȝty *adj.* doughty 724. [OE. *dyhtig.*] See DOȜTY.

duk *n.* duke 552, 678. [OFr. *duc.*]

dulful; dunt(e); durst. See DEL-; DYNT; DAR.

dure 110. See AGRAUAYN.

dust *n.* dust 523. [OE. *dŭst.*]

dut *n.* joy 1020. [OFr. *dedu(i)t.*]

dut(te) *pa. t.* feared 222, 784, 2257 (*subj.*). [OFr. *do(u)ter, duter.*]

E

eft(e) *adv.* again 700, 1340, 1404, 1668, 1875, 2295; afterwards 898, 2388; then 788; secondly 641. [OE. *eft.*]

eftersones, eftsonez *adv.* again (immediately) 1640, (as a second instance) 2417. [OE. *eftsōna* with infl. of *æfter.*]

egge *n.* edge 212; weapon 2392. [OE. *ecg,* edge, (verse) weapon.]

eke *adv.* also, as well 90, 1741. [OE. *ēac; tō-ēacan.*]

elbowes *n. pl.* elbows 184. [OE. *el(n)-boga.*]

elde(e) *n.* age; generation, time 1520; *of hyghe e.*, in the prime of life 844. [OE. *éldo*.]

elles, ellez *adv.* else, besides 384, 1550, 2108; in other things 1082; *oþer elles*, or else 1529; *conj.* provided that 295. [OE. *elles*.]

elnȝerde *n.* measuring-rod an ell (45 in.) long 210. [OE. *eln+gérd*.]

em(e) *n.* (maternal) uncle 356, 543. [OE. *ēam*.]

enbaned *pp.* provided with projecting horizontal coursings 790 n. [OProv. *enbanar*.]

enbelyse *v.* to adorn, grace 1034. [OFr. *embelir, embeliss-*.]

enbrauded *pp.* embroidered 166, 879, 2028; **enbrawded** 78, 856; **enbrawden** 609. [OE. *ge-brogden* infl. by OFr. *broder*.]

enclyne *v. intr.* to bow 340. [OFr. *encliner*.]

ende *n.* end 63, 215, 660, 661, 1301, etc.; ending, result 496; *vpon endez*, at the ends 2039. [OE. *énde*.]

endeles *adj.* endless 630; **endelez** *629. [OE. *énde-lēas*.]

endite *v.* to direct; *to dethe e.*, do to death 1600. [OFr. *enditer*, here blended with phrase *diȝt to deþe*.]

endured *pp.* endured 1517. [OFr. *endurer*.]

enfoubled *pp.* muffled up 959. [OFr. *enfubler*.]

Englych *adj. as n. pl.* the English 629. [OE. *englisc*, adj.]

enker-grene *adj.* bright green 150, 2477. [ON. *einkar*+GRENE.]

enmy *n.* enemy 2406. [OFr. *enemi*.]

enn(o)urned *pp.* adorned, graced 634; set as adornment 2027. [OFr. *ao(u)rner, aürner*, with altered prefix.]

enquest *n.* inquiry 1056. [OFr. *enqueste*.]

entayled *pp.* carved; depicted (in embroidery) 612. [OFr. *entaill(i)er*.]

enterludez *n. pl.* dramatic or mimic displays (at a feast) 472. [AFr. *entrelude; Anglo-Lat. *interludium*.]

entyse *v.* to take, catch (infection) 2436. [OFr. *entic(i)er*.]

entre *v.* to enter 221 (*trans.*), 934. [OFr. *entrer*.]

er(e) *adv.* before 527, 1274; **er** *prep.* before 197; *er þis*, before now 1892, 2528; *conj.* (*with subj.*) 92, 987, 2277, etc.; (*indic.*) 764. [OE. *ǣr*.]

erande. See ERNDE.

erber *n.* gullet 1330. [OFr. *erb(i)ere*.]

erbez *n. pl.* herbs, green plants 517, 2190. [OFr. *erbe*.]

erde *n.* land, region 1808; *in erde*, in the world, actual(ly) 27, 140, 881, 1544, 2416. [OE. *éard*.]

erly *adv.* early (in the day) 567, 1101, 1126, 1474, 1689. [OE. *ǣr-līce*.]

ermyn *n.* ermine 881. [OFr. *ermine*.]

ernd(e) *n.* business, mission, errand 257, 559, 809, 1051, 1067, 2303; *go myn ernde*, go as my messenger 811; *an erande*, on a mission 1808. [OE. *ǣrende*, ON. *erendi*.]

erraunt *adj.* errant; *knyȝt erraunt*, knight journeying (on a mission) 810. [OFr. *errer*, travel.]

erþe *n.* earth, ground 4, 427, 728, 1137, 2098, etc. [OE. *eorþe*.]

ese *n.* ease 1676; *at þyn e., in your e.*, at your ease 1071, 1096; consolation 1798; delight 1539. [OFr. *aise, eise*.]

etayn *n.* ogre, giant 140, 723. [OE. *eoten*, with ending altered.]

ete *v.* to eat, dine 85, 91; **et(t)e** *pa. t.* 113, 1135. [OE. *etan*.]

eþe *adj.* easy 676. [OE. *ē(a)þe*.]

eþe *v.* to conjure, entreat 379, 2467. [OE. *ge-æþan* from *āþ*, oath.]

euel *n.* evil 1552. [OE. *yfel*.]

euen *adj.* even; *even of*, fairly quit of 1641; equal *1266 n.; *adv.* just, right, straight 1004, 1589, 1593; actually, indeed 444, 2464. [OE. *efen; efne*.]

euen *n.* eve (of a festival) 734, 1669. **euensong** vespers 932; **euentide** evening 1641. [OE. *ēfen; ēfensong, -tīd*.]

euenden *pa. t. pl.* made even, trimmed 1345. [OE. *ge-efnan*.]

euer *adv.* ever; always 913, 1844, 2264, etc.; continually 172, 1657; at any time 52, 682, 1544, etc.; *for e.*, 293. **euermore** *adv.* evermore 1547, 2520; *for e.* 669. [OE. *ǣfre*; +*māre*, neut.]

euesed *pp.* clipped, trimmed 184. [OE. *efsian*.]

euez *n. sg.* eaves, border (of a wood) 1178. [OE. *efes*.]

excused *pp.* excused 2131, 2428. [OFr. *excuser*.]

exellently (*of*) *adv.* pre-eminently (above) 2423. [From OFr. *excellent*.]

expoun *v.* to expound 1540; describe 209; *e. much speche of*, have much discussion concerning 1506. [OFr. *espo(u)ndre*.]

F

face *n.* face, mien 103, 445, 2503, etc.; surface 524. [OFr. *face*.]

fade *adj.* (?)bold 149 n. [Obscure, perh. OE. *fāh*+adj. suffix -*ede*.]

fader *n.* father 919. [OE. *fæder*.]

fage *n.* deceit; *no fage*, in truth *531 n. [Origin obscure; *fage* still in dialects.]

fay *n.* faith; *ma fay*, on my word 1495. [OFr. *fei*.]

faye *n.* fairy 2446. [AN. *feie*, OFr. *fée*.]

fayly *v.* to fail, be at fault 455, 641, 1067, 1295, 2356; lack opportunity 278; *fayld neuer*, was nowhere incomplete 658. [OFr. *faillir*.]

fayn *adj.* glad 388, 840; fain, desirous 1067, 2019. [OE. *fægen*.]

fayntyse *n.* frailty 2435. [OFr. *faintise*.]

fayr(e) *adj.* fair, comely, good(ly) 54, 181, 427, 803, 943, 1260, 1694, etc.; courteous 1116; *þe fayrer* (*compar*.), the advantage 99. [OE. *fæger*.]

fayr(e) *adv.* fairly; gracefully, courteously, well 367, 622, 1046, 1556, 1961, 2229, etc.; deftly 2309; *compar.* 1315. [OE. *fægre*.]

fayryȝe *n.* magic 240. [OFr. *faierie*.]

fayþ(e) *n.* faith, plighted word 1783; *in* (*god*) *f.*, in truth 279, 381, 1535, etc.; *bi my* (*þi*) *f.*, on my (thy) honour 2284, 2469. [OFr. *feid*, later *fei* = FAY.]

faythely *adj.* truly 1636. [From prec.]

faythful *adj.* trustworthy 632, 1679. [As prec.]

falce *adj.* untrue, dishonest 2382. [OE. *fals*, from L. *falsus*.]

fale *adj.* pale, faded 728. [OE. *fealu*.]

falle *v.*; **fel(le)** *pa. t.* 430, 1425, etc.;

falled 2243; **fallen** *pp.* 1432, 2528. To fall (down) 507, 728, 1432, etc.; bend low 1758; *f. to*, rally to, rush towards 1425, 1702; *f. on*, fall on 1904; *f. in*, hit on 1699. To happen 23, 2132, 2251, 2528; (*pa. subj.*) might befall 1588; fall to one's lot 2243, 2327, *foule mot hit f.* bad luck to it 2378; be fitting, right (for) 358, 483, 890, 1303, 1358. [OE. *fallan*.]

falssyng *n.* breaking of faith 2378. [ME. *falsie*, v. from OE. *fals*, FALCE.]

faltered *pa. t.* staggered 430. [ON. *faltrask*, be cumbered.]

fange. See FONGE.

fannand *pres. p.* fanning, waving 181. [From OE. *fann*, n.]

fantoum *n.* illusion 240. [OFr. *fanto(s)me*.]

farand *adj.* splendid 101. [ON. *farandi*, fitting.]

fare *n.* track 1703; faring, fortune 2494; fare, entertainment 694; feast 537; behaviour, practices 409, 2386; observances 1116. [OE. *faru*.]

fare *v.* to go, proceed 699, 1973; *farez wel*, farewell 2149; **ferde(n)** *pa. t.* 149, 703, 1282, 1433; **faren** *pp.* 1231. [OE. *faran*, str.; pa. t. from *fēran*. See FORFERDE.]

faste *adj.* fast, binding 1636. [OE. *fæst*.]

fast(e) *adv.* fast, securely 782; pressingly 2403; earnestly 1042; vigorously 1425, loudly 1908; quickly 1585, 1705, 2215. [OE. *fæste*.]

faut(e) *n.* fault, faultiness 1551, 2435, 2488. [OFr. *faute*.]

fautles, -lez *adj.* faultless, flawless 640, 1761; **fautlest** *superl.* in *on þe f.*, the most faultless 2363. [Prec.+ OE. *-lēas*.]

fawne *v.* to fondle, stroke 1919. [OE. *fagnian*.]

fawty *adj.* faulty, lacking integrity 2382, 2386. [From FAUTE.]

fax *n.* hair 181. [OE. *feax*.]

feblest *adj. superl.* feeblest, least capable 354. [OFr. *feble*.]

fech *v.* to bring 1375, 2013; obtain 1857; **fette** *pp.* 1084. [OE. *fetian*, *feccan*.] See FOCH, FOTTE.

fede v. to feed 1359. [OE. *fēdan*.]

fee n. payment 1622; portion of deer to which the huntsman is entitled 1358; *corbeles fee*, the raven's fee 1355 n. [OFr. *f(i)e, fieu*.]

fe(e)rsly adv. proudly 329, 1323; fiercely 832. [From OFr. *f(i)ers*, nom.; cf. FERE *adj.*]

feȝt(yng). See FYȜT.

feye adj. doomed to die; stricken by death 1067. [OE. *fǣge*.]

felaȝe n. companion (hound) 1702. [OE. *fēolaga* from ON. *félagi*.]

felaȝschip n. love of fellow men 652; company 2151. [From prec.]

felde n. field (of battle) 874. [OE. *féld*.]

felde v. to fold, embrace 841. [OE. *féldan*; cf. -*féldan*.]

fele adj. many 122, 890, 1653, 2417, etc.; **felle** 1566; *as sb.* many (people) 428, 1588; **feler** compar. more 1391. [OE. *fela*.]

fele v. to feel, perceive 2193, 2272. [OE. *fēlan*.]

felefolde adj. manifold 1545. [OE. *fela-fáld*.]

felle adj. bold, fierce, formidable 291, 717, 847, 874, 2222; *as sb.* wild beast 1585; **felly** adv. fiercely 2302. [OFr. *fel*.]

felle n.[1] skin 880, 943, 1359, 1737, 1944. [OE. *fell*.]

felle n.[2] fell, precipitous rock 723. [ON. *fjall, fell*.]

felle(n). See FALLE, FELE.

femed pa. t. foamed 1572. [OE. *fǣman*.]

fende n. fiend; *þe f.*, the Devil 1944, 2193. [OE. *fēond*.]

feng. See FONGE.

fer adv. far, afar 13, 714, 2092; **ferre** 1093; **fyrre, fire** compar. further, moreover, besides 411, 1105, 1304, 2121, 2151; *fyrre passe*, proceed (with the business) 378. [OE. *feorr(an); firr*, compar.]

ferde n. fear; *for ferde*, in fear 2130, 2272. [Prob. developed from the phrase with *for*; see next, and *for* prep. (cf. *for olde*).]

ferde pa. t. feared 1588; pp. afraid 1295, 2382. [OE. *fǣran, fēran*.]

ferde(n). See FARE v.

fere adj. proud, bold 103. [OFr. *f(i)er*.]

fere n.[1] companion 695, 915; wife 2411; peer, equal 676; *in fere*, in company, (?) with a force of men 267 n. [OE. *gefēra*.]

fere n.[2] company 267 n. [OE. *gefēre*; *gefēran*, pl., as companions.]

ferk(ke) v. to go, ride 173, 1072, *1973; flow 2173; *ferkez hym vp*, gets up 2013. [OE. *fer(e)cian*.]

ferly adj. extraordinary, unusual 716; n. a marvel, wonder 23, 2414. [ON. *ferligr*, monstrous; OE. *feorlic*, strange.]

ferly adv. wondrously, exceedingly 388, 741, 1694; **ferlyly** 796; of marvellous things 2494. [ON. *ferliga*; OE. *feorlíce*.]

fermed pp. confirmed *2329. [OFr. *fermer*.]

fermysoun n. close-season 1156. [OFr. *fermiso(u)n*.]

fest n. feast, festival 44, 537, 1036, 2401, etc. [OFr. *feste*.]

fest pa. t. made fast, agreed upon 2347. [OE. *fæstan*; ON. *festa*.]

festned pp. made firm, bound 1783. [OE. *fæstnian*.]

fete. See FOTE.

feted pa. t. behaved 1282. [OFr. *faitier* prepare.]

fetled pp. set, fixed 656. [From OE. *fetel*, girdle.]

fetly adv. gracefully, daintily 1758. [From OFr. *fait, fet*, adj.]

fette 1084. See FECH.

fetures n. pl. parts (of the body) 145, 1761. [OFr. *faiture, feture*.]

fyched pp. fixed, established 658. [OFr. *fich(i)er*.]

fyft adj. fifth 651. [OE. *fifta*.]

fiften adj. fifteen 44. [OE. *fiftēne*.]

figure n. figure 627. [OFr. *figure*.]

fyȝed pa. t. fitted 796. [OE. *fēgan*.]

fyȝt n. fight 279. [OE. *fe(o)hte*.]

fyȝt, feȝt v. to fight 278, 717; **foȝt** pa. t. pl. *874; **feȝtyng** n. fighting; *in. f. wyse*, in warlike fashion 267. [OE. *fe(o)htan*.]

fyked pa. t. flinched 2274. [OE. *fician*; cf. *befician*.]

fildore *n.* gold thread or cord 189. [OFr. *fil d'or.*]

fyled *pp.* sharpened 2225. [OE. *fīlian*, file; or OFr. *afiler.*]

fylyolez *n. pl.* pinnacles 796. [OFr. *filloele.*]

fylle *v.* to fulfil, carry out 1405, 1934. [OE. *fyllan.*]

fylor *n.* sharpening tool with whetstone 2225. [Cf. OFr. *afilé*, sharpened, and FYLED.]

fylter *v.* to crowd together; contend 986. [OFr. *feltrer*, press (felt).]

fylþe *n.* impurity, sin 1013, 2436. [OE. *fҳ̄lþ.*]

fynde *v.* to find 123, 449, 660, 1053, etc.; obtain 324; **fonde** *pa. t. sg.* 694 (had served), 716, 1875 (*subj.*); *pl.* 1329; **founden** *pl.* started, dislodged 1704; **funde(n)** *pp.* 396, 640; **founden** 1264. [OE. *findan.*]

fyndyng *n.* finding, dislodgement 1433. [From prec.]

fyn(e) *adj.* perfected; fully ratified 1636; fine, superb, perfect 919, 1761; pure, sheer 1239 n.; *adv.* completely 173; superbly 1737; **fynly** *adv.* completely 1391. [OFr. *fin.*]

fyng(e)res, fyngrez *n. pl.* fingers 641, 1833; finger's-breadths (as measure) 1329. [OE. *finger.*]

fynisment *n.* end 499. [OFr. *finissement.*]

fyr(e), fire *n.* fire 832, 847, 1368, 1653, 1925; sparks 459 (see STON-FYR). [OE. *fy̆r.*]

fire, fyrre. See FER.

fyrst *adj. superl.* first 54 n., 290, 2347, etc.; ⟨*vp*⟩*on f.*, at first, in the beginning 301, 528, 2019; first (of all) 9, 491, 1477, 1934; *as sb.* first day 1072; *adv.* first(ly) 359, 568, 1422, 1592, 2524, etc.; before 2227. [OE. *fyr(e)st.*]

fische *n.* fish 503 (*coll.*), 890. [OE. *fisc.*]

fyskez *pres. t.* scampers 1704. [(?)ON. **fjaska*, cf. Björkman, p. 137.]

fyue *adj. and n.* five 627, 632, etc.; group of five 651. [OE. *fīf(e).*]

flaȝ(e). See FLE, FLYȜE.

flat *n.* plain 507. [ON. *flǫt* (in place-names in England).]

fle *v.* to flee 2125, 2130; flinch 2272; **flaȝ(e)** *pa. t.* 2274, 2276; **fled** 1628. [OE. *flēon*, pa. t. *flēah.*]

flesch(e) *n.* flesh 943, 2313; (opposed to 'spirit') 503, 2435; venison 1363. [OE. *flҳ̄sc.*]

flet(te) *n.* floor 568, 859; *on þe* (*þis*) *f.* 294, 1374, *vpon f.* 832, 1653, 1925 in the (this) hall. [OE. *flett.*]

flete *v.* to fleet, speed; *pa. t. pl.* (*sg. form*) 1566; **floten** *pp.* having wandered 714. [OE. *flēotan.*]

flyȝe *n.* fly, butterfly 166. [OE. *flē(o)ge.*]

flyȝe *v.* to fly 524; **flaȝ(e)** *pa. t.* 459, 2276 (*first*). [OE. (*flē(o)gan*; see FLE.]

flynt *n.* flint 459. [OE. *flint.*]

flod(e) *n.* flood, stream 2173; sea 13. [OE. *flōd.*]

flokked *pa. t.* assembled 1323. [From OE. *flocc*, n.]

flone *n.* arrow 1161, 1566. [OE. *flān.*]

flor(e) *n.* floor (= hall) 834, 1932. [OE. *flōr.*]

flosche *n.* pool 1430. [Cf. OFr. *flache.*]

floten. See FLETE.

flowrez *n. pl.* flowers 507. [OFr. *flo(u)r.*]

fnast(ed) *pa. t.* snorted, panted 1587, 1702. [OE. *fnҳ̄stian.*]

foch(che) *v.* to get, take 396, 1961. [Var. of FECH; cf. OE. *feotian* or *fatian.*] See FOTTE.

fode *n.* food 503. [OE. *fōda.*]

foyned *pa. t.* thrust at; kicked 428. [From OFr. *foi(s)ne*, fish-spear.]

foysoun *n.* abundance 122. [OFr. *foiso(u)n.*]

folde *n.* earth, land 23, 524, 1694; ground 422; *vpon f.*, (tag) on earth, living 196, 396, 642, 676, 1275, 2373 (there). [OE. *fólde.*]

folde *v.* to fold; *f. to*, match, be like 499; befit, be proper to 359; turn, go 1363; **folden** *pp.* plaited, tied 189; enfolded, wimpled 959; plighted 1783. [OE. *fáldan*; here seems equated with both ME. *plihten* (plight), and *plīten* (fold).]

fole *n.*[1] horse 173, 196, 459 (*gen.*), 695, 803. [OE. *fola.*]

fole *n.*[2] fool 2414. [OFr. *fol.*]

folé *n.* folly 1545; **foly** 324. [OFr. *folie.*]

folȝe *v.* to follow, pursue 1164, 1895; *þat f. alle þe sele,* to whom all prosperity came 2422; **folȝande** *pres. p.* in like manner 145; *of f. sute,* of similar sort 859. [OE. *folgian.*]

folk(e) *n.* people, men 54, 816, etc.; throng 1323. [OE. *folc.*]

fonde *v.* to try, test, tempt 291, 565, 986, 1549. [OE. *fóndian.*]

fonde(t). See FYNDE, FOUNDE.

fonge, fange *v.* to take, receive, get 391, 1363, 1556, 1622; welcome, entertain 816, 919, 1315; **feng** *pa. t.* derived *646; **fonge(d)** *pp.* 919, 1315; **fongen** 1265 n. [OE. *fōn,* str.; ON. *fanga,* wk.]

foo *adj.* hostile; forbidding 1430; *adv.* fiercely 2326. [OE. *fāh, fā-.*]

foo *n.* foe 716. [OE. *gefā.*]

for *conj.* for 147, 492, *1514, etc.; because, since 258, 632, 1093, 1266, 1396, 1441, 1827, 1847. [OE. *for þam (þe).*]

for *prep.* for (sake, purpose of), to be, as 240, 479, 537, 1347, 1786, etc.; because of, through 282, 488, 2125, etc.; before 965 n.; (in return, exchange) for 98, 287, 1055, etc.; to prevent 1334 n.; in spite of 1854, 2132, 2251; *for olde,* because of age 1440 n.; *for to,* in order to, so as to, to 124, 1550, 1634, etc.; *for as much as,* in so far as 356. [OE. *for.*]

forbe *prep.* past; beyond, more than 652. [OE. *for(a)n+be.*]

force, forse *n.* necessity 1239; strength 1617. [OFr. *force.*]

forde. See FORÞE.

forest *n.* wild uncultivated land, forest 741, 1149. [OFr. *forest.*]

forfaren *pp.* headed off 1895. [OE. *forfaran²*.]

forferde *pa. t.* killed 1617 [OE. *forfaran¹*; see FARE *v.*]

forfete *v.* to transgress 2394. [From OFr. *forfait, -fet,* n.]

forgat *pa. t.* forgot 2031. [OE. *forgetan,* with substitution of ON. *geta.*] Cf. FORȜATE.

forgoo *v.* to give up 2210. [OE. *forgān.*]

forȝ *n.* channel, bed 2173. [OE. *furh.*]

forȝate *pa. t.* forgot 1472; **forȝeten** *pp.* 1485. [OE. *forgetan.*]

forȝelde *pres. subj.* repay, reward 839, 1279, 1535, 2429. [OE. *forgéldan.*]

forlond *n.* foreland, promontory 699. [OE. *for(e)- +lónd.*]

forme *adj.* first 2373; *n.* beginning 499. [OE. *forma.*]

forme. See FOURME.

forne *adv.* of old 2422. [OE. *forne.*]

forred. See FURRED.

forsake *v.* to deny, refuse 475, 1826, 1846; forsake 2380; **forsoke** *pa. t.* 1826. [OE. *forsacan.*]

forsnes *n.* fortitude 646. [From FORCE.]

forst *n.* frost, rime 1694. [OE. *forst.*]

fortune *n.* fortune 99. [OFr. *fortune.*]

forth *adv.* forth, forward, away, out 66, 428, 1308, 1444, 1703, 2316, 2397, etc.; *forth dayez* (=OE. *forþ dæges*), well on in the day 1072. [OE. *forþ.*]

forþ(e), forde *n.* ford 699, 1585, 1617. [OE. *ford, *forþ.*]

forþi, -þy *conj.* for this reason, and so, therefore 27, 240, 500, 631, 2110, etc. [OE. *forþī, -þȳ.*]

forward(e) *n.* agreement, covenant 1105, 1636, 2347; *watz not f.,* was not in our agreement 1395; *pl. in sg. sense* 378, 409, 1405, 1934. [OE. *foreweard.*]

forwondered *pp.* astonished 1660. [*for-* intens. prefix+WONDER.]

fot(e) *n.* foot 422; (*of measure*) 2151, 2225; **fete** *pl.* 428, 1904; *vnder f.,* under foot 859; **fotez** *d. pl.* 574. **fote** *orig. gen. pl.* in *fowre f. large* 2225; *dat. pl.* in (*vp*)*on* (*his*), *to my f.* 329, 2229, 2276, 2363. [OE. *fōt.*]

fotte *v.* to get 451. [OE. *fettan,* var. of *feccan,* with vowel of FOCH.]

foule, fowle *adj.* evil 717; poor in quality (*superl.*) 1329; vile 1944; *adv.* evilly 2378. [OE. *fūl, fūle.*]

founde *v.* to hasten 1585, 2229; **founded, fondet** *pa. t.* 2125, 2130; *pp.* journeyed 267. [OE. *fúndian.*]

founden. See FYNDE.

fourchez *n. pl.* fork of body; legs 1357. [OFr. *fo(u)rche.*]

fo(u)rme *n.* shape, figure 145; manner, fashion 1295, 2130. [OFr. *fo(u)rme*.]

fourty *adj.* forty 1425. [OE. *féowertig*.]

fowre, foure *adj. and n.* four 1332, 2101, 2225. [OE. *féower*.]

fox *n.* fox 1699, 1895, 1944 (*attrib.*), 1950. [OE. *fox*.]

frayn (*at*) *v.* to ask, inquire (of) 359, 703, 1046, 2494; to make trial of 489, 1549. [OE. (*ge*)*frægnian*.]

frayst *v.* to ask 1395; ask for, seek 279, 324, 391; (*with inf.*) 455; make trial of 409, 1679; test, try 503; **frayst(ed)** *pp.* 324, 391, 1679. [ON. *freista*.]

fraunchis(e) *n.* generosity, magnanimity 652, 1264. [OFr. *fra(u)nchise*.]

fre *adj.* noble, courtly, good 101, 803, 847, 1156, 1885, 1961; *as sb.* noble lady 1545, 1549, 1783; **freest** *superl.* noblest 2422. [OE. *fréo*, free, noble (*verse*); lady (*verse*).]

frek(e) *n.* man, knight 149, 241, 537, 651, 840, etc. [OE. *freca*.]

frely *adv.* readily, courteously 816, 894. [OE. *fréolíce*.]

fremedly *adv.* as a stranger 714. [From OE. *fremede*, alien.]

French *adj.* French; *F. flod*, the English Channel 13; **Frenkysch** in *F. fare*, elaborately polite behaviour 1116. [OE. *Frencisc*.]

frendez *n. pl.* friends 714, 987. [OE. *fréond*.]

frenges *n. pl.* fringes 598. [OFr. *frenge*.]

Frenkysch. See FRENCH.

fres *pa. t.* froze 728. [OE. *fréosan*, pa. t. *fréas*.]

fresch(e) *adj.* fresh, clean 2019; *as sb.* fresh food 122; **freschly** *adv.* quickly 1294. [OFr. *freis*; fem. *fresche*; cf. OE. *fersc*.]

fryth *n.* a wood, woodland 695, 1430, 1973, 2151. [OE. *fyr(h)þ, gefyrþe*.]

fro *prep.* away from, from 524, *1440, 1534, *1863, etc.; (*after its case*) 1797, 2331. [ON. *frá*.]

fro *conj.* (after the time) when, after 8, 62. [Shortened from *fro þat*.]

from *prep.* from 461. [OE. *fram*.]

frote *v.* to rub, stroke 1919. [OFr. *froter*.]

froþe *n.* froth 1572. [ON. *froða*.]

frounse *v.* to pucker 2306. [OFr. *fro(u)nc(i)er*.]

frount *n.* forehead 959. [OFr. *fro(u)nt*.]

fuyt. See FUTE.

ful *adj.* full 2005. [OE. *full*.]

ful *adv.* fully 44; very, quite, full 41, 1820, 2455, etc. [OE. *full*.]

fulsun *v.* to help 99. [ME. *fülstnen*; cf. OE. *fylstan*.]

funde(n). See FYNDE.

furred *pp.* lined with fur 880, 1737, 2029; **forred** 1929. [OFr. *fo(u)rrer, fur-*.]

fust *n.* fist, hand 391. [OE. *fŷst*.]

fute, fuyt *n.* track, trail of hunted animal 1425, 1699. [OFr. *fuite*.]

G

gafe. See GIF.

gay(e) *adj.* gay, bright, fair 74, 167, 791, 1003, *1208, etc.; *adv. or predic. adj.* 179, 935; *as sb.* fair lady 970, *1213, 1822; fair knight 2035; **gayest** *superl.* 2023 n.; **gayly** *adv.* gaily 598, 1760. [OFr. *gai*.]

gayn *adj.* ready, prompt; obedient 178; *at þe gaynest*, by the most direct route 1973; *adv.* promptly 1621; *n.* an advantage, a good thing 1241, 2491. [ON. *gegn*, adj.]

gayn(e) *v.* to profit, be of use to 584, 1829. [ON. *gegna*.]

gayne *n.* gain, what you obtained 2349. [OFr. *gaaigne*.]

gaynly *adv.* appropriately, appositely 476; fitly, rightly 1297. [From GAYN, adj.]

game. See GOMEN.

gargulun *n.* throat of deer, includes gullet (*wesaunt*) and wind-pipe 1335, 1340. [OFr. *garguillun*.]

garysoun *n.* keepsake 1807; treasure 1255 n., 1837. [OFr. *gariso(u)n*, infl. in sense by ON. *gersumi*.]

garytez *n. pl.* watch-towers, turrets along the walls 791. [OFr. *garite*.]

gart *pp.* made, caused 2460. [ON. *gøra, gǫrva*; neut. adj. as pp. *gǫrt*.]

gast *pp.* afraid 325. [OE. *gǽstan*.]

gate *n.* way, road 709, 778, 930, 1967,

gate (*cont.*)
2119; *bi g.*, on the way 696; *haf þe g.*, pass 1154. [ON. *gata.*]

gaudi *n.* ornamentation 167. [OFr. *gaudie.*]

geder(e) *v.* to collect, assemble 1326, 1426, 1566, 1625; lift (with both hands) 421, 2260; *g. þe rake*, pick up the path 2160. [OE. *gæderian.*]

gederez (MS.), 777. See GORDEZ.

gef. See GIF.

gemme *n.* gem 78, 609. [OFr. *gemme.*]

gentyle, ientyle *adj.* of gentle birth, noble 42, 639, 2185; kindly 774; noble, excellent 1022; *as sb.* gentle knight 542. [OFr. *gentil.*]

gerdez. See GORDEZ.

gere *n.* gear; armour 569, 584; doings, behaviour 2205; *pl.* bedclothes 1470. [ON. *gervi.*]

gere *v.* to clothe, attire 1872; *pp.* 179, 957, 2227; fashioned 791, 1832. [From prec.]

geserne. See GISERNE.

gest *n.* guest 921, 1024, 1036, 1127, 2055. [ON. *gestr.*]

get *n.*: *my get*, that I have got 1638. [From next.]

gete *v.* to get 1871; *pa. t.* 1571; **geten** *pl.* seized 1171; **geten** *pp.* 1943; fetched 1625. [ON. *geta.*]

gif *v.* to give, grant 288, 297, 1383, etc.; **gafe** *pa. t. refl.* surrender 1861; **gef** 370, 2349; wished 668, 1029, 2068, 2073 n.; **geuen** *pp.* 920, 1500. [ON. *gefa, gifa.*] See ȜEF.

gift(e), gyft *n.* gift 68, 1500, 1822, 2030; *of (my) g.*, as (my) gift 288, 1799, 1807 (*pl.*). [ON. *gift.*]

gyld, gilt *pp.* gilded, gilt 569, 777, 2062. [OE. *gyldan.*]

gile *n.* guile 1787. [OFr. *guile.*]

gyng *n.* company 225. [ON. *gengi.*]

gyrdez; girdel. See GORDEZ; GORDEL.

giserne *n.* battle-axe 288 n., 375, 2265; **geserne** 326. [OFr. *guiserne.*]

glad *adj.* merry, glad 495, 1079, 1926, 1955. [OE. *glæd.*]

glade *v.* to gladden, cheer 989. [OE. *gladian.*]

gladly *adv.* gladly, with pleasure 225, 370, 415; **gladloker** *compar.* 1064. [OE. *glædlíce, -lucor.*]

glam *n.* din 1426; noise of merry-making 1652. [ON. *glam(m).*]

glauer *n.* babel 1426. [Cf. ME., modern dial. *glaver(en)*, chatter.]

glaum *n.* noise of merrymaking 46. [ON. *glaumr.*]

gle *n.* merriment 46, 1652; gladness 1536. [OE. *glēo.*]

gled(e) *n.* red-hot (char)coal 891, 1609. [OE. *glēd.*]

glem *n.* beam, ray 604. [OE. *glǽm.*]

gleme *v.* to shine 598. [From prec.]

glemered *pa. t.* gleamed 172. [OE. **glimerian*, related to prec.]

glent *pa. t.* glanced; flinched 2292; sprang 1652; glinted 172, 569, 604, 2039; looked 82, 476. [ON. **glenta*; cf. Norw. *glenta.*]

glent *n.* glance 1290. [From prec.]

glyde *v.* to glide 2266; hasten 748, 935; **glod** *pa. t.* came 661. [OE. *glídan.*]

glyfte *pa. t.* glanced (sidelong) 2265. [See next.]

glyȝt *pa. t.* glanced, looked 842, 970. [Obscurely related are ME. *glis(t)en*, *gliȝ(t)en*, *glif(t)en*, assoc. together as equivalents of GLENT; cf. OE. *glisian*; ON. *gljá.*]

glyter *v.* to glitter 604, 2039. [ON. *glitra.*]

glod. See GLYDE.

glode *n.* open space; patch 2181; *on glode*, on the ground 2266. [Obscure.]

glopnyng (*of*) *n.* dismay (at) *2461. [ON *glúpna.*]

glorious *adj.* glorious 46, 1760. [OFr. *glorio(u)s.*]

gloue *n.* gauntlet, glove 583, 1799, 1807. [OE. *glōf(e).*]

glowande *pres. p.* shining *236. [OE. *glōwan.*]

go *v.* to go 448, 2150; depart 1024, 1127; be (alive), 2109; *quasi-trans.* 811; **gos** *3 sg.* goes 935; **gotz** 375, 1293; **gotz** *imper. pl.* 2119; **goande** *pres. p.* walking, 2214; **gon** *pp.* 1872. [OE. *gān.*] See ȜEDE.

God(e), Godde *n.* God 326, 1036, 1110, 2156, 2205, etc.; *for G.*, by God 965, 1822; *gef hym G.*, wished him Godspeed 2073 (cf. 370); *vnder*

G., on earth 2470 (cf. 51). [OE. *god*.]

god(e), good(e), goud(e) *adj.* good 109, 129, 381, 702, 1625, 1766, 2118, etc.; **guod** 2430; *for gode*, as a good knight 633; *go(u)d day*, 'good-day', 'goodbye' 668, 1029, 1290, 2073; *go(u)d moroun*, 'good morning' 1208, 1213. **go(u)dly** *adv.* courteously, graciously 273, 842, 1933, etc. [OE. *gōd*, adj.]

god(e) *n.* possession, property 1064; goodness 1482; advantage 2031, 2127; *pl.* goods (the fox-skin) 1944. [OE. *gōd*, n.]

goddes *n.* goddess 2452. [OE. *god +* OFr. *-esse*.]

godlych *adj.* fine 584. [OE. *gōdlic*.]

godmon *n.* master of the house 1029, 1392, 1635, 1932; **godemon** 1955. [GOD(E) + MON.]

gold(e) *n.* gold 159, 211, 1255, 2150, etc.; *attrib.* 587, 620, etc.; *red g.* 663; *attrib.* 857, 1817. [OE. *góld*.]

golde-hemmed *adj.* bordered with gold 2395. [Prec. and OE. *hemm*, border.]

gome *n.* knight, man 151, 178, 696, *2461, etc. [OE. (verse) *guma*.]

gomen *n.* game, sport, pleasure 273, 283, 692, 1014, 1536; **game** 365, 1314, 1532; **gamnez, gomnez, -es** *pl.* 495, 683, 989, 1319, 1894; quarry 1635; process 661; *in* or *with g.*, merrily 1376, 1933. [OE. *gamen, gomen*.]

gomenly *adv.* merrily 1079. [OE. *gomenlíce*.]

gorde *pp.* girt 1851; **gurde** 588, 597. [OE. *gyrdan*.]

gordel *n.* girdle 2035, 2037, 2429; **girdel** 1829, 2358; **gurdel** 2395. [OE. *gyrdel*.]

gordez (*to*) *v.* strikes (spurs into) 2062; *gerdez 777; **gyrdez** 2160. [Perh. OE. *gyrdan*.]

gorger *n.* gorget, neckerchief enfolding throat 957. [OFr. *gorg(i)ere*.]

gost *n.* spirit, soul 2250. [OE. *gāst*.]

gostlych *adv.* like a phantom 2461. [OE. *gāstlíce*, spiritually.]

gotz, gos. See GO.

goud(e), goudly. See GOD(E).

gouernour *n.* ruler, lord 225. [OFr. *go(u)verneo(u)r*.]

goulez, gowlez *n.* gules, red (in heraldry) 619; *red g.* 663. [OFr. *goules*; Med.L. *gulæ*, ermine dyed red.]

goune *n.* gown 2396. [OFr. *go(u)ne*.]

grace *n.* favour, mercy, gracious gift (of God or fortune) 920, 1215, 1258, 1837, 2480; *druryes greme and g.*, unhappiness and happiness in love-making 1507. [OFr. *grace*.]

gracios *adj.* beautiful 216; **graciously** *adv.* graciously 970. [OFr. *gracio(u)s*.]

gray(e) *adj.* grey 82, 1024, 1714. [OE. *græg*.]

grayes *v.* withers 527. [From prec.]

grayn *n.* blade of axe 211 n. [ON. *grein*, branch, division.]

grayþ(e) *adj.* ready 448, 597, 2047. [ON. *greiðr*.]

grayþe *v.* to get ready (*refl.*) 2259; dress 2014; *pp.* arrayed, prepared 151, 666, 876; set 74, 109. [ON. *greiða*.]

grayþely *adv.* readily, promptly, at once 417, 1006, 1335, 1683; duly, as was right 2292; pleasantly 876, 1470. [ON. *greiðiliga*.]

grame *n.* wrath; mortification 2502. [OE. *grama*.] See GREME.

grant merci, graunt mercy, gramercy *n.* thank you (*lit.* great thanks) 838, *1037, 1392, 2126. [OFr.]

gra(u)nte *v.* to consent 1110, 1861; *trans.* grant 273, 921, 1841, etc. [AN. *graa(u)ntèr*, for OFr. *creanter*.]

grattest. See GRET.

grece, gres *n.* fat, flesh 425, 1326, 1378, 2313. [OFr. *graisse, gresse*.]

gref *n.* grief 2502. [OFr. *gr(i)ef*.]

gre-houndez *n. pl.* greyhounds 1171. [OE. *grīg-, grei-húnd*.]

grem(e) *n.* wrath 312; grief 1507; mortification 2370; hurt 2251; *with g.*, wrathfully 2299. [ON. *gremi*.]

grene *adj.* green 172, 211, 451, 2239, etc.; *as sb.* green man 464; (*compar.*) 235; **grene** *n.* green (hue) 151, 167, 216, 549, 2227, etc.; verdure 207. [OE. *grēne*.]

grenne *v.* to grin 464. [OE. *grennian*.]

gres(se) *n.* grass 235, 527, 2181. [ODan. *græs* (*æ = ę*); OE. *græs*.]

gres. See GRECE.

gret(e) *adj.* great, large, big 9, 139, 1171, 2369, 2470, etc.; **grett** magnificent 2014; *g. wordes*, boasts, threats 312, 325; *as sb.* great one, king 2490; **grattest** *superl.* 1441; *þe g. of gres*, those that were fattest 1326; *adv.* most 207. [OE. *grēat.*]

gret *pa. t.* greeted 842, 1933. [OE. *grētan*, wk.]

grete *v.* to weep 2157. [OE. *grētan*, str.]

greue *n.* grove, thicket 207, 508, 1355, 1707, 1898, 1974. [OE. *græfa.*]

greue *v.* to afflict; *subj.* let it trouble 1070; to dismay 2460; *intr.* be dismayed 1442; take offence 316. [OFr. *grever.*]

greuez *n. pl.* greaves 575. [OFr. *greves.*]

gryed *pa. t.* shuddered 2370. [Rel. to nth. dial. *grue.*]

grymme *adj.* grim 413, 2260; fierce 1442. [OE. *grimm.*]

◆**gryndel** *adj.* fierce 2338; **gryndelly** *adv.* wrathfully 2299. [(?)Backformation from next.]

gryndel-layk *n.* fierceness *312. [ON. *grindill*, storm+-*leikr.*]

gryndel-ston *n.* grindstone 2202. [OE. *grindel*+*stān.*]

gryp(p)e *v.* to grasp 330; *g. to*, lay hold of 421, 1335; *hit bi grypte*, by which [he] gripped it 214. [OE. *grīpan, grippan.*]

grome *n.* lackey, servant 1127; man 1006 n. [Cf. MDu. *grom*; OFr. *gromet.*]

grone *v.* to groan, lament 2157, 2502. [OE. *grānian.*]

gronyed *pa. t.* grunted (fiercely) 1442 n. [OFr. *grognir*, perhaps+ OE. *grunian.*]

grounde *n.* ground 426, 526, 2294; region 705; open land 508; (*vp*)*on g.*, on earth 1058, 1070, 2150; *dresses hym vpon g.*, takes up his stand 417. [OE. *grúnd.*]

grounden *pp.* ground 2202. [OE. *gríndan*, pp. *grúnden.*]

growe *v.* to grow 235. [OE. *grōwan.*]

gruch *v.* to bear ill will 2251; **gruchyng** *pres. p.* with displeasure 2126. [ONFr. *gro(u)ch(i)er.*]

grwe *n.* grain, jot; *no grwe*, not at all 2251. [OFr. *gru*, a grain of oats.]

guod; gurde(l). See GOD(E); GORDE(L).

guttez *n. pl.* guts 1336. [OE. *guttas.*]

ȝ

ȝayned *pp.* met, greeted 1724. [OE. *ge-gegnian*, ON. *gegna.*]

ȝare *adv.* fully 2410. [OE. *gear(w)e.*]

ȝark(k)e *v.* to ordain 2410; set 820. [OE. *gearcian.*]

ȝar(r)ande *pres. p.* snarling 1595; chiding 1724. [OE. *gyrran,* *georran*, str.]

ȝate *n.* gate 782, 820, 1693, 2069. [OE. *gæt.*]

ȝaule *v.* to yowl, howl 1453. [Cf. ON. *gaula.*]

ȝe *adv.* yea, yes, indeed 813, 1091, 1381, 1498, 1729, 1940. [OE. *gæ, gē(a).*]

ȝe *pron.* you 30, 265, 1820, etc.; addressed to one person 343, 470, 545, 814, 835, 897, 1050, etc.; **yow** *acc. and dat.* (to) you 130, 624, 1997, etc.; *reflex.* (for) yourself 470, 1390, 2117; **your(e)** *poss. adj.* your 311, 347, 2450, etc.; **yowre** 836, 1071, etc.; **ȝowre** 1065, *1092; **yourez** *pron.* yours 1106, etc.; **yowrez** 1037; **ȝourez** 1387. **ȝourself** *pron.* you yourself 350; **yourself** 1267; *by y.* beside you 1522; **yowreself** in *if y. lykez*, if you like 1964; **yourseluen** you 1548; *to y.* upon yourself 350; **yorseluen** in *of y.*, of your own *1394. [OE. *gē, ēow*, etc.]

ȝede(n) *pa. t.* went 815, 817, 1122, 1400, 1684; **ȝedoun** = *ȝed doun* 1595 n.; **ȝod** 1146; was, 2333; *on fote ȝ.*, lived 2363. [OE. *ēode.*]

ȝederly *adv.* promptly 453, 1215, 1485, 2325. [From OE. *ēdre, ǣdre.*]

ȝef *v.* to give 1964 n. [OE. *gefan.*]

ȝeȝe *v.* to cry (as wares) 67; *ȝ. after*, cry for 1215. [OE. **gēgan*, rel. to ON. *geyja.*]

ȝelde *v.* to yield; **ȝelde(n)** *pa. t.* 67, 1595, 1981; **ȝolden** *pl.* 820; *pp.* 453. To give back, return 453, 1478

(reply), 1981, 2223, 2325; bring
(back) 498; give 67; repay one (for)
(*subj.*) 1038, 1263, 1292, 1963, 2056,
2410, 2441; ȝ. *hym*, allowed him
(to pass) 820; *refl.* surrender 1215,
1595. [OE! *géldan.*]

ȝelle *v.* to yell 1453. [OE. *gellan.*]

ȝelpyng *n.* vaunt; challenge 492. [OE.
gylpincg, *gelping.]

ȝep(e) *adj.* brisk, bold, valiant 105,
284, 1510; fresh 60, 951; **ȝeply**
adv. promptly 1981, 2244. [OE.
ȝēap, cunning.]

ȝer(e) *n.* year 498, 500, etc.; *þis seuen
ȝ.*, these seven years, for ages 1382;
ȝonge ȝ., New Year's tide 492. [OE.
ȝē(a)r.] See Nw(e) ȝer(e).

ȝeres-ȝiftes *n. pl.* New Year's gifts
67. [Prec.+OE. *gift* infl. by ON.;
see GIFTE. Cf. ME. *ȝeres-ȝiues.*]

ȝern(e) *adv.* eagerly 1478, 1526;
swiftly 498. [OE. *géorne.*]

ȝerne *v.* to long 492. [OE. *géornan.*]

ȝernes *v.* runs, passes 498; **ȝirnez**
529. [OE. (*ge-*)éornan, ge-irnan.]

ȝet *adv.* yet, still 1122, 1894, 2219;
ȝet firre, moreover 1105; all the
same, (and) yet, nevertheless 297,
465, 1489, 1613, 2276, etc.; *and ȝ.*
even if 1009. [OE. *ȝēt.*]

ȝette *v.* to grant 776. [Late OE.
ȝē(a)tan after ON. *játta.*]

ȝif *conj.* (*usually with subj.*) if 406,
1061, 1774, etc.; **if** 30, 272, 360,
1484, etc.; **iif** 2343; if only 1799;
whether, if 704, 1057, 2457; *bot if*,
unless 1054, 1782, 1956. [OE. *gif.*]

ȝirnez. See ȝernes.

ȝisterday *adv.* yesterday 1485; *n. pl.*
passing days 529. [OE. *gestrandæg.*]

ȝod. See ȝED.

ȝol *n.* Yule, Christmas 284, 500.
[OE. *ȝēol*; ON. *jól*, n. pl.]

ȝolden. See ȝELDE.

ȝolȝe *adj.* yellow, withered 951. [OE.
geolu, geolw-.]

ȝomerly *adv.* in pain, piteously 1453.
[OE. *geōmer-líce.*]

ȝon *adj.* that, yon 2144. [OE. *geon.*]

ȝonder *adv.* *as adj.* yonder, that
678, 2440. [Cf. OE. *geónd* and
MLG. *gender.*]

ȝong(e), ȝonke *adj.* young, youthful

89, 1526; *ȝ. ȝer*, New Year 492; *as
sb.* young(er) one 951, 1317; *so ȝ.*,
one so young 1510. [OE. *geong.*]

ȝore *adv.* since long ago, a long while
2114. [OE. *geāra.*]

ȝour-, ȝow(re), etc. See ȝE.

H

habbe(z), haf(e). See HAUE.

hadet *pp.* beheaded 681. [OE. *hĕaf-
dian.*]

haȝer *adj.* skilful; well-wrought 1738;
compar. fitter, readier 352 n. [ON.
hag-r.]

haȝþorne *n.* hawthorn 744. [OE.
hagu-þorn.]

hay *interj.* hey! hi! 1158, 1445. [Cf.
Du. and Germ. *hei.*]

haylse, haylce *v.* to greet 223, 810,
829, 972, 2493. [ON. *heilsa.*]

hal, halle *n.* castle, hall 48, 102, 2329,
etc.; *h. dor*, hall-door 136, 458; *h.
ȝatez*, main entrance (within castle
wall) 1693. [OE. *hall.*]

halce. See HALS.

halche *v.* to embrace 939; enclose
185; loop, fasten round 218, 1852;
fasten 1613; *h. in*, join to 657. [OE.
halsian.]

halde, holde *v.* to hold (up) 436, 2297
(*subj.*), etc.; rule 53, 904, 2056 (*see*
HONDE); keep, fulfil 409, 698, 1677,
2129, etc.; *h. alofte*, maintain 1125;
contain 124, 627; restrain 1043,
1158; consider, account 28, 285,
1274, 1297, 2390, etc.; **helde** *pa. t.
subj.* 2129; **halden, holden** *pp.* 259,
2270, etc.; bound 1040; beholden
1828. [OE. *háldan.*]

hale, halle *v.* to draw 1338; loose
(from bow) 1455; *intr.* rise 788;
come, go, pass 136, 458, 1049 n.
[OFr. *haler*, from Gmc.]

half, halue *adj.* half 185; *as sb.* 165,
1543; *adv.* 140, 2321. [OE. *half.*]

half, halue (*dat. and pl.*) *n.* side 649;
direction 698, 742, 1224, 1552, 2070,
2165; **haluez** sides of boar 1613;
(*vp*)*on Godez h.*, for God's sake 326,
692, 2119, 2149. [OE. *half.*]

half-suster *n.* half-sister 2464. [OE.
half- +swustor.] See SISTER-SUNES.

halȝe *n.* saint 2122. [OE. *hålga.*]

haliday *n.* (religious) festival 805, 1049. [OE. *hālig-dæg.*]

halydam *n.* holy thing (as relic) on which oath could be taken 2123. [OE. *hāligdōm.*]

halle(d). See HAL; HALE.

halme *n.* shaft, handle 218, 330, 2224. [OE. *halm*, stalk.]

halowe, halawe *v.* to shout 1445, 1908, 1914; shout at 1723; **halowing** *n.* shouting 1602. [OFr. *halloer.*]

hals(e), halce *n.* neck 427, 621, 1353, 1388, 1639. [OE. *hals.*]

hame; han; han(de)-. See HOME; HAUE; HONDE(SELLE).

hap *n.* happiness 48. [ON. *happ.*]

hapnest *adj.* most fortunate 56. [ON. *heppinn*, infl. by prec.]

happe *v.* to wrap, clasp, fasten 655, 864, 1224. [Prob. rel. to HASPE.]

hard(e) *adj.* hard 732, 733, 789, 2199; *adv.* 2153; firmly 655 (*compar.*), 1783. [OE. *heard, hearde.*]

harden *v.* to encourage, make bold 521, 1428. [ON. *harðna.*]

hardy *adj.* bold 59, 285, 371; **hardily** *adv.* certainly *2390. [OFr. *hardi.*]

harled *pp.* tangled 744. [(?) Cf. HERLE.]

harme *n.* injury, misfortune 2272, 2277, 2390, 2511. [OE. *hearm.*]

harnays *n.* armour, gear, 590, 2016. [OFr. *harneis.*]

harnayst *pp.* clad in armour 592. [From prec.]

hasel *n.* hazel 744. [OE. *hæsel.*]

haspe *n.* door-pin 1233. [OE. *hæpse.*]

hasp(p)e *v.* to clasp, fasten 281, 590, 607, 831, 1388. [OE. *hæpsian.*]

hast(e) *n.* speed 1569; *in h.* quickly 780, 2218, *with h.* 1756. [OFr. *haste.*]

haste *v.* to hasten 1165, 1424; *refl.* 1897. [OFr. *haster.*]

hasty *adj.* pressing 1051; **hastyly** *adv.* hastily 1135; quickly 605. [OFr. *hasti(f).*]

hastlettez *n. pl.* edible entrails 1612 n. [OFr. *hastelet.*]

hat(t)e *v.* am (is) called 10, 253, 381, 2445; **hattes** *2 sg.* 379, 401. [OE. *hātte*, passive of HETE.]

hatte *n.* hat 2081. [OE. *hætt.*]

hatz. See HAUE.

haþel *n.* knight 221, 234, 323, 829, 1853 n., etc.; master 2065; Lord 2056. [OE. *hæleþ*, infl. by *æþele.*]

hauberghe, hawbergh *n.* hauberk *203, 268. [OFr. *hauberc*, infl. by OE. *halsbeorg*, Med.L. *halsberga.*]

haue, haf(e) *v.* to have 99, 1711, 2135, etc.; *1 sg.* 263, 406, etc.; **habbe** 1252; **habbez, -es** *2 and 3 sg.* 327, 452, 626, *2339; **hatz** 330, 2341, etc.; **hátz, hauen, haf, han** *pl.* 17, 497, 1089, 1255, etc.; **haue, haf** *subj.* 2287, 1944; *imper.* 496, 2143, 2287, 2288; **had(e)** *pa. t.* 52, 72, 442, 657, etc.; *subj.* 677, 680, 1815, 2394, etc.; *pp.* 1962. To possess 836, etc.; take 773, 1051, 1612, 1944, 2247, 2408; accept 1980, put 1446; reach 700; beget 2466; *auxil.* have 17, 327, 452, 1380, etc.; *pa. subj.* would have 677, 680, 725, etc.; if . . had 2263, 2394, etc. *Haf at þe*, let me get at you 2288. [OE. *habban, haf-.*] See NAF.

hauilounez *v.* doubles back 1708. [From OFr. *havilon*, n.]

haunche *n.* haunch 1345, 2032. [OFr. *ha(u)nche.*]

hawtesse *n.* pride 2454. [OFr. *hautesse.*]

he *pron.* he 9, *438, 523, *1389, 1666, etc.; the one 53, 256, 1242, etc.; **him, hym** *acc. and dat.* (to, for) him, the one 237, 294, 399, *862, *865, *1906, etc.; *refl.* (for) himself 8, 221, 303, 1104, 1551, 2305; *pleonastic* 1464, 2013, 2154, etc.; **hymself, hym-, hisselue(n)** himself, the same, this very one, him (in person) 107, 113, 164, 226, 902, 1046, 1298, etc.; *refl.* (to, for) himself 126, 285, 1198, 2031, 2051, etc.; **his, hys** *adj.* his, its 4, 447, 676, *2291, etc.; *þat . . hys*, whose 913; *pron.* his own affairs 1018. [OE. *hē; him*, dat.; *his*, gen.]

hed(e) *n.* head 180, 286, 333, 1721, 2217, etc.; mouth 1523; (arrow) 1162, 1459; (axe) 210, 217; (including antlers) 1154; lord 253. [OE. *hēafod.*]

hedlez *adj.* headless 438. [OE. *hēafodlēas.*]

hef; heȝ-. See HEUE; HIȝ-, HYȝT.

hegge *n.* hedge 1708. [OE. **hecg.*]

helde *v. intr. and refl.* to slant, sink west 1321; bow 972, 1104; turn 2331; proceed, go, come 221, 1523, 1692, 1922. [OE. *héldan.*]

helde 2129. See HALDE.

helder *adv.* rather; *þe h.,* the more for that 376, 430. [ON. *heldr.*]

helez *n.* heels 1899; (spurred) 777, 2062, 2153. [OE. *héla.*]

helme *n.* helmet 203, etc. [OE. *helm.*]

help *n.* aid 987. [OE. *help.*]

help(p)e *v.* to help 2209; *subj.* 256, 1055, 2123. [OE. *helpan.*]

hem *pron. dat. and acc. pl.* (to, for) them 301, 870, 1613, etc.; **him, hym** 49, 229, 493, 1423, 1684, 1897; **hom** 99, 819, 1484, etc.; *refl.* 1130, 1254, 1910, etc.; **hemself** them 976; *refl.* themselves 1085; **her** *adj.* their 54, 706, 976, *1129, etc.; **hor** 130, 1265, 1516, etc. [OE. *heom, heora.*]

heme *adj.* (?)suitable, neat 157; **hemely** *adv.* 1852. [OE. *gehǽme,* customary.]

hemme *n.* border 854. [OE. *hemm.*]

hende *adj.* courteous, gracious, courtly 108, 405, 647, 904, 1633, 1731; *superl.* noblest 26; *as sb.* courteous, gracious (onè) 827, 946; *voc.* 1252, 1813; good sir 2330; *as (þe) h.* kindly 896 n., courteously 1104. **hend(e)ly** *adv.* 773, 895, 1639, etc. [OE. *gehende,* convenient.]

hendelayk *n.* courtliness 1228. [Prec. +ON. *-leikr.*]

heng(e) *v. wk.* to hang 477, 983, 1357, 1614; *intr.* 117, 182, 478, 732, 1345, 1930. [ON. *hengja,* trans.]

henne *adv.* hence 1078. [OE. *heonane.*]

hent *v.* to take, catch (up), receive 605, 827; *pa. t. and pp.* 864, 1597, *1639, 2277, etc. [OE. *hentan.*]

hepes, -**ez** *n. pl.* heaps; *on h.* in a mass 1722; *vpon h.* fallen in confusion 1590. [OE. *héap.*]

her. See HO, HEM.

herber *n.* lodging 755, 812. [OE. *herebeorg.*]

herber *v.* to lodge 805, 2481. [OE. *herebeorgian.*]

here *adv.* here, now, at this point 23, 1056, 1243, *2187, 2385, etc.; **herebiforne** before now 2527; **herinne** in this place 300. [OE. *hér; hér-beforan, -inne.*]

here *n.*[1] company of warriors, host 59, 2271. [OE. *here.*]

here *n.*[2] hair 180, 183, 190, 436, 1587. [OE. *hǽr, hér.*]

here *v.*[1] to hear (of) 46, 755, 2273, etc.; be told 630; **herd(e)** *pa. t.* 31, 690, 1897, etc.; *pp.* 515, 1135; *h. telle,* etc. 26, 263, 1144; **herande** *pres. p.* in the hearing of 450. [OE. *héran.*]

here *v.*[2] to praise 1634. [OE. *herian.*]

heredmen *n. pl.* courtiers 302. [OE. *héord-, híred-mann.*]

herk(k)en *v.* to hear, listen (to) 592, 775, 1274, 1529, 1708. [OE. *hercnian.*]

herle *n.* strand 190. [MLG. *herle.*]

herre. See HIƷ(E).

hersum *adj.* devout 932. [OE. *hérsum.*]

hert *n.* heart 1594; secret thoughts, courage 120, 371, 467, 1781, 1855, etc. [OE. *heorte.*]

hertte *n.* hart, stag 1154. [OE. *heor(o)t.*]

heruest *n.* autumn 521. [OE. *hærfest.*]

hes *n.* obligation, *or* promise 1090. [OE. *hǽs,* order; *behǽs,* promise.]

hest *n.* bidding, behest 1039, 1092. [Extended from prec.]

hete *v.* to promise 2121; **hyƷt** *pa. t.* 1966, 1970, 2218, 2341; future 448; *pp.* 450. [OE. *hátan; hét, héht.*]

hetes *n. pl.* vows, assurances of knightly service 1525. [From prec.]

het(t)erly *adv.* fiercely, vigorously, suddenly 1152, 1446, 1462, 1587, 2291, 2311, 2317. [Cf. OE. *hetol,* fierce; MLG. *hetter.*]

heþe *n.* heath 1320. [OE. *hæþ.*]

heþen *adv.* hence, away 1794, 1879. [ON. *héðan.*]

heue *v.* to lift 1184, 2288; **hef** *pa. t.* 826; made bristle 1587; *intr.* was uplifted 120; **heuen** *pl.* 1346. [OE. *hebban, hef-.*]

heuen *n.* heaven(s), sky 323, 2057,

heuen (*cont.*)
2079, 2442; *vnder h.*, on earth 56, 352, 1853 n. [OE. *heofon(e)*.]

heuened *pp.* raised 349. [OE. *hafenian*, infl. by HEUE.]

heuen-quene *n.* queen of heaven 647. [HEUEN+QUENE, cf. OE. *heofoncyning*.]

heuenryche *n.* heaven; *vnder h.*, on earth 2423. [OE. *heofon-rīce*.]

heuy, heué *adj.* heavy, grievous 289, 496. [OE. *hefig*.]

hewe *n.* See HWE.

hewe *v.* to hew, cut 1351, 1607; **hwen** *pa. t. pl.* 1346, 1353; **hewen** *pp.* cut 477; hammered, made 211; shaped 789. [OE. *hēawan*.]

hyde *n.* skin 1332, 2312. [OE. *hȳd*.]

hyden *v.* to hide, conceal 2511; **hid** *pa. t.* 1875. [OE. *hȳdan*.]

hider(e) *adv.* hither, here 264, 1209, 1537, 2524, etc. [OE. *hider*.]

hyghe *interj.* hi! 1445.

hyȝe *n.* haste; *in h.*, suddenly 245. [From next.]

hiȝe, hyȝe(e) *v.* to hasten, speed 299, 521, 826, 1152, 1351, 1462; *refl.* 1910, 2121. [OE. *hīgian*.]

hiȝ(e), hyȝ(e), heȝ(e) (i) *adj.* high, tall 137, 281, 1138, etc.; high (of special dignity) 108, 222, 250, 593, 2297, 2462, etc.; *h. kyng*, God 1038, 1963; *h. tyde*, festival 932, 1033; noble 5, etc.; important 1051; loud 1165, 1417; mature 844: (ii) *as sb.* height, high ground 1152, 1169, 2004; *(vp)on h.*, on high 1607, 2057; in heaven 256, 2442; loudly 67, 1602; to the highest pitch 48; *h. and loȝe*, great and small, all 302; all matters 1040: (iii) *adv.* high 120, 223, 258, etc.; loudly 307, 468, 1445, 2212; publicly 349: (iv) **herre** *compar.* taller 333; **hyȝest, heȝest** greatest 57; *adv.* highest (at table, on the host's right) 1001. [OE. *hēh*; *hĕrra*.]

hyȝly, heȝly *adv.* erect 1587; highly, deeply 949, 1547, 1828; devoutly 755, 773; gaily 983. [From prec.]

hiȝlich *adj.* noble, splendid 183. [OE. *hēalic*, infl. by *hēh*.]

hyȝt *pa. t.* See HETE.

hyȝt, heȝt *n.* height 788; *(vp)on h.*, towering 332, aloft 421. [OE. *hēhþo*.]

hiȝtly *adv.* fitly 1612. [OE. *hyhtlīce*.]

hil(le) *n.* hill 742, 2081, 2271, etc.; castle-mound 59. [OE. *hyll*.]

hym(self) etc. See HE, HEM.

hind *n.* hind 1158, 1320. [OE. *hind*.]

hypped *pa. t.* hopped 2232; *hypped aȝayn*, rebounded 1459. [OE. **hyppan*; cf. *hoppian*.]

hir, his(seluen). See HO, HE.

hit, hyt *pron.* it 10, 187, 839, 1391, 2511, etc.; *impers.* 73, 843 (he), 948 (she), 988, 1293, etc.; *hit ar(n)*, there are 280, 1251. **hitself** *refl.* itself 1847. [OE. *hit*.]

hit(te) *v.* to hit, smite 2296; *pa. t.* 1455, 1459, 1594, 2153; *pp.* 2287; *h. to*, fell to 427. [ON. *hitta*.]

ho *pron.* she 738, 948, ***1872, etc.; **hir** *acc. and dat.* (to) her 76, 1200, 1289, 1742, etc.; **her** 1002, 1477; *refl.* herself 1193, *(pleonastic dat.)* 1735, etc. **hir** *adj.* her 647, 955, 1862, etc.; **her** 1778. [OE. *hēo, heŏ; heore, hire*.]

hod(e) *n.* hood 155, 881, etc. [OE. *hōd*.]

hode *n.* degree, order (of knighthood) 2297 n. [OE. *hād*.]

hoge. See HUGE.

hoȝez *n. pl.* hocks 1357. [OE. *hōh*.]

holde *v.* See HALDE.

holde *n.* stronghold, castle 771; possession 1252. [OE. *geháld*.]

holde *adv.* loyally 2129. [OE. *hólde*.]

holdely *adv.* faithfully, carefully 1875, 2016. [OE. *holdlīce*.]

hole *n.* hole 1338, 1569, 2180, 2221. [OE. *hol*.]

holȝ *adj.* hollow 2182. [OE. *holh*.]

holyn *n.* holly; *h. bobbe*, holly branch 206. [OE. *hole(g)n*.]

hol(l)e *adj.* whole, intact, healed 1338, 1346, 1613, 2296, 2484; amended 2390; **holly** *adv.* entirely, quite 1049, 1257. [OE. *hāl*.]

holsumly *adv.* healthfully 1731. [OE. *hāl+-sum*; cf. ON. *heilsamr*.]

holt *n.* wood 1320, 1677; *(attrib.)* 1697. [OE. *holt*.]

holtwode *n.* wood 742. [OE. *holtwudu*.]

hom. See HEM.

hom(e), hame *n.* home, dwelling 12, 408, 1924; *adv.* 2121; *to h.*, home 1615, 1922; *at h.*, 268, 2451, etc.; *fro hame* 1534. [OE. *hām.*]

homered *pa. t.* hammered; struck 2311. [From OE. *homor, hamor*, n.]

hond(e) *n.* hand 206, 328, 494, 2291, etc.; **hande** 458, 1203; possession 1270; *bi h.*, in person 67; *tan on h.*, undertaken 490; *out of h.*, straight away 2285; *holden in h.*, govern, dispense 2056; *at þe hondes (of)* from 2499. [OE. *hánd, hónd.*]

hondele *v.* to handle, take hold of 289, 570, 1633, 2505. [OE. *hondlian.*]

hondeselle, hanselle *n.* gift(s) at New Year 66, 491. [OE. *handselen.*]

hone *n.* delay 1285. [(?)Rel. to HOUE.]

honour *n.* honour 1038, 1228; honour shown, hospitality 1963, 2056; *your h.*, worthy of you 1806; **honours** *pl.* 1813. [OFr. *hono(u)r.*]

honour, honowr *v.* to honour 830, 949, 1033, 2412, 2520; celebrate 593. [OFr. *hono(u)rer.*]

hoo *imper.* stop 2330. [ME. *hō*, v. from *ho!* interj.; cf. E. *whoa!*]

hope *v.* to hope (*of* for) 2308; expect, think, believe 140, 352, 395, 926, 2301. [OE. *hopian.*]

hor. See HEM.

hore *adj.* hoar, grey 743. [OE. *hār.*]

horne *n.* (hunting) horn 1165, 1417, 1601, 1923, etc. [OE. *horn.*]

hors(s)e *n.* horse 175, 1138; 180, 1904 (*gen.*), etc.; **horce** 1464; *on hors(e)*, on horseback 1692, mounted 2065. [OE. *hors.*]

hose *n. pl.* hose 157. [OE. *hosa.*]

hostel *n.* lodging, dwelling 776, 805; **ostel** 253. [OFr. *(h)ostel.*]

hot *adj.*; *in h. and colde*, through thick and thin 1844. [OE. *hāt.*]

houe *v.* to tarry, halt 785, 2168. [?]

houes *n. pl.* hoofs 459. [OE. *hōf.*]

hound, hownd *n.* hound 1139, 1359, 1422, 1597, 1897, etc. [OE. *húnd.*]

hous(e) *n.* house 285, 309, 2275, etc.; *in house*, under a roof 2481. [OE. *hūs.*]

how(e) *adv.* how, in what way, what 401, 414, 1379, 2436, etc. *how þat*, how 379, 1752; **how-se-euer** *adv.* however 1662. [OE. *hū.*]

huge, hoge *adj.* great, huge 208, 788, 1536, 2420, etc. [OFr. *ahoge, ahuge.*]

hult *n.* hilt 1594. [OE. *hilt.*]

hundreth *adj. and n.* hundred 743, 1144, 1543, 1597, 2294. [ON. *hundrað.*]

hunt *v.* to hunt 1320, 1677, 1943; **huntyng** *n.* hunting 1102. [OE. *huntian; huntung.*]

hunte *n.[1]* hunt(ing array) 1417 (*or as next*). [From prec.]

hunt(e) *n.[2]* huntsman 1147, 1422, 1604, 1701, 1910. [OE. *hunta.*]

hunter *n.* hunter 1144, 1165, 1428, 1697. [From HUNT, v.]

hurt *n.* wound 2484. [OFr. *hurt.*]

hurt *v.* to hurt, wound 1452, 1462, 2291; *pa. t.* 2311; *pp.* 1577. [OFr. *hurter.*]

hwe, hewe *n.* hue, colour, shade of colour 147, 234, 620, 707, 867, 1471, 1738, 1761. [OE. *hīw, hēow.*]

hwen. See HEWE.

I

I *pron.* I 24, 253, 1962, etc.; **me** *acc. and dat.* (to, for) me 256, 292, 1035, 1214, 2112, 2213, etc.; *ethic dat.* 1905, 1932, 2014, 2144, 2459; *dat. absol.* 1067; *refl.* 474, 1271, 1964, etc. **my** *adj.* my 288, 408, etc.; **my(y)n** (*before vowels*) 257, 1067, etc.; **myn(e)** *pron.* 342, 1816, 1942. **myself(e), -seluen** myself 1052, 1244, 1540, 2361, 2434. [OE. *ic, mē, mīn; mē selfan.*]

iapes *n. pl.* jests 542, 1957. [Obscure.]

iche. See VCHE.

ientyle; i(i)f. See GENTYLE; 3IF.

iisse-ikkles *n. pl.* icicles 732. [OE. *īs+gicel*; cf. *īses gicel.*]

iles *n. pl.* islands 7, 698. [OFr. *i(s)le.*]

ilyche *adj.* the same 44. [OE. *gelīc.*]

ilk(e) *adj.* same, very 24, 819, 2397, 2461, etc.; *pron.* 1385, 1981; same (hue) 173, 1930 (cf. SAME). [OE. *ilca.*]

ille *adv.* ill 346; *n.* in *tas to i.*, take amiss 1811. [ON. *illa; illr*, adj.]

in *prep.* in, on, at 7, 645, 1096, 1421, 2199, 2433, etc.; **inn** 1451; (in)to

in (*cont.*)
924, 1699; within 764, 1198, etc.;
(*of time*) 22, 54, 1641, 1646, etc.
[OE. *in.*]

in *adv.* in 136, 189, 2161, etc. [OE. *inn.*]

inmyddes, -ez *adv. and prep.* in the
middle (of) 167, 1004 n., 1932.
[From OE. *on middan.*]

inne *adv.* in; *þer(þat)* .. *inne*, in which
2196, 2440, 2509. [OE. *inne.*]

innermore *adv. compar.* further in
794. [OE. *innor+māre.*]

innogh(e), i(n)noʒ(e), innowe *adj.*
enough 404, 730; say no more!
1948; many, in plenty 77, 514, 826,
1401, 2123, etc.; *adv.* enough 477,
*803, 1496; exceedingly 289, 888.
[OE. *genōh, genōg-.*]

inore *adj. compar.* inner 649. [OE.
innerra.]

into *prep.* into 62, 435, 697, etc.;
from here to 2023. [OE. *inn tō.*]

inwyth *adv.* within 2182; *prep.* within
1055. [OE. *in+wiþ.*]

ioy(e) *n.* joy, gladness 646, 1022,
1247, 2053, etc.; *maden i.* were de-
lighted 910. [OFr. *joie.*]

ioyfnes *n.* youth 86. [OFr. *joefnesse.*]

ioylez *adj.* joyless 542. [From IOY.]

ioyne *v.* to join (with), encounter 97.
[OFr. *joindre, joign-.*]

ioly *adj.* gay 86; **iolilé** *adv.* gallantly
42. [OFr. *joli(f).*]

ioparde *n.* peril 1856; *in i.* to lay, to
hazard 97. [OFr. *ju(jeu) parti.*]

irke *v. impers.*: *irked burnez to nye*,
men tired of hurting 1573. [Ob-
scure.]

is *3 sg.* is 33, 754, 1319, etc. [OE. *is.*]

iuel *n.* jewel; *fig.* 1856. [OFr. *joel.*]

iugged *pp.* adjudged, assigned 1856.
[OFr. *jug(i)er.*]

iuste *v.* to joust 42; **iustyng** *n.* 97.
[OFr. *jo(u)ster, juster.*]

iwysse *adv.* indeed, certainly 1035,
1065, 1557, 2526, etc.; **iwy(i)s** 252,
264. [OE. *mid* (or *tō) gewisse.*]

K

K. See also C.

kay *adj.* left 422. [ODan. *kei.*]

kanel *n.* pipe, wind-pipe; neck 2298.
[ONFr. *canel*, channel.]

kauelacion *n.* cavilling, objection
2275; ***cauelaciounz** *pl.* trifling
disputes 683. [OFr. *cavillacio(u)n.*]

kene *adj.* bold 321, 482; bitter 2406;
kenly *adv.* daringly 1048; bitterly
2001. [OE. *cēne, cēnlīce.*]

kenel *n.* kennel; *attrib.* 1140. [ONFr.
**kenil*; cf. OFr. *chenil.*]

kenet *n.* (small) dog 1701. [ONFr.
kenet; cf. OFr. *chenet.*]

kenne *v.* to teach 1484; entrust,
commend (= BIKENNE) 2067, *2472;
kende *pa. t.* taught 1489. [OE.
cennan; ON. *kenna.*]

kepe *v.* to keep, hold, preserve 1059,
2148; *subj.* 2298; let him keep 293;
to await 1312; attend to 1688;
care for 2016; care, be anxious (to)
546, 2142; *k. hym with carp*, engage
in conversation with him 307; *kepe
þe*, take care 372. [OE. *cēpan.*]

ker(re) *n.* thicket on marshy ground;
ker(re) syde, side of a marsh 1421,
1431. [ON. *kjarr*, older **ke(a)rr.*]

kerchofes *n. pl.* kerchiefs, coverings
for the head and neck 954. [OFr.
cuevrech(i)ef, AN. *kevre-.*]

kest(en). See CAST *n.* and *v.*

keuer *v.* to recover 1755; obtain 1221,
1254; afford, give 1539; *intr.*
manage (to) 750, 804, 2298; *keuerez*,
makes his way 2221. [OE. *a-cofrian*,
intr.; OFr. *(re-)covrer*, AN. *-kevre*,
trans.]

kyd, kydde *pp.* made known, shown
263; *k. hym cortaysly*, shown him
courtesy 775; behaved 2340; *as adj.*
famous 51; reputed 1520. [OE.
cȳþan, pp. *ge-cȳdd.*]

kylled *pp.* killed 2111. [ME. forms
point to OE. **cyllan*, beat.]

kyn *n.* kind; *gen. sg.*, in *alle kynnes*,
of every kind, every kind of 1886;
originally *gen. pl.* in *fele kyn*, many
kinds of 890. [OE. *cynn.*]

kynde *n.* nature, natural character
321, 2380; kindred, offspring 5; *of
þe worldes k.*, among men 261; *bi
k.*, properly 1348. [OE. *(ge)cýnd.*]

kynde *adj.* natural, proper; seemly,
courtly 473. [OE. *(ge)cýnde.*]

kyndely *adv.* duly, properly 135.
[OE. *(ge)cýndelīce.*]

kyng(e) *n.* king 37, 364, 393, 992
(MS.), 1048, 2492, etc.; the king,
Arthur 57, 2340; *kynges hous Arthor*,
k. Arthur's house 2275; *þe heȝe
k.*, God 1038, 1963. [OE. *cyning,
cyng.*]

kyrf *n.* cut, blow 372. [OE. *cyrf.*]

kyrk *n.* church 2196. [ON. *kirkja.*]

kyrtel *n.* kirtle, a coat or tunic reach-
ing to the knees 1831. [OE. *cyrtel.*]

kysse *v.* to kiss, exchange kisses 605,
974, 1303, 1501, 2472, etc.; **kyssed,
kyst** *pa. t.* 596, 1118, 1758, 2351,
etc.; *pp.* 1869. **kyssyng** *n.* kissing
1489, 1979. [OE. *cyssan.*]

kyth *n.* native land; land 460, 2120.
[OE. *cy̆þþu.*]

knaged *pp.* fastened 577. [From
ME. *knagg*, peg; cf. Swed. *knagg.*]

knape *n.* fellow 2136. [OE. *cnapa.*]

knarre *n.* rugged rock, crag 721,
1434, 2166. [Cf. LG. *knarre*, knot.]

knawen. See KNOWE.

kneled *pa. t.* knelt 368, 818, 2072 n.
[OE. *cnēowlian.*]

knez *n. pl.* knees 577; **knes** 818.
[OE. *cnēo.*]

knyf *n.* knife 1331; **knyffe** *dat.* (*note
rhyme*) 2042; **knyuez** *pl.* 1337.
[OE. (late) *cnīf*, prob. from ON.
knifr.]

knyȝt, kniȝt *n.* knight 42, 51, 62, 96,
1272 (*voc.*), 1279, etc. [OE. *cniht*,
servant.]

knyȝtyly *adj.* knightly, chivalrous
1511; **knyȝtly** *adv.* courteously
974. [From prec.]

knitte, knyt *pa. t.* tied 1331 n.;
made (fast) 1642; **knit** *pp.* knotted,
tied 1831; knit, entwined 1849.
[OE. *cnyttan.*]

knokke *n.* knock, blow 2379. [Stem
of OE. *cnocian.*] See CNOKEZ.

knokled *adj.* knobbed, rugged 2166.
[From ME. *knok(e)le*, knob,
knuckle; cf. OFris. *knokele.*]

knorned *adj.* rough, craggy 2166.
[Cf. O.E.D. *knur.*]

knot *n.* knot 188, 194, 577, 1334 n.,
2376, 2487; rocky (wooded) knoll
1431, 1434; (*endeles*) *k.*, pentangle
630, 662. [OE. *cnotta*; ON. *knottr*,
ball—see Smith, *Pl.-N. Elements.*]

know(e) *v.* to acknowledge, recognize
357, 937; know 325, 400, 454, 546,
1095, 1484, etc.; **knew** *pa. t.* 682,
1849; **knwe** 460, 2008; **knawen,
knowen** *pp.* discovered 1272;
acknowledged (to be) 348, 1511;
k. for, known to be 633. [OE.
cnāwan.]

koynt *adj.* skilful; skilfully made,
beautiful 877; **coynt** (*of*) polite,
gracious (in) 1525; **quaynt** finely
prepared 999; **coyntly(ch)** *adv.*
elegantly 578; gracefully 934;
koyntly adroitly 2413. [OFr. *cointe*,
AN. *queinte.*]

koyntyse (*of*), *n.* skill, ability (in)
2447. [OFr. *cointise.*]

kort, kourt. See CORT.

kowarde *adj.* cowardly, recreant
2131. [OFr. *co(u)ard.*]

L

lace *n.* thong 217, 2226; belt 1830,
2487, 2505, etc. [OFr. *laz, las.*]

lach(che) *v.* to catch; **laȝt, laght**
pa. t. 127, 667, etc.; **leȝten** *pl.* 1410;
pp. **laȝt** 971, etc.; caught back 156.
To take hold of 292 (*subj.*), 936,
1029, *1906, etc.; take, get 127, 234,
595, etc.; receive 2061, 2499, etc.;
accept 1772; *l. at, to*, seize 328, 433.
[OE. *læccan.*]

lachet *n.* latchet 591. [ONFr. *lachet.*]

lad(de). See LEDE *v.*

lady, ladi *n.* lady 49, 346, 1187, 2030,
etc.; **ladé** 1810. [OE. *hlǣfdige.*]

laft. See LEUE *v.*[1]

lagmon 1729. See note.

laȝe *v.* to laugh 316, 988, 2514; smile
1207, etc.; *pa. t. wk.* 69 etc.; **loȝe**
2389. **laȝyng** *n.* 1954. [OE. *hlæhhan.*]

laȝter *n.* laugh 1217; laughter *1623.
[OE. *hlæhtor.*]

lay *v.* to lay, stake 97, 156, 419; utter
1480; *l. vp*, put away safe 1874;
l. hym bysyde, put aside, parry 1777;
refl. lie down 1190. [OE. *lecgan.*]

laye *n.* lay; poem 30. [OFr. *lai.*]

layk *n.* sport, entertainment 262, 1023,
1125, 1513. [ON. *leikr.*]

layke *v.* play, amuse oneself 1111,
1178, 1554, 1560; **laykyng** *n.*
playing 472. [ON. *leika.*]

layne *v.* to conceal 1786, 1863; *layne yow (me)*, keep your (my) secret 2124, 2128. [ON. *leyna.*]

layt *n.* lightning 199. [OE. *lēget.*]

layt(e) *v.* to seek 411, 449; wish to know 355. [ON. *leita.*]

lakked *pa. t.* found fault with 1250; *impers.* in *yow l.*, you were at fault 2366. [From MLG. *lak.*]

lance. See LAUNCE *v.*

lante *pa. t.* gave 2250. [OE. *lǣnan.*]

lappe *n.* loose end or fold (of garment) 936, (of skin) 1350. [OE. *læppa.*]

lappe *v.* to fold, wrap, embrace 217, 575, 973. [From prec.]

large *adj.* broad, wide 210, 2225. [OFr. *large.*]

larges(se) *n.* great size 1627; generosity 2381. [OFr. *largece, -esse.*]

lasse *adj. compar.* less, smaller 1284, 1524, 2226; *adv.* 87, 1829, 1848, 2368; **lece** *see* NEUER. **lest** *adj. superl.* smallest 355, 591. [OE. *lǽssa, lǣs(es)t.*]

lassen *v.* to ease 1800. [From prec.]

last(e) *adj. superl.* last 1133; *as sb.* 1023; *at þe l.*, at last, finally 1027, 1120, 2497, etc. [OE. *lætest.*]

last(e) *v.* to endure, last, live 1061, 1235, 2510; **last** *pa. t.* 1665; **lested** 805; **lasted** extended 193. [OE. *lǽstan.*]

late *adj.* late 1027; **later** *adv. compar.* less readily 541. [OE. *læt.*]

laþe *v.* to invite 2403. [OE. *laþian.*]

laþen. See LOþE.

laucyng *n.* loosening 1334. [LAUSEN.]

laumpe, *n.* lamp *2010. [OFr. *la(u)mpe.*]

launce *n.* lance 667, 2066, 2197. [OFr. *la(u)nce.*]

la(u)nce *v.* to cut 1343, 1350; (fling), utter 1212, 1766, 2124; *intr.* fly 526; dash, gallop 1175, 1464, 1561. [OFr. *la(u)ncer.*]

launde *n.* glade, lawn, field 765, 1894, 2146, 2154, 2171, 2333. [OFr. *la(u)nde.*]

lausen, lawse *v.* to undo 2376; break (troth) 1784. [From ON. *lauss.*]

lawe *n.*[1] law; style 790; *bi. l.*, duly 1643. [OE. *lagu*, from ON.]

lawe *n.*[2] mound, knoll 765, 2171, 2175. [OE. *hlǣw.*]

lece; lede *n.* See NEUER; LEUDE.

lede *v.* to lead, conduct 936, 947, 977; pursue 1894; hold 849; experience, have 1927, 2058; **lad(de)** *pa. t.* 1729, 1927, etc.; *pp.* 1989. [OE. *lǣdan.*]

leder *n.* leader 679. [From prec.]

lee *n.* protection, shelter; *in l.*, in castle 849 n.; comfortable place 1893. [OE. *hlēo.*]

lef, leue (*wk.*) *adj.* dear, beloved, delightful 909, 1111, 1133, 1924, 2054; **leuer** *compar.* dearer 1782; *þat l. wer*, whom it would delight more 1251; **leuest** *superl.* 49, 1802. [OE. *lēof.*]

leg(e) *adj.* entitled to feudal allegiance; sovereign 346, 545. [OFr. *l(i)ege.*]

leg(g)e *n.* leg 575, 2228. [ON. *leggr.*]

leȝten 1410; **leke.** See LACH, LOUKE.

lel(e) *adj.* loyal, faithful 1513, 1516; true 35 n.; **lelly** *adv.* 449, 1863, 2124, 2128. [OFr. *leal*, AN. *leёl.*]

leme *v.* to shine 591, 1119, 1137, 1180, 2010, 2226. [ON. *ljóma.*]

lemman *n.* loved one, mistress 1782. [OE. *lēofman; early ME. *leofmon.*]

lende *v.* to arrive; dwell, stay 1100, 1499; **lent** *pa. t.* went *971; took his place 1002; *pp.* 2440; *is l. on*, is occupied in 1319. [OE. *lendan.*]

lene *v.*; *l. with*, incline 2255; *l. to*, lean on 2332. [OE. *hleonian.*]

leng(e) *v.* to make stay, keep 1683; *hym l.*, let him stay 1893; *intr.* stay 254, 411, 1068, 1672, 2446, etc. [OE. *lengan.*]

lenger. See LONGE *adv.*

len(k)þe *n.* length 210, 1627, 2316; *on lenþe*, far away 1231; for a long time 232. [OE. *lengþu.*]

lentoun *n.* Lent 502. [OE. *lencten.*]

lepe *v.* to leap, run 292 (*subj.*), 328, 981, 1131, 1709; **lopen** *pp.* 1413; *lepez hym*, gallops 2154. [OE. *hlēapan.*]

lere *adj.* empty; *as sb.* (something) worthless 1109. [OE. *gelǣr.*]

lere *n.*[1] ligature 1334 n. [OFr. *lieure.*]

lere *n.*[2], *n.*[3] See LYRE *n.*[1] and *n.*[2]

lern(e) *v.* to learn 908, 918, 927,

1532; teach 1878; *pp.* well in-structed, skilful 1170, 2447. [OE. *léornian*.]

lese *v.* to lose 2142; **lost** *pp.* 69, 675. [OE. (*for*)*léosan*; *losian*.]

lest *conj.* (*with subj.*) lest 750, 1304, 1773, etc. [OE. *þe-læs-þe*.]

lest. See LASSE.

let(e), lette *v.*[1] (*pres. and pa. t.*) to let (fall) 817, 2309; let, allow 248, 423, 468, 1063, 1154, 1733, 2208, 2387, etc.; let be 360; *forming imper.* 1994; *l. se*, show (me) 299, 414; *l. be*, cease from 1840; *l. one*, let be 2118; cause to 1084; utter 1086; look and speak, behave 1206, 1634; *l. as* (*lyk*), behave as if, pretend 1190, 1201, 1281, 2257. [OE. *lætan, lētan*, str.]

lette *v.*[2] to hinder 2142, 2303; dis-suade 1672. [OE. *lettan*, wk.]

letteres *n. pl.* letters 35. [OFr. *lettre*.]

lettrure *n.* lore, learning 1513. [OFr. *lettreüre*.]

leþe *v.* to soften, make humble 2438. [OE. *geliþian, -leoþian*.]

leþer *n.* skin; *l. of þe paunchez*, tripe 1360. [OE. *leþer*.]

leude *n.*[1] man, knight, prince 675, 851, 1023, 1306, 2499, etc.; **lede** 38, 98 n., 126, 258, *1516, etc.; **lude** 133, 232, 449. [OE. (verse) *léod*, m.]

leude *n.*[2], **lede** people, company 833, 1113, 1124. [OE. *léod*, f.; *léode*, pl.]

leudlez *adj.* companionless 693. [From LEUDE *n.*[1]]

leue *adj.* See LEF.

leue *v.*[1] to leave 1583, 1870, 2154; leave off 1502; **laft** *pa. t.* gave up 369; omitted 2030. [OE. *læfan*.]

leue *v.*[2] to allow 98. [OE. *léfan*.]

leue *v.*[3] to believe 1784, 2128, 2421. [OE. *geléfan*.]

leue *v.*[4] to live 1035, 1544. [OE. *lifian, leofian*.]

leue *n.* leave 133, 971, 1218, 1670; leave to go 545; leave-taking 1288; *take* (*etc.*) *l.*, take leave, depart 595, 993, 1118, 1556, 1960, 1978, etc. [OE. *léaf*, f.]

leuez *n. pl.* leaves 519, 526. [OE. *léaf*, neut.]

lewed *adj.* ignorant 1528. [OE. *læwede*.]

lewté *n.* loyalty, fidelity 2366, 2381. [OFr. *leauté*, AN. *leuté*.]

liddez *n. pl.* eyelids 2007. [OE. *hlid*.] See Y3E-LYDDEZ.

lyf, lif *n.* life(time) 87, 98, 545, 675, etc.; person 1780; **lyue** *dat.* 706, 2480, etc.; **lyues** *pl.* 1516, 2112; *l. haden*, lived 52; (*vp*)*on l.*, alive, on earth (often a tag) 385, 1719, 1786, 2054, 2095. [OE. *līf*.]

liflode *n.* food 133. [OE. *līflād*.]

lyft(e) *adj.* left (hand, etc.) 698, 947, 2146, 2487. [OE. *lyft*.]

lyft(e) *v.* to lift, raise 2309; build 12; *pa. t.* 369, 433, 446; *pp.* extolled 258. [ON. *lyfta*.]

lyfte *n.* heaven(s) 1256. [OE. *lyft*.]

ly(3)e *v.* to lie (down, idle) 88, 1096, 1780, 1994; *imper.* 1676; **lyg3ez** *3 sg. pres.* 1179; **lys, lis** 1469, 1686; **le3** *pa. t.* 2006; **lay** 1195, 2088; was lodged 37. [OE. *licgan, lig-; lyg3ez* prob. from ON. *liggja*.]

ly3t *adj.*[1] bright 199; cheerful 87; gay 1119. [OE. *lĕ(o)ht*, adj.[1]]

ly3t *adj.*[2] light, active 1119 (*or prec.*), 1464; *set at l.*, think light of 1250. [OE. *lĕ(o)ht*, adj.[2]]

ly3t *n.* light(s) 992, 1649, 1685, 1989, 2010; dawn 1675. [OE. *lĕ(o)ht*.]

ly3t(e), li3t(e) *v.* to dismount 254, 329, 1175, 1583, 1906, 2176; come down 1373, 2220; land (on) 423, 526; *pa. t.* 822; *pp.* in *is l.*, has arrived 1924. [OE. *līhtan*.]

ly3tez *n. pl.* lights, lungs 1360. [LY3T *adj.*[2] as *sb.*]

ly3tly *adj.* light (gleaming *or* of fine texture) 608. [OE. *lĕ(o)htlic*, shining; light.]

ly3tly *adv.* lightly; swiftly 292, 328, 423, 1131, 1830, 2309; easily 1299. [OE. *lĕ(o)htlice*.]

lyk *v.* to taste 968 n. [OE. *liccian*.]

lyke *adj.* (with *to*) like 187; *as sb.* similar (events) 498; *adv.* in *lyk as*, as if 1281. [OE. *gelīc*; *gelice*, adv.]

lyke *v.* to please 87, 893, 1084, 1234, etc.; *impers.* 289, 814, 976, etc.; *lyked ille*, it might displease 346; *pers.* like 694 (*and perhaps* 893, 1682, 2134). [OE. *līcian*.]

lykkerwys *adj.* delicious, sweet 968. [ONFr. **lekerous* (OFr. *lecheros*) with anglicized suffix.]

lym(m)e *n.* limb, member 139, 868, 1332. [OE. *lim.*]

lymp(e) *v.* to befall 907; *subj.* falls to our lot 1109. [OE. *limpan.*]

lynde *n.* lime-tree; (*allit.*) tree 526, 2176; **lynde-wodez** woods 1178. [OE. *linde.*]

lyndes *n. pl.* loins 139. [OE. *lendenu*; ON. *lendir.*]

lyne *n.*[1] line 628. [OFr. *ligne.*]

lyne *n.*[2] linen (attire); *lufsum vnder l.,* fair lady 1814 n. [OE. *līn.*]

lyppe *n.* lip 962, 1207, 2306. [OE. *lippa.*]

lyre *n.*[1] cheek, face 943, 2228; **lere** 318. [ON. *hlýr,* OE. *hlēor.*]

lyre *n.*[2] flesh 2050 (coat); **lere** 418. [OE. *līra*; confused with prec.]

list *n.* joy 1719. [ON. *lyst.*]

lyst(e) *pres. sg. impers.* it pleases (*yow l.,* you desire) 1111, 1502, 1784, 2133, 2142; *pa. t.* 941, 2049. [OE. *lystan.*]

lyste *v.* to hear; *l. his lyf,* hear his confession **1878. [OE. *hlystan.*]

lysten *v.* to listen to 30; *intr.* 2006. [OE. *hlysnan*; cf. LYSTE.]

lystyly *adv.* craftily 1190; skilfully, deftly 1334. [OE. *listelīce.*]

lyt(e) *adj.* little 1777; *pl.* few 701. [OE. *lȳt,* indecl.]

lyte *n.* expectation; *on l.,* in delay 2303; back (in fear) 1463. [From ON. *hlíta,* to trust.]

littel, lyt(t)el *adj.* little, small 30, 1183, 1250, 1338, 1709, 1848; *adv.* 2007; *a littel,* a little 418, 973, 1185, 2267, 2366; some way (away) 2146, 2171. [OE. *lȳtel,* adj.]

lyþen *v.* to hear 1719. [ON. *hlýða.*]

liþernez *n.* ferocity 1627. [OE. *lȳþernes.*]

lyuer *n.* liver 1360. [OE. *lifer.*]

lo, loo *interj.* lo! look 1848, 2378, 2505; *we loo,* ah well! 2208. [OE. *lā.*]

lode *n.* leading: *on l.,* (in tow), with her 969; way, journey: *in his l.,* with him 1284. [OE. *lād.*]

lodly *adv.* horribly: *let l.,* professed horror 1634; offensively 1772. [OE. *lāþlīce.*]

lofden. See LUF *v.*

loft(e) *n.* upper room 1096, 1676; (*vp*)*on l.,* aloft 788, 2261. [ON. (*á*) *loft.*] See ALOFTE.

loȝe, loghe *adj.* low(lying) 1170; *as sb.* 302, 1040 (*see* HIȜE); *on l.,* down (to the hall) 1373; **lowe** *adv.* low 972, 2236; **loȝly** *adv.* humbly, with deference 851, 1960. [ON. *lágr.*]

loȝe 2389. See LAȜE.

loke *n.* look 1480; *þe loke to,* a glance at 2438. [From next.]

loke *v.* to look 223, 446, 970, 1172, 1194, 2146; (*with subj.*) see to it that 448; appear 199; *l. on (at, to),* look at, see 479, 941, 950, 1063, 2333; *trans.* look after, guard 2239; **lokyng** *n.* staring 232. [OE. *lōcian.*]

loken. See LOUKE.

lokkez *n. pl.* locks of hair 156, 419, 2228. [OE. *locc.*]

lome *n.* tool, weapon 2309. [OE. *lōma.*]

londe *n.* land, ground, country 411, 1055, 2440, etc.; *pl.* countryside 1561; *in (vpon) londe,* in the land, on earth 36, 486, 679, 1802, 2058. [OE. *lónd.*]

long(e) *adj.* long 139, 419, 796, 1195; *hym boȝt l.,* he was impatient 1620. [OE. *láng, lóng.*]

long(e) *adv.* a long while 36, **88, 1554, etc.; **lenger** *compar.* 1043, 2063, 2303. [OE. *lónge;* compar. adj. *lengra.*]

longe *v.* to belong to, befit 1524, 2381, 2515. [From OE. *ge-lóng,* adj.]

longynge *n.* grief 540. [OE. *lóngung.*]

lopen. See LEPE.

lord(e) *n.* lord, noble, ruler 38, 316, 850, **992, etc.; Lord 753, 2185; *oure l.,* 1055; husband 1231, 1271, 1534, 1863. [OE. *hláford.*]

lore *n.* learning; *with l.,* learned 665. [OE. *lār.*]

lortschyp *n.* lordship, command 849. [OE. *hláfordscipe.*]

los *n.* renown 258, 1528. [OFr. *los.*]

losse *n.* damage 2507. [OE. *los.*]

lost. See LESE.

lote *n.* sound, noise 119, 1917, 2211; noise of talk 244, word, saying, speech 639, 988, 1086, 1116, 1399, 1623, 1954. [ON. *lát(pl.*), behaviour, cries.]

loþe *adj.* hateful; *þuʒt l.*, were loath 1578. [OE. *lāþ.*]

loþe, laþe *n.* injury 2507; grudge 127. [OE. *lāþ.*]

loude *adj.* loud 64. [OE. *hlūd.*]

loude, lowde *adv.* loudly, aloud 69, 1088, 1623, 1724, etc. [OE. *hlūde.*]

loue-, louy(e). See LUF, LUFLYCH, etc.

louke, lowke *v.* to shut 2007; *intr.* (be) fasten(ed) 628; *pa. t. wk.* 217, 792; *str.* leke 1830; loken *pp.* fastened 35 n., 2487; shut 765. [OE. *lūcan.*]

loupe *n.¹* loop 591. [Obscure.]

loupe *n.²* loop-hole, window 792. [?]

loute *v. intr.* to bow, bend 1306, 1504; turn, go 833, 933; *trans.* bow before, reverence 248; lut(te) *pa. t.* 2255; saluted 2236; *l. with*, bent 418. [OE. *lūtan*, str.]

louue, lowe *v.* to praise 1256; *to l.*, praiseworthy 1399. [OFr. *lo(u)er.*]

lowande *pres. p.* shining 236 (MS.); brilliant 679, 868. [ON. *loga.*]

lowe. See LOʒE, LOUUE.

lowkez; lude. See LOUKE; LEUDE.

luf *n.* love: affection, regard generally 540, 2054, etc.; friendliness, amiability 1086; love between the sexes 1284, 1513, 1524, etc.; *for l.*, because of (my) love 1733, 1810; *for þy l.*, out of regard for you, for your sake 1802; *for alle lufez vpon lyue*, for all loves there are 1786 n. [OE. *lufu.*]

luf, louy(e) *v.* to love 1780, 2095, 2099, 2421, 2468; be in love 1795; lou(i)ed *pa. t.* 87, 702, 1281, liked 126; lufed 2368; lofden *pl.* 21. [OE. *lufian.*]

luf-lace *n.* love-lace, girdle as love-token 1874, 2438. [LUF+LACE.]

luf-laʒyng *n.* loving laugh 1777. [LUF+LAʒYNG.]

lufly(ch), louely(ch) *adj.* pleasing, gracious, fair 38, 419, 433, 1218, 1480, etc.; loueloker *compar.* 973; louelokkest, loflyest *superl.* 52, 1187. lufly(ch) *adv.* graciously,

courteously 254, 595, 981, 1002; willingly, gladly 1606, etc. [OE. *luflic, -līce.*]

luflyly *adv.* graciously, amiably, in seemly manner 369, 2176, 2389, 2514. [From prec.]

lufsum *adj.* lovely 1814. [OE. *lufsum.*]

luf-talkyng *n.* (art of) lovers' conversation 927. [LUF+TALKYNG.]

lur *n.* loss, disaster 355, 1284; sorrow 1682. [OE. *lyre.*]

lurk(k)e *v.* to lie snug 1180; *pp.* lurking 1195. [Cf. Scand. dials. *lúr* (extended *lurk-*) (i) doze, etc.; (ii) sneak off.]

lut(te). See LOUTE.

M

ma fay by my faith 1495. [OFr. *ma fei.*]

mace. See MAKE.

mach *v.* to match 282. [OE. *gemæcca*, n.]

madame *n.* (*voc.*) my lady 1263. [OFr. *ma dame.*]

madde *v.* to act madly 2414. [From OE. *gemǣdd*, mad.]

maʒtyly *adv.* powerfully, forcibly 2262, 2290. [OE. *mæhtiglīce.*]

may *n.* woman 1795. [ON. *mær, meyj-*; OE. (verse) *mǣg.*]

may(e) *v.* can, may 380, 409, 926, 1795, etc.; *pl.* 70, 2396; mowe *pl.* 1397; myʒt *pa. t.* 79, 201, 1569, 1903, etc.; *if .. might* *1858; *quat he m.*, what he was doing 1087; moʒt(en) 84, *872, 1871, 1953. [OE. *mæg*, etc.]

mayme *v.* to injure 1451. [From ME. *maym*, OFr. *mahaym, mayhem*, etc., maiming.]

mayn *adj.* great, strong 94, 187, 336, 497. [ON. *megn*; OE. *mægen.*]

maynteine *v.* to support, keep 2053. [OFr. *maintenir, maint(i)en.*]

mayster *n.* lord, knight 136; master 1603, 2090. [OFr. *maistre.*]

maystrés *n. pl.* arts 2448. [OFr. *maistrie; maistrise*, sg.]

make *v.* to make, do, perform 43, 1073, 1674, etc.; commit 1774; cause to be 2455; mas *3 sg.* 106;

make (*cont.*)

mace 1885; **make** *subj. 1 pl.* let us make 1105, 1681; **mad(e)** *pa. t.* 71, 562, 687, etc.; created 869; **madee** compelled 1565; **maked** 1142, 1324; *pp.* 1112; **made** 982. [OE. *macian.*]

male *adj.* male 1157. [OFr. *ma(s)le.*]

male *n.* bag 1129, 1809. [OFr. *male.*]

malt *pa. t.* melted 2080. [OE. *mieltan, mæltan*; pres. is *malte* in this MS.]

mane *n.* mane 187. [OE. *manu.*]

maner *n.* custom 90; kinds 484; way 1730; *pl.* manners 924. [OFr. *manere.*]

manerly *adj.* seemly 1656. [Prec.]

mansed *pa. t.* threatened 2345. [OFr. *manec(i)er, manac(i)er.*]

mantyle *n.* mantle, robe 153, 878, 1736, 1831. [OFr. *mantel.*]

marre *v.* to destroy 2262. [OE. *merran.*]

mas; masse. See MAKE; MESSE.

masseprest *n.* priest 2108. [OE. *mæsse-prēost.*] See MESSE.

mat(e) *adj.* daunted 336; exhausted 1568. [OFr. *mat.*]

matynez, matynnes *n. pl.* matins (first of the canonical 'hours', recited at midnight or before daybreak) 756, 2188. [OFr. *matines.*]

mawgref *prep.* in *m. his hed* (extension of *his*, gen.), in his despite, do what he might 1565. [Alteration (assoc. with GREF) of *maugreþ* from OFr. **malgred, maugré.*]

Meȝelmas *n.* Michaelmas (Sept. 29); *m. mone*, harvest moon (full at or near the equinox) 532. [Cf. OE. *Michaeles mæsse*; forms with *ch* treated as spirant, as OFr. *Mihiel*, are used exclusively of the archangel.]

me(y)ny *n.* company, household, court 101, 1372, 1625, 1729, 1957, 2045, 2468, etc. [OFr. *mai(s)n(i)ee, me(s)nie.*]

mekely *adv.* humbly 756. [ON. *mjúkliga*, older **mēuk-.*]

mele *n.* mealtime 999. [OE. *mēl.*]

mele *v.* to speak, say 447, 543, 974, 1280, 2295, 2336, 2373. [OE. *mælan.*]

melle *n.* in *inn melle*, in the midst, on all sides 1451. [ODan. *i melle.*]

melle *v.* to mingle; stream (together) 2503 (cf. 2371). [OFr. *me(s)ler.*]

melly *n.* contest, battle 342, 644. [OFr. *me(s)lée.*]

membre *n.* limb 2292. [OFr. *membre.*]

men. See MON.

mended *pa. t.* improved 883. [Shortened from AMENDE.]

mene *v.* to mean 233; **menyng** *n.* understanding 924. [OE. *mǣnan.*]

menged *pp.* mingled 1720. [OE. *méngan.*]

mensk *adj.* honoured 964. [ON. *mennskr*, human; cf. next.]

mensk(e) *n.* courtesy, honour (shown) 834, 2052; honour, fame 914; *pl.* 2410. [ON. *mennska*, humanity, generosity.]

mensked *pp.* adorned 153. [From prec.]

menskful *adj.* of worth 1809; *as sb.* noble (knights) 555; (lady) 1268. [As prec.]

menskly *adv.* courteously 1983; worthily 1312. [As prec.]

merci, mercy *n.* mercy 1881, 2106; *see* GRANT. [OFr. *merci.*]

mere *adj.* noble 924, (?) 1495 (*but see* MERY). [OE. *mǣre, mēre.*]

mere *n.* appointed place 1061. [OE. *gemǣre*, landmark.]

mery, meré, miry, myry *adj.* merry, joyful, cheerful 497, 1086, 1447, 1623, 1891, 1915; gay, fair 142, 153, 878, 1263, 1495, 1736; fine, pleasant 1691; *make m.*, enjoy oneself 1313, 1681, 1953, 2468; (*with refl. pron.*) 1885. **meryly, muryly** *adv.* gaily, playfully 2295, 2336, 2345; handsomely 740. [OE. *myrge.*]

merk *n.* appointed place 1073. [ON. *merki*; OE. *gemerce.*]

merkke *v.* to aim (a blow) at 1592. [ON. *merkja*; OE. *me(a)rcian.*]

merþe, mirþe, myrþe *n.* joy, pleasure, amusement 40, 45, 541, 1007, 1656, 1763, 1871, 1952; **myerþe** 860; *meue m.*, provide fun 985; *make m.*, make merry, revel 71, 106, 899, 982. [OE. *myrgþ.*]

meruayl(e) *n.* wonder, marvel 94, 466, 479, 718, 2307; *to m.* marvellous

1197; *had m.*, wondered 233 (cf.
WONDER). [OFr. *merveille*.]

meschaunce *n*. disaster 2195. [OFr.
mesch(e)a(u)nce.]

meschef *n*. harm; *his m.*, the disaster
to himself 1774. [OFr. *mesch(i)ef*.]

mes(se) *n*. table, buffet 999; food
1004; *pl.* dishes of food 999. [OFr.
mes.]

messe *n*. Mass 1690; **masse** 592,
755, 1135, 1311, 1414, 1558. [OE.
messe, mæsse; OFr. *messe*.]

messequyle *n*. time for Mass 1097.
[Prec.+WHYLE.]

mesure *n*. stature 137. [OFr. *mesure*.]

metail *n*. metal 169. [OFr. *metail*.]

mete *adj*. equal; extending (to) 1736;
metely *adv*. duly 1004, 1414. [OE.
gemēte; cf. *gemetlīce*.]

mete *n*. food, meal 45, 474, 543, 887,
n312, 1414, etc.; *attrib*. dinner- 71
1.; *pl*. dishes 121, 1952. [OE. *mete*.]

mete *v*. to meet 1061, 1753, 1932;
greet 834, 2206 n., 2235; **met(te)**
pa. t. 703, 1723, 1984; *m. wyth*
1370; *intr*. 1407, 1592; *pp*. come
upon 1720. [OE. *mētan*.]

methles *adj*. immoderate, ruthless
2106. [OE. *mǣþlēas*.]

meue *v*. to move; arouse 985; in-
fluence 90; *intr*. move, pass (on)
1312, 1965, mwe 1565; *m. to*, result
in 1197; interfere with 1157. [OFr.
mo(u)veir; *muev*-, AN. *mev*-.]

mych, miche. See MUCH(E).

myddelerde *n*. the world 2100. [Cf.
OE. *middangeard* and ERDE.]

myddes: *in þe m.*, in the midst 74.
[Var. of INMYDDES.]

myd-morn *n*. midmorning, nine a.m.
1073, 1280. [OE. *midd+morgen*.]

myd-nyȝt *n*. midnight 2187. [OE.
mid-niht.]

myd-ouer-under *n*. mid-afternoon
1730. [OE. *mid+ofer undern*.]

myȝt *n*. power 2446; *at my m.*, as
far as I can 1546; *for myȝtez so
wayke*, because of (their) powers
(that are) so weak 282. [OE. *miht*.]

myȝt. See MAY.

myldest *adj. superl*. gentlest 754.
[OE. *milde*.]

myle *n. pl*. miles 770, 1078. [OE. *mīl*.]

mylk-quyte *adj*. milk-white 958
(MS.). [OE. *milc-hwīt*.]

mynde *n*. mind, memory 497, 1484;
in m. hade, reflected 1283; *gotz in
m.*, is a matter of doubt 1293. [OE.
gemýnd.]

mynge *v*. to draw attention to (by
giving tongue) 1422. [OE. *myndgian*.]

myn(n)e *v*. to declare 141; exhort
982; remember, think of 995, 1992;
m. (vp)on, give one's mind to 1681;
be reminded of 1800; *m. of*, have
thought for 1769 (*subj*.). [ON.
minna, remind; *minnask*, remember.]

mynne *adj*. less; *þe more and þe m.*,
all 1881 n. [ON. *minni*.]

mynstralsye, mynstralcie *n*. min-
strelsy 484, 1952. [OFr. *menestral-
sie*.]

mynt, munt *n*. aim; feint, pretence
at a blow 2345, 2350, 2352. [From
next.]

mynte *v*. to aim, swing (axe) 2290; *pa.
t.* 2274; **munt** 2262. [OE. *myntan*.]

myre *n*. mire, swamp 749. [ON. *mýrr*.]

miry, mirþe. See MERY; MERþE.

mysboden *pp*. ill-used 2339. [OE.
misbēodan, pp. *misboden*.]

mysdede *n*. sin 760, 1880. [OE.
misdēd.]

misy *n*. swamp, bog 749. [Cf. Mod.
Lancs. dial. *mizzy*; (?)OE. **mysig*,
adj. rel. to *mos*, MOSSE.]

mislyke *v*. to displease 1810; *impers.
(subj*.) 2307. [OE. *mislīcian*.]

mysses *n. pl*. faults 2391. [OE. *miss*,
and *mis*- prefix.]

mist *n*. mist 2080. [OE. *mist*.]

myst-hakel *n*. cloak of mist 2081.
[OE. *mist+hacele*.]

mo *adj*. more (in number) 23, 730,
2322, 2324; *adv*. 770. [OE. *mā*.]

mode *n*. mood, mind 1475. [OE. *mōd*.]

moder *n*. mother 754, 2320. [OE.
mōdor.]

moȝt(en). See MAY.

molaynes *n. pl*. ornamented bosses at
each end of horse's bit 169. [OFr.
molein.]

molde *n*. earth; *on (þe) m., vpon m.*,
on earth 137, 914, 964; in life 1795.
[OE. *mólde*.]

mon *n.* man 57, 141, 2349, etc.; *voc.*
1746, 1800, etc.; *as pron.* one 565,
1077, 1160, 1209, 1682, 2355, *2511,
etc.; *vche (no) m.*, everybody, nobody 84, 233, etc.; **men** *pl.* men,
people 28, 45, 914, 1447, 1690, etc.;
menne 466. [OE. *mon(n).*]

mon *3 sg.* must 1811, 2354. [ON. *mun.*]

mone *n.*¹ moon 532, 1313. [OE. *mōna.*]

mone *n.*² complaint 737. [OE. **mān,*
rel. to *mǽnan*, v.]

moni, mony *adj. and pron.* many 14,
284, 351, 454, 2448, etc.; *mony a*,
(with sg.) many, many a 710, 1217;
(without a) 22, 38, 442, 1447, 2493,
etc. [OE. *monig.*]

monk *n.* monk 2108. [OE. *munuc.*]

mor *n.* moor 2080. [OE. *mōr.*]

more *adj. compar.* greater, larger 615,
677, 1804, 1881, 2100, etc.; more,
further 1308, etc.; *as sb.* 130; *lasse
ne m.*, (not) any, at all 1524; *adv.*
more, further 333, 2316, etc.; *forming compar.* 503, 968, etc.; *no m.*,
not in return 560; no further, not
again 546, 2286, 2443, etc.; none
the more for that 2311. **most** *superl.*
greatest, most 137, 141, 985, etc.;
adv. 51, 638. [OE. *māra, mǽst* (late
Nth. *māst).*]

morn(e), moroun *n.* morning 453,
740, 1024, 1208; next day 995, 1670,
2350, etc. [OE. *morgen*, dat. sg.
morne.]

mornyng *n.*¹ morning 1691, 1747.
[From prec.]

mornyng *n.*² See MOURNE, *v.*

morsel *n.* a bite, small meal *1690.
[OFr. *morcel.*]

mosse *n.* moss, lichen 745. [OE. *mos.*]

most(e). See MORE, and next.

mot *pres. t.* may 342; *(in wishes)*
387, 2053, 2120, 2239, 2378; must
1965, 2510; **most(e)** *pa. t.* had to
1287, 1958. [OE. *mōt*, pa. t. *mōste.*]

mote *n.*¹ whit 2209. [OE. *mot.*]

mote *n.*² moat 764; castle 635, 910,
2052. [OFr. *mot(t)e.*]

mote *n.*³ moot, (single) note on hunt-
ing-horn 1364; *pl.* 1141. [OFr. *mot.*]

mount(e) *n.* hill 740, 2080; *bi m.*,
bi þe mountes, among the hills 718,
1730. [OFr. *mo(u)nt*, OE. *munt.*]

mounture *n.* mount, horse 1691.
[OFr. *mo(u)nteüre.*]

mourne *v.* to sorrow 1795; **mo(u)rn-
yng** *n.* sorrow 543, 1800; *in m. of*,
troubled with 1751. [OE. *múrnan.*]

mouþ(e), muthe *n.* mouth 447,
1446, 1572, 1778, 1907; voice 1428,
1447. [OE. *mūþ.*]

mowe. See MAY(E).

much(e) *adj.* great, powerful 182,
2336; much, abundant 558, 684,
899, 1017, 1506, etc.; **miche** 569;
as sb. much 1255, 1265, 1992; *þus
m.*, to this purpose 447; *so m. spellez*,
go so far as to say 2140; *adv.* much,
greatly, to a great extent 187, 726,
1795; **mych** 1281; *for as m. as*, in
so far as 356. [OE. *mycel, micel.*]

muchquat *n.* many things 1280.
[Prec.+WHAT.]

muckel *n.* size 142. [OE. *myc(e)lu.*]

muged *pa. t.* drizzled, was damp 2080.
[Cf. Norw. *mugga*, and *mug* v.² in
E.D.D.]

mulne *n.* mill 2203. [OE. *mylen.*]

munt; muryly. See MYNT(E); MERY.

mused *pa. t.* thought, i.e. lived 2424.
[OFr. *muser.*]

mute *n.* hunting-pack 1451, 1720;
baying of hounds 1915. [OFr.
muete.]

muthe; mwe. See MOUÞ; MEUE.

N

naf *v.* have not 1066; **nade** *pa. t.* 763;
subj. 724. [OE. *nabban*; see HAUE.]

naȝt. See NYȜT.

nay *pa. t.* denied 1836 n. [OFr. *nier.*]

nay(e) *adv.* nay, no 256, 279, 706,
1222, 1813, 2250, 2407, 2471. [ON.
nei.]

naylet *adj.* studded with nails 599.
[OE. *nægled.*]

naylez *n. pl.* nails 603. [OE. *nægel.*]

nayted *pp.* named, mentioned 65 n.
[ON. *neyta.*]

naked *adj.* naked, bare 420, 730, 962,
1740, 2498; *as sb.* bare flesh 423;
the ill-clad 2002. [OE. *nacod.*]

nakerys *n. pl.* kettledrums 1016;
nakryn *adj.* 118 n. [Cf. OFr.
nacaire.]

name. See NOME.

nar v. are not 2092. [OE. *naron*.]

nas v. was not *726. [OE. *næs*.]

nase n. nose 962. [OE. *nasu*.]

nauþer, nawþer, nouþer adj. (n)either 1552; adv. in ne .. *nauþer*, nor .. either 203, *659, 2367; conj. nor 1552; *nauþer* .. *ne*, neither .. nor 430, 1095, 1837, 2157, 2274. [OE. *nāwþer*.]

ne adv. not 488, 750, *1053, 2105, 2142, 2511, etc.; with other neg. 1991, 2236; conj. nor (with neg. or, and) 196, 400, 1087, 1812, 2340, 2431, etc. [OE. *ne*.]

nede adv. of necessity (with BIHOUE) 1216, 1771; **nedes, -ez** needs 1287, 1965, 2510. [OE. *nēde, nēdes*.]

nedes v. in hit n., there is need of 404. [From next.]

nedez n. pl. needs, business 2216. [OE. *nēd*.]

neȝ(e), neghe, nieȝ adv. near, close *697, 929, 1671; nearly 1922; prep. 1771 (see ÞRED). [OE. *nēh*.] See NER.

neȝe, negh(e) v. intr. to approach 132, 697, 1998; watz neȝed, had drawn (near) 929; trans. 1575; reach 1054; touch 1836. [From prec.]

nek, nec n. neck 420, 2255, 2310, 2484, 2498, 2506. [OE. *hnecca*.]

neked n. little 1062, 1805. [ON. *nekkvat*, something.]

neme v. to name (for, as) 1347. [OE. *nemnan*; cf. NEUEN.]

ner(e), nerre adv. (compar.) nearer 1305; close at hand 1995; nearly 729; as prep. nearer to, near 237, 322; com n., approached 556. **nexte** superl. as prep. next, beside 1780. [OE. *nēr (nĕrra*, adj.), compar.; ON. *nær* compar. and positive. OE. *nĕxt*.]

neuen v. to name, call, mention 10, 58, 65, 541. [ON. *nefna*.]

neuer adv. never 91, 659, 706, 2216, 2320, etc.; not at all 399, 470, 1487, etc.; none 376, 430; n. one, no one 223; n.bot, only 547; n.so, no matter how 2129; n. þe lece, none the less 474, 541. [OE. *næfre*; cf. *nā þe læs*.]

newe; nexte. See NWE; NER.

nye, nyȝe n. harm 2141; bitterness 2002; hit were n., it would be hard 58. [OFr. *anui*.]

nye v. to annoy 1575. [OFr. *anuier*.]

nieȝ. See NEȜ(E).

nif conj. unless 1769. [NE+(ȝ)IF.]

nyȝt n. night 730, 751, 1177, 1887, 2347, etc.; ni(y)ȝt 929, 1687; naȝt 1407; on nyȝtez, at night 47, 693. [OE. *niht, næht*.]

nikked, nykked pa. t. in n. hym (wyth) nay, said no to him 706, 2471. [OE. (once) *niccan* from *nic*, not I.]

nyme v. to take 993; n. to þyseluen, bring upon yourself 2141; **nome** pa. t. 809; obtained 1407; **nomen** pp. taken on (himself) 91. [OE. *niman*.]

nirt n. slight cut 2498. [Cf. Norw. dial. *nerta*, v. and SNYRT.]

nys adj. foolish 323, 358. [OFr. *nice*.]

nys v. is not *1266 n. [OE. *nis*.]

no adj. no 201, 696, 1809, etc.; any 1157; **non** 438, 657, 1552; (foll. noun) none 2106; see OÞER, WAY. [OE. *nān*.]

no adv. no 336, 411, 2063, 2226, 2303, etc.; see MO, MORE. [OE. *nā*.]

nobelay n. nobility; þurȝ n., as a point of honour 91. [OFr. *nobleie*.]

nob(e)le adj. noble 623, 675, 917, 1264, etc.; glorious, splendid 118, 514, 853, 1858, 1873; as sb. 1750. [OFr. *noble*.]

nobot conj. only 2182. [Next+BOT.]

noȝt adv. not (at all), by no means 358, 694, 1472, 2257, etc.; not 85, 134, 400, *2131, 2290, etc.; noȝt bot, only 1833. [OE. *nāht, nōht*.]

noȝt(e) n. nothing 680, 961, *1815, 1823, 1943; neuer .. for n., never on any account 1865; n. bot, nothing but, only 1267. [As prec.]

noyce, noyse n. noise 118, 132, 134, 1423, 2200, etc. [OFr. *noise*.]

noke n. angle, point 660. [Cf. Norw. dial. *nōk*, hook, bent figure.]

nolde pa. t. would not 1661, 1825, 1836, 2150, 2471; n. bot if, would not have it happen that .. not 1054. [OE. *nolde*.] See WIL.

nome n. name 10, 408, 937, 1347, 2443; **name** 400, 2453. [OE. *noma, nama*.]

nome(n). See NYME.

non(e) *pron.* none, no one 307, 352, 1790, 1823, 2170, etc. [OE. *nān.*]

nonez: *for þe nonez,* for the nonce, indeed 844. [OE. *for þan ānum.*]

norne, nurne *v.* to announce, propose; offer 1823; urge, press 1771; *n. hir aȝaynez,* refuse her 1661; *n. on þe same note,* propose same terms 1669; call 2443. [Cf. Swed. dial. *norna, nyrna,* inform (secretly).]

norþe *n.* north 2002. [OE. *norþ,* adv.]

not. See NOȝT.

note *n.*[1] business 358; *to þe n.,* in readiness 420; *for þat n.,* for the purpose, specially 599. [OE. *notu.*]

note *n.*[2] (musical) note 514; tenor, fashion 1669. [OFr. *note.*]

note *pp.* noted 2092 n. [OFr. *noter.*]

noþyng *n. as adv.* no whit, not at all 2236. [OE. *nā(n)þing.*]

noumbles *n. pl.* offal from back and loins of deer 1347. [OFr. *no(u)mbles.*]

nouþe, nowþe *adv.* now 1251, 1784, 1934, 2466. [OE. *nū þǎ.*]

nouþer. See NAUþER.

now(e) *adv.* now, still 10, 494, 1998, 2304, etc.; in these days 58; moreover, now 299, 656, 776, 1242, etc.; *oþer n. oþer neuer* 2216; *conj.* now that 2296; since 2420. [OE. *nū.*]

nowel *n.* Christmas 65. [OFr. *noel.*]

nowhere *adv.* nowhere 2164; **nowhare** in no case, not at all 2254. [OE. *nāhwǣr, -hwǎra.*]

nurne. See NORNE.

nurture *n.* good breeding 919, 1661. [OFr. *no(u)rreture.*]

nwe *adj.* new, fresh, novel 118, 636, 1401; **newe** 132, 1655; *adv.* newly, anew, 60, 599, 1668, 2223; **nwez** *as sb. gen.* in *what n.,* whatever new thing 1407. [OE. *nēowe; hwæt nēowes.*]

Nw(e) ȝer(e), New ȝere *n.* New Year's tide, New Year's day 60, 105, 284, 453, 1075, 2244, 2400, etc. [Prec.+ȝER(E); cf. ON. *nýjár.*]

O

of *adv.* off 773, 983, 1346, etc. [OE. *of.*]

of, o (615) *prep.* of; from, out of 183, 903, 1087, etc.; (consisting, made) of 121, 159, etc.; by, with 172, 1455, 2167, etc.; about, concerning 93, 108, 927, etc.; for 96, 975, 1032, 2308, etc.; *as equiv. of gen.* 25, 63, 424, etc.; *partitive* from, among 29, 38, 1816, etc.; some of 1452; in, as regards 86, 143, 1478, 1940, 2238, etc.; in, on (*confused with* ON) 1329, 1457. [OE. *of.*]

offre *v.* to offer 593. [OFr. *offrir.*]

oft(e) *adv.* often 18, 23, 65, 1123, 2482, etc. [OE. *oft.*]

oghe *v.* to have, owe; ought 1526; **aȝt(e)** *pa. t.* owned 767, 843, 1775; had (*or* owed) 1941. [OE. *āgan; āhte.*]

oȝt *n.* anything 300, 1815 (MS.), 2215. [OE. *ā(wi)ht, ō(wi)ht.*]

okez *n. pl.* oaks 743, 772. [OE. *āc.*]

olde *adj.* old 1001, 1124, 2182, 2183. [OE. *ǎld.*]

on *adj.* one, a single 30, 314, 372, 2151, 2252, etc.; one, as opposed to 'other' 206, 771, 2312. [OE. *ān.*]

on *adv.* on, away 2219, 2300; (with *infin.* or *rel.*) on 170, 173, 950, 968. [OE. *on.*]

on *prep.* (up)on 4, 236, 353, 1589, 2232, etc.; (*postponed; orig. adv.*) 953; to 1701, etc.; (think) of 1800, 2052, etc.; at 479, 491, 2180, etc.; in(to) 517, 683, 1722, 1730, etc.; a- 385, 1102, 1143, 2363, etc.; (*of time*) on, in, by 47, 537, 1675, 1680, 1732, 1868, etc. [OE. *on.*]

on(e) *pron.* one (person *or* thing) 223, 442, 864, 1340, 1964, 2416, 2439, etc.; *with superl.* 137 n., 1439, 2363; some one 2202, 2217; *þat on,* the one 952, 954, 2412. [OE. *ān.*]

one *adj.* alone, only 2074; *a .. one,* a single 2249, 2345; *al one, al hym (his) one,* alone 749, 1048, 2155; *hym one* 904; *oure one,* by ourselves 1230, 2245. [OE. *āna.*]

ones, onez *adv.* once 2280, 2512; formerly 2218; *at onez,* at the same time, together 895, 1425, 1913; *at þys onez,* at this very moment 1090. [OE. *ānes.*]

onewe *adv.* anew 65. [OE. *on+nīwan.*]

on-ferum *adv.* from a distance 1575. [OE. *on+feorran.*]

only *adv.* only 356. [OE. *ānlic,* adj.]

on-stray *adv.* out of his course, in a

new direction 1716. [OFr. *estraié*, ME. *astraie*, altered by assoc. with *a-*, *on-*.]

onsware. See ANSWARE.

open *adj.* open 2070. [OE. *open*.]

oquere *adv.* anywhere *660. [OE. *ōhwǣr*.]

or *conj.*[1] or 88, 661, 2183. [Reduced form of OÞER, conj.]

or *conj.*[2] than 1543 n. [Same as ARE.]

oryȝt. See ARYȝT.

oritore *n.* oratory, chapel 2190. [OFr. *oratur*.]

orpedly *adv.* boldly, aggressively, 2232. [OE. *orpedlīce*.]

ostel. See HOSTEL.

oþer *adj. and pron.* other (one), other kinds of 24, 90, 190, 208, 555, 655, 2342, etc.; different 132; *pl.* others 64, 551, 1249, 1445, 2423, etc.; one another 673. *An o.*, otherwise 1268; *non o.*, nothing else, what I say 1396; *þat o.*, the other 110, 386, 2389, 2412, etc.; latter 1591; second 1020, 2350; *of alle o.*, than any other 944 n.; *ayþer o.*, each (the) other 841, 939, 1307, 2472; *vch(on) . . oþer*, each . . the other 98, 501, 628. [OE. *ōþer*.]

oþer, auþer *adv. and conj.* or, or else 96, 456, *591, etc.; either (foll. by *oþer, or*) 88, 702, 1772, 2216; else (prec. by *oþer*) 1956, 2293; *oþer oþer*, or any one else 2102. [OE. *āhwæþer, ā(w)þer, ō-*.]

oþerquyle *adv.* at other times 722. [OÞER *adj.*+WHYLE *n.*]

oþez *n. pl.* oaths 2123. [OE. *āþ*.]

ouer *adv.* above (them) 223; across 2232; over there 700. *prep.* above 76, 732, 1908, 2217, etc.; over 182, 419, 957, 1758, etc.; over, across 13, 1561, 1709, 1896, etc. [OE. *ofer*.]

oueral *adv.* all over, entirely 150; everywhere 630. [OE. *ofer all*.]

ouerclambe *pa. t.* climbed over 713. [OE. *oferclimban*.]

ouergrowen *pp.* overgrown 2181, 2190. [OE. *ofer*+*grōwen*, pp.]

ouerȝede *pa. t.* passed by 500. [OUER +ȝEDE; cf. OE. *oferēode*.]

ouertake *v.* to regain 2387. [OE. *ofer*+ON. *taka*.]

ouerþwert *prep.* (*after its case*) through (a line of) 1438. [OE. *ofer*+ ON. *þvert*.]

ouerwalt *pp.* overthrown 314. [OE. *ofer*+*wæltan*.]

oure. See WE.

out *adv.* out 432, 458, 1333, 1438, etc.; *hatz out*, removes 1612; *out of out* of 802. [OE. *ūt*.]

oute *adv.* far and wide 1511. [OE. *ūte*.]

outtrage *n.* excess; *as adj.* exceedingly strange 29. [OFr. *outrage*.]

owen *adj. and pron.* own 408, 2359; **awen** 836, 1036, 1488, 1519, 2301, etc.; **auen** 293; **aune** 10. [OE. *āgen*.]

P

pay *n.* pay 2247. [OFr. *paie*.]

paye *v.* to please 1379; *pp.* satisfied 2341; paid up 1941. [OFr. *payer*.]

payne *n.* hardship 733. [OFr. *peine*.]

payne *v. refl.* to take pains; endeavour 1042. [OFr. *se pener*, 3 sg. *peine*.]

paynte *v.* to paint 800; depict 611. [OFr. *peindre*; *peint*, 3 sg., pp., sb.]

payre *v.* to be impaired, fail 650, 1456, 1734. [OFr. *empeir(i)er*.]

payttrure *n.* breast-trappings of horse 168, 601. [OFr. **peitreüre*, cf. *peitrel*.]

palays *n.* a fence of pales, palisade 769. [OFr. *paleïs*.]

pane *n.* fur edging, facing 154, 855. [OFr. *pan(n)e*.]

papiayez *n. pl.* parrots 611. [OFr. *papegai, papejaye*.]

papure *n.* paper 802. [OFr. *pap(i)er*, suff. altered.]

paradise *n.* paradise, heaven 2473. [OFr. *paradis*.]

paraunter, parauenture *adv.* perhaps 1009, 1850, 2343. [OFr. *par aventure*.]

pared *pp.* cut 802. [OFr. *parer*.]

park *n.* park 768. [OFr. *parc*.]

parte *v.* to part 2473. [OFr. *partir*.]

passage *n.* journey 544. [OFr. *passage*.]

passe *v.* to pass (by, away), proceed 266, 378, 1998, 2129, etc.; *trans.* cross 2071; surpass 654; *watz passande*, surpassed 1014; **passed**

passe (*cont.*)
 pa. t. 715, etc.; **past(e)** 1667; was
 over 1280. [OFr. *passer.*]
pater *n.* the Pater Noster, 'Our
 Father' 757.
patrounes *n. pl.* lords 6. [OFr.
 patro(u)n.]
paumez *n. pl.* 'palms' (broad flat
 parts) of horns of fallow deer 1155.
 [OFr. *paume.*]
paunce *n.* armour covering abdomen
 (properly *pauncer*) 2017. [OFr.
 pa(u)nc(i)er; see next.]
paunchez *n. pl.* stomachs (of a rumi-
 nant) 1360. [ONFr. *pa(u)nche.*]
pece *n.* piece 1458; (of armour) 2021.
 [OFr. *p(i)ece.*]
pelure *n.* fur (esp. for lining or trimming) 154, 2029. [OFr. *pelure.*]
penaunce *n.* penance 2392; peniten-
 tial fare 897. [OFr. *pen(e)a(u)nce.*]
pendauntes, -aund- *n. pl.* pendants
 168, 2038, 2431. [OFr. *penda(u)nt*,
 pres. p.]
penyes *n. pl.* pennies, money 79.
 [OE. *peni(n)g.*]
penta(u)ngel *n.* five-pointed star
 620 n., 623, 636, 664. [Alteration
 of OFr. *pentacle*, Med.L. *pentācu-
 lum*, by assoc. with *angle.*]
pented *pa. t.* had to do with, belonged
 204. [OFr. *apent* 3 sg., APENDE.]
peple *n.* people 123, 664. [OFr. *pueple.*]
pere *n.* peer, equal 873. [OFr. *per.*]
perelous *adj.* perilous 2097. [OFr.
 perillo(u)s.]
perile, peryl *n.* peril 733, 1768.
 [OFr. *peril.*]
perle *n.* pearl 954, 2364. [OFr. *perle.*]
persoun *n.* person 913. [OFr. *per-
 so(u)ne.*]
pertly *adv.* openly, plainly 544, 1941.
 [From OFr. *apert*, APERT.]
peruyng *n.* periwinkle 611 n. [OE.
 peruince, L. *pervinca.*]
pes *n.* peace 266. [OFr. *pais, pes.*]
pese *n.* pea 2364. [OE. *pise, peose.*]
piched *pp.* attached 576; **pyched** set
 up, erected 768; **py3t** *pa. t.* pitched,
 struck 1456; was (fixed) 1734. [OE.
 *piccan; cf. (late) *pīcan.*]
pyked *adj.* with spikes 769. [From
 OE. *pīc.*]

piked *pp.* polished 2017. [See O.E.D.
 pick, v.¹]
pynakle *n.* pinnacle 800. [OFr.
 pinacle.]
pine, pyne *n.* pain, grief, trouble 747,
 1812, 1985; *pine to*, it was difficult
 to 123. [OE. **pīn*; cf. next.]
pyne *v. refl.* to trouble oneself 1009,
 1538. [OE. *pīnian*; cf. PAYNE.]
pyned *pp.* enclosed 769. [OE. *pýndan*,
 ME. *pinden* (pp. *pind*) and *pin(n)en*,
 partly infl. by *pinnen*, pin.]
pipes *n. pl.* pipes 118. [OE. *pīpe.*]
pipe *v.* to pipe 747; **pypyng** *n.* music
 of pipes 1017. [OE. **pīpian.*]
pysan *n.* armour for upper breast
 and neck 204. [OFr. *pisa(i)ne* (sc.
 gorgerette), L. *pisanum*, of Pisa.]
pité *n.* pity, compassionateness 654.
 [OFr. *pit(i)é.*]
pyth *n.* toughness 1456. [OE. *piþa.*]
pitosly *adv.* piteously 747. [From
 OFr. *pito(u)s.*]
place *n.* room 123; place, dwelling
 252, 398, 1052, 2240, etc. [OFr.
 place.]
play *n.* play, sport 1014, 1379. [OE.
 plega.]
play *v.* to sport, amuse oneself 262,
 1538, 1664. [OE. *pleg(i)an.*]
playnez *n. pl.* level lands, fields 1418.
 [OFr. *plaine.*]
plate *n.* steel plate, piece of plate
 armour 204, 583, 2017. [OFr.
 plate.]
plede *v.* to plead 1304. [OFr. *plaid(i)er*,
 pled-.]
plesaunce *n.* pleasure 1247. [OFr.
 plaisa(u)nce, ples-.]
plesaunt *adj.* civil 808. [OFr.
 plaisa(u)nt, ples-.]
plese *v.* to please 1249, 1659. [OFr.
 plaisir, ples-.]
ply3t *n.* offence 2393; danger, hos-
 tility 266. [OE. *pliht.*]
plytes *n. pl.* (evil) conditions, hardships 733. [AN. *plit*; OFr. *pleit.*]
poynt *n.* (i) (sharp) point 1456, 2392;
 point of angle 627, 658: (ii) quality
 654; (good) condition 2049; question 902; *bryng me to þe p.*, come
 to the point with me 2284. [OFr.
 (i) *pointe*; (ii) *point.*]

poynte *v.* to describe (in detail) 1009. [OFr. *point(i)er.*]

polaynez *n. pl.* pieces of armour for knees 576. [OFr. *polain.*]

policed, polyst *pp.* polished 576, 2038; **polysed** cleansed 2393. [OFr. *polir, poliss-.*]

pore, pouer *adj.* poor, humble 1538, 1945. [OFr. *povre,* AN. *poure.*]

porter *n.* porter (at the gates) 808, 813, 2072. [OFr. *port(i)er.*]

poudred *pp.* powdered, scattered 800. [OFr. *poudrer.*]

pray(e) *v.* to pray, beg 254, 757, 1219, 1785, 2439, etc. [OFr. *preier.*]

prayere *n.*[1] prayer 759. [OFr. *preiere.*]

prayere *n.*[2] meadow 768. [OFr. *praiere.*]

prayse *v.* to praise 913, 1228, 1630, 1633, 2072; esteem 1850; *to p.,* praiseworthy 356. [OFr. *preis(i)er.*]

praunce *v.* to prance 2064. [Obscure.]

prece, prese *v.* to press forward, hasten 830, 2097. [OFr. *presser.*]

presense *n.* presence 911. [OFr. *presence.*]

prest *n.* priest 1877. [OE. *prēost.*]

prestly *adv.* promptly 757, 911. [From OFr. *prest.*]

preue *adj.* valiant 262. [OFr. *preu.*]

preué *adj.* discreet 902; **preuély** *adv.* privately 1877. [OFr. *privé.*]

preued, proued *pp.* proved 79; given proof of, shown 1630. [OFr. *pro(u)ver, pruev-,* AN. *prev-.*]

pryde *n.* pride 681, 2038, 2437; *with p.,* splendidly 587. [OE. *prȳdo.*]

prik, pryk *v.* to pierce, stir (heart) 2437; to spur (*intr.*), gallop 2049. [OE. *prician.*]

pryme *n.* prime, first division of the day, 6–9 a.m. 1675. [OE. *prīm,* from L. *prīma (hōra).*]

prynce *n.* prince 623, 873, 2398, etc.; *attrib.* princely 1014; *p. of paradise,* Christ 2473. [OFr. *prince.*]

prynces *n.* princess *1770. [OFr. *princesse.*]

pris, prys *n.*[1] value 79, 1277, 1850; excellence 912, 1249, 1630; praise 1379; *your p.,* politely for 'you' 1247; *o(f) prys,* precious 615, 2364;

noble 1770, 2398; **prys** *adj.* precious 1945. [OFr. *pris.*]

prys *n.*[2] capture; blast on horn when hunted animal is taken 1362, 1601. [OFr. *prise,* pp. stem of *prendre.*]

prysoun *n.* prisoner 1219. [OFr. *priso(u)n.*]

profered *pa. t.* offered 1494, 2350; made the offer 2346. [OFr. *parofrir,* AN. *prof(e)rir,* infl. by *pro-.*]

proude, prowde *adj.* proud, haughty 830, 1277, 2049, 2104, 2269; superb, splendid 168, 601. [OE. *prūt, prūd,* from OFr. *prout, prou(d);* cf. PREUE.]

proued 1630. See PREUED.

prouinces *n. pl.* realms 6. [OFr. *province.*]

prowes *n.* prowess 912, 1249, 2437. [OFr. *pro(u)ece.*]

pure *adj.* pure 620; faultless, fair, noble 262, 654, 664, 2398; sheer 1247; *as adv.* faultlessly 808; **purely** *adv.* entirely, certainly 802, 813. [OFr. *pur.*]

pured *pp.* purified, refined 633, 912, 2393; (of fur) trimmed, or cut down, so as to show one colour only 154, 1737. [OFr. *purer.*]

purpose *n.* purpose 1734. [OFr. *po(u)rpos.*]

put *v.* to set, put 1277; *pp.* 902. [OE. *pŭtian, pȳtan.*]

Q

qu-. See also WH-.

quaynt. See KOYNT.

quaked *pa. t.* trembled 1150. [OE. *cwacian.*]

quel. See WHIL(E).

queldepoyntes *n. pl.* quilted coverings 877. [OFr. *coiltepointe.*]

quelle *v.* to quell, end 752; kill 1324, 1449, 2109. [OE. *cwellan.*]

queme *adj.* pleasant 2109; fine 578. [OE. *cwēme.*]

quene *n.* queen 339, 469; **whene** 74, 2492. [OE. *cwēn.*]

querré *n.* quarry, assemblage of game killed in chase 1324. [OFr. *cuir(i)ée.*]

quest *n.* searching of hounds after game; baying of hounds (on scenting or viewing) 1150; *calle of a q.,* give tongue 1421. [OFr. *queste.*]

quethe *n.* utterance 1150. [Stem of OE. *cweðan*.]

queþer *pron.* which (of two) 1109. [See WHEÞER.]

quik, quyk *adj.* alive 2109; lively, restive 177; *adv.* quickly 975; **quikly, quykly** *adv.* 1324, 1490. [OE. *cwic(u)*; *cwiclīce*.]

quyssewes *n. pl.* thigh-pieces 578. [OFr. *cuissel*, pl. *cuisseus*.]

quit-clayme *v.* to declare settled; renounce 293. [Pp. of next+ CLAYME.]

quyte *v.* to requite, repay 2244, 2324. [OFr. *quiter*.]

quoþ. See COÞE.

R

rabel *n.* rabble 1703, 1899. [Cf. OFr. *rabler*, make confused noise.]

race *n.* headlong course 1420; stroke 2076. [ON. *ras*, *rás*.]

rach *n.* hound that hunts by scent 1903, 1907 (*gen. pl.*); **rach(ch)ez** *pl.* 1164, 1362, 1420, 1426. [OE. *ræcc*.]

rad *adj.* afraid 251. [ON. *hræddr*.]

rad *adv.* promptly 862. [OE. *hrade*.]

radly *adv.* swiftly, promptly 367, 1341, 1744, 1907, etc. [OE. *hrædlīce*.]

raged *adj.* ragged, shaggy 745. [ON. *raggaðr*; OE. *raggig*.]

raȝt. See RECH(E).

rayke *v.* to wander; depart 1076; *out r.*, make for the open 1727; *rayked hir*, went 1735. [ON. *reika*.]

rayled *pp.* arranged, arrayed, set 163, 603, 745, 952. [OFr. *reill(i)er*.]

rayn *n.* rain 506. [OE. *regn*.]

rayne *n.* rein 457, 2177. [OFr. *re(s)ne*.]

rayse *v.* to raise 1916; bid rise 821. [ON. *reisa*.]

raysoun. See RESOUN.

rak *n.* drifting clouds 1695. [Cf. ON. *rek(i)*, Norw. dial. *rak*, flotsam.]

rake *n.* path 2144, 2160. [Prob. ON. *rák* stripe, Norw. dial. *raak* path; but cf. OE. *racu*, water-course.]

ran. See RENNE.

rande *n.* border, edge 1710. [OE. *rand*.]

rape *v. refl.* to hasten, hurry 1309, 1903. [ON. *hrapa*.]

rapely *adv.* hastily, quickly 2219. [ON. *hrapalliga*.]

rase *v.*[1] to rush 1461. [ON. *rasa*.]

rase *v.*[2] to snatch 1907. [Shortened from ONFr. *arac(i)er*, OFr. *es-rach(i)er*.]

rasor *n.* razor 213. [OFr. *rasor*.]

rasse *n.* level; (?) ledge of rock 1570; cf. *Purity* 446. [OFr. *ras*.]

raþeled *pp.* entwined 2294. [See O.E.D. s.v. *raddle* v.[1], *ratheled*.]

rawez *n. pl.* hedgerows 513. [OE. *rāw*.]

rawþe *n.* ruth, grief; *r. to here*, grievous to hear 2204. [OE. *hrēow*+ n. suff. *-þ(u)*.]

rech(e) *v.* to reach; offer, give 66, 1804, 2059, 2324; *intr.* extend 183; *r. to*, come up to, merit (*or* presume to accept) 1243; **raȝt** *pa. t.* offered, gave 1817, 1874, 2297, 2351; *r. out*, reached out 432. [OE. *ræcan*.]

rechate *v.* to blow the recall, indicating where hunters should assemble 1446, 1466, 1911. [OFr. *rechater*.]

rechles *adj.* care-free, joyous 40. [OE. *recceleas*.]

recorded *pa. t.* recalled, mentioned 1123. [OFr. *recorder*.]

recreaunt *adj.* confessing oneself vanquished, faint-hearted 456. [OFr. *recrea(u)nt*.]

red(e) *adj.* red 304, 663, 1205, 2036; *n.* 1695; (of face) 952; *on red*, against red background 603. [OE. *rēad*.] See GOLD.

red(e) *v.* to advise; direct 738 (*subj.*); manage, deal with 373, 2111 n.; **redde** *pa. t.* advised 363; *pp.* declared 443. [OE. *rǣdan*, *rēdan*.]

redé *adj.* ready 1970. [From OE. *ge-rǣde*.]

redly *adv.* fully 373; **redyly** promptly 1821, 2324; willingly 2059; rightly 392. [OE. *gerǣdelice*.]

refourme *v.* to restate 378. [OFr. *refo(u)rmer*.]

refuse *v.* to refuse 1772. [OFr. *refuser*.]

rehayte *v.* to encourage 1422; exhort 895; rebuke, rally 1744. [OFr. *rehait(i)er*.]

reherce, reherse *v.* to repeat 392; describe 1243. [OFr. *reherc(i)er*.]

rekenly *adv.* promptly, courteously 251, 821; worthily, fittingly 39. [OE. *recenlīce*.]

rele *v.* to roll 229, 304; *intr.* turn suddenly 1728; sway (in combat) 2246 (*subj.*). [From OE. *hrēol*, a reel.]

relece *v.* to release 2342. [OFr. *re-laiss(i)er, reless-*.]

remene *v.* to recall, recount 2483. [OFr. *remener*, bring back.]

remnaunt *n.* remainder, rest 2342, 2401. [OFr. *remena(u)nt*.]

remorde *v.* to call to mind with remorse 2434. [OFr. *remordre*.]

remwe *v.* to change, alter (mood) 1475. [OFr. *remuer*.]

renay(e) *v.* to refuse 1821, 1827. [OFr. *reneier*.]

Renaude *n.* Reynard, the fox 1898, 1916 (*gen.*); **Reniarde** 1728; **Reynarde** 1920. [OFr. *Renart, Renard*; assim. to OFr. *Renaud*.]

rende *v.* to rend 1608; **rent** *pa. t.* 1332; *pp.* 1168. [OE. *rendan*.]

renk *n.* knight, man 303, 2206 n., etc.; **renkes** *pl.* 2246, **renkkez** 432, 862, 1134. [OE. *rinc*; ON. *rekkr*, older *renk-*.]

renne *v.* to run, slide, flow 731, 857, 1568, 1570; be current 310, 2458; **ran** *pa. t. pl.* 1420; **runnen** 66, 1703; *pp.* 1727. [ON. *renna*.]

renoun *n.* renown, glory 231, 313, 2434, 2458, 2519; *of renoun*, noble 2045. [OFr. *reno(u)n*.]

repayre *v.* to resort; be present 1017. [OFr. *repair(i)er*.]

repreued *pa. t.* rebuked 2269. [OFr. *repro(u)ver, repruev-*, AN. *-prev-*.]

require *v.* to ask 1056. [OFr. *requerre*, 3 *sg. requ(i)er*, L. *requir-*.]

rered *pp.* raised 353. [OE. *rǣran*.]

res *n.* rush 1164, 1899. [OE. *rǣs*.]

resayt *n.* reception; receiving stations 1168 n. [OFr. *receite*.]

resayue *v.* to receive 2076. [OFr. *receivre*.]

rescowe *n.* rescue 2308. [Stem of OFr. *rescourre*, v.]

resette *n.* refuge, shelter 2164. [OFr. *recet*.]

resoun, raysoun *n.* reason; speech, statement 227, 392; *bi r.*, correctly 1344; *by rights* 1804; **resounz** *pl.* speech 443. [OFr. *raiso(u)n, res-*.]

respite *n.* respite 297. [OFr. *respit*.]

rest *n.* rest 1990. [OE. *rǣst, rest*.]

restaye *v.* to stop, turn back 1153; *resteyed to lenge*, bade remain and linger 1672. [OFr. *r-ester*, 3 *sg. -estait*; see O.E.D. s.v. *stay*, v.[1]]

rested *pa. t.* rested, leaned 2331. [OE. *rǣstan, restan*.]

restore *v.* to restore 2283, 2354. [OFr. *restorer*.]

reue *v.* to take away 2459. [OE. *rēafian*.]

reuel *n.* revelry, revelling 40, 313, 538. [OFr. *revel*.]

reuel *v.* to revel 2401. [OFr. *reveler*.]

reuerence *n.* honour 1243; *at þe r.*, out of respect, in honour 2206. [OFr. *reverence*.]

reuerenced *pa. t.* saluted 251. [From prec.]

rewarde *n.* reward 1804, 2059. [ONFr. *reward*.]

rewarde *v.* to reward 1610, 1918. [ONFr. *rewarder*.]

ryal *adj.* royal 905; **ryol** splendid 2036; **ryally** *adv.* 663. [OFr. *reial*, AN. *rial*.]

ryalme *n.* realm 310, 691. [OFr. *reialme*, AN. *rialme*.]

rybbe *n.* rib 1356; *pl.* 1343, 1378. [OE. *ribb*.]

richche, rych(e) *v.* to direct, decide, intend, prepare 599, 1223, 2206; *refl.* prepare (oneself), dress 1130, 1309, 1873; *refl. and intr.* make one's way, proceed 8, 1898. [Prob. same as RUCH, but senses also due to OE. *reccan*.]

rich(e), rych(e) *adj.* of high rank, noble 8, 20, 39, 347, 360, 397, 905; wealthy 1646; splendid, costly, rich 40, 243, 882, 2036, etc.; flourishing 513; resounding 1916; pleasant 1744; high (feast) 2401; *as sb.* noble (steed) 2177 n.; *pl.* nobles, courtly folk 66, 362; *adv.* richly 159, 220, 879; **rychest** *superl. as sb.* those of highest rank 1130. [OE. *rīce*; OFr. *riche*.]

rychely *adv.* richly 163; with festive peal 931; in lordly fashion *308. [OE. *rīclīce*.]

ride, ryde v. to ride 142, 160, 738, etc.; **rod(e)** pa. t. 689, 821, *1466, etc.; **rydyng** n. 1134. [OE. *rīdan*.]

ryd(d)e v. to relieve (of the contest) 364; separate (combatants) 2246; r. of, clear away 1344. [OE. *ryddan*.]

rygge n. back 1344 (attrib.), 1608. [OE. *hrycg*.]

ry3t adj. true 2443; actual, very 1703. [OE. *riht*.]

ry3t, ri3t adv. properly 373; right, just, even 667, 931, 1899, 1903, 2328, 2473, etc.; at all 1790; r. to, as far as 1341, 2162. [OE. *rihte*.]

ry3t, ri3t n. justice 2346; claim (upon a person) 2342; right, privilege (of the Christmas season) 274; obligation, duty 1041. [OE. *riht*.]

ry3t pa. t. directed; refl. proceeded 308. [OE. *rihtan*.]

rimed pa. t. refl. drew himself up 308. [OE. *rȳman*.]

rymez n. membranes 1343. [OE. *rēoma*.]

ryne v. to touch 2290. [OE. *hrīnan*.]

rynk n. ring 1817, 1827; **ryngez** pl. rings of mail-shirt 580, 857, 2018. [OE. *hring*.]

rynkande pres. p. ringing *2337; **ronge** pa. t. sg. 2204; **r(o)ungen** pl. 195, 1427, 1698; trans. rang (the bells) 931. [OE. *hringan*, wk.]

ryol. See RYAL.

rype adj. ripe 522. [OE. *rīpe*.]

rype v. to ripen 528. [OE. *rīpian*.]

rys n. branch, twig; bi rys, in the woods 1698. [OE. *hrīs*.]

rys(e), rise v. to rise, stand up, get up (from bed) 306, 366, 1076, 1101, 1219, 1695, etc.; **ros** pa. t. 1148, 1427, 1735; grew 528; **rysed** rose 1313. [OE. *ārīsan*.]

rytte pa. t. cut 1332. [OE. *rittan*.]

ryue adv. abundantly, much 2046. [Late OE. *rȳfe*, *rīfe*, adj.]

ryue v. to rip, cut (open) 1341; **roue** pa. t. 2346. [ON. *rīfa*.]

robe n. robe 862. [OFr. *robe*.]

roche n. rock 2199. [OFr. *roche*.]

roché adj. rocky 2294. [From prec.]

rocher n. rocky hillside 1427, 1432, 1698. [OFr. *roch(i)er*.]

rod(e). See RIDE.

rode n. rood, cross 1949. [OE. *rōd*.]

roffe n. roof 2198; **rouez** pl. 799. [OE. *hrōf*.]

rof-sore n. gash, wound 2346. [ON. *rof*+OE. *sār*.]

ro3(e), rogh, ru3e, rugh adj. shaggy 745; rough, rugged 953, 1432, 1898, 2162, 2166, 2177, 2198; **roghe** adv. roughly 1608. [OE. *rūh*, *rūg-*.]

rokk(e) n. rock 730, 1570, 2144. [Cf. OE. *stānrocc*; ONFr. *roque*.]

rokked (of) pp. burnished, made clean (from) by rolling under pressure 2018. [Late OE. *roccian*.]

rol(le) v. intr. to roll 428; hang in loose folds 953. [OFr. *rol(l)er*.]

romaunce n. romance 2521. [OFr. *roma(u)nz*.]

rome v. to wander, make one's way 2198. [ME. forms point to OE. *rāmian*.]

ronez n. pl. bushes, brushwood 1466. [ON. *runnr*.]

ronge. See RYNKANDE.

ronk adj. luxuriant 513. [OE. *ronc*.]

ronkled pp. wrinkled 953. [Cf. ON. *hrukka*, *hrunka*, a wrinkle.]

ropez n. pl. cords 857. [OE. *rāp*.]

ros. See RYS(E).

rote n. custom; bi rote, with ceremony 2207. [OFr. *rote*.]

rote v. to decay 528. [OE. *rotian*.]

rotez n. pl. roots 2294. [ON. *rót*.]

roue. See RYUE v.

rouez. See ROFFE.

roun v. to take whispered counsel 362. [OE. *rūnian*.]

rouncé n. horse 303. [OFr. *ro(u)nci*, -in.]

rounde adj. round; þe Rounde Table 39, 313, 538, 905, 2458, 2519. [OFr. *rōo(u)nt*, fem. *rōo(u)nde*.]

roungen. See RYNKANDE.

rous n. fame, talk 310. [ON. *hrós* or *raus*.]

roust n. rust 2018. [OE. *rūst*.]

rout n. violent movement, jerk 457. [Obscure; see O.E.D. s.v. *rout* sb.³.]

ruch(ch)e v. refl. to turn (oneself) 303; proceed 367. [OE. *ryccan*; cf. ON. *rykkja*.] See RICHCHE.

rudede pp. reddened, fiery 1695. [OE. *rudian*.]

rudelez *n. pl.* curtains 857. [OFr. *ridel*.]

ruful *adj.* grievous 2076. [OE. *hrēow* +*-full*.]

rugh, ruȝe; rungen; runnen. See RO3(E); RYNKANDE; RENNE.

runisch *adj.* rough, violent 457; **runischly** *adv.* fiercely 304, *432. [See note to 304.]

rurd(e) *n.* voice 2337; noise 1149, 1698, 1916, 2219. [OE. *réord*.]

rusched *pa. t.* made a loud rushing noise 2204; *r. on þat rurde*, went on with that rushing noise 2219. [Echoic; cf. OFr. *russer*, OE. *hryscan*.]

ruþe *v.* to bestir 1558. [See note.]

S

sabatounz *n. pl.* steel shoes 574 n. [OProv. *sabató*.]

sadel *n.* saddle 164, 303, 437, 597, 2110. [OE. *sadol*.]

sadel *v.* to saddle 1128, 2012. [OE. *sadelian*.]

sadly *adv.* steadily, firmly 437, 1593; vigorously 1937; sufficiently, long enough 2409. [From OE. *sæd*.]

saf. See SAUE, WOWCHE.

sage 531 (MS.). See FAGE.

saȝe *n.* saying, words 1202; *s. oþer seruyce*, word or deed 1246; *pl.* words 341. [OE. *sagu*.]

say *v.* to say, tell 84, 130, 1797, 1991, etc.; **sayn** *pres. pl.* 1050; **sayd(e)** *pa. t.* 200, 252, 673, etc.; *herde say*, heard tell, read in 690. [OE. *secgan*.]

saylande *pres. p.* sailing; flowing 865. [OE. *seglian*.]

sayn. See SAY; SAYNT.

sayned *pa. t.* blessed (with sign of cross) 761, 763, 1202. [OE. *segnian*.]

saynt *adj.* Saint 1644; **sayn** *774, 1022, 1788. [OFr. *saint*.]

saynt *n.* girdle 2431; **sayn** 589. [OFr. *ceint*.]

sake *n.* in *for . . . sake*, for (one's) sake 537, 997, 1862, 2518. [ON. *fyrir sakir*.]

sale *n.* hall 197, 243, 349, 558, 1005, 1372, 1651. [OE. *sæl*; OFr. *sale*.]

salue *v.* to salute; wish good morning to 1473. [OFr. *saluer*.]

salure *n.* salt-cellar 886. [OFr. *sal(i)ere*, with altered suffix.]

same *adj.* same 1405, 1669; *pron.* in *of þe (þat) s.*, with the same 881, 1640; (of, with) the same colour 157, 170 (cf. ILKE). [ON. *samr*.]

same(n) *adv.* together 50, 940, 1318; *al(le) s.*, (all) together 363, 673, 744, 1345. [OE. *æt samne*; ON. *saman*.]

samen *v. trans.* to gather 1372; **samned** *pa. t. intr.* came together, joined 659. [OE. *samnian*.]

sanap *n.* over-cloth to protect table-cloth 886. [OFr. **sa(u)ve-nape*.]

sate. See SITTE.

saue(n) *v.* to preserve, keep safe, bring to salvation 1879, 2040, 2139; *subj.* 1548, 2073. [OFr. *sa(u)ver*.]

saue, saf *prep.* except 2171; *s. þat*, save that 394, 2229. [OFr. *sa(u)f*.]

sauer *adj. compar.* safer (from temptation) 1202. [OFr. *sauf*, fem. *sauve*.]

sauered *pp.* flavoured 892. [OFr. *savo(u)rer*.]

sauerly *adv.* with relish 1937; to his liking 2048. [From OFr. *savo(u)r*.]

saule *n.* soul 1916; **sawle** 1879. [OE. *sāwol*.]

sawes *n.* sauce 893 n. [OFr. *sauce*.]

scaþe *n.* injury 2353; *hit is s.*, it is disastrous 674. [ON. *skaði*.]

schad(d)e. See SCHEDE.

schaft(e) *n.* shaft (of arrow) 1458; handle 2332; spear 205. [OE. *scæft*.]

schafted *pa. t.* set 1467 n. [From prec.]

schaȝe *n.* shaw, small wood 2161 (see SIDE). [OE. *scaga*.]

schal *v. 1 sg.* shall, will 31, 288, 2094, etc.; shall be 1544; *2 sg.* 374, 389, 675, etc.; *3 sg.* 374, 898, 925, 2437, etc.; *pl.* 255, 922, 1071, etc.; shall come 2400; **schyn** *pl.* (OE. *scylon*) 2401; *and schale*, and I will be 1240. **schulde** *pa. t.* should, would 238, 248, 398, 931, *1286, 2349, etc.; had to go 1671 n., 2084; was to 2244. [OE. *sceal, scólde*.]

schalk *n.* man 160, 424, 1454, 1776, 2061, 2268, 2372. [OE. *scealc*.]

scham(e) *n.* shame 317, 2504; **schome** 2372; *for schame*, for shame! 1530. [OE. *scamu, scomu*.]

schamed *pa. t.* was embarrassed 1189. [OE. *scamian*, impers.]

schankes, schonkez *n. pl.* legs 431, 846; *vnder schankes*, on his feet 160. [OE. *scanca, sconca*.]

schape *v.* to make; give (account) 1626; contrive 2138; *intr.* be arranged 1210; **schop** *pa. t.* appointed 2328, **schaped** 2340; **schapen** *pp.* adorned, fashioned 213, 662. [OE. *sceppan*.]

schaped *pp. adj.* 'chaped', trimmed 1832 n. [From OFr. *chape*.]

scharp *adj.* sharp 213, 1337, 2267, etc.; *as sb.* sharp blade 424, 1593, 1902, 2313, 2332. [OE. *scearp*.]

schaterande *pres. p.* dashing and breaking 2083. [OE. **scaterian*.]

schaued *pa. t.* scraped 1331; **schauen** *pp.* shaven, smooth 1458. [OE. *scafan*, str.]

schawe. See SCHEWE.

schede *v.* to sever, shed; *intr.* be shed, fall 506, **956*; **schadde** *pa. t.* was shed 727; **schade** severed **425*. [OE. *scādan, scēadan*.]

schelde *n.* shield 205, 619, 637, 2061, etc.; **(s)cheldez** tough skin and flesh at shoulders 1456 n.; slabs of boar's flesh 1611, 1626. [OE. *scéld*.]

schemered *pa. t.* shimmered 772. [OE. *scimerian*.]

schende *v.* to destroy 2266. [OE. *scéndan*.]

schene *adj.* bright 662, 2314; *as sb.* bright blade 2268. [OE. *scēne*.]

schere *v.* to cut 213; **scher** *pa. t. pl.* 1337; **schorne** *pp.* cut 1378. [OE. *sceran*.]

schere. See CHER(E).

schewe, schawe (27) *v.* to look at 2036; bring out for one, produce 619, 2061; show, lay bare, declare 27, 1378, 1626, 1880, 2256, 2498, 2504; offer 315, 1526; *intr.* show, be seen, appear 420, 507, 885. [OE. *scēawian, sceāwian*.]

schylde *v.* to defend; *God schylde*, God forfend 1776. [OE. *scíldan*.]

schyn. See SCHAL.

schinande *pres. p.* shining 269; **schon** *pa. t.* 772, 956. [OE. *scínan*.]

schynder *v. trans. and intr.* cleave, burst asunder 424, 1458, 1594. [OE. *syndrian*, infl. by words of similar

sense in *sch-* (SCHEDE, *schiueren*, etc.).]

schyr(e), schyree, schyire *adj.* bright, fair, white 317, 506, 619, 772, 2083; *s. grece* 425, 1378, 2313; *as sb.* (white) flesh 1331, 2256; **schyrer** *compar.* 956; **schyrly** *adv.* clean 1880. [OE. *scír*.]

scho *pron.* she 969, 1259, 1550, 1555, 1556. [OE. *hēo* with shift of stress.] See HO.

scholes *adj.* without shoes 160 n. [OE. *sc(e)ōh+-lēas*; cf. ON. *skólauss*.]

schome; schon; schonkez; schop. See SCHAM; SCHINANDE; SCHANKES; SCHAPE.

schore *n.* shore, bank 2083; hillside, slope 2161; *vpon s.*, on the ground (by the river) 2332. [Cf. MDu., MLG. *schore*.]

schorne. See SCHERE.

schort *adj.* short 966. [OE. *scort*.]

schote *v. trans.* to shoot (arrows) 1454; **schot** *pa. t.* jerked 2318; *intr.* shot, sprang 317, 2314; **schotten** *pl. trans.* 1167. [OE. *scēotan*, str., *scotian*, wk.]

schowre *n.* shower 506. [OE. *scúr*.]

schowen, schowue. See SCHWUE.

schrank(e) *pa. t.* shrank; flinched, winced 2267, 2372; sank, penetrated 425, 2313. [OE. *scrincan*.]

schrewe *n.* villain 1896. [OE. *scrēawa*, shrew-mouse; see O.E.D.]

schrof *pa. t.* shrove, confessed 1880. [OE. *scrífan*.]

schuld(en). See SCHAL.

schulder *n.* shoulder 156, 1337, 1930, 2061, 2318, etc. [OE. *sculdor*.]

schunt *n.* sudden jerk and swerve 2268. [See next.]

schunt *pa. t.* swerved 1902; flinched 2280. [Prob. rel. to OE. *scunian*.]

schwue *v.* to thrust 205; **schowue** *intr.* press, make one's way 2161; **schowued** *pa. t.* 2083; **schowen** *pl.* (OE. *scufon*) 1454. [OE. *scúfan*, str.]

scowtes *n. pl.* jutting rocks 2167. [ON. *skúti*.]

scrape *v.* to scrape, paw the ground 1571. [OE. *scrapian*; ON. *skrapa*.]

se *v.* to see, look at 226, 751, 963, 1160,

etc.; **sene** (OE. *sēonne*) 712; *let se,*
let me (us) see 299, 414; **segh(e)**
pa. t. 1632, 1705; **se3(e)** 672, 707,
1382, 1624, 1911, etc.; **sy3(e)** 83
(*subj.*), 200, 1582. [OE. *sēon.*] See
SEN(E).

sech(e) *v. trans.* to seek, look for 266,
395, 549, 2169; *intr.* go 1052; **so3t**
pa. t. was making for 1284, 1995;
out s. tried to get out 1438; came,
went 685, 2493. [OE. *sēcan, sõhte.*]

seche. See SUCH.

sedez *n. pl.* seeds; seeding grasses and
plants 517. [OE. *sǣd.*]

seg(g)e *n.* siege 1, 2525. [OFr. *s(i)ege.*]

segg(e) *n.* man, knight 96, 115, 226,
574 (*gen.*), 1882 (priest), etc.; in
appos. to *he* 763; *voc.* 394; *vch s.*,
everybody 1987; *pl.* men, people
673, 822, 888, etc. [OE. (verse)
secg.]

segh, se3(e). See SE, SEYE.

seye *v.* to go 1879; **si3ed** *pa. t.* had
gone *1440 n.; **se3en** *pp.* come
1958. [OE. *sīgan; sǣgan*, trans.]

seker. See SYKER.

selden *adv.* seldom 499. [OE. *seldan.*]

sele *n.* happiness, good fortune 1938,
2409, 2422. [OE. *sǣl.*]

self, seluen *adj.* same, very 751, 2147;
as sb. self 2156, 2301; *þe burne(s) s.*,
Krystes s., the knight (etc.) himself
51, 1616, 2377. [OE. *self(a).*] See
3E, HE, HEM, HIT, I, ÞOU.

selly *adj.* marvellous; excellent *1962;
strange 2170; *as sb.* wonder, marvel
28, 475; *pl.* 239; **sellokest** *adj.*
superl. 1439; **selly** *adv.* exceedingly,
very 1194; **sellyly** 963, 1803. [OE.
sel(d)-lic, -lucost; sellīce, adv.]

selure *n.* (ceiling) canopy 76. [L.
cēlātura, OFr. **cel(e)ure*.]

semb(e)launt *n.* appearance, looks
148; sign of his feelings 468; (kindly)
demeanour, manner 1273, 1658,
1843. [OFr. *sembla(u)nt.*]

semblé *n.* company, throng 1429.
[Shortened from OFr. *assemblée.*]

seme *adj.* seemly; fair, excellent 1085;
semly(ch) *adv.* becomingly, excellently 865, 882, 888; pleasantly,
sweetly 916, 1658, 1796. [ON. *sœmr.*]

seme *v.* to beseem, suit 1929; *impers.*

679, 848 (*subj.*); seem fitting 73,
1005; seem, appear 201, 235, 840,
866, 1827, 1847, etc.; *semed*, was
to be seen 1551. [ON. *sóma* (pa. t.
subj. *sœmdi*) infl. by prec.]

semez *n. pl.* ornamental stitching about
seams, *or* embroidered stuff laid over
them 610, 2028. [OE. *sēam.*]

semly *adj.* seemly, fitting 348, 1198;
comely, fair 685; *as sb.* in *þat s.*, that
fair knight 672; **semloker** *compar.*
as sb. one more fair 83; **semlyly**
adv. becomingly 622. [SEME+OE.
-lic, -lucor; ON. *sœmiligr.*]

sen(e) *adj.* visible; plain to see 148;
plain, clear 341; *used as pp. of* SE,
seen 197, 239, 468, 475. [OE. *gesēne*,
adj. (late as pp.).]

sendal *n.* a kind of thin rich silk 76.
[OFr. *cendal.*]

sende *pa. t.* sent 2362; *subj.* should
send 1837. [OE. *sendan.*]

sene. See SE.

sengel *adj.* single, all alone 1531.
[OFr. *sengle.*]

serched *pa. t.* searched, examined,
1328. [OFr. *cerch(i)er.*]

sere *adj.* separate, individual 1985;
various 124, 889; several 761, 822;
fele sere, many and various (women)
2417; *adv.* in each case 632 n.; *sere
twyes*, on two separate occasions
1522. [ON. *sér* (dat. sg.) for oneself,
separately.]

serlepes *adv.* separately, in turn 501.
[Prec.+OE. *-lēpes*, in *sundor-lēpes.*]

sertayn *adv.* assuredly, indeed 174.
[OFr. *certain*, adj.]

seruaunt *n.* servant 976, 1240, 1971,
2139, etc. [OFr. *servant.*]

serue(n) *v.*[1] to serve (God) 724; wait
on 827, 851, 1986; *s. of (with)*, serve
with 482, 888, 1640; *pp.* served (with
food) 61, 85, 114, 1006; served (up)
135, 1559; *intr.* wait at table 1651.
[OFr. *servir.*]

serue *v.*[2] to deserve 1380. [Shortened
from DESERUE.]

seruyce, seruyse *n.* serving, service
1246, 1985; (at table) 130; (in
church) 940; *s. of þat syre etc.*,
celebration of Christmas *751,
[OFr. *servise.*]

sese *v.* to seize, take 822, 1083, 1330, 1825, 2407. [OFr. *seisir*.]

sesed *pp.* ceased; *watz s.*, had come to an end 1, 134, 2525. [OFr. *cesser*.]

sesoun *n.* season 501, 516, 1382; due time 1958, 2085. [OFr. *saiso(u)n, ses-*.]

sesounde *pp.* seasoned 889. [OFr. *saiso(u)ner, ses-*.]

sete *adj.* fitting, excellent 889. [OE. **(ge)sǽte*; cf. *andsǽte*.]

sete *n.* seat, place at table 72, 493. [ON. *sǽti*.]

sete(n). See SITTE.

sette *v.* to set, etc.; **sett(e)** *pa. t.* 422, 574, etc.; *pp.* 148. To set in a seat 1083; set, put 124, 1607, 2230, 2332, etc.; lay table 1651; establish, found 14; plant 1593, 1937; make 1883; inflict 372; do 1246; *refl.* seat oneself, sit down 437, 1193, 1479; *s. at ly3t*, were to esteem lightly 1250; *s. hym on*, rush at 1589; *s. on*, called down on 1721; *s. solace*, made merry 1318; *s. in (þe) waye*, put on the right road 1077, 1971. [OE. *settan*.]

settel *n.* seat, chair 882. [OE. *setl*.]

seuen *adj.* seven 613, 1382. [OE. *seofon*.]

seuer *v.* to sever (*or intr.*) 2312; *intr.* separate 1958; depart (from) 1797; part (with) 1987. [OFr. *sevrer*.]

sewe *n.* broth, stew 124, 889, 892. [OE. *sēaw*.]

sidbordez *n. pl.* side-tables 115 n. [OE. *sīd-+bord*.]

syde *adj.* long, dangling 2431. [OE. *sīd*.]

side, syde *n.* side, flank 110, 152, 771, 1338, 1356, 1632, etc.; *pl.* waist 1830; *at (bi, in) . . . side*, at the side of, beside 1421, 1431, 1697, 2144, 2161 (orig. with gen., cf. 589, 2486); *in no s.*, in no direction 659, 2170. [OE. *sīde*.] See BISYDE.

syfle *v.* to whistle, blow gently 517. [OFr. *sifler*.]

sy3(e); si3ed. See SE; SEYE.

sy3t *n.* sight 1721; *se wyth (in) s.*, set eyes on 197, 226, 1705; *in si3t, to see* 28. [OE. *gesihþ, -siht*.]

syke *v.* to sigh 672, 753, 1796;

sykyngez, *n. pl.* sighs 1982. [OE. *sīcan*.]

syker, seker *adj.* sure; assured 265; true 403; trusty 96, 111, 115, 2493; *in a s. wyse*, securely 2048; *adv.* certainly 1637. [OE. *sicor*.]

siker *v.* to assure; *s. my (bi þi) trawþe*, give my (your) word 394, 1673. [From prec.]

sylence *n.* silence 243. [OFr. *silence*.]

silk(e), sylk(e) *n.* silk 854, 959, 1832, 2035, 2431; piece of silk 1846; *as adj.* 159, 164, 589. [OE. *seolc*.]

sylkyn *adj.* silk 610. [OE. *silcen*.]

sille *n.* sill, flooring; *on s.*, in the hall 55; *cf.* FLET. [OE. *syll*.]

syluerin *adj.* silver 886; *as sb.* in *þe sylueren*, the silver (things) *124. [OE. *silfren*.]

symple *adj.* plain (food) 503; of no great value 1847. [OFr. *simple*.]

syn *conj.* since 919, 1892, 2440 (*with subj.*); *syn þat* 2320; *as prep.* 24. [Reduction of SIÞEN.]

syng(e) *v.* to sing 472, 509, 923. [OE. *singan*.]

syngne *n.* sign, token 625, 2164, 2433. [OFr. *signe*.]

synne *adv.* since then 19. [Extended from SYN on anal. of ÞENNE, etc.]

synne *n.* sin 1774. [OE. *synn*.]

syre *n.* lord, knight 685, 751, 1083; **sir** *as title before name* 377, 552, 554, etc.; *polite voc.* 276, 415, 477, 811, 1481, etc.; *beau sir* 1222; *sir swete* 2237. [OFr. *sire*.]

sister-sunes *n. pl.* nephews 111. [ON. *systra-synir*.] See HALF-SUSTER.

sitte, sytte *v.* to sit (down, at table) 110, 906, 936, 1001, 2110, etc.; sit idle 88; sit here 290, 1531; be throned 256, 2442; **sate** *pa. t.* 339; **sete(n)** 242, 882, 940, 1003, 1402; *pp.* 1522; *sete on*, fitted 865. [OE. *sittan*.]

syþe *n.* scythe 2202. [OE. *sigþe*.]

siþen, syþen *adv.* afterwards, next, then 6, 43, 115, 194, 791, 1559, etc.; since 1094; *long s.*, since long ago 1440; *conj.* since 1642, 2394, 2524; (*causal*) 358, 1234; after 1; now that 2094. [OE. *siþþan*.] See SYN(NE).

syþez *n. pl.* times, occasions 632, 761, 982; cases, conjunctures 656; *bi s.*, at times 17; syþe *dat. pl.* 1868. [OE. *sīþ*.]

skayned (*of*) *pp.* grazed (by) 2167. [ON. *skeina*.]

skere *adj.* pure 1261. [ON. *skærr*.]

skete *adv.* quickly 19. [ON. *skjótt*, older **skēut-*.]

skyfted *pp.* shifted, alternated 19. [ON. *skifta*.]

skyl(le) *n.* reason 1509; *bi þis s.*, for this reason 1296. [ON. *skil*.]

skyrtes, -ez *n. pl.* skirts, lower part of flowing garment or covering 865; flaps of a saddle, saddle-skirts *171, 601. [ON. *skyrta*.]

skwez *n. pl.* clouds 2167. [ON. *skí*, earlier **skiw-*.]

slade *n.* valley 1159, 2147. [OE. *slæd*.]

slayn *pp.* slain, killed 729, 1854, 1950; slowe *pa. t. sg.* 1321. [OE. *slægen*; *slōgon*, pa. t. pl.]

slaked *pa. t.* slackened; were stilled 244. [OE. *slacian*.]

sleȝe *adj.* skilfully made 797, *893; sleȝly *adv.* (made) warily 1182. [ON. *slœgr*.] See VNSLYȜE.

sleȝt, slyȝt *n.* skill 1542; device 1858; *for s. vpon erþe*, by any means 1854; *sleȝtez of*, acts of practised skill in 916. [ON. *slœgð*.]

slentyng *n.* slanting flight 1160. [ON. *sletta*, earlier **slenta*.]

slepe *n.* sleep 1095; *vpon slepe*, asleep 244. [OE. *slēp*.]

slepe *v.* to sleep 1686, 1731, 1733, 1746, 2007; sleped, slepte *pa. t.* 729, 1190 (*subj.*); slepe *pa. t. subj.* 1991. [OE. *slēpan*, str. and wk.]

sleper *n.* sleeper 1209. [OE. *slēpere*.]

slete *n.* sleet 729. [OE. **slīet-*, **slēt*; cf. MLG. *slōte*.]

slyde *v. intr.* to glide, steal 1209; slode *pa. t. sg.* in *s. in slomeryng*, slept softly on 1182. [OE. *slīdan*.]

slyȝt. See SLEȜT.

slypped *pp.* slipped; escaped 1858; fallen 244; slypte *pa. t.* were loosed 1160. [Cf. MLG., MDu. *slippen*.]

slyt *pa. t.* slit 1330. [OE. **slittan*.]

slokes *imper. pl.* stop, enough! 412 n. [(?)ON. *slokna*.]

slomeryng *n.* slumber 1182. [From OE. **slŭmerian*; cf. *slŭma*.]

slot *n.* hollow above breast-bone at base of throat 1330, 1593. [OFr. *esclot*.]

slowe. See SLAYN.

smal(e) *adj.* small, slender 144, 1207; fine (in texture) 76. [OE. *smæl*.]

smartly *adv.* promptly 407. [From OE. *smeart*, sharp.]

smeþely *adv.* gently, pleasantly 1789. [From OE. *smēþe*.]

smyle *v.* to smile 1789; smylyng *n.* 1763. [OE. **smīlan*; cf. OHG. *smīlan*.]

smyte *v.* to smite, strike 205, 2260; smeten *pa. t. pl. intr.* in *s. into merþe*, fell quickly to merry speech 1763; smyten *pp.* 407. [OE. *smītan*, smear.]

smolt *adj.* gentle 1763. [OE. *smolt*.]

smoþe *adj.* gentle; courteous 1763; smoþely *adv.* (?) neatly 407. [OE. *smōþ*.]

snayped *pa. t.* nipped cruelly 2003. [ON. *sneypa*.]

snart *adv.* bitterly 2003. [ON. *snarr*, neut. and adv. *snart*.]

snaw(e) *n.* snow 956, 2003, 2088, 2234, 2315. [OE. *snāw*.]

snyrt *pa. t.* snicked, cut lightly 2312. [Cf. ON. *snerta*, str.]

snitered *pa. t.* (snow) came shivering down 2003. [Cf. Norw. dial. *snitra*, shiver with cold.]

so *adv.* so, thus, in this way, this, that 680, 998, 1108, 1259, 1847, 2281, etc.; as 36; then 218; (that being) so *1304, 2296; to such an extent, so 59, 89, *282, 1048, 1728, 1848, 2140, etc.; so too 2365; such 1761, 2454; *intensive*, so 103, 258, etc.; *neuer so*, no matter how 2129; *half so* 2321; *so . . . to*, so as to 291; *so þat, so . . . þat* 60, 717, 1414, etc.; without *þat* 139, etc.; *so . . . as*, as (so) . . . as 199, 592, 1510, etc., *in asseveration* 387–8; *as . . . as if* 612, 1883; *with indef. prons.* etc. *384, 1107, 1109, 1167, 1406, 1407, 1851. [OE. *swā*.]

soberly *adv.* gravely, with propriety 940, 1278; without exaggeration 2051. [From OFr. *sobre*.]

soft(e) *adj.* soft, gentle, unwarlike 510, 516; *compar.* 271; *adv.* softly 1929; in comfort 1121, 1687; **softly** gently, quietly 1193, *1479; in a whisper 915. [OE. *sŏfte*.]

so3t. See SECHE.

soiorne *n.* sojourn, stay 1962. [OFr. *sojo(u)rn*.]

soio(u)rne *v.* to stay 2409; lodge, stable 2048. [OFr. *sojo(u)rner*.]

solace *n.* pleasure, delight 510, 1085, 1318; kindness 1985; *with s.*, joyfully 1624. [OFr. *so(u)las*.]

somer *n.* summer 510, 516. [OE. *sumor*.]

son, sun *n.* son 113, 1064. [OE. *sunu*.]

sone *adv.* at once, quickly 433, 521, 534, 807, 935, 1289, 1309, 1872, 1906; soon 884, 1421, 1704, 2085; *s. as*, as soon as 864. [OE. *sōna*.]

songez *n. pl.* songs 1654. [OE. *sáng, sóng*.]

sop *n.* morsel of food, light meal 1135 (*cf.* 1690). [OE. *sopp*.]

soper *n.* supper 1400, 1654. [OFr. *so(u)per*.]

sore *adj.* painful, grievous 1793, 2116. [OE. *sār*.]

soré *adj.* sorry, grieved 1826, 1987. [OE. *sārig*.]

sor3e *n.* sorrow, grief 2383, 2415; imprecation 1721. [OE. *sorg*.]

sostnaunce *n.* sustenance, food 1095. [OFr. *so(u)stena(u)nce*.]

sop(e) *adj.* true, *and n.* (the) truth, a fact 348, 355, 1385, 1488, 2457, etc.; *by his s.*, on his word 1825, 2051; *for s.*, truly 403, 2094; indeed 415, 1222, 1793, 2302, etc.; *adv.* with truth 84; certainly 2110. **soply** *adv.* with truth 673; truly 976, 1095, 2362. [OE. *sōp, sōplīce*.]

sopen *pp.* boiled 892. [OE. *sēopan*, pp. *soden*; ON. *soðinn*.]

souerayn *n.* sovereign; liege lady 1278. [OFr. *so(u)verain*.]

sounde *quasi-sb.* in *al in sounde*, in safety 2489. [*in* reflects *ge-* in OE. *ge-súnd*, adj.; cf. FERE.]

sounder *n.* herd of wild pigs 1440. [OE. *sunor*.]

soundyly *adv.* soundly 1991. [OE. *gesúndlīce*.]

soure *adj.* sour, unpleasant, *or* sore 963. [OE. *sūr*; *sūr-ēge*, bleared.]

sourquydrye *n.* pride 311; **surquidré** 2457. [OFr. *surcuiderie*.]

sowme *n.* number 1321. [OFr. *so(u)me*.]

space *n.* space, short while; *in space*, soon after 1418; soon, straightway *1199, 1503. [OFr. *(e)space*.]

spare *adj.* sparing; *vpon s. wyse*, without undue pressing, tactfully 901. [OE. *spær*.]

spare *v.* to spare 1935. [OE. *sparian*.]

sparlyr *n.* calf (of leg) 158. [OE. *spær-līra*.]

sparred *pa. t.* sprang *1444 (1442 n.). [Obscure.]

sparþe *n.* battle-axe 209. [ON. *sparða*.]

spech(e) *n.* speech, conversation 314, 410, 918, 1292; *pl.* expressions, words 1261, 1778. [OE. *sp(r)ēc*.]

specially *adv.* particularly 2093. [From OFr. *(e)special*.]

specialté *n.* partiality; fondness 1778. [OFr. *(e)specialté*.]

spede, speed *n.* success; profit 918; speed (*good s.*, at great speed) 1444. [OE. *spēd*.]

spede *v. trans.* to prosper, bless 762 (*subj.*), 1292, 2120; further, get done 2216; *intr.* in *spedez better*, will be better off 410; **speded** *pa. t. refl.* sped, hastened 979. [OE. *(ge)spēdan*.]

spedly *adv.* with good result, to our good fortune 1935. [OE. *spēd-līce*.]

speke(n) *v.* to speak 226, 544, 1242, 2302, etc.; **spek(ed)** *pa. t.* 1288, 2461; **speken** *pl.* 1117; **spoken** *pp.* agreed upon 1935. [OE. *sp(r)ecan*.]

spelle *n.* speech, words 1199; *expoun in s.*, describe 209; *deme hit with s.*, say which 2184. [OE. *spell*.]

spelle *v.* to say 2140. [OE. *spellian*.]

spende *v.* to spend; lose 2113; utter 410. [OE. *spéndan*.]

spenet (*on*) *pa. t.* were fastened, clung (to) 158; **spend** *pp.* fastened 587. [ON. *spenna*.]

spenne *n.* fence, hedge 1709, 1896; (enclosed) ground; *in spenne*, there 1074 n. [Cf. ON. *spenni*.]

spenne-fote *adv.* (?) with feet together 2316 n. [ON. *spenna+* FOT(E).]

spere *n.* spear 269, 983, 2066, 2143; *attrib.* 2316. [OE. *spere.*]

sperre *v.* to strike 670. [OE. *sperran.*]

spetos *adj.* cruel 209. [Shortened from OFr. *despito(u)s.*] See SPYT.

spyces *n. pl.* spices 892; spiced cakes 979. [OFr. *(e)spice.*]

spye *v.* to look out for 2093; get a sight of 1896; inquire 901 (cf. *York Plays,* xxi. 23). [OFr. *(e)spier.*]

spyt *n.* doing harm 1444. [Shortened from OFr. *despit.*]

spoken. See SPEKE.

sponez *n. pl.* spoons 886. [OE. *spōn,* chip; ON. *spón-n,* chip, spoon.]

sporez. See SPUREZ.

sprenged *pa. t.* sprang; (day) broke 1415, 2009. [OE. *sprengan.*]

sprent *pa. t.* leapt 1896. [ON. *spretta,* older **sprenta.*]

sprit *pa. t.* sprang 2316. [OE. *spryttan, *spring,* sprout.]

sprong *pa. t. sg.* sprang 670; **sprange** *pl.* 1778. [OE. *springan.*]

spured *pp.* asked 901; **spuryed** *(after)* 2093. [OE. *spyrian (æfter).*]

spurez *n. pl.* spurs 158, 670; **sporez** 587. [OE. *spura, spora.*]

stabeled *pa. t.* put in a stable 823. [OFr. *(e)stabler.*]

stabled *pp.* established; agreed upon 1060. [OFr. *(e)stablir.*]

stablye *n.* ring of beaters 1153 n. [OFr. *establie.*]

stad *pp.* placed; put down (in writing) 33; present 644; standing there 2137. [ON. *steðja;* pp. *staddr.*]

staf *n.* staff 214; **staue** *dat.* club 2137. [OE. *stæf.*]

staf-ful *adj.* cram-full 494. [Rel. obscurely to prec.]

stayne *v.* to colour 170. [ON. *steina.*]

stalke *v.* to walk cautiously 237; stalk 2230. [OE. *stalcian.*]

stal(l)e *n.* standing; *in s.,* standing up 104, 107. [OE. *stall; in stalle.*]

stalworth *adj.* stalwart 846; *as sb.* 1659. [OE. *stælwyrþe.*]

stange *n.* pole 1614. [ON. *stǫng.*]

stapled *pp.* fastened, *or* strengthened, with staples 606 n. [ME. *stapel,* staple; prob. same as OE. *stapol,* post.]

starande *pres. p.* staring; blazing 1818. [OE. *starian.*]

start(e) *v.* to start (aside), flinch 1567, 2286; leap forward 2063; *pa. t.* sprang 431; swerved 1716. [OE. **stertan;* cf. *styrtan.*]

statut *n.* statute; solemn agreement 1060. [OFr. *(e)statut.*]

staue. See STAF.

sted(e) *n.* steed 176, 281, 670, 823; *on stedes to ryde,* among knights 260. [OE. *stēda.*]

sted(de) *n.* place; *in (þis) s.,* here, there 439, 2213, 2323. [OE. *stede.*]

stek. See STOKEN *pp.*[2]

stel(e) *n.*[1] steel 211, 426, 575; armour 570; *as adj.* 580. **stel-bawe** *n.* stirrup-iron 435 (cf. 2060). **stel-gere** *n.* armour 260. [OE. *stēle;+* OE. *boga;* +ON. *gervi.*]

stele *n.*[2] handle, haft 214, 2230. [OE. *stela.*]

stele *v. intr.* to steal 1710; **stel** *pa. t. sg.* 1191; **stollen** *pp.* as *adj.* stealthy, sly 1659. [OE. *stelan.*]

stem(m)ed *pa. t. intr.* stopped, halted 230; stood about, hesitated 1117. [ON. *stemma.*]

steppe *v.* to step 435, 570, 2060; *wk. pa. t.* 1191. [OE. *steppan,* str.]

steropes. See STIROP.

steuen *n.*[1] voice 242, 2336. [OE. *stefn,* f.]

steuen *n.*[2] appointment, tryst 1060, 2194, 2213, 2238; appointed day 2008. [ON. *stefna* appointment; OE. *stefn,* m., time.]

stif(fe), styf *adj.* stiff; unweakened 431; unflinching 294; stout, strong, firm 176, 214, 846, 2099, etc.; fearless, bold 104, 322, 823, 2369, etc.; *s. and strong,* brave (story) 34; *superl.* 260, 1567; *adv.* vigorously 671; **stifly** *adv.* strongly 606; fearlessly 287; undaunted 1716. [OE. *stīf.*]

stiȝtel, styȝtel *v.* to order, control; deal with 2137; rule, be master 2213; *s. in stalle,* stand 104; *s. þe vpon,* limit yourself to 2252. [OE. **stihtlian;* cf. *stihtan.*]

stille *adj. and adv.* (stand) still 2252, 2293; without stirring, undisturbed 1367, 1687, 1994; without protest, humbly 2385; secret(ly) 1188, 1659; privately 1085; silent (and motion-less) 301 (*compar.*), 1996. **stilly** *adv.* softly, secretly 1117, 1191, 1710. [OE. *stille, stillīce.*] See STON(E).

stirop *n.* stirrup 2060; **steropes** *pl.* 170. [OE. *stig-rāp.*]

styþly *adv.* stoutly, undismayed 431. [OE. *stīþ-līce.*]

stod(e). See STONDE.

stoffed *pp.* stuffed 606 n. [OFr. *(e)s-toffer.*]

stoken *pp.*¹ shut 782. [OE. **stecan* in *bestecan*, perh. same as next.]

stoken *pp.*² stuck; set down, fixed (in writing) 33; *s. of*, full up, fully pro-vided with 494; *s. me*, imposed on me 2194; **stek** *pa. t. intr.* clung, fitted close 152. [OE. **stecan.*]

stollen. See STELE *v.*

stonde *v.* to stand 107, 1058, 2252, etc.; stand up 1797; stand and take from 294, 2286; **stod(e)** *pa. t.* 170, 237, 432, 1951, etc.; waited 2063; went and stood 322; (?)*subj.* would have been present 1768 n.; *stond-ande alofte*, set in it 1818. [OE. *stándan, stóndan.*]

ston(e) *n.* stone 789, 2166; (stony) ground 2230, 2282 (*pl.*); pavement 2063; gem 162, 193, 1818, 2027, etc.; *stylle as þe s.*, stock-still 2293. **ston-fyr** *n.* sparks struck out of stones 671; **ston-stil** *adj.* in stony silence (and stock-still) 242. [OE. *stān.*]

stonyed. See STOUNED.

stor(e) *adj.* mighty 1923; strong, severe 1291. [ON. *stórr.*]

stori *n.* story 34. [OFr. *(e)storie.*]

stoundez *n. pl.* times 1517; *bi s.*, at times 1567. [OE. *stúnd.*]

stouned, stowned, stonyed *pa. t.* astonished, amazed 301, 1291; *pp.* 242. [OFr. *esto(u)ner.*]

stoutly *adv.* proudly, valiantly, vigor-ously 1153, 1364, 1614, 1923. [From OFr. *(e)stout.*]

stray. See ON-STRAY.

strayne *v.* to restrain, manage 176. [OFr. *estreindre, estreign-.*]

strayt *adj.* tight, close-fitting 152. [OFr. *(e)streit.*]

strakande *pres. p.* sounding call (on horn) 1364, 1923. [Obscure.]

straunge *adj.* strange 709, 713; **stronge** 1028 n. [OFr. *(e)stra(u)nge.*]

streȝt *adj.* straight 152. [OE. *streccan*, pp. *streht.*]

strenkþe *n.* strength 1496. [OE. *strengþ.*]

stryde *v.* to stride 1584, 2232; *s. alofte*, stride into the saddle 435, 2060. [OE. *strīdan.*]

strye *v.* to destroy 2194. [Shortened from OFr. *destruire.*]

stryf *n.* resistance 2323. [OFr. *(e)strif.*]

strike, stryke *v.* to strike 287, 331, 2099, 2305; **stroke** *pa. t. intr.* was struck, sprang 671. [OE. *strīcan.*]

stryþ(þ)e *n.* stance 2305; *stif on þe s.*, standing firm 846. [(?) Rel. to OE. *stride*, stride, pace.]

strok(e) *n.* stroke, blow 287, 294, 1460, 2252, 2286, 2323, 2327, 2341. [OE. **strāc*, rel. to STRIKE.]

stroke *v.* to stroke 334, 416. [OE. *stroccian*, rather than *strācian*; cf. rhyme 416; but 965 n.]

stronge *adj.* strong 34 (see STIF), 1618. [OE. *stráng, stróng.*]

strothe *n.* small wood; *attrib.* or *gen.* 1710 n. [ON. *storð.*]

stubbe *n.* stock, stump 2293. [OE. *stybb, stubb.*]

study *n.* study, silent thought 2369. [OFr. *(e)studie.*]

studie *v.* to look carefully (to discover) 230; watch intently 237. [OFr. *(e)studier.*]

stuffe *n.* stuff 581. [OFr. *estoffe.*]

sture *v.* to brandish (to try its weight) 331. [OE. *styrian.*]

sturn(e) *adj.* grim, of forbidding ap-pearance, stern 143, 334, 846, 2099, 2136; serious 494; *as sb.* grim knight 214; **sturnely** *adv.* grimly 331. [OE. *styrne, *stiorne; styrnelīce.*]

such(e), seche (1543), *adj. and pron.* such, so great, of the same kind 92, 239, 396, 1631, 2528, etc.; such (as), as great (as if) 1166, 1721; with *þat* 1011, 1426, 1658; *þat* omitted

46, 1321, 1393 n. [OE. *swelc,
swylc.*]

sue *v.* to follow, pursue 501, 510, 1467,
1705; **swez** *3 sg.* 1562. [OFr. *sivre,
siu-,* AN. *suer, suir.*]

suffer *v.* to suffer, permit 1967; submit 2040. [OFr. *so(u)frir, suf-.*]

sum, summe *adj.* some 28, 93,
1301, 1527, 2119, etc.; *pron.* 891,
1328, etc.; *adv.* in part 247. **sumquat**
n. something 1799; *adv.* somewhat
86. **sumquyle** *adv.* once upon a
time 625; **sumwhyle** sometimes
720, 721. **sumtyme** *adv.* formerly
2449. [OE. *sum.*] See WHAT, WHYLE.

sumned *pp.* summoned 1052. [OFr.
so(u)mo(u)ndre, sum-, infl. by OE.
somnian.]

sun. See SON.

sunder *adv.* in *in sunder,* asunder
1563. [OE. *on-sundran;* ON. *í sundr.*]

sunder *v. trans.* separate 1354; **sundred** *pa. t. intr.* 659. [From prec.;
cf. ON. *sundra,* OE. *syndrian.*]

sunne *n.* sun 520, 1467, etc. [OE. *sunne.*]

sure *adj.* trusty 588; **surely** *adv.*
securely 1883. [OFr. *seür.*]

surfet *n.* transgression 2433. [OFr.
surfait, surfet.]

surkot *n.* surcoat, flowing outer robe
of rich stuff 1929. [OFr. *surcote.*]

surquidré. See SOURQUYDRYE.

sute *n.* suit; *of a sute, of folȝande s.,*
to match 191, 859; **swete** in *of his
hors s.,* to match his horse 180; *in
swete,* following suit 2518. [OFr.
siute.]

swange *n.* middle, waist 138, 2034.
[ON. *svangi.*]

swap *v.* to exchange, swap 1108.
[Same as ME. *swappen,* strike.]

sware *adj.* squarely built 138. [OFr.
(*e*)*square,* n.; (*e*)*squarré,* adj.]

sware *v.* to answer 1108 n., 1756,
1793, 2011. [ON. *svara.*]

sweȝe *v.* to sink; **sweȝe** *pa. t. str.*
stooped 1796; **sweyed** *wk.* fell,
rushed, swung 1429. [See O.E.D.
s.v. *sway.*]

swenge *v.* to rush, hasten 1439, 1615;
come suddenly 1756. [OE. *swengan.*]

swere *v.* to swear 403, 2051, 2122;
swere *pa. t.* 1825. [OE. *swerian.*]

swete *adj.* sweet, lovely 1204; *as sb.*
fair lady 1222; (*sir*) *swete,* good sir
1108, 2237; *adv.* sweetly 1757.

swetely *adv.* with delight 2034.
[OE. *swēte; swētelīce.*]

swete. See SUTE.

sweþle *v.* to wind, wrap 2034. [From
OE. *sweþel,* wrapping.]

sweuenes *n. pl.* dreaming 1756. [OE.
swefn, often pl. with sg. sense.]

swez. See SUE.

swyerez *n. pl.* esquires 824. [OFr.
esquier.]

swyft(e) *adv.* swiftly 1354, *1825.
[OE. *swift,* adj.]

swyn *n.* swine, boar 1439, 1467, 1562,
1589, 1615, 1628, 1632. [OE. *swin.*]

swynge *v.* to rush 1562 n. [OE.
swingan.]

swyre *n.* neck 138, 186, 957. [OE.
swira.]

swyþe *adv.* greatly 1866; earnestly
1860; hard 1897; quickly 8, 815,
1424, 2034, 2259; **swyþely** quickly
1479. [OE. *swiþe, swiþlice.*]

swoghe *adj.* swooning, dead (silence)
243. [OE. *ge-swōgen.*]

sworde *n.* sword 2319. [OE. *swurd.*]

T

ta. See TAKE.

tabil, table *n.* (i) table 112, *884,
etc.; *hyȝe t.,* high table on dais 108,
2462; *see* ROUNDE: (ii) projecting
cornice-moulding 789. [OFr. *table.*]

tacche, tach(ch)e *v.* to attach, fasten
219, 579, 2176, 2512. [OFr.
atach(i)er.]

taȝtte. See TECHE.

tayl *n.* tail 191, 1726; *pl.* 1377. [OE.
tægl.]

taysed *pp.* harassed; driven 1169.
[See O.E.D. s.v. *teise,* v.²]

tayt *adj.* merry 988; vigorous, well-
grown 1377. [ON. *teitr.*]

take *v.* to take 682, 1823, etc.; **tas** *3
sg.* 2305; **tan** *pl.* 977, 1920; **take,
ta(s)** *imper.* 413, 897, 1390, 2357,
etc.; **tok(en)** *pa. t.* 709, 1333, 2243,
etc.; **taken** *pp.* 2448; **tan(e)** 1210,
1396, 1978, etc.; **tone** 2159. To take,
accept, receive 709, 828, 897, 1690,
1811, etc.; capture 1210; detect

take (*cont.*)
2488, 2509; acquire 2448; assign
1966; commit 2159; *t. to yourseluen*,
take upon yourself 350; *t. to myself*,
presume 1540; *take at*, (I) will take
from 383; *tan*, circumstanced 1811;
tan on honde, undertaken 490. [ON.
taka.]

takles *n. pl.* equipment, gear 1129.
[MLG. *takel*.]

tale *n.* talk, speech, word(s) 638, 1236,
1301, 2133; account, report 1057,
1626, 2124; story 93, 1541, 2483.
[OE. *talu*.]

talenttyf *adj.* desirous 350. [OFr.
talentif.]

talk *n.* speech 1486. [From next.]

talk(ke) *v.* to talk, speak (of) 108,
2133, 2372; **talkyng** *n.* conversation
917, 977. [OE. **talcian*, rel. to TALE.]

tame *adj.* tame 2455. [OE. *tam*.]

tapit *n.* tapestry, figured cloth; as
wall-hanging 858; as carpet 77, 568.
[OE. *teppet*; OProv. *tapit*.]

tap(p)e *n.* tap, knock 406, 2357.
[Echoic; cf. OFris. *tap*; OFr. *taper*, v.]

tary *v.* to delay 624, 1726. [See
O.E.D. s.v. *tarry*.]

tars *n.* silk of Tharsia 77 n., 571, 858.
[OFr. *Tarse*.]

tas. See TAKE.

tassel *n.* tassel 219. [OFr. *tassel*.]

teccheles *adj.* spotless, irreproach-
able 917. [From next.]

tech *n.* spot, stain, guilt 2436, 2488.
[OFr. *teche*.]

teche *v.* to teach 1527, 1533; inform
407; show (the way), direct 401,
1069, 1966, 2075; direct the attention of 1377; **ta3t(te)** *pa. t.* 1485,
2379. [OE. *tæcan*.]

tel. See TIL.

telde *n.* tent; dwelling, house 11,
1775. [OE. *téld*.]

telde *v.* to erect, set up 795, 884, 1648.
[OE. *téldian*, set up tent.]

telle *v.* to tell, relate 26, 31, 272, 480,
643, etc.; recite 2188; speak of (it)
291, 2130, 2501; say to, tell 279,
380, etc.; *t. of*, tell, speak of 165,
1514, 1656, etc.; *telles*, tells them of
it 2494; **tolde** *pa. t.* 1951. [OE.
tellan; *tálde*.]

temez *n. pl.* themes 1541. [OFr.
teme.]

tender *adj.* susceptible, liable 2436.
[OFr. *tendre*.]

tene *n.* harm, trouble 22, 547, 1008;
as adj. troublesome, rough 1707;
painful, perilous 2075. [OE. *téona*.]

tene *v.* to torment, harass 1169, 2002;
intr. suffer torment 2501. [OE.
téonian, ténan.]

tent *n.* intention, purpose; *in t. to
telle*, bent on telling 624. [OFr.
atente.]

tente *v.* to attend to, mind 1018, 1019.
[From OFr. *atente*, n.; see prec.]

tenþe *adj.* tenth 719. [ME. *ten+-þe*.]

terme *n.* appointed place 1069; appointment 1671; *pl.* expressions,
terms 917. [OFr. *terme*.]

teuelyng *n.* labour, deeds 1514.
[Prob. from ON. *tefla*, play (at
tables); but see O.E.D. s.v. *tevel*.]

th-. See þ-.

tyde *n.* time; (*at*) *þat t.*, then 585,
736, 2168; at that season 2086; *hy3e
t.*, festival 932, 1033. [OE. *tíd*.]

tyde *v.* to befall; *yow tydez*, is due to
you 1396. [OE. *tídan*.]

tyffe *v.* to prepare, make ready 1129.
[OFr. *tiffer*, adorn.]

ty3t *v.* to arrange; intend 2483; *pp.*
spread 568; *t. to*, hung on 858.
[OE. *tyhtan*; in ME. infl. by *dihtan*.]

til(le), tyl *prep.* to 673, 1979 (*after its
case*); until 734; *til þat*, until 697,
991; **til, tel** (1564) *conj.* until 85,
532, 1280, 1581, etc.; *with subj.* 449,
2287. [ON. *til*; OE. (rare Nth.) *til*.]

tyme *n.* time, period, occasion 22, 41,
991, 1069, 1156, etc; *at þis t.*, on this
occasion, now 264, 1510, **1810*,
2091, etc.; *at þat t.*, then 1409. [OE.
tíma.]

tymed *pp.* timed 2241. [From prec.]

tyrue *v.* to strip (off) 1921. [(?) OE.
*tyrfan; see O.E.D. s.v. *tirve*, v.[1]]

tit(e) *adv.* quickly 299, 1596. [ON.
títt.] See AS-TIT.

tytel *n.* evidence 480; **tytle** right: *bi
t. þat hit habbez*, justly 626. [OFr.
title.]

tytelet *pp.* inscribed 1515. [OFr.
titler.]

titleres *n. pl.* hounds from a relay 1726 n. [From OFr. *title*.]

tyxt *n.* text, very words 1515; story, romance 1541. [OFr. *texte, tixte*.]

to *prep.* to 8, 413, 1377, 1446, etc.; *(after its case)* 292, 2050; (in)to 2, 680, 1855, 2313; at 1455, 2333, 2438; (hold) of 421, 433, 1335, 2376; on(to) 228, 728, 858, 2332; towards 340, 1482; down (up) to, as far as 138, 222, 786, 1341, 1928, etc.; until 71, 1177, 1887; for 420, 548, 932, 1247, 1558; as 1197, 1811; *with inf.* 43, 58, 141, 472, 1130, 1338, etc.; as to 291; *for to* 863, etc.; *in split inf.* 88, 1540, 1863. *adv.* to them 579; up, to the spot 1454, 1903; *þat . . . to*, to which 1671 n., 2097. [OE. *tō*.]

to *adv.* too 165, 719, 1529, 1827, 2300. [OE. *tō*; orig. same as prec.]

to-day *adv.* today 397, 470. [OE. *tō dæg*.]

to-fylched *pa. t.* tore down 1172. [Obscure.]

togeder *adv.* together 362, 481, 743, 1011, 1613, etc. [OE. *tō gædere*.]

to3t *adj.* stout 1869. [OE. **toht*, taut, rel. to *tēon*; in ME. infl. by *tōh*.]

to-hewe *v.* to cut down; slay 1853. [OE. *tō-hēawan*.]

tok(en). See TAKE.

token *n.* token, sign, indication 1527, 2398, 2509; teaching 1486; *tytelet t.*, inscribed title 1515. [OE. *tācn*.]

tokenyng *n.* indication; *in t.*, as a sign that 2488. [OE. *tācnung*.]

tole *n.* weapon 413, 2260. [OE. *tōl*.]

tolke. See TULK.

tolouse *n.* (?) fabric of Toulouse 77 n.

to-morn(e) *adv.* tomorrow morning 548, 756, 1097, 1965. [OE. *tō mor(g)ne*.]

tone. See TAKE.

tonge *n.* tongue 32. [OE. *tunge*.]

toppyng *n.* forelock of horse 191. [Cf. OE. *topp*, top; *toppa*, tuft.]

to-raced *pp.* pulled down 1168. [OE. *tō-*+RASE, v.² or OFr. *raser*, tear.]

tor(e) *adj.* hard, difficult 165 n., 719. [ON. *tor-*; cf. TORUAYLE.]

torches *n. pl.* torches 1119, 1650. [OFr. *torche*.]

toreted *adj.* with embroidered edge *960 n. [OFr. *to(u)ret*+adj. suff.]

tornaye *v.* to double back 1707; **tournaye** tourney, joust 41. [OFr. *to(u)rneier*.]

torne *pp.* torn 1579. [OE. *toren*, pp.]

torne, t(o)urne *v. trans.* to turn 457; *intr.* turn 1200; return 1099; go 2075; *turned towrast*, might go awry, come to no good 1662; *turned tyme*, time that came to pass 22. [OE. *turnian*; OFr. *to(u)rner*.]

tortors *n. pl.* turtle-doves 612. [L. *turtur*.]

toruayle *n.* hard task 1540. [ON. *torveldi*, infl. by OFr. *travail*.]

tote *v.* to peep 1476. [OE. *tōtian*.]

toun(e) *n.* dwellings (of men), court 31, 614, 1049 n. [OE. *tūn*.]

tourn-. See TORN-.

toward(e) *prep.* towards 445, 1189; *to hir warde* 1200. [OE. *tōweard, tō hire weard*.]

towch *n.* touch; burst of music 120; allusion, hint 1301; *pl.* (terms of) agreement 1677. [OFr. *touche*.]

towche *v.* to touch; treat of 1541. [OFr. *toucher*.]

towen *pp.* journeyed 1093. [OE. *tēon*, pp. *togen*.] See VMBETE3E.

to-wrast *pp.* twisted awry; amiss 1663. [OE. *tō-*+*wrǣstan*.]

towre *n.* turret 795. [OFr. *tour*.]

trayle *v.* to (follow a) trail 1700 n. [From ME. *traile*, a trail.]

trayst *adj.*; *þat be 3e t.*, be sure of that 1211. [ON. *traustr*, assim. to *traiste*, v. (ON. *treysta*).]

trayteres (MS). See TRAUERES.

traytor *n.* traitor 1775. [OFr. *traître*, acc. sg. *traïtor*.]

trammes *n. pl.* cunning devices, machination 3. [OFr. *traime*, later *trame*, woof.]

trante *v.* to practise cunning, dodge 1707. [From TRAUNT.]

trased *pp.* set (as ornament) 1739. [Uncertain.]

trauayl *n.* (toilsome) journey 2241. [OFr. *travail*.]

trauayle *v.* to travel (toilsomely) 1093. [OFr. *travaill(i)er*.]

traueres *adv.* in *a traueres*, across, backwards and forwards *1700 n. [OFr. *a travers.*]

traunt *n.* (cunning) practice 1700. [Uncertain; cf. MDu. *trant*, step.]

trawe, trowe(e) *v.* to believe (in), be sure, think 70, 94, 373, 813, etc.; expect 1396; *t. me þat*, take my word for it 2112; *trawe of*, trust with regard to 2238. [OE. *trēowan*, *truwian.*]

trawþe, trauþe, traweþ (403) *n.* fidelity 626, 2470; truth 1050, 1057; plighted word 394, 1545, 1638, 1673, 2287; compact 2348. [OE. *trēowþ.*]

tre *n.* tree 770. [OE. *trēo.*]

treleted *pp.* latticed, meshed 960. [OFr. *tre(i)llette*+adj. suff.]

tresoun *n.* treason 3. [OFr. *tresoun.*]

tressour *n.* fret enclosing hair 1739 n. [OFr. *tress(e)or.*]

trestes, -ez *n. pl.* trestles 884, 1648. [OFr. *treste.*]

trewest. See TRWE.

tricherie, trecherye *n.* treachery 4, 2383. [OFr. *tricherie, trecherie.*]

tried, tryed *pp.* tried (for crime) 4 n.; *adj.* of proven quality, fine 77, 219. [OFr. *trier.*]

trifel, tryfle *n.* trifle, small matter 108, 1301; detail (of ornament) 165, 960; *neuer bot t.*, except for a small point 547. [Cf. OFr. *trufle.*]

tryst *v.* to believe 380; *þerto ȝe t.*, be sure of that 2325. [OE. *trȳstan*, or ON. *trýsta*, rel. to TRAYST.]

trystyly *adv.* faithfully 2348. [From ME. *tristi*, rel. to prec.]

trystor, tryster *n.* hunting station 1146, 1170, 1712. [OFr. *tristre.*]

trochet *pp.* provided with 'troches', the tines of a deer's horn; (towers) provided with ornamental pinnacles 795. [OFr. *troche.*]

trowe(e). See TRAWE.

true *n.* truce 1210. [OE. *trēow.*]

trumpes *n. pl.* trumpets 116, 1016. [OFr. *tro(u)mpe, trumpe.*]

trusse *v.* to pack 1129. [OFr. *tro(u)s-ser, truss-.*]

trwe(e), truee *adj.* faithful 1845; true (to one's word), trusty, honest 638, 1514, 1637, 2354; true, ac-curate 392, 480, 1274; **trewest** *superl.* most certain, veriest 4; *adv.* honestly 2354. [OE. *trēowe.*]

trwly, truly, trwely *adv.* faithfully 2348; with belief 2112; truly, rightly 380, 401, 406, 1785, 2444. [OE. *trēowlīce.*]

trwluf, trweluf *n.* true love 1527 (*attrib.*), 1540; **trulofez** *pl.* true-love knots or flowers 612 n. [OE. *trēow-lufu.*]

tulé, tuly *adj.* made of rich red stuff (usually silk), perhaps originally imported from Toulouse 568; *as sb.* 858. [?; cf. TOLOUSE.]

tulk, tolke *n.* man, knight 3, 41, 638, 1093, 1775, 1811, 1966, 2133. [ON. *tulkr*, spokesman.]

turne. See TORNE.

tusch *n.* tusk 1573, 1579. [OE. *tŭsc.*]

twayne, tweyne *adj.* two 962, 1864. [OE. *twēgen*, masc.]

twelmonyth *n.* twelvemonth, year 298; *at þis tyme t.*, a year hence 383; a year ago 2243. [OE. *twelf mōnaþ.*]

twelue *adj.* twelve 128. [OE. *twelfe.*]

twenty *adj.* twenty 1739 (see BE), 2112. [OE. *twentig.*]

twyges *n. pl.* twigs, branches 746. [ONth. *twicg.*]

twynne *adj.* double; *in t.*, in two 425, 1339. [ON. *tvinnr*; OE. *getwinn.*]

twynne *v.* to be separated, depart 2512. [From prec.]

twynnen *pp.* (were) twined, plaited 191. [ME. *twīnen*, v. from OE. *twīn*, n.]

twy(e)s *adv.* twice 1522, 1679. [OE. *twiga*+adv. *-es.*]

two *adj.* two 128, 770, 1019, 1316, 2352, etc.; *in two* 1351. [OE. *twā.*]

þ

þad. See PAT.

þaȝ(e) *conj.* (*with subj.*) though, even if 350, 1391, 2112, 2136, 2282, etc.; **thaȝ** 493; (*with wonder*) 496, 2307. [OE. *þē(a)h*, unaccented *þæh, þah.*]

þay *pron. pl.* they 50, 1019, 1452, etc.; **þayr** *adj.* their 1359, 1362; **þayres** *pron.* theirs; their affairs 1019. [ON. *þeir*; gen. *þeira.*]

þanne. See PEN.

þar *3 sg. pres.* need 2355. [OE. *þearf*.]

þare, þore *adv.* there 463, 667, 1889, 2173, 2356, 2508. [OE. *þǣr*, *þǎra*.]

þat, þad (686) *adj.* that, the 9, *1069, 1775, 2256, etc.; *þat ilk(e)*, that (same) 24, 1256, 2358, etc.; *as def. art.* (*before* ON, OÞER, etc.) 110, 173, 771, 1385, 2412, etc. [OE. *þæt*, neut.]

þat *conj.* that 83, 131, 234, 726, 1045, 1111, etc.; so that 120, 869, etc.; seeing that 1209; after *so*, *such* 60, 316, *1014, 1427, etc.; *with subj.* that, to (*with inf.*) 371, 380, etc.; so that, in order that 133, 345, 424, 2073, etc.; *pleonastic with other conj. or interrog.* (q.v.) 379, 1752, etc. See also the preps. (*as* BI, TIL, etc.). [OE. *þæt*, *þætte*.]

þat *pron.* that, it 70, 165, 264, 1834, 2112, etc.; at that, moreover 142, 717; of that 1211. See BI, WITH. [OE. *þæt*.]

þat *rel. pron.* that, which, who(m) 3, 22, *877, *1032, 1171, 1312, 2529, etc.; to whom 1251; (time) when *996, 2085; that which, what 291, 391, 836, *1386, etc.; she whom 969; (that) he that 926; at what 2372; *þat . . . hym, hys, hit*, whom, whose, which 28, 912, 2105, 2195; *with postponed prep.* (q.v.) 170, 1780, 2196, 2465, etc. [Substitution of prec. for OE. *þe*.]

þe *def. art.* the 1, 2057, 2069, 2153, etc.; *generic* 235, etc.; *with abstract sb.* (as OFr.) 1528, 2134, 2206, etc.; *with part of body* 621, 962, 2255, etc. [Late OE. *þe* (for *se*).]

þe *adv. with compar.* the, so much (the), for that 87, 376, 541, 1035, 1284, etc. [OE. *þȳ*, *þě*.]

þe. See ÞOU.

þede *n.* country 1499. [OE. *þēod*.]

þeder. See ÞIDER.

þef *n.* thief 1725. [OE. *þēof*.]

þen, þen(n)e *adv.* (i) then, next, in that case 116, 250, 462, 619, 1076, 1870, 2033, 2248, 2288, etc.; þanne 301: (ii) than 24, 236, 730, etc.; than if 337. [OE. *þanne*, *þænne*, *þon*.]

þenk(ke) *v.* to take heed 487; remember 1680; *þ. of* (*on*, *vpon*), be mindful of, remember 534, 2052, 2397; þoзt(en) *pa. t.* 1023; intended 331, 1550. [OE. *þencan*; *þǒhte*.] See ÞYNKEZ.

þer(e) *adv. demonstr.* there 3, 44, 109, 240, etc.; *indef.* 232, 852, etc.; *þer(e) as*, where 432, 731, 1432, 1897; *rel.* where, when 195, 334, 349, 694, 1875, etc.; *introducing wish* 839; *þer . . . inne*, in which 2440; *with preps.* it, them, etc.: þeraboute engaged on it 613; round it 2485; thereabouts 705; þerafter behind, after it (that) 671, 1021, 1342, 1826; þeralofte on it 569; þeramongez with it 1361; þerat 909, 1463, 2514; þerbi on them 117; þer-byside 1925; þer-fore, -forne therefore, for that reason 103, 1142, 2279, etc.; (?) (in exchange) for it 1107; þerinne in it, there 17, 21, 1652, 1767; þerof of it, to it 480, 547, 2523, etc.; þeron 570; þeroute out (of it, them) 518, 1140, 2044; out-of-doors 2000, 2481; þertylle to it 1110, 1369; þerto to it (them) 219, 576, etc.; at it 650; in that 2325; to this end (*or* moreover) 757; *as . . . þerto*, as . . . (to do) 1040; þer-vnder under it 185, 2079; þerwyth (together) with it, thereupon 121, 980, 1610. [OE. *þǣr*, *þěr*.]

þer-riзt *adv.* at once 1173. [OE. *þǣr-rihte*.]

þes(e). See ÞIS.

þewez *n. pl.* manners, knightly conduct 912, 916. [OE. *þēawas*, pl.]

þy, þyseluen, etc. See ÞOU.

þider, þeder *adv.* thither 402, 935, 1424, 1735, 1910. [OE. *þider*.]

þiderwarde *adv.* in that direction 1186. [OE. *þiderweard*.]

þyзez *n. pl.* thighs 579, 1349. [OE. *þē(o)h*.]

þik(ke) *adj.* thick, stout 138, 175, 579, etc.; *adv.* thick(ly), densely, closely 612, 769, 795, 801, 1702; continually 1770. [OE. *þicce*.]

þyng, þing *n.* thing, matter 93, 1512, 1802; þynk creature 1526; þyng(e) *pl.* 652, 1080; þinges, þyngez 645, 1809, 1945. [OE. *þing*.]

þynk(k)ez, þinkkez 2 *sg. pres.* you seem to 2362; *impers.* it seems good to 1502; seems to 1111, 1241, 1793, etc.; þink in *me þynk*, etc., I think 348, 1268, 2109, 2428; þoȝt, þuȝt *pa. t. impers.* it seemed to 49, 692, 870, 1245, 1620, 2491; (*merging into*) *pers.* thought (it) 803, 848, 945, 1578, etc. [OE. *þyncan*, pa. t. *þŭhte*.]

þis, þys *adj.* this, the 20, 1394, 1448, 1514, etc.; the (customary) 1112; *pron.* 100, 1385, 2398, etc.; *er þis* (OE. *ær þissum*), before now 1892, 2528. þis(e), þyse, þes(e) *pl.* these, the 42, 654, 656, 1386, 1445, 1514, etc.; *pron.* these (folk, things) 114, 1103, 2420, 2422; *þis seuen ȝere*, this many a day 1382. [OE. *þis*, neut.]

þo *adj. pl.* those, the 39, 68, 466, 1419, etc. [OE. *þā*.]

þof, þoȝ *conj.* even though 69, 624. [ON. *þó*, older *þoh*.]

þoȝt *n.* thought 645, 1751, 1867, 1993. [OE. *þŏht*.]

þoȝt(en). See þENK, þYNKEZ.

þoled *pa. t.* suffered, allowed 1859; endured 2419. [OE. *þolian*.]

þonk(e) *n.* thanks 1380; *made a þ.*, gave his thanks 1984; þonkkez *pl.* thanks 1980. [OE. *þonc*.]

þonk(ke) *v.* to thank 773, 939, 1031, 1080, 1975, 2020, etc. [OE. *þoncian*.]

þore. See þARE.

þorne *n.* thorn 1419, 2529. [OE. *þorn*.]

þose *adj. pl.* those 495; *pron.* 963. [OE. *þās*, or *þā* with anal. ending.]

þou, þow *pron.* thou 277, 1485, 1676, etc.; þe *acc. and dat.* 254, 258, 324, 2110, 2286, etc.; *refl.* 372, 396, 413, 2252, 2341, 2351. þi(n), þy(n) *adj.* thy 255, 394, 1071, 2303, 2467, etc.; þiself *nom.* thyself 395; þyseluen *refl.* 2141; *þyn awen seluen* 2301. [OE. *þū*, *þē*, *þīn*.]

þrast *n.* thrust 1443. [Stem of OE. *þrǣstan*, v.]

þrawen, þrowen *pp.* bound tight 194; thrown, laid 1740; well-knit, muscular 579. [OE. *þrāwan*, twist.]

þre *adj.* three 1066, 1141, 1443, 1713, 1946. [OE. *þrēo*.]

þred *n.* thread; *so neȝe þe þred*, so near

to the limit, *i.e.* to a definite offer of love 1771. [OE. *þrǣd*.]

þrepe *n.* importunity 1859; contest 2397. [From next; cf. ON. *þrap*.]

þrepe *v.* to quarrel; contend 504. [OE. *þrēapian*, rebuke.]

þresch *v.* to thrash; smite 2300. [OE. *þerscan*, late *þrescan*.]

þrete *n.* force, compulsion 1499. [OE. *þrēat*.]

þrete *v.* to threaten 2300; þrat *pa. t.* urged, pressed 1980; attacked 1713; þreted *pp.* reviled 1725. [OE. *þrēatian* with changed conjug.]

þrich *n.* thrust; rush 1713. [Stem of OE. *þryccan*, v.] See þRYȜT.

þrid, þryd *adj.* third 1021, 1680, 2356. [OE. *þridda*.]

þrye *adv.* thrice 763; þryes, þryse 1412, 1936. [OE. *þria*;+adv. *-es*.]

þryȝt *pa. t.* thrust 1443; *pp.* pressed on 1946. [OE. *þryccan*.]

þrynge *v.* to press, make one's way 2397; þronge *pa. t.* 1021. [OE. *þringan*.]

þrynne *adj.* threefold, three; *on þ. syþe*, thrice 1868. [ON. *þrinnr*.]

þryuande *adj.* abundant, hearty 1980; þryuandely *adv.* 1080, 1380. [Pres. p. of next.]

þryue *v.* to thrive; *so mot I þ. as I am*, on my life I am 387. [ON. *þrífask*.]

þryuen *adj.* fair 1740. [ON. *þrifinn*, pp. of prec.]

þro *adj.* intense, steadfast 645; oppressive 1751; fierce 1713 (*as sb. pl.*), 2300; *as adv.* earnestly, heartily 1867, 1946; *as þro*, equally crowded with delight 1021; þroly *adv.* heartily 939. [ON. *þrár*; *þráliga*.]

þrote *n.* throat 955, 1740. [OE. *þrote*.]

þrowe *n.* time; *a þrowe*, for a time 2219. [OE. *þrāg*.]

þrowe *v.* (*subj.*) in *þrid tyme þ. best*, third time turn out best, third time pays for all 1680 n. [OE. *þrāwan*.]

þrowen. See þRAWEN.

þuȝt. See þYNKEZ.

þulged *pa. t.* was patient (with) 1859. [OE. *geþyldgian*.]

þurȝ(e) *prep.* through(out), over 243, 691, 772, 1005, 1418, etc.; because of, for, by (means of) 91, 998, 1258,

1617, etc.; *þ. alle oþer þynge(z)*, (for this) beyond all else 645, 1080; *adv.* through 1356. [OE. *þurh.*]

þurled *pa. t.* made a hole in, pierced 1356. [OE. *þyrlian.*]

þus *adv.* thus, so, in this way 107, 529, 733, 1177, etc. [OE. *þus.*]

þwarle *adj.* intricate 194. [(?) Rel. to OE. *þweorh*; cf. mod. Lancs. dial. *wharl-knot.*]

þwong *n.* thong, lace 194, 579. [OE. *þwong.*]

V

vayles *n. pl.* veils 958. [OFr. *veile.*]

vayres: *in vayres*, in truth, truly 1015. [OFr. *en veires.*]

valay *n.* valley 2145, 2245. [OFr. *valée.*]

vale *n.* vale; *by hylle ne be v.*, in no circumstances 2271; *in vale*, in the land, by the way 2482. [OFr. *val.*]

vch(e) *adj.* each, every 101, 233, 501, 634, 980, 1014, etc.; *iche* 126, 1811; *vche a*, every 742, 997, 1262, 1491.

vchon(e) *pron.* each one, every one 657, 1028; *in appos. to sb.* 829, 1113, 1413; *v. (in) oþer*, (in) each other 98, 657. [OE. *ælc*, (rare) *ylc.*]

veluet *n.* velvet 2027. [Cf. Med.L. *velvetum.*]

venysoun *n.* venison 1375. [OFr. *veneiso(u)n, veniso(u)n.*]

venquyst *pa. t.* won victories 2482. [OFr. *veintre*, pa. t. *venquis.*]

ver *n.* spring-time 866 n. [L. *ver.*]

verayly *adv.* truly, assuredly 161, 866, 1342, 1375, 2245. [From OFr. *verai.*]

verdure *n.* verdure, green 161. [OFr. *verdure.*]

vertue *n.* (knightly) virtue *634, 2375. [OFr. *vertu.*]

vertuus *adj.* of special power (of stones) 2027. [OFr. *vertuo(u)s.*]

vesture *n.* vesture, raiment 161. [OFr. *vesture.*]

vewters *n. pl.* keepers of greyhounds 1146. [OFr. *veutr(i)er, veutre.*]

vgly *adj.* gruesome 441; threatening 2079; evil-looking 2190. [ON. *uggligr*, causing apprehension.]

vyage *n.* journey 535. [OFr. *veiage*, AN. *viage.*]

vylany(e) *n.* lack of (chivalrous) virtues, ill breeding 634, 2375; discourtesy 345. [OFr. *vilanie, vilenie.*]

vilanous *adj.* boorish, ill-bred 1497. [OFr. *vilano(u)s, vilen-.*]

visage *n.* appearance 866. [OFr. *visage.*]

vyse *n.* vice 2375. [OFr. *vice.*]

vmbe *prep.* about, round 589, 1830, 2034. [Blend of OE. *ymb(e)* and ON. *umb.*]

vmbe-clyppe *v.* to encompass, surround 616. [OE. *ymb(e)-clyppan.*]

vmbe-folde *v.* to enfold 181. [VMBE +FOLDE.]

vmbe-kesten *pa. t.* cast about, searched all round 1434. [VMBE+ CAST.]

vmbe-lappe *v.* to enfold, overlap 628. [VMBE+LAPPE.]

vmbe-teȝe *pa. t.* surrounded 770. [VMBE+OE. *tēah*, pa. t. of *tēon.*]

vmbe-torne *adv.* all round 184. [Blend of OFr. *en tour(n)* and ME. *umbe-trin* (Orm); cf. MLG. *umme trint*, Dan. *om trind.*]

vmbe-weued *pa. t.* enveloped 581. [OE. *ymbe-wæfan.*]

vnbarred *pp.* unbarred 2070. [OE. *on- (un-)*+OFr. *barrer.*]

vnbene *adj.* inhospitable, dreary 710. See BENE.

vnbynde *v.* to undo, cut in two 1352. [OE. *on-, un-bindan.*]

vnblyþe *adj.* unhappy, mournful 746. [OE. *unblīþe.*]

vncely *adj.* ill-fated, *or* disastrous 1562. [OE. *unsēlig.*]

vnclose *v.* to open 1140. See CLOSE.

vncouple *v.* to uncouple, unleash 1419. See COWPLED.

vncouþe *adj.* strange 93, 1808. [OE. *uncūþ.*] See COUÞE.

vnder *prep.* under 202, 1831, 2487, etc., *(after its case)* 748; in (clothes, etc.) 260, 1814; see CRYST, HEUEN, SCHANKES; *adv.* underneath 868 n.; under (his arm) 2318; at their feet 742; below, on his heels 158. [OE. *under.*]

vndertake *v.* to take in, perceive (what are) 1483. [OE. *underniman* with substitution of TAKE.]

vndo *v.* to undo; *didden hem v.*, had them cut up 1327. [OE. *on-*, *undōn*.]

vneþe *adv.* hardly 134. [OE. *unēaþe*.]

vnfayre *adj.* hideous 1572. [OE. *un-fæger*.]

vnhap *n.* mishap 438. [ON. *úhapp*.]

vnhap *v.* to unfasten 2511 n. See HAPPE.

vnhardel *v.* to unleash hounds 1697. [From OFr. *hardel*, leash.]

vnlace *v.* to unlace; cut up (boar) 1606. [From OFr. *lac(i)er*.]

vnleuté *n.* disloyalty 2499. See LEWTÉ.

vnlyke *adj.* unlike, different 950. [OE. *ungelīc*.]

vnlouked *pa. t.* opened 1201. [OE. *on-*, *unlūcan*, str.]

vnmanerly *adv.* discourteously 2339. See MANERLY.

vnmete *adj.* monstrous 208. [OE. *un(ge)mǣte*.]

vnrydely *adv.* in rough confusion 1432. [OE. *unrȳdelīce*.]

vnslayn *adj.* not slain 1858. See SLAYN.

vnslyȝe *adj.* unwary 1209. See SLEȜE.

vnsoundyly *adv.* disastrously 1438. See SOUNDYLY.

vnsparely *adv.* unsparingly 979. [OE. *un-*+*spærlīce*.] See SPARE.

vnspurd *adj.* unasked, without asking 918. See SPURED.

vntyȝtel *n.* unrestraint, lightheartedness; *dalten vnt.*, revelled 1114. [ME. *untühtle* (Laȝ. 24655), lack of discipline; *cf.* OE. *tyht*.]

vnto *prep.* to 249. [OE. **untō*.]

vntrawþe *n.* perfidy 2383, 2509. [OE. *untrēowþ*.]

vnþryuande *adj.* unworthy, ignoble 1499. See ᵽRYUANDE.

vnworþi *adj.* of no value 1835; unworthy 1244. [From OE. *unweorþe*.]

voyde *v.* to make empty; vacate, leave 345; get rid of 1518; *v. out*, clear out 1342; *voyded of*, free from 634. [OFr. *void(i)er*.]

vp *adv.* up 369, 884, 1131, 2260, etc.; up from table 928; out of bed 1128, 2009; open 820, 1341, 1743; away safe 1874; *vp to* 789, etc.; *vp and doun* 229. [OE. *up(p)*.]

vpbrayde *pp.* pulled up 781. [Prec.+ BRAYDE.]

vphalde *v.* to hold up 2442. [VP+ HALDE.]

vphalt *pp. adj.* high 2079. [VP+HALE.]

vplyfte *v. intr.* to lift, rise 505. [VP+LYFT(E).]

vpon *prep. equiv. of* ON; upon, on 159, 164, 431, 581, etc.; over 1831; to 2252; at 793, 2039, etc.; in 901, 1272, 1605, etc.; into 244; *(time)* at, in, on 37, 92, 301, 982, etc.; by 47; *þat . . . vpon*, by whom 2466; *adv.* on (them) 1649; on (him) 2021. [OE. *upp-on*.]

vpon *v.* to open 1183 n. [OE. *openian*, infl. by VP, open.]

vpryse *v.* to rise up 1437; **vpros** *pa. t. sg.* 367; **vprysen** *pl.* 1126. [OE. *upp arīsan*.]

vrysoun *n.* embroidered silk band on helmet 608. [OFr. *horso(u)n*.]

vse *v.* to use; have dealings with 2426; show, practise (a virtue) 651, 1491, 2106. [OFr. *user*.]

vtter *adv.* out, into the open 1565. [OE. *ūtor*, *ŭtter*.]

W

wade *v.* to wade 2231; **wod** *pa. t.* stood (in water) 787. [OE. *wadan*.]

wage *n.* pledge, earnest 533; *pl.* wages, payment 396. [ONFr. *wage*.]

way(e) *n.* way, road 689, 1077, 1876, 2479, etc.; *on his w.* 670, 1028, 1132, 2074; *went his (hir) w.*, departed 688, 1557; *bi non way(es)*, by no means 1045, 2471. [OE. *weg*.]

way *adv.* away; *do w.*, enough of 1492. [Shortened from AWAY.]

wayke *adj.* weak 282. [ON. *veikr*.]

wayne *v.* to bring, send 264, 2456, 2459 (*me ethic*); *pa. t.* urged, challenged 984. [OE. in *be-wægnan*.]

wayte *v.* to look 306, 1186, 2163, 2289. [ONFr. *wait(i)er*.]

wayth *n.* (meat gained in) hunting 1381. [ON. *veiðr*.]

wayue *v.* to wave; *w. vp*, swing open 1743; *pa. t.* swept from side to side 306; *pp.* offered, shown 1032 n. [ON. *veifa*, AN. *waiver*.]

waked *pp.* kept awake, revelled at

night 1094; **woke** *pa. t.* 1025. [OE. *wacian,* infl. by *wæcnan.*]

wakened(e), wakned *pa. t. intr.* woke up 1200; would wake up 1194 (*subj.*); was aroused, arose 2000, 2490; *trans.* kindled 1650; *pa. t.* awakened 119. [OE. *wæcn(i)an,* intr.]

wakkest *adj. superl.* weakest, most insignificant 354. [OE. *wāc,* compar. *wǎccra.*] See WAYKE.

wal, walle *n.* wall 783, 787, 809. [OE. *wall.*]

wale, walle *adj.* choice 1403; excellent, fair 1010, 1712, 1759. [For ME. *to wale,* inf. of next.]

wale *v.* to choose 1276; take 1238; find 398. [ON. *velja,* pa. t. *valdi.*]

walke *v.* to walk 2178; be spread abroad 1521. [OE. *walcan.*]

wallande *pres. p.* welling up warm 1762. [OE. *wallan.*]

walour *n.* valour 1518. [OFr. *valour.*]

walt. See WELDE.

walt *v.* to toss, fling; *pa. t.* 1336. [OE. *wieltan, wæltan.*]

walter *v.* to welter; roll in streams 684. [Rel. to prec.; cf. MLG. *waltern.*]

wande *n.* wand, branch; *vnder w.,* in the wood 1161; **wandez** *gen.* stave's 215. [ON. *vǫndr.*]

wane *adj.* lacking 493 n. [OE. *wana.*]

wap *n.* blow 2249. [As next.]

wappe *v.* to rush 1161, 2004. [Echoic.]

war *adj.* (a)ware; *watz w. of,* perceived 764, 1586, 1900; *war!,* ware! (hunting cry) 1158; **ware** on (my) guard 2388; **warly** *adv.* warily 1186, 1900; **warloker** *compar.* more carefully 677. [OE. *wær, wærlīce, -lucor.*]

warde *adv.* See TOWARDE.

ware *v.* to deal 2344; spend, employ 402, 1235. [OE. *warian*[2].]

waryst *pp.* cured, recovered 1094. [ONFr. *warir, wariss-.*]

warme *adj.* warm 506, 684. [OE. *wearm.*]

warme *v.* to warm 1762. [OE. *werman.*]

warne *v.* to warn 522. [OE. *warenian.*]

warp *v.* to cast; utter 2253; **warp** *pa. t.* uttered 224 n., 1423; cast, put 2025. [OE. *weorpan.*]

warþe *n.* ford 715 n. [OE. *waroþ,* shore, infl. by ON. *vað,* ford.]

waschen *pp. intr.* washed 72; **wesche** *pa. t.* 887. [OE. *wascan.*]

wast *n.* waist 144. [OE. **wæ(c)st.*]

waste *n.* waste, uninhabited land 2098. [ONFr. *wast,* adj.]

wat. See WHAT.

water *n.* water, stream 715, 727, etc.; **watter** 2231; **wattrez** *pl.* 1169; *warme w.* tears 684. [OE. *wæter.*]

watz *pa. t. sg.* was 4, 603, 652, ***1315, etc.; **was** 169, 573, etc.; had been 2016, 2488; *with intr. pp.* had 1, 62, 461, 1413, etc.; **wer(en)** *pl.* were 78, 320, 1138, 1328, etc.; **wer(e)** *pa. t. subj.* would, (should) be ***58, 165, 1251, 1545, 1773, 2131, etc.; was 92, 131, 143, 149, etc.; might be 1509; *as hit were* ***2171; *if hit w.,* if only 1799. [OE. *wæs, wæron, wǣre.*]

waþe. See WOþE.

wax *v.* to grow 518, 522; increase 997; **wex** *pa. t.* grew, became 319. [OE. *weaxan, wēox.*]

waxen *adj.* of wax 1650. [OE. *weaxen.*]

we *interj.* ah! alas! 2185; *we loo,* ah well 2208. [OE. *wæ; wæ lā, wel lā.*]

we *pron.* we 255, 378, 1681, etc.; **oure** *adj.* our 378, 1055, 1230, etc.; (subject of the story) 1469; **vus** *acc. and dat.* (to) us 920, 925, 1210, etc.; **vs** 2246. [OE. *wē, ūre, ǔs.*]

wede *n.* garment ***987, 2358; raiment 1310; *heʒ wede,* armour 831; *pl.* raiment, clothes (and armour) 151, 271, 508, 861, 2013, 2025. [OE. *wǣd, ge-wǣde.*]

weder *n.* (good) weather 504; *pl.* storms 2000. [OE. *weder; gewider,* storm.]

weʒed *pa. t.* brought 1403. [OE. *wegan,* str.]

wel *adv.* well 188, 679, etc.; without doubt, clearly 70, 270, 1820, etc.; certainly 1847; fully 1094; very much 1276, 2095, etc.; very 179, 684; *wel connez* 1267 n.; *wol þe wel,* wish you well 2469; *w. worþ þe,* good fortune befall you 2127. [OE. *wel.*]

wela *adv.* very 518, 2084. [OE. *wellā.*]

welcum, -com *adj.* welcome 252, 814, 835, 1237 n., *2240; *superl.* 938. [OE. *wilcuma*, n.; ON. *velkominn*.]

welcum *v.* to welcome 819, 1477, 1759. [OE. *wilcumian*; see prec.]

welde *n.* control; *to haue at yowre wylle and w.*, to use as you please 837. [OE. *gewáld*, infl. by next.]

welde *v.* to wield 270; possess, use 835, 1528, 1790, 2454, etc.; **walt** *pa. t.* possessed 231; spent 485. [OE. *wéldan*, *wæ̆ldan*.]

wele *n.* wealth, riches 7, 1270, 1394, 1820; costliness 2037, 2432; joy, delight 50, 485, 997, 1371, 1767, 2490; *w. oþer wo* 2134. [OE. *wela*.]

wel-haled *adj.* pulled up properly, drawn tight 157. [WEL+HALE.]

welkyn *n.* heavens 525, 1696. [OE. *wolcen*, *welcn*, cloud.]

welneȝ(e) *adv.* almost 7, 867. [OE. *wel-nēh*.]

wende *n.* turn 1161. [OE. *wend*.]

wende *v.* to turn 2152; *intr.* go 559, 1053, 1102, etc.; **wende** *pa. t.* in *w. in his hed*, went to his head 900; **went(en)** 72, 493, 688, 887, 1143, 1718, etc.; *pp.* in *watz w.*, came 1712. [OE. *wendan*.]

wene *v.* to expect, think 2404; *w. wel*, know well 270, 1226; **wende, went** *pa. t.* 669; *w. haf*, hoped to have 1711. [OE. *wēnan*.]

wener *adj. compar.* more lovely 945. [ON *vænn*; cf. OE. *wēn-lic*.]

wenge *v.* to avenge oneself 1518. [OFr. *veng(i)er*.]

weppen *n.* weapon 270, 292, 368, 384, 1586, 2222. [OE. *wēpn*.]

wer, were(n). See WATZ, WERRE.

werbelande *pres. p.* blowing shrill 2004. [OFr. *werbler*.]

werbles *n. pl.* warblings, shrill tremulous notes 119. [OFr. *werble*.]

were *v.*[1] to ward off 2015; defend 2041. [OE. *werian*[1].]

were *v.*[2] to wear 2358, 2510, 2518; **were** *pa. t.* 1928; **wered** 2037. [OE. *werian*[2].]

werk(e) *n.* work 494; *wylyde w.*, skilfully made object 2367 n.; **werk(k)ez** *pl.* deeds 1515; workmanship 1817, 2432; embroidery

164, 2026; designs 216. [OE. *we(o)rc*.]

werne *v.* to refuse 1494, 1495, 1824; **wernyng** *n.* resistance 2253. [OE. *wernan*.]

werre *n.* strife, fighting 16, 726; **were** 271, 1628. [ONFr. *werre*.]

werre *v.* to fight 720. [From prec.]

wesaunt *n.* oesophagus 1336. [OE. *wāsend*, *wæsend*, suff. infl. by Fr.]

wesche. See WASCHEN.

west *adj.* west 7 n. [OE. *west*, n.]

weterly *adv.* clearly 1706. [ON. *vitrliga*, wisely.]

weue *v.* to offer, show (honour) 1976; give 2359. [OE. *wǣfan*, *wave, equated with WAYUE.]

wex. See WAX.

wharre *v.* to whirr 2203. [Echoic.]

what *pron. interrog.* what 238, 462, 1487, etc.; **quat** 233, 563, 1087, etc.; what! 309; *interj.* (echoing noise) 1163, 2201–4; *indef.* what(ever) 1073, 1082; *adj.* what 460, 1047. **what-so** *pron.* whatever 1550; **quat-so** 255, 382; *what (wat) . . . so* 384, *1406, 1407, etc.; *quat . . . so* 1107, 1851; **quat-so-euer** 1106. [OE. *hwæt*; *swā-hwæt-swā*.]

whederwarde *adv.* whither, where 1053; **whiderwarde-so-euer** wherever 2478. [OE. *hwider*; *swā-hwider-swā*.]

when, quen *adv. interrog.* when 1194; *indef. and rel.* when(ever) 20, 72, 517, 650, 1098, 1727, 1753, 1857, 2437, etc. **when-so** whenever 1682. [OE. *hwanne*, *hwænne*.]

whene. See QUENE.

wher(e) *adv. interrog.* where 224, 311, 398, 399, 1394; **quere** 1058; *indef. (with subj.)*, wherever 100; *rel.* in *where . . . þerinne*, where 16; **where-so** wherever 395; **quere-so** 1227, 1490; **where-euer** 661; **were-so-euer** 1459; **quere-so-ever** 644. [OE. *hwǣr*; *swā-hwǣr-swā*.]

wherfor, querfore *adv. interrog.* wherefore 1294; *rel.* in *wh. . . . þerfore*, and so 2278. [Prec.+OE. *fore*.]

whette *v.* to sharpen, whet 1573; **whette** *pa. t. intr.* made a grinding

noise 2203; **quettyng** *n.* grinding
(his axe) 2220. [OE. *hwettan.*]

wheþen, queþen *adv. interrog.*
whence; *from queþen* 461; *indef.* (*with
subj.*) from wherever 871. [ON.
hvaðan; ODan. *hueden.*]

wheþer *adv.* yet, all the same 203.
[OE. *hwæþere.*]

wheþer *adv. interrog.* whether; *introd.
direct question* (no modern equivalent) 2186. [OE. *hwæþer.*]

why, quy *adv. interrog.* why 623;
interj. why! (*incredulous*) 1528. [OE.
hwī.]

whiderwarde. See WHEDERWARDE.

whil(e), wyle, quyl(e), quel (822)
conj. while, as long as 60, 351, 805,
814, 1035, 1469, 1852, 2025, etc.;
until 1180, 1435; *quyle þat*, as long
as 1115; *prep.* until 536, 1072, 1075,
1097, 1730. [OE. *þā-hwīle-þe.*]

whyle, quile *n.* time 1235; *adverbially* 30, 1195, 2369; *a wh.*, a moment 134, 1996; *any qu.*, any length
of time 257, 2058; *in a wh.*, pre-
sently 1646; *þe qu.*, at present 1791;
þe seruise (*etc.*) *qu.*, during the service time 940, 985. [OE. *hwīl*, (*þā*)-
hwīle.]

whyrlande *pres. p.* whirling 2222.
[OE. *hwyrftlian*; ON. *hvirfla.*]

whyssynes *n. pl.* cushions 877 (*allit.
with* qu). [OFr. *cuissin.*]

whyte *adj.* white 1573; *quit(e)* 1205
(*as sb.*), 2364; *quyt(e)* 799, 885,
2088. [OE. *hwīt.*]

who, quo *pron. interrog.* who 231,
682, 2213; *indef.* whoever 355. **who-
so, quo-so** *indef.* whoever, if anyone 209, 1112, 1849; *interrog.* who
(ever) 306. [OE. *hwā, swā-hwā-swā.*]

wy *interj.* ah! 2300. [Cf. WE.]

wich *adj.* what 918. [OE. *hwilc.*]

wyde *adv.* wide 820. [OE. *wīde.*]

wyf *n.* woman 1001, 1495; wife 1098,
2351, 2359, 2361, 2404. [OE. *wīf.*]

wyȝ(e), wyghe (1487) *n.* man, knight
249, 314, 581, 1039, 2074, etc.; person, one 131, 384, 1087, etc.; (of
God) 2441; *voc.* sir (knight) 252,
1508, 2127, etc.; *pl.* men, persons,
1167, 1403, etc. [OE. (verse) *wiga.*]

wyȝt *adj.* lively, loud 119; *superl.* most

valiant 261, fiercest 1591; *as adv.*
ardently 1762; **wyȝtly** *adv.* swiftly
688. [ON. *vigr*, neut. *vigt.*]

wyȝt *n.* creature; *þat wyȝt*, she 1792.
[OE. *wiht.*]

wykez *n. pl.* corners 1572. [ON.
munn-vik.]

wil, wyl(le) *1 & 3 sg. pres.* will, etc.,
130, 1547, etc.; **wol** 2469; **wyl(t)**
2 sg. 273, 384, etc.; **wyl** *pl.* 30, 1090,
etc.; **wolde, woled** *pa. t.* 85, 1508,
etc. *Pres.* wish (for), desire 384,
1822, 2469, etc.; intend to, will 130,
1102, etc.; *merging into auxil. of
future*, will 30, 549, 2512, etc.; *I
wyl to*, I mean to go to 2132. *Pa. t.*
wished (to), would (wish, be willing)
85, 271, 347, 1127, 2478, etc.;
wolde of his wyte, was likely to go
out of his senses 1087. [OE. *wil(l)e,
wyl(le)*; *wolde.*]

wylde *adj.* wild 119, 741, 1423, 1467,
1628, 2000, 2163, 2479; restless 89.
[OE. *wilde.*]

wylde *n.* wild beast 1167, 1586, 1900;
pl. wild creatures 1150, 2003. [OE.
*wild, wilder, pl. *wildru*; cf. MHG.
wilt.]

wyldrenesse *n.* wilderness 701. [OE.
wildeornes; see prec.]

wylé, wyly *adj.* wily 1728; *as sb.*
1905. [From next.]

wylez *n. pl.* wiles 1700, 1711, 2415,
2420. [OE. *wīgel*; ONFr. *wile*, OFr.
guile.]

wylyde *adj.* skilful 2367. [From
ME. *wīle*; see WYLEZ.]

wylle *adj.* wandering, perplexing
2084. [ON. *villr.*]

wylle *n.* desire, pleasure, (good) will
255, 1665, 2158, 2387; *of w.*, in
temper (of mind) 57, 352; *at his* (*etc.*)
wylle, to his pleasure 836, 1371,
1952; at his good pleasure 887, 1039,
1081, 1214; *bi ȝowre w.*, by your
leave 1065; *with* (*a*) *god w.*, gladly
1387, 1861, 1969, 2430. [OE. *willa.*]

wylnyng *n.* desire 1546. [OE. *wilnung.*]

wylsum *adj.* bewildering, leading one
far astray 689. [WYLLE *adj.* + OE.
-sum; cf. ON. *villusamr.*]

wylt *pp.* strayed, escaped 1711. [ON.
villask.]

wymmen *n. pl.* women 1269, 2415, 2426. [OE. *wíf-men, wimmen.*]

wyn(e) *n.* wine 129, 338, 900, 980, 1025, 1403. [OE. *wín.*]

wynde *n.* wind 516, 525, 784, 2004; *as wroth as w.* 319. [OE. *wind.*]

wynde *v.* to wind (back), return 530; **wounden** *pp.* wound, bound round 215. [OE. *windan.*]

wyndow *n.* window 1743. [ON. *vindauga.*]

wynne *adj.* delightful, lovely 518, 1032, 2430, 2456. [Next in compounds as *wynn-wyrt,* pleasant herb.]

wynne *n.*¹ joy 15, 1765. [OE. *wynn.*]

wynne *n.*² gain 2420. [OE. *gewinn.*]

wynne *v.* to gain, win, get 70, 984, 1106; win over, bring (to) 1550; bring 831, etc.; *refl.* in *wynne me,* find my way, get 402; *intr.* get with effort (to), reach 1569; come, go 1537, 2044, 2050, 2215 (*subj.*); **wan** *pa. t. sg.* 70, 2231 (came); **wonnen** *pl.* brought 831; **wan** got 1394; **won(n)en** *pp.* won, brought 1379, *1386, 1550, 2091, 2415; *watz w.,* had come 461, 1365. [OE. *ge-winnan,* ON. *vinna.*]

wynnelych *adj.* pleasant 980. [OE. *wynnlic.*]

wynter *n.* winter 504, 530, 726, 1382; *gen.* 533; *pl.* years (with numeral) 613. [OE. *winter.*]

wynt-hole *n.* wind-hole, windpipe 1336. [OE. *wind*+*hol.*]

wyppe *v.*¹ to whip, slash 2249. [Cf. ON. *svipa,* MDu. *wippen,* and ME. variation *wap, swap.*]

wyppe *v.*² to wipe, polish 2022 n. [OE. *wípian.*]

wyrde *n.* fate 1752, 2418; *þe wyrde,* Fate 2134; *pl.* as *sg.* 1968. [OE. *wýrd.*]

wys (*vpon*) *adj.* skilled (in) 1605. [OE. *wís.*]

wyse *n.* manner, fashion 185, 267, 901, 2014, etc.; *on fele w.,* in many ways 1653; *in no w.,* by no means 1836. [OE. *wíse.*]

wysse *v.* to guide, direct 549, 739 (*subj.*). [OE. *wissian.*]

wysty *adj.* desolate 2189. [OE. *wēstig.*]

wit, wyt *v.* to know, learn 131, 255, 1864; *wyt at,* learn from 1508; **wot** *1 sg. pres.* 24, 354, 1053, etc.; **wot** *pl.* 1965; **wyst** *pa. t. sg.* 1087, 1712, 2125; **wyst(en)** *pl.* 461, 1435, 1552 (were aware of), 2490, etc.; *wyt ȝe wel,* be assured, 1820. [OE. *witan; wāt,* sg.; *wiste,* pa. t.]

wyt(e), wytte *n.* (right) mind 1087; sense, reason 677; intelligence, understanding, cleverness 354, 402, 1394, 1533, 2096; *pl.* reason, wits 2459; consciousness 1755; *fyue wyttez,* five senses 640 n., 2193. [OE. (*ge*)*witt.*]

wyte *v.* to look 2050. [OE. *wítan.*]

with, wyth *prep.* with; (i) (= OE. *mid*) with, having, among 38, 116, 364, 375, 816 (*after its case*), etc.; in, amid 9, 50, 538, etc.; by, through 32, 78, 681, 949, etc. *w. hymseluen,* in his own mind 1660, *similarly* 2301. (ii) (= OE. *wiþ*) with, against 97, 262, 1253, etc.; at 1573; from 384; *wyth þis* (*þat*), thereupon 316, 1305. *adv.* wherewith 2223. [OE. *mid, wiþ.*]

withalle *adv.* entirely, altogether 106, 1926. [OE. *mid alle,* ON. *með ǫllu.*]

wythhalde *v.* to hold back, check 2268; **withhelde** *pa. t.* 2291; **wythhylde** 2168. [OE. *wiþ*+*háldan.*]

withinne, wythinne *adv.* in, inside, within 153, 573, 606, 880, 1192, 2029; inwardly 2370; *prep.* *1435, 1732, 1742; (*after its case*) 804, 1386, 1388. [OE. *wiþinnan.*]

withoute(n) *prep.* without 127, 315, 345, 873, etc. [OE. *wiþūtan.*]

wyttenesse *n.* witness, testimony 2523. [OE. *gewitnes.*]

wlonk *adj.* noble 1977, 1988 (*as sb.*); glorious, lovely 515, 581, 2022, 2432; *superl.* 2025. [OE. *wlonc.*]

wo *n.* woe 1717, 2134. [OE. *wā.*]

wod. See WADE.

wodcraftez *n. pl.* woodcraft, hunting practice 1605. [WOD(E) + CRAFT.]

wod(e) *n.* wood, forest 764, 1106, 1415, 1711, 1718, 2152; *in* (*bi*) *wod,* in the wood(s) 515, 1628, 2084. [OE. *wudu.*]

wode *adj.* mad 2289. [OE. *wōd.*]

wodwos *n. pl.* satyrs, trolls of the forest 721. [OE. *wudu-wāsa*.]

woȝe, wowe *n.* wall 858, 1180; *bi woȝez*, on the walls 1650. [OE. *wāg*.]

woȝe *v.* to woo, make love 1550 n. [OE. *wōgian*.]

woke; wol(ed), wolde. See WAKED; WIL.

wolues *n. pl.* wolves 720. [OE. *wulf*.]

wombe *n.* paunch 144. [OE. *wámb*.]

won(e) *n.* course (of action) 1238; multitude, host 1269. [ON. *ván*, hope, fair prospect, etc.] See WONE *n.*

wonde *v.* to shrink from, fear 563; neglect (through fear) 488. [OE. *wándian*.]

wonder *n.* wonder, amazement 238; *have w. (of)*, be amazed (at) 147, 467, 496; prodigy, marvel, wondrous deed (*or* tale) 16, 480, 2459; *of Arthurez wonderez*, from among the marvellous tales concerning A. 29; *predic.* (a) wonderful (thing) 1322, 1481; *adv.* wonderfully 2200. [OE. *wundor*; *wundrum*, adv.]

wondered *pa. t. impers.*; *hym w.*, he was surprised 1201. [OE. *wundrian*, pers.; ON. *undra*, pers. and impers.]

wonderly *adv.* marvellously 787, 1025. [OE. *wunder-lice*.]

wone *n.* dwelling, abode 257, 739, 764, 906, 997, 2490; *pl. in sg. sense*, 685, 1051, 1386, 2198, 2400. [ON. *ván*; see note on 257.]

wone *v.* to remain, dwell, live 257, 814, 2098; **wonyes** 2 *sg.* 399; **wonde, woned** *pa. t. pl.* 50, 701, 721; **wonyd, wonde, wont** *pp.* 17, 1988, 2114. [OE. *wunian*.]

wont *n.* lack (of good things) 131. [ON. *vanr*, neut. *vant*.]

wont *v. impers.* there lacks; *er me w. ere I have to go without, lose 987; neked wontez of*, it wants little (time) till 1062; *yow wonted*, you lacked, fell short of 2366. [From prec.]

worch(e) *v.* to work, make; do 1039, 1546; *absol.* act, do 238, 2253; *w. bi*, act according to 2096; *let God worche*, let God act (as He will) 2208 n.; **wroȝt** *pa. t. and pp.* made 399; wrought, devised, brought (about) 3, 22, 2344, 2361; acted

677, 1997 (*pl.*). [OE. *wyrcan, worhte* (late *wrohte*).]

worchip, worschyp *n.* honour, honourable treatment 1032, 1267 n., 1521, 1976, 2441; honour (conferred by possession) 984, 2432. [OE. *weorþ-, wurþ-scipe*.]

worchip *v.* to honour 1227. [From prec.]

word(e) *n.* word 224, 314, 2373; a thing to say 1792; fame 1521; *pl.* words, speech, conversation 493 n., 1012, 1423, 1766, 2269; *grete w.*, boasts 312, 325. [OE. *wórd*.]

worie *v.* to worry 1905. [OE. *wyrgan*.]

worlde *n.* world 261, 504, 530 n., 2000, 2479; *alle þe w.*, all men 1227; *in (þis) w.*, in the world 871, 2321, etc.; *of (in) þe w.*, in the world 50, 238, etc. [OE. *woruld*.]

wormez *n. pl.* dragons 720. [OE. *wyrm*.]

worre *adj.* worse; *þe w.*, the worst of it (in a fight) 1588, 1591. [ON. *verri*, infl. by next.]

wors *adj. compar.* worse 726; **worst** *superl.* worst 1792, 2098. [OE. *wyrsa, wyrsta*.]

wort *n.* plant 518. [OE. *wyrt*.]

worth *adj.* worth 1269, 1820. [OE. *weorþ(e), wyrþe*.]

worþe, worth(e) *v.* to become, be made (done) 1202; (*as future of 'be'*) will be: *me worþez þe better*, I shall be the better 1035; *worþez to*, shall become 1106, 1387; *me schal w.*, it shall be done to me 1214; *subj.* let it be (done) 1302 be (*with pp.*) 2374; *wel w. þe*, may good fortune befall you 2127; *w. hit wele oþer wo*, come what may 2134; **worþed** *pa. t.* came (to pass), was made 485; *subj.* would fare 2096; *pp.* become, been made 678. [OE. *weorþan*, str.]

worþy, worthé (559) *adj.* worthy; of value 1848; honoured, noble 559, 1537; *as sb.* noble lady 1276, 1508; becoming, fitting 819; **worþyest** most excellent 261; *adv.* courteously 1477. [OE. *wyrþig*, merited, infl. by *wyrþe*, worth(y).]

worþily, worþyly *adv.* in honour 1988; courteously 1759; with honour

worþily (*cont.*)
1386; becomingly 72, 144. [OE. *weorþlīce*, infl. by prec.]

worþilych *adj.* honoured, glorious 343. [OE. *weorþlic*; as prec.]

woþe *n.* danger 222, 488, 1576; **waþe** 2355. [ON. *váði*.]

wouen *pp.* woven 2358. [OE. *wefan.*]

wounded *pp.* wounded 1781. [OE. *wúndian*.]

wounden. See WYNDE.

wowche *v.* to vouch; *I w. hit saf*, I would vouchsafe (freely grant) it 1391. [OFr. *voucher sauf*.]

wowes 1180. See WO3E *n.*

wowyng *n.* wooing, (unlawful) love-making 2367; *þe w. of*, your temptation by 2361. [See WO3E *v.*]

wrake *n.* distress 16. [OE. *wracu*.]

wrang *adj.* (in the) wrong 1494. [ON. *rangr*, older *vrangr*.]

wrast *adj.* strong; loud (noise) 1423. [OE. *wræst*.]

wrast *pp.* turned, disposed (to) 1482. [OE. *wrǣstan*, twist.]

wrastel *v.* to wrestle, strive 525. [OE. *wrǎstlian, wrǣstlian*.]

wrathed *pa. t.* angered, grieved; afflicted 726; *impers.* in *you w.*, you

were angry 1509; *pp.* brought to disaster 2420. [From OE. *wrǣþþu*; cf. *gewrǣþan*.]

wre3ande *pres. p.* denouncing 1706. [OE. *wrēgan*.]

wro *n.* nook 2222. [ON. *(v)rá*.]

wro3t(en). See WORCH(E).

wroth(e), wroþe *adj.* angry, wroth 319, 1660; displeased 70; fierce 525, 1706, 1905; **wroþely** *adv.* fierce(ly) 2289; **wroþeloker** *compar.* more harshly 2344. [OE. *wrāþ*; *wrāþlīce, -lucor*.]

wroth *pa. t.* writhed; stretched himself 1200. [OE. *wrīþan.*]

wruxled *pp.* wrapped, clad 2191. [OE. *wrixlan*, wind to and fro, alternate; cf. related *wrigels, wrēon*.]

Y

y3e *n.* eye 198; *pl.* 228; **y3er** 82, 304, 684, 962. [OE. *ē(a)ge*.]

y3e-lyddez *n. pl.* eyelids 446, 1201. [Late OE. *ēge(h)lid*.]

ymage *n.* image 649. [OFr. *image*.]

your-, yow(re). See 3E.

yrn *n.* iron 215; weapon 2267; *pl.* (pieces of) armour 729. [OE. *īren*.]

INDEX OF NAMES